AMERICAN FAMILIES AND THE ECONOMY

The High Costs of Living

Richard R. Nelson and Felicity Skidmore
Editors

Conference on Families and the Economy
Committee on Child Development Research and Public Policy
Commission on Behavioral and Social Sciences and Education
National Research Council

NATIONAL ACADEMY PRESS
Washington, D.C. 1983

National Academy Press, 2101 Constitution Avenue, NW, Washington, DC 20418

NOTICE: The project that is the subject of this report was approved by the Governing Board of the National Research Council, whose members are drawn from the councils of the National Academy of Sciences, the National Academy of Engineering, and the Institute of Medicine. The members of the committee responsible for the report were chosen for their special competences and with regard for appropriate balance.

This report has been reviewed by a group other than the authors, according to procedures approved by a Report Review Committee consisting of members of the National Academy of Sciences, the National Academy of Engineering, and the Institute of Medicine.

The National Research Council was established by the National Academy of Sciences in 1916 to associate the broad community of science and technology with the Academy's purposes of furthering knowledge and of advising the federal government. The Council operates in accordance with general policies determined by the Academy under the authority of its congressional charter of 1863, which establishes the Academy as a private, nonprofit, self-governing membership corporation. The Council has become the principal operating agency of both the National Academy of Sciences and the National Academy of Engineering in the conduct of their services to the government, the public, and the scientific and engineering communities. It is administered jointly by both Academies and the Institute of Medicine. The National Academy of Engineering and the Institute of Medicine were established in 1964 and 1970, respectively, under the charter of the National Academy of Sciences.

Library of Congress Cataloging in Publication Data

Conference on Families and the Economy (1980 : Woods
Hole, Mass.)
American families and the economy.

Bibliography: p.
1. Family—United States—Congresses. 2. Family policy—United States—Congresses. 3. Child welfare—United States—Congresses. 4. United States—Economic conditions—1971–1981—Congresses. 5. Young adults—Employment—United States—Congresses. I. Nelson, Richard R. II. Skidmore, Felicity. III. National Research Council (U.S.). Committee on Child Development Research and Public Policy. IV. Title.

HQ536.C73 1980 306.8′5′0973 83–12134
ISBN 0–309–03376–4

Printed in the United States of America

COMMITTEE ON CHILD DEVELOPMENT RESEARCH AND PUBLIC POLICY

ALFRED J. KAHN (*Chair*), School of Social Work, Columbia University
ELEANOR E. MACCOBY (*Vice-Chair*), Department of Psychology, Stanford University
DORIS R. ENTWISLE, Department of Social Relations, Johns Hopkins University
FRANK F. FURSTENBERG, Department of Sociology, University of Pennsylvania
JOEL F. HANDLER, School of Law, University of Wisconsin
JOHN H. KENNELL, School of Medicine, Case Western Reserve University Rainbow Babies' and Children's Hospital
WILLIAM KESSEN, Department of Psychology, Yale University
FRANK LEVY, School of Public Affairs, University of Maryland
SAMUEL J. MESSICK, Educational Testing Service, Princeton, N.J.
ROBERT H. MNOOKIN, School of Law, Stanford University
JOHN MODELL, Department of History, University of Minnesota
WILLIAM A. MORRILL, Mathematica Policy Research, Inc., Princeton, N.J.
CONSTANCE B. NEWMAN, International Business Services, Inc., Washington, D.C.
JOHN U. OGBU, Department of Anthropology, University of California, Berkeley
T. M. JIM PARHAM, School of Social Work, University of Georgia
LAUREN B. RESNICK, Learning Research and Development Center, University of Pittsburgh
MICHAEL L. RUTTER, Institute of Psychiatry, University of London
JACK L. WALKER, Institute for Policy Studies, University of Michigan
CAROL K. WHALEN, School of Social Ecology, University of California, Davis

W. ANDREW COLLINS (*ex officio*), *Chair*, Panel to Review the Status of Basic Research on School-Age Children; Institute of Child Development, University of Minnesota

Preface

The Committee on Child Development Research and Public Policy has, over the years, undertaken many studies to help inform the discussion bearing on policies as they affect children and their families and to identify important avenues for future research. This volume is concerned with recent trends in the economic status and well-being of children and their families.

The enterprise had its origins in a meeting of the committee held at Woods Hole in summer 1980. The objective of the meeting was to chart future directions for the committee. Much of the discussion concerned propositions put forth, then questioned, to the effect that the difficult economic times of the 1970s had significantly worsened the economic status of children and their families. The discussion highlighted the facts that information bearing on the relevant questions was scattered and that there were probably significant holes in our knowledge. The committee decided to commission a set of papers to highlight what is known and not known and to sponsor a conference at which these papers would be discussed.

The Conference on Families and the Economy, and this volume that resulted from it, were made possible through the support of the MacArthur Foundation, which provided funds for the committee to conduct a series of forums on salient national issues of both research and policy concern with respect to the welfare of children and families.

The conference was deliberately organized as a small working group (see the participants list in the appendix). Members of the multidisciplinary group were chosen by the committee for their research expertise in the various behavioral and social sciences. Some of the participants were designated as formal discussants of particular papers; others were invited to make their contributions to the conference discussions more generally. The conference consisted of five sessions in two days: The first four sessions included presentation and discussion of the material in Chapters 2-8 of this volume. The final session comprised a panel of policy analysts assessing the broad significance of the conference papers and discussions for future federal policy; Chapter 9 captures the issues discussed.

Many people contributed to the success of this endeavor. First, I wish to thank the authors of the papers, for their hard work, cooperation, and willingness to meet our schedule, and the formal discussants, for providing copies of their comments, which was a great help in drafting the discussion summaries.

Second, I wish to thank members of the committee for their assistance in developing plans for the conference, especially Frank Levy, for his particular interest in and advice on the project, and Alfred Kahn, chair of the committee. In addition, many committee members made valuable contributions in their comments on the early drafts of the papers.

Third, I wish to thank the staff and consultants to the committee. Cheryl D. Hayes, the executive officer of the committee, organized the whole effort. Her help in particular was invaluable in securing the participation of the authors and conference attendees and in making the conference into the smoothly run and fruitful event that it turned out to be. Felicity Skidmore, consultant, organized and synthesized the manuscript review process both before and after the conference, edited the papers, drafted the discussion summaries, and, with me, coauthored the introductory essay and final chapter. Her buoyant sense of humor, her superb organizational skills, and her meticulous editing ensured the smooth and timely completion of the volume. Her tireless assistance was essential throughout the project. Suzanne Magnetti, research associate/consultant, assisted in the proofreading and production of the several drafts when time constraints would have made the job extremely difficult without her help. Ginny Peterson, staff assistant, was invaluable in her attention to administrative detail for the project as a whole and her efficient coordination of the typing and production of numerous drafts and redrafts. Janie Marshall provided secretarial support in the early stages of the project. Irene Martinez shouldered most of the typing burden in an exceptionally rapid and accurate manner.

Finally, I wish to acknowledge the support and encouragement of the executive office of the Commission on Behavioral and Social Sciences and Education.

RICHARD R. NELSON, *Chair*
Conference on Families and the Economy

Contents

AMERICAN FAMILIES AND THE ECONOMY

The High Costs of Living

1
Overview

RICHARD R. NELSON AND FELICITY SKIDMORE

In the 1960s the American economy performed remarkably well. Unemployment rates, which were uncomfortably high at the start of the decade, shrank and in the late 1960s averaged less than 4 percent of the work force. Inflation was kept under reasonably good control, although in the latter half of the decade there were inflationary spurts that some observers thought boded ill. Productivity growth was rapid, and per capita income grew at a near record pace—reflecting both rising productivity and increasing labor force participation rates, particularly among young women.

Of special note was the reduction in poverty during the decade: The incidence of measured poverty in the United States declined from 17 percent to 13 percent of the population. At least three broad forces were behind this development. The general economic prosperity and rising income levels described above certainly were a large part of the story. A progressive closing of the average income gap between black and white Americans also contributed. And, during this decade, a number of programs were established or enlarged that either specifically channeled income (in money or in kind) to poor Americans or aimed to increase their earning potential.

As the decade of the 1960s ended, the economic waters became choppy. The oil and materials price shocks of 1973-1974 hit an economy that already was showing signs of foundering. In contrast with the 1960s, the 1970s saw relatively high unemployment and inflation rates, slow productivity growth, and relatively slow income growth. Black/white average income differentials ceased to narrow. The incidence of poverty ceased to decline for both money income and more inclusive income measures. At the same time, the 1960s programs aimed at helping the poor and reducing poverty became increasingly controversial and came under heavy political attack as expensive, ineffective, and even possibly counterproductive. Spending on them ceased to grow. The 1980s have thus far seen a magnification of all these changes.

This volume is concerned with marshaling information about what the changing climate has meant for the economic welfare of families with children. Obviously, many children raised in conditions of economic hardship emerge from the experience unscathed and possibly strengthened. But the environment of material deprivation does put the children of those who suffer from it at greater developmental risk—not only from the possible direct physical consequences of the deprivation, but also from the possible indirect consequences deriving from the additional stress that hard (and worsened) economic circumstances can inflict on the relationships between parents and their children.

Major Findings

First, while the generally adverse economic trends of the 1970s, compared with the 1960s, were an important background condition influencing the economic status of children and their families, changing demographic conditions and patterns of work force participation played a perhaps more important role. In particular, many more women with young children were in the work force, and many more families with young children were mother-only families. These developments occurred at the same time that general economic trends were getting worse, but they had at least partially independent roots.

Second, the experience of blacks and whites diverged significantly in the decade of the 1970s. The incidence of poverty among children and their families is strikingly higher among blacks than among whites, and it seems to be increasingly associated with families in which the mother is present and the father is not.

Third, a large fraction of child poverty occurs in generally poor and segregated communities. Our knowledge about child poverty and its incidence is limited by the fact that we have few data on the irregular, unrecorded economy in such communities. In any case, child poverty often is a community problem, which compounds the individual and family aspects.

Demographic and Labor Force Developments

The period since 1970 has seen a slow, steady increase in average per capita income of families with children—slightly more than 1 percent per year. It is important to note, however, that this increase in part reflects two trends that are unlikely to continue. First, the decade of the 1970s witnessed an enormous influx of women, including mothers, into the labor market. This meant that a steadily increasing proportion of family income over the decade was made up of the earnings of mothers. Second, the average number of children per family declined between 1970 and 1980.

At the same time that average per capita income of families with children was rising slightly, there was a significant increase in the relative size of one group of children who were especially vulnerable to poverty—children in households with only one parent present, usually the mother. In the early 1970s these mother-only families came about largely as the result of separations and divorces, but during the decade of the 1970s the incidence of families headed by mothers who had never married increased (see Chapter 2). Average levels of per capita income were much lower in mother-only families than in two-parent families; thus their rising incidence led to increasing numbers of children who were vulnerable to poverty. Not only did children in mother-only families have lower average income levels; they also had incomes that fluctuated much more widely from year to year than did children in two-parent families.

This is not to say that mother-only households now are the norm; many more children continue to live in households headed by two parents. Nor is it to say that, in general, families must choose between having the mother work or going on welfare. For many families the choices are far less crude, involving a difficult trade-off between desires for higher family income and concerns about how to raise and care for children. We do want to highlight, however, that a sizable fraction of children in poverty live in mother-only households and that these families are dependent on the mother's earnings or on welfare.

The data for the 1970s show that these families' choices are not an either/or proposition. A good fraction of the mothers did work a good portion of the time, and many of them from time to time drew on welfare, particularly when they were out of work. Contrary to popular belief, in most cases dependence on welfare was episodic. Yet there were also female-headed families that were dependent on welfare for more than half the decade; most of these families were black.

These facts suggest that some rethinking is needed. First, the widespread notion of women as secondary earners is not a satisfactory frame of reference. Particularly in poor families, the mother now often is the primary or sole potential earner. Women's unemployment rates and wage rates, therefore, should be understood as important determinants of the income levels of poor families with children. Second, the major public assistance program for these families, Aid to Families with Dependent Children (AFDC), should be understood as serving two different kinds of needs. One role of such public assistance payments to families with poor children is that of a fill-in when the mother is out of work or when her income falls to very low levels. Another role is as the principal long-term source of income for some families, usually female-headed and usually black. Third, many poor families are in a real predicament regarding how to care for their children. If the mother stays home, it is virtually impossible to make ends meet. If the mother works, alternative child care arrangements must be found.

The first part of the 1970s did see a significant increase in public funding going into AFDC and related programs. There was also a significant increase in public support of day care. By the mid-1970s, however, spending on these programs had leveled off. And even at their peak they did not amount to very much. Current discussion about these programs, both in support and in opposition, has not proceeded in awareness of the demographic facts about child poverty in the 1970s and 1980s described above.

Black and White Differences

As noted earlier, during the 1960s the difference between the average income levels of blacks and whites narrowed somewhat, and the percentage of blacks in poverty declined significantly. During the 1970s these trends toward convergence not only stopped but also reversed. Developments during the 1970s have put a growing percentage of black children at risk. A black child is 5 times more likely than a white child to be poor; 5 times more likely to be supported, at least partially for a short period of time, through welfare; and 10 times more likely to be completely dependent over a long period of time on welfare. The data do not show, however, that child poverty is a black problem. In 1981, for example, of the 12 million poor children under 18, 7.4 million were white. More white children than black are also being supported, in part or in whole, through welfare. But poverty is a disproportionately large possibility for black children. Two major factors are involved in the widening gap.

First, the higher and more rapidly rising incidence of mother-only families among blacks certainly is one important reason why such a large fraction of black children grow up in very poor households. Over the decade, a much higher proportion of never-married black women than white women had children, suggesting, in turn, that many black children may never have lived with their fathers (see Chapter 2 and discussion following).

Second, employment rates among two important classes of black people—unmarried mothers and teenagers—are significantly lower than among whites. For unmarried mothers, this shows up largely in lower work force participation rates. For teenagers, the major difference is in their unemployment rate. According to data for the 1970s, about half the unemployed black teenagers were in school, but this does not mean that it was not important to them and their families that they earn income. There also is the difficult question of why white teenagers, most of whom were in school, were able to find jobs much more readily than black teenagers. There obviously are many reasons behind these differences, but research has not yet sorted them out or weighted them. There is strong reason to believe, however, that an important part of the reason is that a significant fraction of young blacks live in situations and environments that make it difficult for them to find jobs in the regular economy.

While these two factors provide a good part of the explanation, however, the total difference cannot be so explained. Even if the demographic profile for blacks over the decade had been identical to that of whites, the per capita income of black families would have been distinctly lower on average and more unstable. And the incidence of child poverty would have been strikingly higher. For a society that a decade ago prided itself on the effectiveness of its march toward racial equality, this should come as bad news.

Poverty as a Community Problem

Existing studies have not been very successful in sorting out the reason for the particularly high incidence of poverty among black families with children. There are certain obvious correlates; however, the basic reasons are not well understood. One route to better understanding certainly lies in analyses that try to take into account individual and family differences in such variables as education level, characteristics of housing location, etc. It seems unlikely, however, that differences in easily measured characteristics of individuals and families will provide a full explanation. It is more likely that different family and community histories and different cultural adaptations to these histories are an important part of the story. These differences are likely to be overlooked in statistical analyses unless the researcher has them firmly in mind. And if they are overlooked there is grave danger that, since the variables treated explicitly will account for only a portion of black/white differences, prejudicial interpretations will be made.

A significant fraction of the American black population today is crowded together in the segregated neighborhoods of aging industrial cities. A large portion of economic activity in these ghettos is unrecorded, and, in the nature of the case, we know very little about such unrecorded economic activity. It is thus difficult to interpret the numbers of families with children living in such areas reporting very low incomes, high poverty rates, or low employment rates. To what extent are low reported income rates and employment rates compensated for by mothers' and teenagers' working "off the books"? It is highly unlikely that activities in the unrecorded economy account for the lion's share of the recorded inequalities, but we do not know how much of the difference is one of reporting and how much of it is real.

Even if the activity in the unrecorded economy lifts black incomes and employment rates a significant distance closer to national averages, the very separateness of these economies warrants some unease. The warning of the Kerner Commission, some time ago, that the nation was in danger of splitting, may not have been far off the mark. As indicated in the discussion following Chapter 5, the skills one needs to survive in the unrecorded economy are different from, and to some extent antithetical to, the skills needed in the regular economy. These differences are bound to have major effects on how families and their children develop and function in the world.

Ghetto society also clearly has a different familial support structure from that prevailing in the rest of society. If the presumption that virtually all American families with young children include both parents—with the father working and the mother staying home to care for the children—is increasingly too simple a characterization of life among the population at large, this situation is no longer even the norm among black families living in cities. This is not to say that such families lack a familial support structure, but that the support structure is quite different from the one that has long been regarded as customary. And not much is known about exactly how it works.

Organization of the Volume

Chapter 2, by Martha Hill, presents information on what happened to the income distribution of families with children over the course of the 1970s. The data are broken down by family type and race, and the sources of family income are explored. In Chapter 3, David Wise and David Ellwood focus on what has been happening to youth employment and unemployment. The specific concern of the committee was to gather more information about the meaning and significance of the unusually high unemployment rates for male teenagers, especially black male teenagers, that had been reported. Chapter 4, by Mary Jo Bane, Julie Wilson, and Neal Baer, is concerned with the changing patterns of expenditure on government programs affecting children and their families. While we knew what the broad trends were, we thought it important to get more information on the details. Together these three chapters provide the basic numbers needed to analyze the changing economic status of children.

Chapter 5, by Ann Witte and Carl Simon, is concerned with the unrecorded economy. We are not the first to ask the question: To what extent do available measures give a distorted picture, by neglect or undercounting, of certain kinds of economic activities? We do think it important to extend the question to include the implications of this growing sector for the lives of children. Chapter 6, by James Zais, discusses housing. The sharp rise during the 1970s in housing prices, the collapse in public housing, and perceptions that rental housing has become increasingly scarce and expensive led to the commissioning of a special study on how these trends were affecting families and young children.

In choosing housing as a focus, we expected to find evidence that families with children were badly housed, in terms of physical structure, compared with the rest of society. And there are families, indeed, who are poorly housed; these are the poor families. Since the incidence of poverty is high in mother-only families and minority families, these families are most likely to be found in poor housing. But on reflection, it is apparent that this is not well defined as a housing problem; it is a poverty problem. In fact, average housing quality has been increasing steadily from World War II through the 1970s. Viewed simply as a matter of the existence of adequate structures, the housing problem for poor people does not seem to have gotten worse.

Although there may not be problems of housing per se, there certainly is a problem of neighborhoods. Segregation by race and income has many causes, but the phenomenon has been exaggerated by housing policies that have focused on providing more adequate physical housing structures for poor families. The construction of low-income housing has had the result of crowding the poor together in neighborhoods in which the schools are bad, the streets are unsafe, and there are fewer and fewer jobs to be had in the regular economy. Again, it is not clear exactly what the implications are. It is clear, however, that poverty, particularly child poverty, must be understood in terms of community. The leading cause of death among black youth is homicide, much of it in the crowded ghetto environment. This alone should make us reconsider the goals of housing policy.

While the theme of the conference was the economic status and well-being of families, much of the committee's concern was with how families and children coped with the economic adversity and the effects on the development of children. This is the topic of Chapter 7, written by Phyllis Moen, Edward Kain, and Glen Elder, Jr. Also, it was recognized that the economic troubles of the 1970s came about at the same time that the postwar baby boom cohort was coming into the work force. Some scholars have postulated that particular demographic patterns set in train by the baby boom have had a lot to do with the economic conditions that have faced young people over the decade; Chapter 8, by Richard Easterlin, articulates the argument.

As stated, early versions of each of these chapters were presented at a conference held in January 1982. Following each chapter in this volume, a summary of the conference discussion of the paper is presented. These discussions help to place the individual papers in context, highlight the most important findings, and point out important questions that were left unanswered.

The concluding chapter is concerned with two broad questions. What new light has been shed on policy issues? What important puzzles and questions have been identified that ought to be placed high on someone's research agenda? We do not put forth any specific policy proposals, nor do we draw up any plans for research. Rather, the discussion aims to identify some warranted changes in the orientation of thinking, given what we now know and don't know about what has been happening to the economic status and well-being of children and their families.

2

Trends in the Economic Situation of U.S. Families and Children: 1970-1980

MARTHA S. HILL

> Worry about the family is mostly worry about the next generation. Falling birth rates, rising divorce rates, increasing numbers of working mothers, and other indicators of the alleged decline of the family would probably seem much less alarming if adults alone were affected. . . . People are distressed by these trends not because they signal a decline in the quality and richness of adult lives but because they seem to threaten the next generation. (Bane, 1976, p. 3)

The economic well-being of a family with children depends on the number of providers (primarily parents) and their ability to acquire income, plus the total number of dependents (primarily children) in the family. Over time, this means that major factors influencing children's paths of economic well-being include: (1) changes in conditions in the economy that influence the parents' access to income and (2) changes in the family that alter the number of parents, the ability of the parents to acquire income, or the number of children in the family. During the past decade, there have been large aggregate changes in each of these.

The U.S. economy has fluctuated widely during this period, with recessionary conditions prevailing at several points. In addition, even during nonrecessionary times the unemployment rate has been high, and, despite a traditional reciprocal association between unemployment and inflation, high unemployment rates have been accompanied by high inflation rates.

During the same period, U.S. family units have themselves undergone pervasive changes. Despite an atmosphere continuing to foster the notion of a "typical" U.S. family consisting of a breadwinning husband, a homekeeping wife, and two children, in March 1981 only one-fifth (22 percent) of the families with children satisfied both the number-of-parents and labor-force-participation criteria of this definition.

The decade's shift in the demographic characteristics of families with children has primarily reflected increases in the number of mothers heading households and increases in the labor force participation of mothers with children. Changes of this kind are strongly associated with changes in the economic well-being of family members and appear to be considerably more important to individual economic well-being than are changes in the general conditions of the economy. This suggests that analysis of the economic situation of children during the 1970s should focus on the pervasive changes in family composition—mothers becoming increasingly household heads and participating more in the labor force.

This chapter concentrates on the economic well-being of children during the decade of the 1970s and the relationship between their well-being and family composition. After a discussion of the demographic trends associated with changing family life-styles, we focus on economic well-being. Emphasis is placed on the relationship between family life-style and the time path of economic well-being and how they differ according to the race of the child. The analysis includes cross-sectional comparisons of children's economic situations at the beginning and end of the 1970s plus longitudinal analysis of the experiences of cohorts of children during the same time span. Findings reported in the literature are used to supplement this analysis. Data for this analysis come from the Panel Study of Income Dynamics (PSID), which has been following family members (adults as well as children) who were part of a nationally representative sample of 1968 families or have subsequently been born to one of the original 1968 family members. These data provide information each year on the families in which the children are living, as well as information about the children themselves.

Demographic Trends Affecting Children

In order to understand the factors associated with changes in the family circumstances of children, it is useful to examine several of the demographic trends of recent years. The most prominent of these include:

- an increase in the population of young women as the baby boom generation enters adulthood;
- increasing proportions of women, particularly those married with children, in the labor force;
- the declining incidence of marriage, both first marriage and remarriage, among women of childbearing age;

• a sharp rise in the incidence of separation and divorce among married women of childbearing age;

• a strong decline in the incidence of childbearing among young married women, with the birthrate reaching the lowest level ever recorded in 1975-1976 and then increasing slightly as the women who delayed childbearing began having the children they had postponed;

• a rise in the proportion of births that occur out of wedlock, reflecting a fairly constant birthrate for unmarried women coupled with a large decline in the birthrate for married women; and

• a general increase in the propensity of adults to maintain separate households, including an increase in the likelihood of women who are divorced or who bear an out-of-wedlock child to head their own household rather than live with their parents, friends, or relatives.

These factors have, singly and collectively, resulted in many changes over the past decade in the family life of children. Despite increases in the population of young women, lower birthrates have meant that children are now not only a smaller proportion of the population but also fewer in number. Children are also growing up with fewer siblings due to the higher propensities for small families and delayed childbearing. The declining incidence of marriage combined with the increasing incidence of divorce and separation, as well as out-of-wedlock births, has meant that more children are in families without the father present. Coupled with the increased propensity for independent living arrangements, this has meant that more children are living in households headed by their unmarried mothers.[1] In addition, the pattern of increased labor force participation of women, especially of married women with children, has substantially increased the proportion of children with working mothers.

The growth in female-headed households with children and the increased labor force participation of mothers have received the most attention as factors affecting the family life of children. These trends, although continuations of changes begun earlier, accelerated during the past decade.[2] In 1960, it was relatively rare for children to be living in

[1] See Ross and Sawhill (1975), Bradbury, et al. (1979), and Cutright (1974) for discussion of the relative importance of the various demographic factors to the increase in female-headed households with children.

[2] Between 1960 and 1970 the number of one-parent, predominantly female-headed families increased by 49 percent, compared to only an 8 percent increase in two-parent families. During the next 8 years not only did one-parent families increase at an even faster rate (by 76 percent), but at the same time two-parent families actually declined by 3 percent.

one-parent families; since then it has become increasingly common. The percentage of children in one-parent families has increased from 9 percent in 1960 to 14 percent in 1970 to 20 percent in 1980. About 90 percent of the one-parent families were headed by a woman throughout this period. In the 1970s, the proportion of children in two-parent households, while still in the majority, declined steadily from 85 percent in 1970 to 76 percent in 1980. Thus, while the two-parent family remains the typical situation for the majority of children, the one-parent, female-headed family has become frequent enough to warrant attention in its own right.

During the last decade, there have been continuous increases also in women's labor-force-participation rates, with the sharpest rise among married women with children, particularly those with young children.[3] This has led to continuous increases both in the proportion and in the number of children with working mothers. Their number has grown by more than 5 million, despite a decrease of 7.5 million in the total number of children. This has also meant the narrowing, although not the complete elimination, of long-established differentials regarding age of the child and marital status of the mother.

Historically, mothers with young children and those with a husband have been less likely than other mothers to participate in the labor force. This continues to be the case, but the differences are much smaller. By March 1980, differences by age of child had decreased to the point that the percentage with mothers in the labor force varied only from 43 percent for those under age 6 to 56 percent for those 6-13 to 59 percent for those 14-17.[4,5] By 1980 as well, the percentage of children in two-parent households with mothers in the labor force had risen to 52, compared to 62 for the children in mother-only households.

The ultimate outcome of these changes has been that children with working mothers are now in the majority; as of 1980, 52.8 percent of children had mothers who were labor force participants. What this means

[3] Whereas in 1960 about 28 percent of married women with children were labor force participants, in 1970 the percentage had risen to about 40, and in 1978 the percentage was up to about 53.

[4] Work hours of the working mothers as well as the proportion of mothers working have varied substantially by age of child (Masnick and Bane, 1980). Between 1970 and 1978 married women with children of all ages registered sharp increases in full-time as well as part-time work. Among married mothers with children aged 6-17, as well as those with children aged 3-5, the proportion working full time increased more sharply than the proportion working part time. Among mothers with the youngest children, those under age 3, the sharper increase was in part-time work. Throughout this period, mothers with school-age children continued to be the group most likely to be full-time

is that mothers have been increasingly taking on labor market responsibilities while continuing to have family obligations that require their presence in the home a substantial part of the time. Across all income levels and life-cycle stages, working wives have indicated that they face greater time pressures than nonworking wives (Strober and Weinberg, 1980:346):

> The primary strategies used by employed wives to cope with time pressures seem to be decreasing the time spent on household production, the time allocated to volunteer and community work, and the time allocated to leisure and sleep.

The time pressures, as well as the coping reaction, may well mean an increase in stress for the mother and her children when she increases her labor force participation, especially if poor economic circumstances are the major motivation behind the increase in market work.

Race and Family Situation

The long-established racial differential in mother's work status has also narrowed since 1970. Historically, black mothers have been more likely to be labor force participants than white mothers. While this continues to hold, the difference by race is now smaller, due to a narrowing of the race difference in participation among married mothers plus no reversal in the race difference among unmarried mothers.

Among both married and unmarried mothers, participation rates for blacks and whites increased over the decade. Among married mothers, though, the increase was considerably greater for whites than blacks

---

workers, with the proportion working full time exceeding the proportion working part time. Mothers with children under age 3 remained the group most likely to be part-time workers, with a greater tendency toward part-time than full-time work. Mothers with children aged 3-5 continued to be the intermediate group, although among this group there was a somewhat greater tendency toward part-time than full-time work.

[5] These differences in work commitment can be further examined in terms of average weeks worked over the year (Bradbury et al., 1979). Comparing the 1975 work weeks of women ages 25-44 with children by marital status and sex of head reveals marital status differences in labor force commitment among mother-only households. Never-married mothers averaged considerably fewer workweeks (20 as opposed to 28) than did separated/divorced/widowed mothers. In fact, the never-married mothers averaged about the same number of work weeks as currently married mothers (21), who worked fewer weeks than mothers in mother-only households as a whole.

after the mid-1970s.[6] This led to reductions in the degree to which black married mothers were the more likely participants. The rate of increase in participation for unmarried mothers, in contrast, was quite similar for blacks and whites.[7] Of the unmarried mothers, though, whites have for some time been the more likely participants. The end result is that, by 1980, the percentage of white children with a mother in the labor force was up to 52 percent, compared to the 57 percent of black children in the same situation.

While differences between black and white children were diminishing with respect to mother's labor market participation, they were widening in terms of the likelihood of being in a two-parent versus a mother-only family. Each year since 1970, a larger proportion of white than black children has been living with two parents. Despite an increase in mother-only, female-headed households among white families with children, this differential grew because of an even larger shift in the same direction among blacks. By the end of the decade, this shift among blacks resulted in equal proportions of black children living in two-parent and mother-only households.[8]

Among the mother-only households, there are also important race differences having to do with the marital status of the mother. During the 1970s there was a shift in the marital status mix of mother-only households that affected black and white children differently. At the end of the decade, as at the beginning, the majority of both black and white children in mother-only families were living with a divorced or separated mother. However, there was an increase in the proportion of white children with a divorced or separated mother, while the proportion of black children with a divorced or separated mother actually declined. This differential shift was due to the greater increase for blacks in the proportion with a never-married mother as head of the household. The increase in black households of this type was so large that by the end

[6] For white children in two-parent households, the portion with mothers working outside the home increased from 36 percent in 1970 to 51 percent in 1980; for black children the corresponding increase was from 52 percent to 62 percent.

[7] Among the children living with their mother only, 57 percent of the whites, as opposed to 47 percent of the blacks, had working mothers in 1970. As of 1980 these percentages both had increased, to 67 percent for whites and 57 percent for blacks.

[8] By 1979 the percentage of black children living with two parents had dropped to 43, whereas the percentage in mother-only households had risen to 42. Changes for white children were in the same direction but much smaller in magnitude, with 84 percent in two-parent households in 1979, as opposed to 13 percent in one-parent households. Standardizing for changes in the age distribution of children, Bianchi and Farley's (1979) figures provide further evidence of the large race differentials in living arrangements of children widening in recent years.

of the decade more than 25 percent of black children in mother-only households were living in households headed by a never-married mother.[9] This meant that 10 percent of all black children, compared to less than 1 percent of all white children, were in never-married, mother-only families.

Movement of Mothers In and Out of the Labor Force and One-Parent Status

While the changes noted for children in terms of the work status of the mother and two-parent/one-parent living arrangements were pervasive, they were not permanent. Mothers moved both in and out of the labor force and many married, became divorced, and then remarried.

Analyses of women's work histories, both retrospective (e.g., Corcoran, 1978) and longitudinal (e.g., D. H. Hill, 1979; Masnick and Bane, 1980), show considerable movement in and out of market work. Though their longitudinal examination of women's work patterns is confined to women either stably married or persistently household heads, Masnick and Bane's figures for the period 1968-1977 are helpful in assessing the extent of labor force movement by women with children. Using PSID data, they found that about four out of five women aged 18-47 in stable living arrangements worked at least 1 year during the 10-year period, but less than one-third worked all 10 years. Separate calculations for stably married women and those persistently heads of households showed a much greater prevalence of permanent labor force attachment among the latter group, particularly among younger women.

Just as the changes in labor force participation of women were more pervasive but less permanent than cross-section figures suggest, so too were changes in their living arrangements. Female-headed families are strikingly transient, with most ever-married mothers remarrying eventually (Bane and Weiss, 1980; Ross and Sawhill, 1975; Wattenberg and Reinhardt, 1979). Thus, an increasingly familiar pattern for children has been to experience the dissolution of their parents' marriage while they are young, spend several years in a mother-only/female-headed household, and then spend the rest of their childhood in the family formed by their mother's remarriage. The average length of the time-

[9] Of the white children in mother-only households, 76 percent were living with a divorced or separated mother in 1970 and 81 percent were in 1979. The comparable change for blacks was a decrease from 71 percent to 61 percent. At the same time, the proportion of white children living with never-married mothers increased from 3 to 6 percent of all white children in mother-only households. The comparable change for blacks was an increase from 15 to 28 percent.

between marriages for the mother is 4.5 years. As Bane and Weiss (1980:11) state:

> This may be a relatively brief interval for an adult, but it is a significant one in a child's life.

Economic Well-Being

A common belief seems to be that being raised in a family without a father present or with the mother spending substantial time away from home is damaging to children not only while they are growing up but after they reach adulthood as well. However, the findings concerning impaired school performance, reduced scores on intellectual indices, and increased antisocial behavior, while extensive, are not consistent. Indeed, some hypotheses and research suggest that a working mother exerts positive as well as negative effects on child development. In addition, many of the ills associated with single-parenthood may in fact be due to the lower economic status of one-parent families: Lower economic status for these families is a very consistent finding.

The level of material resources available to children is clearly important to their development. By affecting the degree to which their basic physical needs—for food, clothing, and shelter—are satisfied, the available resources influence their immediate and possibly longer-term health. Deprivation resulting from low family income during childhood may be detrimental to a child's personality and emotional development as well. The family's economic resources also can influence educational attainment and skill development.

With the many changes in family life during the past decade, a major cause for concern is what has happened to the level of economic resources available to children. While this topic has been addressed by many researchers, the amount of dispersion in economic well-being, whether it has changed, and if so by how much, are topics that have not been thoroughly investigated.

Well-Being Measures

The typical level of family money relative to family needs,[10] a measure of per capita income, is a fairly good indicator of children's economic well-being. Economic well-being, though, can be affected not only by

[10] This measure is the ratio of total family cash income divided by estimated total family money needs. The needs estimate is based on the Orshansky "thrifty" needs standard.

the typical level of resources available but also by the degree of deviation from this typical level.

A family income stream with substantial year-to-year variation complicates the choice of the optimal allocation path for a given level of lifetime income. Uncertainty and institutional barriers combine to preclude currently low-income families, even those with high expected lifetime income, from borrowing against future income. Thus, children in families with substantial income instability are in a weaker economic position than children in otherwise similar families with the same expected lifetime incomes but more income stability.

The distribution of income across children is also an important indicator of social welfare. For children even more than for adults, equality of opportunity depends strongly on equality of access to income because income affects access to education. Because measures of lifetime income are better than measures of 1-year income for analyzing children's well-being, longitudinal data are more appropriate than cross-sectional data.

While most of the recent changes in the composition of children's families have resulted from divorce or separation, out-of-wedlock births have also contributed. These differing sources of the increase in mother-only households can have different implications for the well-being of the children living in the households. Recent findings, for example, indicate that out-of-wedlock birth, particularly among teenagers, creates a family form likely to need public assistance (Moore and Hofferth, 1978). Out-of-wedlock births are associated with low levels of educational attainment for the mother as well as larger completed family size, and these are important factors leading to the disproportionately large number of teenage mothers receiving welfare income. Out-of-wedlock birth is more frequent among black women than white. However, early childbirth, with its large proportion of out-of-wedlock births, seems to have a less detrimental effect for blacks over the long run (Hofferth and Moore, 1979). Among black women, early childbirth fosters greater work experience, leading to somewhat higher subsequent income. Early childbirth imparts no such long-run benefits for white women.

Unfortunately, the PSID data do not permit a clear analysis concerning out-of-wedlock birth nor unambiguous identification of never-married mothers. Consequently, the following analysis focuses on the distinction between two-parent and mother-only households, with no separation of the latter according to marital status.

The number, age, and sex of family members are factors used to determine an estimate of total family weekly money and food needs on the basis of the Orshansky standard. Adjustments for "economies of scale" are made for large families, and the weekly food needs are then translated to a total annual money needs value.

Data

This analysis uses several samples from the PSID. All data have been weighted to be representative of the U.S. population as a whole. An initial cross-sectional view of changes in the economic well-being of children during the last decade compares the economic situation of all children aged 1-16 in the sample in 1970 with the economic situation of all children aged 1-16 in the sample in 1979. Like the Current Population Survey, the PSID gathers income information each year by asking about the income of all family members during the preceding year. Thus, the cross-sectional family income/family needs comparisons apply to the years 1969 and 1978 for children in 1970 and 1979, respectively. The longitudinal analysis follows three cohorts of children across time. The primary cohort consists of all sample individuals aged 1-6 at the start of the 10-year analysis period, 1970-1979. These individuals were the only ones to remain within the age range 1-16 throughout those 10 years. The other two longitudinal samples follow children for 8 years only. One consists of children aged 1 in either 1969, 1970, or 1971. Members of this cohort are followed through their first 8 years of life. The other 8-year sample consists of children aged 9 in either 1969, 1970, or 1971. Members of this cohort are followed through ages 9-16. These samples of single-year birth cohorts[11] are used primarily to observe the long-run living arrangements that children born in the 1970s were likely to experience.

We view children's economic well-being first from a cross-sectional perspective and then from a longitudinal one. As we shall see, the cross-sectional view can be deceptive. This is because three cohorts of children are involved in a cross-sectional comparison of beginning and end years of a decade—the cohort born during the decade, the cohort there throughout the decade, and the cohort reaching an age beyond the upper limit of the childhood range before the decade ended.[12]

[11] Three successive single-year birth cohorts were combined to represent children born in the middle year of the 3-year range. This was done in order to produce a large enough sample size to allow disaggregation by the desired characteristics.

[12] These different cohorts can be identified by age at the end of the decade: The born-in cohorts would be aged 9 or younger, the continuing-on cohort would be aged 10-16, and the growing-up-and-out cohort would be aged 17 or older.

Cross-Sectional Analysis

Table 1 presents the view of a cross-sectional analysis using information about the economic situation of children at the beginning and end of the decade. The figures in this table indicate that children as a group began the decade fairly well off economically and that the economic position of children had improved somewhat by the end of the decade. At the beginning of the decade, family income was almost three times as high as needs. The change in this ratio throughout the decade (an increase from 2.9 to 3.4) is consistent with increases amounting to 1.6 percent per year, or 17.5 percent during the 10 years. Per capita income was as evenly distributed across children in 1979 as it was in 1970. The percentage of poor was somewhat lower in 1979 than in 1970.[13] Accompanying this improvement were increases in the percentage of children receiving welfare[14] as well as in those dependent on welfare.[15]

We see a rise in the average level of per capita income in the cross section despite the dramatic shift of children from higher-income two-parent households to lower-income mother-only households. Other cross-sectional analyses have shown that: (1) The average annual income level for two-parent families was about $20,000 and for mother-only households about $8,000 toward the end of the 1970s decade; (2) per capita income differences were also quite large (Bianchi and Farley, 1979); (3) the proportion of families who were poor was six times greater among mother-only households (Bane and Weiss, 1980), despite the longer work hours and higher personal income of mothers heading their own households relative to those living with their husbands (Bradbury et al., 1979); and (4) a married woman could expect about a 40 percent reduction in economic well-being as a result of becoming a single head of family (Bradbury et al., 1979).

In the cross section, detrimental economic effects of the shifts in household headship were somewhat ameliorated by increases in the average level of economic well-being across all categories of households.

[13] The poverty measure corresponds to the official definition of poverty, with the poverty line set at a ratio of family income/needs equal to 1. A child is counted as in poverty in a given year if his/her family income that year is less than family needs.

[14] Welfare status is based on reports of income from the following sources: AFDC, SSI, General Assistance payments, Old Age Assistance, Aid to the Disabled, or food stamps. A child is counted as a welfare recipient in a given year if he/she is living with a parent who is either the household head or wife and who received income from any of these sources during the previous year.

[15] Welfare dependency is determined on the basis of the portion welfare income is of total annual income of the household head and wife. If the portion is one-half or more, all children in the household are counted as welfare dependents.

TABLE 1 Various Measures of Family Situation and Economic Well-Being for All Children in 1970 and in 1979 (Cross-Section Samples)

	1970			1979		
	Nonblack	Black	All	Nonblack	Black	All
Income/needs ratio:						
Average	3.07	1.63	2.85	3.60	1.86	3.35
Two-parent families	3.20	2.02	3.08	3.86	2.51	3.66
Mothers only	1.89	1.12	1.59	1.99	1.20	1.72
Other families	2.52	1.11	1.82	3.36	1.59	2.58
GINI coefficient	0.307	0.389	0.330	0.306	0.371	0.330
Top 10 percent/bottom 10 percent	2.04	0.05	1.0	1.98	0.04	1.0
Percent poor	6.4	36.8	10.9	5.3	31.9	9.1
Percent receiving welfare	6.7	36.8	11.2	12.1	44.1	16.7
Percent dependent on welfare	3.1	20.1	5.6	4.3	24.7	7.2
Family situation:						
Percent two-parent	89.5	56.9	84.7	84.7	47.9	79.5
Percent mother only	8.2	30.4	11.5	12.6	39.7	16.5
Percent other	2.3	12.8	3.9	2.7	12.4	4.1
Children in family:						
Two-parent families	3.3	4.3	3.4	2.5	3.0	2.5
Mother only	2.9	4.2	3.4	2.2	2.7	2.4
Other families	3.0	3.9	3.5	1.6	2.9	2.2
All families	3.3	4.2	3.4	2.4	2.9	2.5
Percent with mother's work hours:						
Less than 500	65.9	58.2	64.8	53.7	45.8	52.6
500–1,499	16.2	19.0	16.6	20.2	20.3	20.2
1,500 or more	17.9	22.8	18.6	26.1	33.9	27.2
Average age of child (years)	8.5	8.7	8.5	8.4	8.4	8.4
N	3,357	3,310	6,667	3,056	2,497	5,553

There was a large increase in average per capita income for children in two-parent families. This, combined with a small increase for children in mother-only families, more than counteracted the downward effect of the shift toward mother-only families.

Although the cross-sectional increase in per capita income for children in mother-only households seems inconsistent with Bradbury et al.'s (1979) report of large economic losses from a marital disruption, it is not in fact necessarily so. It could well be that the groups of children who entered the cross section (those born during the decade) in mother-only households were economically better off than the groups of children who were initially in mother-only households. The decline in the birthrate in conjunction with the rise in the labor-force-participation rate of mothers is a likely source for the apparent inconsistency.

Within each headship category, as well as overall, the average number of children in a child's family (equivalently, the average number of a child's siblings plus one) declined. This helped reduce the average needs level of families, thus increasing the family income/needs ratio.

The greater labor force participation of mothers over the decade also led to increases in the income portion of the family income/needs ratio. A cross-sectional examination of mother's work status and its relationship to median family income (Grossman, 1981) has shown consistently higher incomes for children with working mothers, regardless of the race and the living arrangement of the child. In addition, large numbers of children were found to have a substantial share of their support coming from their mother's earnings. This occurred most often when the child was either in a mother-only household or in a two-parent household with the father unemployed or out of the labor force.

Race Differences in 1970 and 1979

During the 1970s there were persistent dramatic differences in the levels of economic well-being between black and nonblack children. In both 1970 and 1979, the average level of per capita income for nonblack children was almost twice that of black children. Inequality in the distribution of income/needs around its modal value (GINI coefficient) remained somewhat greater for black than nonblack children; and inequality at the ends of the distribution (top 10 percent/bottom 10 percent)[16] remained much greater for blacks. Both in 1970 and 1979, almost no black children occupied the top decile of the income/needs distri-

[16] This figure was calculated on the basis of the percentages the racial subgroup that fell in the top or bottom decile of the distribution of income/needs across *all* children.

bution for children, and about 33 percent were poor. While the percentage of black children who were poor did fall somewhat over the decade, black children continued to be more likely than white children to be in poverty. The greater likelihood of black children being in a household receiving welfare income declined some, as did the greater likelihood of black children being in a household dependent on welfare income. Thus the economic position of black children improved somewhat during the 1970s, although it remained much worse than that of white children.

A Longitudinal View of Children's Economic Well-Being

Cross-sectional information at two points in time tells us virtually nothing about individual change. An unchanging estimate of the size of the poverty population at two points in time, for example, is consistent both with *no* turnover in the poverty population and with *complete* turnover. The number of individuals who fell into poverty equaled the number who climbed out. Longitudinal data are, thus, crucial for a reliable study of the empirical patterns of childhood access to economic resources. Analysis of the mean level of childhood per capita income (family income relative to needs), the trend in annual per capita income, and a measure of the degree of instability in annual per capita income are all required for a full description of the typical stream of income available during childhood years. Investigation of additional measures, such as long-run exposure to poverty, welfare receipt, and welfare dependency, can help round out the picture of the typical childhood experience. All these measures will be examined in the pages that follow, as we now turn our focus to the group of children included in the 10-year longitudinal sample.

Flow of Family Income/Needs

From the figures in Table 2, we see that the economic environment of the 1970s was mildly favorable as measured by income relative to need for the children aged 1-6 at the start of the decade. These children averaged a level of 10-year family income three times as large as their 10-year family needs. However, growth in their annual level of family income/needs was small, increasing only about 1 percent per year. In addition, many children had negative trends in per capita income.[17] Part

[17] Trend in family income/needs is calculated by adjusting annual family income/needs by the CPI, then regressing annual income/needs, measured in logarithms, on time.

TABLE 2 Various Income/Needs Measures Over the Decade of the 1970s (10-Year Longitudinal Sample)

	Initially Aged 1–6		
	Nonblack	Black	All
Average income/needs			
Mean	3.32	1.65	3.10
GINI coefficient	0.283	0.298	0.305
Top 10 percent/bottom 10 percent	2.30	0.00	1.0
Instability of income/needs	0.67	0.85	0.69
Mean	0.497	0.261	0.467
GINI coefficient	8.8	17.3	10.0
Trend in income/needs			
Mean	0.014	−0.001	0.012
Percent with trend 0	38.8	52.2	40.6
Average number of children in household	2.9	3.9	3.1

of the rise in income/needs seen in the cross section, therefore, is apparently due to the positive trend in income/needs for a large share of the cohort of individuals who were children both at the beginning and end of the decade. Here we are able to see a strong inconsistency between the cross-sectional and longitudinal results—an inconsistency in the rate of growth in children's per capita income. The cross-sectional results showed an increase of 1.6 percent per year, whereas the longitudinal analysis shows an increase of 1.0 percent per year. While this difference may seem small, when we transform these annual rates to 10-year, compounded rates, we see that the differences implied for the change in children's economic well-being are *not* so small. The cross-sectional annual rate of 1.6 percent means a 10-year rate of increase of 17.5 percent; this compares with a 10.5 percent increase produced by the annual longitudinal rate of 1.0 percent. Thus, the cross-sectional analysis erroneously implies an increase in per capita income for children one and one-half to two times as large as the increase children actually experienced.

Besides level and trend in per capita income, another aspect of economic well-being that can be measured only with longitudinal data is the extent of instability in the flow of per capita income across time.[18]

[18] Instability in family income/needs is a measure based on the standard error of the trend regression. It equals the square root of the sum of squared deviations around the trend. It is a measure of the extent to which an individual's per capita income deviates from his or her own trend in per capita income.

The PSID data show a considerable degree of instability, and the amount of instability differs much more across children than does the level of 10-year per capita income.

The figures in Table 2 show astounding race differences:

- Average long-run family income/needs was half as large for black children as for nonblack children.
- Among nonblacks, there were two and one-third times as many children in the highest income/needs decile as there were in the lowest decile. There were virtually no black children in the highest income/needs decile.
- Instability in family income/needs was one and one-third times as large for black children as it was for nonblack children.
- Twice as large a percentage of black children as of nonblack children fell in the top decile of instability in family income/needs.
- Among nonblack children, the trend in income/needs was positive, but this was not so among black children.

Thus, black children averaged much lower levels of long-run per capita income, with a less positive trend and greater instability over time.

Poverty and Welfare Use

We can also look at the long-run incidence of poverty, welfare use, and welfare dependency, including welfare income as part of family income when determining poverty status. From Table 3, we see that between one-quarter and one-third of the children aged 1-6 in 1970 were poor at some time during the 1970s. Six percent of all children—one-fifth of the poor ones—were poor at least half of the 10 years of the decade. Welfare was received by a large fraction of children (33 percent), but only 10 percent were dependent on welfare at some time. In addition, long-term welfare dependency (defined as 6 or more years out of the 10) was much less common among children than was long-term welfare receipt; only 5 percent of the children were long-term welfare dependents, whereas twice that number were long-term welfare recipients. Interestingly enough, poverty was a much more frequent occurrence for children than was welfare dependency.

So we see that, despite a high average level of economic well-being for children during the 1970s, poverty was widespread among children, most of it of a temporary nature. Welfare receipt was common for children also, but long-term welfare dependency, like long-term poverty, was rare.

Experiences of black and nonblack children regarding poverty and welfare use were dramatically different during the 1970s. As Table 3 shows:

- Even with cash welfare benefits added to family income, the majority (70 percent) of black children were poor at some time during the decade. This compares to 20 percent of nonblack children.
- Black children were much more likely to be in persistent poverty than were nonblack children (30 percent compared to 2 percent). For both groups of children, though, poverty was more likely to be a temporary than a permanent state.
- The majority (75 percent) of black children spent some time with a welfare-recipient parent. This compares to 25 percent of nonblack children.
- Almost half of the black children (46 percent) spent some time with a parent who depended on welfare as the major source of income; only 8 percent of nonblack children did so.

TABLE 3 Long-Run Poverty and Welfare Status, by Race (10-Year Longitudinal Sample)

	Nonblack	Black	All
Percent in poverty—			
Number of years poor			
0	79.1	30.3	72.5
1–5	18.8	40.1	21.5
6–10	2.3	29.7	5.8
Average number of years poor			
All	0.6	3.5	0.9
Those ever in poverty	2.6	5.0	3.4
Percent receiving welfare			
0	73.6	25.6	67.1
1–5	20.6	31.4	22.1
6–10	5.8	43.0	10.9
Average number of years receiving welfare			
All	0.9	4.6	1.4
Those ever receiving welfare	3.6	6.2	4.4
Percent dependent on welfare			
0 years	92.1	54.0	87.0
1–5 years	5.6	25.1	8.3
6–10 years	2.2	20.8	4.8
Average number of years dependent on welfare			
All	0.3	2.4	0.6
Those ever dependent on welfare	4.1	5.2	4.6

Despite these large race differences regarding poverty and welfare use, black and nonblack children were quite similar in one important regard: The majority of children who were long-term welfare recipients, whether black or nonblack, were *not* long-term welfare dependents. This indicates that welfare is but one source of income, and not even the largest one, for most children who are long-term recipients.

These large race differences in the poverty and welfare experiences of children are confirmed by other research using the PSID data. Martha S. Hill (1981), for example, finds that blacks are much more susceptible than whites to long-term poverty: during a 10-year period, 20 percent of the individuals temporarily poor were black, whereas 60 percent of those persistently poor were black. In addition, at the end of the 10 years, almost half of the individuals poor the entire time were in female-headed households with children present. Coe's (1981) analysis of differences in long-run patterns of welfare receipt shows further evidence of strong racial differences for children. He finds that children in general, and black children in particular, were much more likely than adults, either black or white, to be in households receiving welfare at some time during the 1970s decade. Further, children—and again, black children especially—were more likely than adults to be long-term welfare recipients. This was especially true for welfare in the form of food stamps. In an analysis of factors distinguishing short- and long-term welfare users, Coe finds that presence of young children is a primary factor causing the racial difference in long-term welfare receipt; black household heads are more likely to have young children at home.

According to Coe (1981:160):

> The presence of young children in households headed by unmarried persons, particularly females and blacks, has a considerable impact on both the incidence and length of time of welfare receipt.

A Longitudinal View of Children's Living Situations

Analysis of the PSID data by others has shown that income changes substantially over time for individuals throughout the income distribution and that these changes are not well explained by differences in the attitudes or skills of family members or by events such as unemployment or migration. As stated by Duncan (1981:42):

> The single most important set of events in accounting for changes in well-being were fundamental changes in family structure: divorces, deaths, marriages, births, and children leaving home.

Analysis of the PSID data has shown, repeatedly, that changes in family composition are critically important in explaining changes in economic well-being (Duncan and Morgan, 1980; Lane and Morgan, 1975; Morgan, 1974) and that these changes are particularly important for women and children.

Until recently, however, very little was known about the pervasiveness and frequency of family composition changes. Little is known still about the family composition changes children undergo, and many estimates are speculative. A need specifically identified at the 1978 Census Bureau Conference on Issues in Federal Statistical Needs Relating to Women was data on the rapidity of household change and how individuals move over time among various types of households and the average length of the intervals adults and children spend in different types of households. With 20 percent as the highest annual percentage of children in a mother-only household, tentative estimates of the fraction living in a mother-only household at some time during childhood range from one-quarter (Bane, 1976) to one-third (Glick, 1980). Indications are that the length of time spent in these households is much greater for black children than for white children (Bumpass and Rindfuss, 1978) because of the lower remarriage rates of black women (Thornton, 1978). As many as 60 percent of black children are estimated to experience the disruption of their parents' marriage, and one-third of all black children are estimated to remain in mother-only households from the time of the disruption to the end of their childhood years (Bumpass and Rindfuss, 1979).

Examination of the long-run living arrangements of the 8-year and 10-year PSID samples (Tables 4-7) yields substantially more precise estimates:

- During the first 8 years of their lives, as many as one-quarter of the children born near the start of the 1970s decade spent some time in a household with at most one parent present. More than one-fifth spent some time in a mother-only household, and 3 percent spent all 8 years in mother-only households (Table 4).
- Among children aged 9 at the start of the decade, almost 30 percent spent some time in the 8 years prior to reaching age 16 in a household with at most one parent present. About one-quarter spent some time in a mother-only household, and almost 10 percent spent all 8 years in mother-only households (Table 5).
- The children born in 1970 who spent some time in a mother-only household averaged almost 4 of their first 8 years in such a household. The children aged 9 in 1970 who spent time in a mother-only household

TABLE 4 Percent of Children in Various Family Situations Over the Long Run (8-Year Longitudinal Sample Initially Aged 1)

	Number of Years				
	0	1–2	3–4	5–7	8
Nonblack children (N = 570)					
Father and mother present	3.3	1.7	3.6	12.0	79.3
Mother present, father not present	82.8	8.5	4.4	3.0	1.4
Black children (N = 421)					
Father and mother present	32.1	8.7	8.5	11.3	39.3
Mother present, father not present	51.8	8.6	10.5	14.3	14.7
All children (N = 991)					
Father and mother present	7.2	2.7	4.3	11.8	74.0
Mother present, father not present	78.7	8.5	5.2	4.5	3.1

TABLE 5 Percent of Children in Various Family Situations Over the Long Run (8-Year Longitudinal Sample Initially Aged 9)

	Number of Years				
	0	1–2	3–4	5–7	8
Nonblack children (N = 497)					
Father and mother present	7.2	4.2	2.4	7.8	78.3
Mother present, father not present	81.0	4.1	4.1	4.9	5.9
Black children (N = 529)					
Father and mother present	38.6	5.9	9.7	7.3	38.5
Mother present, father not present	49.8	5.8	5.2	10.3	28.9
All children (N = 1,026)					
Father and mother present	12.3	4.5	3.6	7.8	71.9
Mother present, father not present	76.0	4.4	4.3	5.8	9.6

averaged an additional year there, making it more than half of their 8 years prior to age 16 (Table 7).

If the 1980s are similar to the 1970s in terms of changes in family living situations, the previous estimate of one-quarter of the children born in the 1970s spending some time in a mother-only household is clearly too low. An estimate of one-third may, in fact, not be high enough. By age 8, more than 20 percent of the children born in 1970 had spent time

TABLE 6 Percent of Children in Various Family Situations Over the Long Run (10-Year Longitudinal Sample)

	Number of Years					
	0	1–2	3–5	6–7	8–9	10
Nonblack children (N = 1,285)						
Father and mother present	3.8	2.0	5.5	5.3	5.9	77.4
Mother present, father not present	79.9	5.7	7.1	2.5	1.7	3.1
Black children (N = 1,086)						
Father and mother present	32.5	7.7	12.0	4.4	9.9	33.6
Mother present, father not present	43.4	9.7	9.9	7.6	11.0	18.4
All (N = 2,371)						
Father and mother present	7.7	2.8	6.4	5.2	6.5	71.5
Mother present, father not present	75.0	6.3	7.6	3.1	2.9	5.2

TABLE 7 Average Number of Years in Various Family Situations Over the Long Run for Those Spending at Least 1 Year in That Family Situation (8-Year Longitudinal Samples)

	Average Number of Years	
Sample Spending at Least 1 Year in Situation	Father and Mother Present	Mother Present, Father Not Present
Initially aged 1		
Nonblack (N = 570)	7.5	3.2
Black (N = 421)	6.2	5.3
All (N = 991)	7.4	3.8
Initially aged 9		
Nonblack (N = 497)	7.4	5.1
Black (N = 529)	6.4	6.4
All (N = 1,026)	7.3	5.5

in mother-only households. For the cohort 8 years older, the percentage in mother-only households at some time during those same 8 chronological years (for them, ages 9-16) was even larger—about 25 percent. Thus, the likelihood of spending time in a mother-only household seems somewhat greater in the second half of childhood than in the first half. Consequently, one-fifth is certainly a lower bound for the fraction of the 1970 birth cohort ever in mother-only households. While these figures cannot establish a clear upper bound, they suggest that the upper limit could go as high as one-half for this cohort.

We can add information about mother's work status to get a more complete picture of children's living situations (see Tables 8 and 9). Doing so, we find that:

- Between ages 1 and 8, about 15 percent of the 1970 birth cohort were never in a "traditional" living situation, that is, with both parents present and the mother not working.
- Only about one-quarter (26.8 percent) of the 1970 birth cohort spent all of their first 8 years in two-parent, mother-not-working households.
- More than two-thirds of the 1970 birth cohort who lived in a mother-only household spent some time with the mother working while heading the household. This compares with about 60 percent of the children in a two-parent household with a working mother.

Figures were similar for the cohort aged 1-6 in 1970, with differences mainly reflecting a somewhat greater frequency of market activity among mothers of the older children. Thus, we see that never having a working mother is a rare situation for children of the 1970s. It was somewhat less common for the children in mother-only households never to have had a working mother than it was for the children always living with both parents. Overall, children spending their entire childhood in a two-

TABLE 8 Family Type and Mother's Annual Hours Worked (8-Year Longitudinal Sample Initially Aged 1) (Percentage in Group)

Headship and Mother's Work Status	Number of Years in Status					
	0	1–2	3–4	5–7	8	
Nonblack						
Father present, mother worked 500 hours	10.5	11.9	12.1	27.3	28.2	(5.7)[a]
Mother only, mother worked 500 hours	87.7	7.3	3.0	1.9	0.0	(2.6)
Black						
Father present, mother worked 500 hours	42.5	16.8	8.3	14.6	17.8	(4.8)
Mother only, mother worked 500 hours	68.7	14.7	9.0	6.8	0.6	(3.2)
All						
Father present, mother worked 500 hours	14.7	12.5	11.7	34.3	26.8	(5.6)
Mother only, mother worked 500 hours	85.2	8.3	3.8	2.6	0.1	(2.8)

[a] Numbers in parentheses are average number of years in status, for those with more than 0 years in it.

TABLE 9 Number of Years in Various Headship/Mother's Work Hours Situations (10-Year Longitudinal Sample)

	Number of Years in Status						
	0	1–2	3–5	6–7	8–0	10	
Nonblack							
Father head and mother's work hours 500	14.6	10.2	16.4	14.8	17.8	26.1	(6.9)[a]
Mother head and mother's work hours 500	83.7	7.1	4.7	2.5	1.4	0.6	(3.9)
Black							
Father head and mother's work hours 500	48.3	14.4	14.4	6.7	8.1	8.2	(5.2)
Mother head and mother's work hours 500	60.1	10.6	11.1	9.7	4.8	3.6	(5.1)
Total							
Father head and mother's work hours 500	19.1	10.7	16.2	13.8	16.5	23.7	(6.8)
Mother head and mother's work hours 500	80.5	7.5	5.6	3.5	1.9	1.0	(4.2)

[a] Numbers in parentheses are average number of years in status, for those with more than 0 years in it.

parent, mother-not-working household constitute a small minority of children.

Racial differences regarding time spent in mother-only households are much more striking than the racial differences concerning mother's work status:

- Only 40 percent of the black children born in 1970 spent all of their first 8 years of life in two-parent households. This compares with about 80 percent of the nonblack children.
- Almost 30 percent of the black children born in 1970 spent more than half of their first 8 years of life in mother-only households. This compares to about 5 percent of the nonblack children.
- Almost 30 percent of the black children were in mother-only households the entire 8 years between ages 9 and 16. The comparable figure for nonblack children was 6 percent.

Adding the work status of the mother as yet another dimension, we find the following race differences:

- About 20 percent of the black children (as opposed to 30 percent of the nonblack children) who were born in 1970 spent all of their first 8 years of life in two-parent, mother-not-working households.

- About 7 percent of the black children as opposed to 2 percent of the nonblack children who were born in 1970 spent more than half of their first 8 years of life in mother-only, mother-working households.
- Almost 4 percent of the black children were in mother-only, mother-working households the entire 8 years between ages 9 and 16. The comparable figure for nonblack children was about 1 percent.

These latter differences in living arrangements reflect the influences of two factors—race differences in propensities for living in mother-only households and race differences in the likelihood of the mother working, given the type of household. While black children are substantially more likely to live in mother-only households, and mothers in mother-only households are substantially more likely to be working than those in two-parent households, black children are only modestly more likely to live in mother-only, mother-working households. These findings are quite consistent with the racial differentials that were cited in the earlier section concerning demographic trends. Thus, the family composition situations of children differ very dramatically by race, and this contributes to the differences in mothers' work status for black and nonblack children. However, racial differences in mothers' work status within the different categories of family composition are relatively small.

Long-Run Relationship Between Economic Well-Being and Children's Living Situations

A comprehensive analysis of the relationship between family composition change and change in economic well-being (Morgan, 1974) has shown that marriages and remarriages of parents are the most economically beneficial of family composition changes, whereas marital disruptions are often detrimental for women and children. An analysis of the National Longitudinal Survey (NLS) young and mature women data sets (Mott, 1979) yields similar findings. In accordance with many other authors using differing data sources to investigate the economic well-being of female-headed households, Mott (1979:xii) concludes:

> In the final analysis, a woman heading her own household (and in particular a woman becoming head of her own household) in all too many instances is living in dire economic circumstances.

Following the fate of mothers subsequent to marital disruption, Bane and Weiss (1980) find sharp drops in family income—drops of 43 percent for divorced women, 51 percent for separated women, and 30 percent for widows. For all three groups there are small increases in income during the 2 years after the initial decrease, but without remarriage these mothers never again approach their income level before the marriage dissolved. The level of the decline in income subsequent to the disruption varies with race as well as type of disruption. The absolute decline is greater for white women than black women. However, since the income level of black women prior to the disruption is lower than that of white women, the reduction in income subsequent to the divorce is more likely to place newly formed black female households in poverty. Other race differences include a larger portion of black female heads receiving income from welfare and a smaller portion of black female heads receiving income from nonwelfare sources.

Evidence indicates that the ability of mothers to provide support for children equal to what it was before a marital disruption is limited. The primary source of income for previously married mothers is their own earnings, especially if the mother is divorced (Bane and Weiss, 1980). The percentage of mothers working increases from 66 to 90 percent following a divorce.[19] Increases in the percentage working are much smaller for mothers becoming separated or widowed, but as many as half of them do have income from their own work subsequent to their marital disruption.

The long-term separated tend to rely more heavily on public assistance, especially food stamps and AFDC, than do other groups of previously married mothers. While increased work effort by the mother would improve the economic situation of these families, the improvement would not be very large. Sawhill (1976) estimates that only one-quarter of such women could increase their income by as much as $1,000 per year by going to work full time. A factor in the decline of the economic resources available to children upon a marital disruption is the more favorable labor market conditions for men than women. If women were able to earn the higher wages of men with similar qualifications, more than one-half of these women would be able to improve

[19] There are race differences in the changes in employment status of women subsequent to a marital disruption. NLS longitudinal evidence (Mott, 1979) shows larger percentages of white women either becoming employed (in the case of mature women) or remaining employed (in the case of young women) right after the transition from being a wife to being a household head. Finding that such differences were present only among the less educated, though, Mott attributes much of this race differential to the higher proportion of black women with less than a high school education.

their economic well-being by distinctly more than $1,000 a year by going to work full time. Morgan (1974) also concludes that, in addition to two parents having greater earning capacity than one, men's wage levels being higher than women's is important to changes in income accompanying a change in marital status.

From analysis of changes in the well-being of children, 1968-1974, and changes in their living arrangements (Duncan and Morgan, 1976), we find that nearly one-quarter of the children losing a father through separation or divorce fell into poverty as a result. Marriage of an unmarried household head, in contrast, helped children climb out of poverty. Analysis of the later period, 1971-1978 (Duncan and Morgan, 1981), reaffirmed the strong relationship between changes in living arrangements and changes in the economic well-being of children: Whereas real per capita income grew by 4.7 percent per year for children in stable two-parent households, it fell by 4 percent per year for children with parents who became divorced or separated.

The PSID data also show a strong negative long-run relationship between economic well-being and the amount of time spent in a mother-only household (Tables 10-13). Average per capita income declines sharply and the percentage of poor increases dramatically as children spend more of their childhood in a mother-only household. The degree of variability in income across time is greater for children spending some but not most of the 10 years in a mother-only household, as measures of both instability and trend indicate.

Welfare is an important income source—but not the only one, even for children usually in mother-only households. Of these children, more than two-thirds received welfare at some time. Almost half were long-term welfare recipients, but only one-third were long-term welfare dependents. Apparently income sources other than welfare (and the literature suggests that the major one is mother's earnings) are essential to the economic well-being of children even in welfare-recipient, mother-only households.

Long-Run Relationships Between Race Differences in Economic Well-Being and Living Arrangements

We have seen that black children tend to fare much worse economically than nonblack children and that they have a much higher propensity for living in mother-only households—which fare worse economically than two-parent ones. This raises a question about the importance of racial differences in children's living arrangements. To what extent are racial differences in the economic situation of children the result of racial differences in family living arrangements? One way to try to an-

TABLE 10 Ten-Year Measures of Income/Needs by Usual Family Situation (10-Year Longitudinal Sample)

Subgroup	Family Situation 1970–1979 Always Both Parents	Occasionally Mother Only	Mostly Mother Only	Other	Total
Mean of average income/needs ratio					
Nonblack	3.50	2.97	2.23	2.93	3.32
Black	2.08	1.77	1.29	1.25	1.65
Total	3.41	2.74	1.81	2.29	3.10
Percent in top decile average income/needs ratio relative to percent in bottom decile					
Nonblack	3.1	1.8	0.0	0.6	2.3
Black	0.0	0.0	0.0	0.0	0.0
Total	2.1	0.9	0.0	0.1	1.0
Mean of instability of income/needs ratio					
Nonblack	0.61	0.94	0.75	0.63	0.67
Black	0.68	0.98	0.89	0.99	0.85
Total	0.62	0.94	0.82	0.77	0.69
Percent in top 10 percent of instability of income/needs ratio					
Nonblack	6.3	22.7	12.5	2.7	8.8
Black	8.0	20.0	22.4	24.1	17.3
Total	6.4	22.2	16.9	10.9	9.9
Mean of trend in income/needs ratio					
Nonblack	0.021	−0.021	−0.007	0.023	0.014
Black	0.024	−0.023	−0.016	0.013	−0.001
Total	0.021	−0.022	−0.011	0.019	0.012
Trend in income/needs					
Nonblack	33.2	65.6	53.7	29.5	38.8
Black	35.6	66.1	63.4	39.5	52.2
Total	33.5	65.7	57.9	33.3	40.6

swer this question is to decompose the mean value of an economic variable into two components: one based on the distribution of the individuals across household types (mother-only and two-parent) and the other based on the mean values of the economic variable for the individuals within each household type (the mean value for children in mother-only households and the mean value for children in two-parent

TABLE 11 Long-Run Poverty and Welfare Status, by Usual Family Situation, All Children (10-Year Longitudinal Sample)

	Family Situation				
	Always Both Parents	Occasionally Mother Only	Usually Mother Only	Other	Total
Percent in poverty—					
Number of years poor					
0 years	81.9	53.5	41.0	58.1	72.5
1–5 years	15.5	39.6	38.1	19.5	21.5
6–10 years	2.5	6.9	20.9	22.4	5.8
Average number of years poor					
Total	0.5	1.3	2.8	2.2	0.9
Those in poverty	2.9	2.8	4.7	5.2	3.4
Percent receiving welfare					
0 years	77.9	46.5	30.7	44.9	67.1
1–5 years	18.4	35.0	23.4	41.3	22.1
6–10 years	3.7	18.5	45.9	13.7	10.9
Average number of years receiving welfare					
Total	0.7	2.4	4.8	2.3	1.4
Those receiving welfare	3.1	4.5	7.0	4.2	4.4
Percent dependent on welfare					
0	96.4	71.7	48.3	81.3	87.0
1–5	3.0	24.0	21.5	13.7	8.3
6–10	0.6[a]	4.3[a]	30.1	5.0[a]	4.8
Average number of years dependent on welfare					
Total	0.1	0.9	3.3	0.7	0.6
Those dependent	3.3	3.0	6.3	3.7	4.6

[a] Fewer than 20 observations.

households). This decomposition of an economic measure is done separately for black and nonblack children; then, the mean values for black children by household type are applied to the distribution for nonblack children across the household types. Mean values for black children derived in this way are then compared to the actual mean values for nonblack children. Any reduction in the racial difference identified this way is then attributable to racial differences in living arrangements, because that is the only change that has been allowed. Racial differences in the economic variable by household type have been held constant.

TABLE 12 Long-Run Poverty and Welfare Status, by Usual Family Situation, Nonblack Children (10-Year Longitudinal Subsample of Nonblack Children)

	Family Situation				
	Always Both Parents	Occasionally Mother Only	Usually Mother Only	Other	Total
Percent in poverty					
0	83.6	61.2	62.2	82.5	79.1
1–5	15.1	33.0	31.5	16.2[a]	18.8
6–10	1.3[a]	5.8	6.3[a]	1.2[a]	2.3
Average number of years poor					
Total	0.4	0.9	1.5	0.4	0.6
Those in poverty	2.5	2.4	3.9	2.1[a]	2.6
Percent receiving welfare					
0	80.1	53.6	44.9	57.8	73.6
1–5	17.3	34.9	23.6	39.3[a]	20.6
6–10	2.5	11.4	31.4	2.9[a]	5.8
Average number of years receiving welfare					
Total	0.6	1.8	3.6	0.9	0.9
Those receiving welfare	2.9	3.8	6.5	2.1[a]	3.6
Percent dependent on welfare					
0	97.3	79.0	59.0	97.1	92.1
1–5	2.0	20.4	20.4	1.7[a]	5.6
6–10	0.7[a]	0.6[a]	20.6	1.2[a]	2.2
Average number of years dependent on welfare					
Total	0.1	0.5	2.3	0.2	0.3
Those dependent	3.9	2.4	5.7	5.5	4.1

[a] Fewer than 20 observations.

Table 14 presents the results of this procedure for several economic variables. Comparing the percentage of the race difference due to differences in living arrangements, we find substantial variation across the different economic measures. Differences in living arrangements account for very little of the overall race difference in economic measures based on the *level* of family income relative to need—the average income/needs ratio and poverty status. Turning to other dimensions of family income relative to needs, however, we find that differences in the long-run likelihood of living in a mother-only household account for a great deal of the race differences in both the trend and instability of the

TABLE 13 Long-Run Poverty and Welfare Status, by Usual Family Situation, Black Children (10-Year Longitudinal Sample of Black Children)

	Family Situation				
	Always Both Parents	Occasionally Mother Only	Usually Mother Only	Other	Total
Percent in poverty					
0 years	57.0	21.0	14.1	18.4	30.3
1–5 years	21.4	67.5	46.3	24.8	40.1
6–10 years	21.5	11.4	39.6	56.9	29.7
Average number of years poor					
Total	2.3	2.9	4.5	5.1	3.5
Those in poverty	5.3	3.6	5.2	6.2	5.0
Percent receiving welfare					
0 years	45.6	16.5	12.6	24.1	25.6
1–5 years	34.5	34.6	23.2	44.7	31.4
6–10 years	19.8	48.7	64.2	31.3	43.0
Average number of years receiving welfare					
Total	2.4	4.9	6.5	4.5	4.6
Those receiving welfare	4.5	5.9	7.4	6.0	6.2
Percent dependent on welfare					
0 years	82.5	40.8	34.8	55.6	54.0
1–5 years	17.1	39.2	22.9	33.1	25.1
6–10 years	0.5[a]	20.0[a]	42.3	11.2[a]	20.8
Average number of years dependent on welfare					
Total	0.3	2.3	4.5	1.5	2.4
Those dependent	1.9	3.9	6.9	3.5	5.2

[a] Fewer than 20 observations.

income/needs ratio. Thus, it seems that differences regarding *variation* in the flow rather than the general level of economic resources are what the race differences in living arrangements generate. This suggests that reduction in black children's greater long-run propensity for living in mother-only families, with no other change, would be of limited help in reducing the racial gap in economic well-being. Bringing the living arrangements of black children more in line with those of white children would help stabilize the flow of income to black children and raise the trend in their income, but it would not substantially increase their income level. Other changes apparently are needed to bring the family income level of black children up to that of nonblack children. The findings so

TABLE 14 Race Differences in Various Income/Needs Measures With and Without Adjustments for Race Differences in Children's Living Arrangements[a] (10-Year Longitudinal Sample)

	Total Race Difference in Means[b]	Percent of Total Due to Differences in Living Arrangements
Average income/needs ratio		
Mean	1.67	19
Top 10 percent/bottom 10 percent	2.3	0
Instability of income/needs ratio		
Mean	−0.18	61
If in top 10 percent	−8.5	74
Trend in income/needs ratio		
Mean	0.015	100
Percent with trend 0	−13.4	79
Number of years poor		
Mean	−2.9	31
Percent 0	48.8	37
Percent 6–10	−27.4	27
Number of years received welfare		
Mean	−3.7	41
Percent 0	48.0	28
Percent 6–10	−37.2	43
Number of years dependent on welfare		
Mean	−2.1	71
Percent 0	38.1	50

[a] Here "living arrangement" refers to being in a mother-only versus two-parent family.
[b] This equals the mean value for nonblack children minus the mean value for black children.

far suggest that it is factors associated with race differences in the level of economic resources within each kind of household that would need to be changed. This suggests, in turn, that what is needed to raise the family income level of black children up to that of white children are changes in the wage levels and skills of black household heads, both male and female.

Factors Associated with Long-Run Level of Family Income/Needs Ratio

To pursue further the issue of what factors, holding family type constant, affect the family income/needs ratio over time, multiple classification analysis was performed separately for the four major categories: black/two-parent, white/two-parent, black/sometime-one-parent, and white/

sometime-one-parent. The coefficients and the percentage of cases in each subcategory are shown in Table 15 for the following independent variables: parent's education (average education of the household head),[20] father's average annual work hours for the years when he is present in the child's household,[21] mother's work hours, number of siblings, and years spent in a mother-only household. As can be seen, a child's level of economic well-being increased with parent's education, father's work hours, and mother's work hours. It decreased with number of siblings and years spent in mother-only households. These general patterns were consistent across the differing race and living arrangement subgroups, and their collective explanatory power was quite large for all subgroups.[22] The patterns of R^2s indicate that there must be more important factors missing for nonblack children always in two-parent families than for the other subgroups. For example, the wage rates of the father and mother are not specified because they were unavailable for all children and inappropriate for some (e.g., children with never-married mothers). Another omitted predictor is the average wealth level of the child's household. This factor could affect the flow of asset income over time—directly as well as indirectly via eligibility for welfare—and also the ability to compensate for periods with low labor market earnings. Data limitations, however, precluded its inclusion in the analysis.

Other analysis of the PSID data (Corcoran and Duncan, 1979) documents large gender and race differentials in wages that persist even with extensive controls for work experience, training, and labor force attachment: Women's wages are lower than men's and blacks' wages are lower than nonblacks'. There are several indications in Table 15 that these differentials are important. For children within each household

[20] Education level of the household head is measured by summing years of education of each year's household head, then dividing by 10. The individual who was the household head could, of course, vary by year.

[21] If no father was present in a given year, father's work hours are counted as zero in that year.

[22] Parent's education was relatively more important for children never in a mother-only household, i.e., those always in two-parent families. For children in two-parent households, this measure reflects father's education only, whereas for children ever in mother-only households it combines father's and mother's education in proportion to the fraction of time each parent was head of the child's household. To the extent that mother's and father's education differ, the education predictor used in the analysis will contain a larger measurement error component for children ever in mother-only households than for children always in two-parent households. This could be the source of the difference in predictive power according to the living arrangement of the child. Since some children never had their father present in the household, though, father's education could not be clearly measured for all children.

TABLE 15 Factors Affecting 10-Year Average Income/Needs Ratio, by Race and Family Situation (10-Year Longitudinal Sample)

	Always Two Parents				Mother Only at Some Time			
	Nonblack		Black		Nonblack		Black	
	Percent of Cases	Coefficients	Percent of Cases	Coefficients	Percent of Cases	Coefficients	Percent of Cases	Coefficients
Average formal education of head								
No high school	12.0	−1.082	37.9	−0.397	14.5	−0.640	20.1	−0.263
Some high school	20.1	−0.746	22.2	−0.214	38.5	−0.258	51.4	−0.138
High school	30.9	−0.309	32.8	0.395	28.8	−0.166	21.3	0.332
Some college	18.9	0.518	6.8	1.006	14.2	1.179	7.2	0.749
College or more	18.1	1.536	0.4	[a]	4.0	[a]	0.0	[a]
(Beta^2)		(0.208)		(0.147)		(0.186)		(0.120)
Average work hours of father								
0	0.2	[a]	0.6	[a]	16.4	−0.762	48.7	−0.358
1–499	0.4	[a]	0.8	[a]	12.4	−0.317	16.0	0.045
500–1,499	2.7	−0.490	15.1	−1.079	37.3	0.050	21.8	0.496
1,500–1,999	21.3	−0.258	27.4	−0.253	21.6	0.453	10.4	0.512
2,000–2,499	44.6	−0.154	46.0	0.440	9.2	0.183	0.2	[a]
2,500 or more	30.7	0.472	10.1	0.435	3.1	[a]	2.9	[a]
(Beta^2)		(0.030)		(0.246)		(0.083)		(0.199)
Average work hours of mother								
0	16.8	−0.097	18.3	−0.306	1.9	[a]	10.2	0.048
1–499	47.1	−0.142	26.5	−0.048	39.3	−0.179	31.5	−0.221
500–1,499	26.6	0.022	34.1	−0.058	36.8	0.038	43.0	0.011
1,500–1,999	7.7	0.779	19.1	0.388	16.5	0.256	14.0	0.422
2,000 or more	1.8	[a]	2.0	[a]	5.4	[a]	1.3	[a]
(Beta^2)		(0.020)		(0.045)		(0.026)		(0.056)

TABLE 15 *Continued*

	Always Two Parents				Mother Only at Some Time			
	Nonblack		Black		Nonblack		Black	
	Percent of Cases	Coefficient	Percent of Cases	Coefficients	Percent of Cases	Coefficients	Percent of Cases	Coefficients
Average unemployment days of father								
0	56.5	0.148	32.2	−0.095	49.5	0.422	67.3	0.045
1–30 days	31.5	−0.125	55.0	0.021	43.4	−0.409	17.3	−0.040
1 month–60 days	8.5	−0.272	7.2	0.325	5.7	−0.248	11.1	−0.157
2 months–183 days	3.1	−0.606	5.6	−0.077	1.4	[a]	4.4	[a]
6 months or more	0.4	[a]	0.0	[a]	0.0	[a]	0.0	[a]
($Beta^2$)		(0.010)		(0.009)		(0.083)		(0.007)
Number of years father disabled								
0	77.0	0.062	61.2	−0.035	78.1	0.041	78.6	0.058
1–2	11.7	−0.176	9.6	0.167	11.3	−0.159	9.8	0.028
3–5	6.2	−0.259	19.5	0.016	7.7	[a]	5.4	−0.361
6 or more	5.1	−0.239	9.7	0.024	2.9	[a]	6.3	[a]
($Beta^2$)		(0.004)		(0.003)		(0.003)		(0.032)
Average age of head								
Less than 25	0.6	[a]	0.0	[a]	1.9	[a]	5.0	0.070
25–34	38.7	−0.030	34.4	−0.101	51.6	0.053	42.7	−0.030
35–44	40.5	0.017	36.9	−0.136	35.0	−0.036	37.7	0.094
45 or more	20.2	0.014	28.8	0.295	11.4	−0.088	14.7	−0.179
($Beta^2$)		(0.000)		(0.027)		(0.002)		(0.012)

Initial age of child								
1 day–2 years	32.4	−0.061	28.4	0.155	25.7	0.052	28.7	0.002
3–5 years	38.8	−0.004	36.8	−0.160	41.5	−0.078	42.2	−0.069
6 years	28.8	0.075	34.9	0.043	32.8	0.057	29.1	−0.103
($Beta^2$)		(0.001)		(0.013)		(0.002)		(0.007)
Average number of siblings in family								
0	4.3	1.193	2.5	[a]	9.7	0.670	0.9	[a]
1	15.2	0.110	7.0	0.418	11.1	0.366	11.7	0.345
2	10.2	0.223	6.6	0.019	8.2	−0.501	11.5	0.058
3 or more	70.4	−0.129	83.9	−0.070	71.0	−0.091	76.0	−0.067
($Beta^2$)		(0.022)		(0.036)		(0.038)		(0.027)
Number of years in mother-only household								
0	100.0		100.0		0.0		0.0	
1–2					28.3	0.221	17.1	0.247
3–7					47.6	0.147	30.9	−0.022
8–10					24.1	−0.550	51.9	−0.068
($Beta^2$)						(0.043)		(0.018)
(Eta^2)						(0.101)		(0.134)
Mean		3.498		2.083		2.698		1.455
R^2 (adjusted)		0.350		0.557		0.540		0.703
N		932		561		317		411

[a] Based on 20 or fewer cases.

type, for example, father's work hours exerted a stronger effect on a child's level of long-term per capita income than did mother's work hours. The gender differential in wages would seem a plausible explanation for additional hours of work having a stronger effect on a child's economic status when they are hours of the father rather than the mother.

Wage differentials may also be responsible for the racial difference in importance of the length of a father's absence from the child's household: The effect of years in a mother-only household was considerably stronger among nonblack children than among black children. Lower wages of black men may help account for this, as lower wages would mean a smaller loss of income when the father is no longer present in the child's household.

Other evidence in Table 15 of important racial differences in the role of the father in a child's average level of per capita income are father's unemployment hours and years of disability. Both are measures of the extent to which the father was in adverse economic circumstances and both are seen to be important only for children with a father absent at some time. This suggests that income losses from a marital separation are lower, and long-term income is likewise lower, for a child whose father had extensive unemployment or disability prior to separation. Where the racial difference comes in is in the relative importance of these two types of adversity: unemployment of the father is what matters for nonblack children, whereas disability of the father is what matters for black children. Thus, conditions inhibiting further income contributions from fathers to children from broken homes differ by race. As a method of raising the contribution from father's earnings, unemployment-induced earnings losses would seem more amenable to reduction than would earnings losses due to severe disability. However, concentration on the former, to the neglect of the latter, would place black children from broken homes in an even more disadvantageous position relative to nonblack children.

There is also one important race differential that appears regardless of household type—a difference in the relative importance of father's education and father's work hours. While both are quite important in determining the long-term per capita income of children, regardless of race, the former is much more important for nonblack children, whereas the latter is much more important for black children. If we look at the distribution of children across the various categories of each of these variables, we see relatively greater spread of nonblack children into high levels of father's education and relatively greater spread of black children into the lower levels of father's work hours. It is this sort of relatively greater variance that seems to account for a large part of the racial difference in effects of father's education and father's work hours. This suggests that if the distribution of black children in terms of their father's education—or at least higher levels of wages that correlate with levels of education—were closer to that of white children, the racial gap in the economic well-being of children would be reduced. In addition, increases in the work hours of black fathers, both those in stable marriages and those in unstable marriages, would also be a big help in reducing this gap. However, the figures in Table 15 suggest caution about the extent to which large gains in black father's work hours could be achieved: Many black children have a disabled father, and the disability may be severe enough to preclude large increases in work hours.

It should be recognized that there are also important constraints to increasing mother's work hours, at least as a means of achieving large economic gains for children, especially black children. We have already seen that father's work hours have a much stronger effect than mother's work hours. That there is an important effect of mother's work hours, especially among black children, suggests that increases in mother's work hours should be considered as a possible means of improving the economic well-being of children, especially black children. However, a closer look at circumstances brings to light several limitations to such an approach. Black mothers averaged at least as long, if not longer, work hours than did nonblack mothers. In addition, black mothers were younger than other groups of mothers and they had more children than the nonblack mothers heading their own families. These types of constraints tend to preclude large increases in labor market work, especially when no father is present to share the responsibilities of providing both income and child care. Further, even though black children in two-parent households had mothers who worked the longest hours of all, the children of these mothers averaged long-term per capita income even lower than that of nonblack children in mother-only households.

Summary

During the 1970s the trend in children's per capita income was only slightly upward, and a large proportion of children experienced severe economic difficulties some time in the decade. More than one-quarter of the children were poor at least 1 of the 10 years. However, poverty was usually a short-term rather than a long-term occurrence for children.

Although the 1970s was a time of highly fluctuating conditions in the economy, changes in family situation—most notably shifts toward mother-only families and greater labor force participation by mothers—had a stronger impact on the economic well-being of children than did changes in the economy. While neither the working-mother nor the mother-only status was usually a permanent one for children, both conditions tended to last several years—and several years loom large in a childhood.

Increased divorce and separation plus growth in out-of-wedlock births resulted in an increasingly larger number of children spending part of their childhood in mother-only families, and mother-only families were more likely than others to be low income. Increased labor force participation by mothers helped reduce the economic problems of children, but longer work hours of the mother often were not able to prevent large drops in the economic position of children.

Children in mother-only families averaged 10-year per capita income much lower than that of children in two-parent families the entire 10 years. Large reductions in children's per capita income often followed the divorce or separation of parents, and family income after a marital disruption did not usually approach its former level unless the mother subsequently remarried. Most ever-married mothers did eventually remarry, although black mothers were less likely to do so than others.

While level of per capita income is the most crucial determinant of economic well-being, stability in the flow of income over time is also important. Children in mother-only households experienced lower economic well-being on both counts, with greater instability in the flow of income over time adding to problems of a lower level of long-term income.

Some of these families relied on welfare income for help. Contrary to popular beliefs, episodes of welfare use were rather brief in most cases, and welfare income was often mixed with income from other sources, most notably work. Longer-term dependence on welfare was the exception rather than the rule.

The large difference in economic well-being of black and nonblack children that existed prior to 1970 persisted into the 1970s decade. Black children were in a much worse economic position at the beginning, at the end, and throughout the decade. This is a consistent finding across all measures of economic well-being—long-term level, trend, and instability in per capita income, as well as poverty status. Average long-term per capita income for black children was half that of other children, and trend in per capita income was positive for nonblack children but zero for black children. Greater instability of income further compounded the poorer economic condition of black children. And, in terms of poverty status, the majority—70 percent—of black children spent part of the decade in poverty, compared to 20 percent of nonblack children. Most of the greater instability of income for black children was due to the mother-only household being a more common living arrangement for them than for other children. One-half of the black children born in 1970 spent at least 1 of their first 8 years of life in a mother-only household. This compares to one-fifth of nonblack children.

While this greater tendency for being in a mother-only household was largely responsible for black children experiencing more instability in the flow of income over time, it was not the major factor behind their lower level of long-term income. The long-term income of black children in two-parent families throughout the decade was even lower than the long-term income of nonblack children who spent most of the decade in mother-only families. Thus, increasing the proportion of black children growing up in two-parent families would not by itself eliminate very much of the racial gap in the economic well-being of children; changes in the economic circumstances of the parents are needed most to bring the economic status of black children up to the higher status of nonblack children.

The 1970s were a time of large increases in the labor force participation of mothers, both those with and those without husbands. During the decade, mother's labor market activity was an important component of the economic status of many children, both black and white. Mother's work hours were especially important in determining the level of income available to children when no father was present in the household. Among nonblack children, the 1970s were a time when those in mother-only households had mothers working longer hours than those in two-parent households. Still, the economic status of the children in mother-only households lagged a great deal behind that of children in two-parent households. Children with mothers who worked the most were black children in two-parent families all 10 years of the decade; yet these children averaged lower per capita income than nonblack children who were in mother-only households more often than two-parent ones. These findings are quite consistent with multivariate analysis showing that father's work hours were of greater importance to children's economic status than were mother's work hours. What seems to be a major factor here is that the wages of women were and continue to be only 60 percent those of men.

Wage differentials may also be responsible for several of the other findings of the multivariate analysis of children's long-term level of per capita income. The lower wages of black men relative to nonblack men seem to account for the effects of education and number of years the father was absent from the child's household. The findings suggest that increases in the wages of black fathers would help reduce the large racial gap in the economic well-being of children. Increases in the work hours of black fathers would also help, but health problems may prevent large increases in black father's work hours.

Conclusions

There are several trends to consider in formulating policies to improve the economic position of children in the 1980s. During the 1970s, the circumstances of unmarried mothers were of critical importance to the well-being of children, and indications are that they will be during the 1980s as well. The work hours of these mothers, as well as married mothers, increased substantially as the 1970s decade progressed. Most children now have mothers who are balancing child-rearing and market work responsibilities, many with no father present to assist in fulfilling these responsibilities. The increase in mother's work hours was accompanied by a sizable drop in the birthrate, which reduced the size of families with children and increased the age of parents when they began having children. At the same time these changes were taking place, large racial and gender differences in wage levels continued to hold.

Several implications of these trends stand out. For one, we must look to changes other than mothers entering the labor force or couples having fewer children as primary means of achieving better economic circumstances for children. Most of the economic gains to be made by such changes have already been realized: The changes of the 1970s were large enough to preclude further changes of the same magnitude in the near future. In addition, we cannot expect to see increases in the earnings of fathers as large as those during the 1970s because delays in child-bearing have resulted in fathers being older at the start of the 1980s decade, and thus having less potential for large increases in earnings.

Other sources of economic improvements for children in low-income families would include such things as increases in the wages of mothers and black fathers, increases in economic support by fathers of children from broken homes, and earnings supplements to low-income parents for work they do themselves taking care of their children,[23] as well as transfer payments to low-income families with children. Future as well as past policy changes in each of these areas should be evaluated with

[23] A great deal of work occurs in the home, with no income being received for this work. This includes the time parents spend in child care and housework. Further improvements in measuring such time inputs would be especially helpful for determining the amount of this work that is being done and how much the amount varies across differing types of families. Estimates of these time inputs could then be used as the basis for transfers designed to supplement the income of low-income families by paying for some of the currently unpaid work done by these families.

the effect on the economic well-being of children in mind. Take recent changes in the AFDC program as an example. Effective as of September 1981, the AFDC earned income disregard was dropped to zero after 4 months of work by the mother while participating in the AFDC program. This means that each dollar of earned income causes the loss of a dollar of benefits. Such a provision locks the family more tightly into a low level of income while reducing the incentive for greater reliance on market work as a major income source. Is this what we want for children in need of income assistance?

References and Bibliography

Allison, Paul D.
1978 Measures of inequality. *American Sociological Review* 43:865-880.

Bane, Mary Jo
1976 *Here to Stay: American Families in the Twentieth Century*. New York: Basic Books, Inc.

Bane, Mary Jo, and Robert S. Weiss
1980 Alone together: The world of single-parent families. *American Demographics* (May):11-15,48.

Bergman, Barbara, Judith Radlinski Devine, Patrice Gordon, Diane Reedy, Lewis Sage, and Christina Wise
1980 The effect of wives' labor force participation on inequality in the distribution of family income. *Journal of Human Resources* 15(3):452-455.

Bianchi, Suzanne M., and Reynolds Farley
1979 Racial differences in family living arrangements and economic well-being: an analysis of recent trends. *Journal of Marriage and the Family* (August):537-551.

Bradbury, Katharine, Sheldon Danziger, Eugene Smolensky, and Paul Smolensky
1979 Public assistance, female headship, and economic well-being. *Journal of Marriage and the Family* (August):519-535.

Bumpass, Larry L., and Ronald R. Rindfuss
1979 Children's experience of marital disruption. *American Journal of Sociology* 85:49-62.

Bureau of the Census
1980a *Statistical Abstract of the United States: 1980*. 101st ed. Washington, D.C.: U.S. Government Printing Office.
1980b Current Population Reports, Series P-60, No. 125. *Money Income and Poverty Status of Families and Persons in the United States: 1979* (Advance Report). Washington, D.C.: U.S. Government Printing Office.
1981a Current Population Reports, Series P-60, No. 127. *Money Income and Poverty Status of Families and Persons in the United States: 1980* (Advance Report). Washington, D.C.: U.S. Government Printing Office.
1981b Current Population Reports, Series P-20, No. 365. *Marital Status and Living Arrangements: March 1980*. Washington, D.C.: U.S. Government Printing Office.
1981c Current Population Reports, Series P-20, No. 366. *Household and Family Characteristics: March 1980*. Washington, D.C.: U.S. Government Printing Office.

1981d Current Population Reports, Series P-23, No. 107. *Families Maintained by Female Householders 1970-79*. Washington, D.C.: U.S. Government Printing Office.

Burr, Wesley R., Reuben Hill, F. Ivan Nye, and Ira J. Reiss, eds.
1979 *Contemporary Theories About the Family*, vol. 1. New York: The Free Press.

Coe, Richard D.
1976 Sensitivity of the incidence of poverty to different measures of income. Pages 357-409 in Greg J. Duncan and James N. Morgan, eds., *Five Thousand American Families—Patterns of Economic Progress*, vol. 4. Ann Arbor: Institute for Social Research.
1978a The poverty line: Its functions and limitations. *Public Welfare* (Winter):32-36.
1978b Dependency and poverty in the short and long run. Pages 273-296 in Greg J. Duncan and James N. Morgan, eds., *Five Thousand American Families—Patterns of Economic Progress*, vol. 6. Ann Arbor: Institute for Social Research.
1981 A preliminary empirical examination of the dynamics of welfare use. Pages 121-168 in Martha S. Hill, Daniel H. Hill, and James N. Morgan, eds., *Five Thousand American Families—Patterns of Economic Progress*, vol. 9. Ann Arbor: Institute for Social Research.

Corcoran, Mary
1978 Work experience, work interruption, and wages. Pages 41-104 in Greg J. Duncan and James N. Morgan, eds., *Five Thousand American Families—Patterns of Economic Progress*, vol. 6. Ann Arbor: Institute for Social Research.

Corcoran, Mary, and Greg J. Duncan
1979 Work history, labor force attachment, and earnings differences between the races and sexes. *Journal of Human Resources* 15(1):3-20.

Cutright, Phillip.
1974 Components of change in the number of female family heads aged 15-44: United States 1940-1970. *Journal of Marriage and the Family* 36:714-721.

Danziger, Sheldon
1980 Do working wives increase family income inequality? *Journal of Human Resources* 15(3):444-451.

Danziger, Sheldon, Robert Haveman, and Eugene Smolensky
1977 The measurement and trend of inequality: Comment. *The American Economic Review* 67(3):505-512.

Duncan, Greg J.
1981 An overview of family economic mobility. *Economic Outlook USA* (Spring):42-43.

Duncan, Greg J., and James N. Morgan
1976 Young children and "other" family members. Pages 155-182 in Greg J. Duncan and James N. Morgan, eds., *Five Thousand American Families—Patterns of Economic Progress*, vol. 6. Ann Arbor: Institute for Social Research.
1980 The incidence and some consequences of major life events. Pages 183-240 in Greg J. Duncan and James N. Morgan, eds., *Five Thousand American Families—Patterns of Economic Progress*, vol. 8. Ann Arbor: Institute for Social Research.
1981 Persistence and change in economic status and the role of changing family composition. Pages 1-44 in Martha S. Hill, Daniel H. Hill, and James N. Morgan, eds., *Five Thousand American Families—Patterns of Economic Progress*, vol. 9. Ann Arbor: Institute for Social Research.

Garfinkel, Irwin, and Robert Haveman
1978 Capacity, choice, and inequality. *Southern Economic Journal*, 45(2)(October):421-431.

Glick, Paul C.
1980 Demographic shifts: Changes in family structure. Pages 39-46 in Cheryl D. Hayes, ed., *Work, Family, and Community: Summary Proceedings of an Ad Hoc Meeting*. Washington, D.C.: National Academy of Sciences.

Grossman, Allyson Sherman
1981 Working mothers and their children. *Monthly Labor Review* (May):49-54.

Haveman, Robert H.
1977 Tinbergen's income distribution: Analysis and policies—A review article. *Journal of Human Resources* 12(1):103-114.

Hayes, Cheryl D., ed.
1980 *Work, Family, and Community: Summary Proceedings of an Ad Hoc Meeting*. Washington, D.C.: National Academy of Sciences.

Hill, C. Russell, and Frank P. Stafford
1974 Time inputs to children. Pages 319-344 in James N. Morgan, ed., *Five Thousand American Families—Patterns of Economic Progress*, vol. 2. Ann Arbor: Institute for Social Research.
1978 Parental Care of Children: Time Diary Estimates of Quantity Predictability and Variety. Working Paper Series. Ann Arbor: Institute for Social Research.

Hill, Daniel H.
1977 Labor Force Participation of Married Women: A Dynamic Analysis. Ph.D. dissertation, University of Michigan.

Hill, Martha S.
1981 Some dynamic aspects of poverty. Pages 93-120 in Martha S. Hill, Daniel H. Hill, and James N. Morgan, eds., *Five Thousand American Families—Patterns of Economic Progress*, vol. 9. Ann Arbor: Institute for Social Research.

Hofferth, Sandra L., and Kristin A. Moore
1979 Early childbearing and later economic well-being. *American Sociological Review* 44(4):784-815.

Johnson, William R.
1977 The measurement and trend of inequality: Comment. *The American Economic Review* 67(3):502-504.

Kakwani, Nanak C.
1980 *Income Inequality and Poverty*. New York: Oxford University Press.

Kurien, C. John
1977 The measurement and trend of inequality: Comment. *The American Economic Review* 67(3):517-519.

Lane, Jonathan P., and James N. Morgan
1975 Patterns of change in economic status and family structure. Pages 3-60 in Greg J. Duncan and James N. Morgan, eds., *Five Thousand American Families—Patterns of Economic Progress*, vol. 3. Ann Arbor: Institute for Social Research.

Lazear, Edward P., and Robert T. Michael
1980 Family size and the distribution of real per capita income. *The American Economic Review* (March):91-107.

Masnick, George, and Mary Jo Bane
1980 *The Nation's Families: 1960-1990*. Joint Center Outlook Reports. Cambridge, Mass.: The Joint Center for Urban Studies of MIT and Harvard University.

Minarik, Joseph J.
1977 The measurement and trend of inequality: Comment. *The American Economic Review* 67(3):513-516.

Mirer, Thad
1974 Aspects of the variability of family income. Pages 201-24 in James N. Morgan, ed., *Five Thousand American Families—Patterns of Economic Progress*, vol. 2. Ann Arbor: Institute for Social Research.

Moore, Kristin A., and Sandra L. Hofferth
1978 The Consequences of Age at First Childbirth: Female Headed Families and Welfare Recipiency. Working Paper No. 1146-05. Washington, D.C.: The Urban Institute, August.

Moore, Kristin A., Linda J. Waite, Sandra L. Hofferth, and Steven B. Caldwell
1978 The Consequences of Age at First Childbirth: Marriage, Separation, and Divorce. Working Paper No. 1146-03. Washington, D.C.: The Urban Institute, July.

Morgan, James N.
1974 Family composition. Pages 99-122 in James N. Morgan, ed., *Five Thousand American Families—Patterns of Economic Progress,* vol. 1. Ann Arbor: Institute for Social Research.

Morley, Samuel A.
1981 The effects of changes in the population on several measures of income distribution. *The American Economic Review* 71(3):285-294.

Mott, Frank
1979 *The Socioeconomic Status of Households Headed by Women.* U.S. Department of Labor R&D Monograph 72. Washington, D.C.: U.S. Government Printing Office.

Nelson, Eric R.
1977 The measurement and trend of inequality: Comment. *The American Economic Review* 67(3):497-501.

Paglin, Morton
1977 The measurement and trend of inequality: Reply. *The American Economic Review* 67(3):520-531.

Ross, Heather L., and Isabel V. Sawhill
1975 *Time of Transition: The Growth of Families Headed by Women.* Washington, D.C.: The Urban Institute.

Sawhill, Isabel V.
1975 *Income Transfers and Family Structure.* An Urban Institute Paper. Washington, D.C.: The Urban Institute.
1976 Discrimination and poverty among women who head families. *Signs* 1(3)(Spring): 201-211.

Smith, James P., and Michael P. Ward
1980 Asset accumulation and family size. *Demography* 17(3):243-260.

Spanier, Graham B., and Paul C. Glick
1980 The life cycle of American families: An expanded analysis. *Journal of Family History* (Spring):97-111.

Strober, Myra H., and Charles B. Weinberg
1980 Strategies used by working and non-working wives to reduce time pressures. *Journal of Consumer Research,* 6(March).

Taussig, Michael K.
1976 Trends in Inequality of Well-Offness in the United States Since World War II. Institute for Research on Poverty Special Report Series. Madison, Wis.: Institute for Research on Poverty.

Thornton, Arland
1978 Marital dissolution, remarriage, and childbearing. *Demography* 15(3)(August):361-380.

Wattenberg, Esther, and Hazel Reinhardt
1979 Female-headed families: Trends and implications. *Social Work* (November):460-467.

Watts, Harold W., and Felicity Skidmore.
1979 Household structure: Necessary changes in categorization and data collection: Postscript. In U.S. Census Bureau, Current Population Reports, Special Studies, Series P-23, No. 83, December. *Issues in Federal Statistical Needs Relating to Women*. Washington, D.C.: U.S. Government Printing Office.

DISCUSSION

There was no disagreement among conference participants with respect to the analysis and findings of the Hill paper. The conference discussion, therefore, centered on the underlying meaning of the trends and what they portend for the next 10 years in terms of future trends, needed policy initiatives, and priority areas for research.

Frank Levy opened the discussion by noting that Hill's finding that per capita income of families with children grew by 17.5 percent over the decade (somewhat more than 1 percent per year) should not be taken as evidence that the sluggishness of the economy as a whole over the period did not have an adverse effect on family well-being. As Levy pointed out, there are two major reasons for the contrast between rising per capita income of families with children and stagnant real family income over the decade as measured by the Bureau of Labor Statistics. The first was a decrease in average family size (from 3.4 children in 1970 to 2.5 children in 1979). This accounted for 15 percentage points of the 17.5 percent increase in the economic well-being of families with children over the period. The second was an enormous increase in the proportion of women in the labor force.

Levy brought home the latter point by tracing through the 1970s experience of the "typical" family as reflected in the 1970 Census. This family had a father between 29 and 34 years old in 1970 and slightly less than two children. During the decade of the 1970s it added one child and had an income/needs ratio that increased by an estimated 15 percent. "When this case is translated into Census income statistics, we find that the family had a 1970 income of 19,000 (1979) dollars, which grew to 25,500 dollars by 1979. This difference of 6,000 1979 dollars was the result of an increase of 1,800 dollars in the earnings of the husband (through age-related promotions, etc.) and 4,200 dollars in the earnings of the wife. Thus, about 70 percent of the family's real income growth over the 1970-79 period was due to increased earnings from the wife." The conclusion Levy drew from this example was that we could not expect the increase in per capita of families with children to continue in the decade to come if the economy remained as sluggish in the 1980s as it had been in the 1970s. Family size cannot continue to fall indefinitely, and fewer families have a "wife in reserve" to beat inflation. Levy's comments, in turn, stimulated considerable discussion.

The first major point concerned the role of changed tastes in the whole process. Perhaps the decrease in average family size over the decade was not a response to bad economic conditions, but rather a change in tastes for children. Perhaps the increased labor force participation by women was a change in attitudes of women to work in the marketplace versus work in the home. Perhaps the increase in the number of single-parent families noted by Hill is a measure of how bad those marriages were and what the mothers were willing to sacrifice in terms of living standards in order to be out of them. And perhaps the decrease in family size in part reflects the phenomenon of undoubling—the value people place on a separate dwelling who in the past would have married again or returned to their own parental family. To the extent that any of these are correct, Hill's estimates of the increase in welfare would be biased downward and the economic well-being of the families with children would have increased more during the 1970s than her estimates would indicate.

The second major point concerned Levy's predictions for the 1980s. First, Richard Easterlin raised the point (elaborated further in his conference paper, which appears as Chapter 7 of this book) that the earnings rates of both young men and women may have been unusually depressed during the 1970s by the fact that these parents belong to an unusually large cohort competing for the available jobs. The cohort entering young adulthood in the 1980s is smaller, and, therefore, other things equal, earning *rates* of young parents will tend to increase over the next decade. However, if in fact economic constraints affect family size, we may find family size rising again in the 1980s and counteracting to some extent the positive effects on per capita income coming from the increased earnings rates. David Ellwood added the point that the great influx of women into the labor force in the 1970s may have had a supply side shock on the labor market, depressing wage rates. To the extent that a majority of women now work and the capacity for continued increase in their labor force participation is limited, wage rates may improve, relatively speaking, in the 1980s.

The discussion then turned to the disquieting persistence in Hill's trend figures of black-white differences and to the possible implications of those differences. Mary Jo Bane pointed out that the Hill paper documented very different rates of formation of single-parent families, very different percentages using welfare at some time, and very different percentages persistently dependent on welfare. These statistics, she suggested, were "consistent with a picture showing a group of mostly minority, mostly single-parent families who are mostly poor and mostly dependent on welfare for long periods of time. The trends we have been talking about are essentially mainstream phenomena. But there is a tangle of poverty and welfare use, low employment rates, and high teenage pregnancy rates which is a different phenomenon and which we ought to think about differently."

John Ogbu added emphasis to this point by noting that the Hill paper talked about income differences and race differences, but did not address class differences. "I think that mothers' decisions to reduce family size and go into the labor market are essentially middle-class decisions. I would like to see more analyses or breakdowns on the basis of class factors, so that we are not taking to be an overall improvement what is in fact an improvement for middle-class mainstream people while those at the bottom are left in even worse conditions." Conference participants pursued that issue to some extent, although it was clear that none of the information in the Hill paper (or in the other conference papers) shed much light on race versus class issues.

It was noted that the Hill figures indicate that any permanent underclass was certainly small, since less than 1 percent of the Michigan sample was poor for more than 8 out of 10 years, even though 25 percent was poor at some time or another. It was pointed out that the decrease in family size was a black as well as a white phenomenon. But it was also noted that two out of three black children were born to unmarried women, a rapidly increasing proportion of whom had never been married, and that there was evidence that for blacks, but not to the same extent for whites, parenthood seemed to be increasingly separated from marriage. As Andrew Cherlin put it, "We have to think about this very basic difference in family life, and the implications of this kind of change from the family system we are used to thinking about—where marriage is the key—to one where an extended network of kin may be the central attribute of the families." (The problem of a possible group outside the mainstream came up again in the conference discussion of the underground economy; see Chapter 5 of this volume.)

Myra Strober, the second formal discussant of the Hill paper, changed the focus of the discussion somewhat by pointing out that the increased labor force participation by mothers during the 1970s had to come from somewhere—and the evidence was that it came from housework and child care. The traditional neoclassical labor supply model has now recognized that housework exists and holds that a woman decides to enter the labor market when the perceived value of the housework she does is less than the wage she would get by going out to work. But this, according to Strober, is not the correct link between housework and labor force participation for two reasons. First, if a family is not eligible for welfare and is in dire need of money, the mother will go out to work because, however high a value she places on her work in the home, she cannot buy food or anything else with it. Second, and more importantly, the evidence is that women do not decide to do market work instead of housework—they do both. Women who are employed full time do less housework than women who are not, but they still do an average 25 hours worth of housework a week.

The reason these implications are still far from fully recognized, according to Strober, is that in spite of the changes that took place in the 1970s, "our ideology and institutions are still firmly predicated on the proposition that children's mothers are at home and that these mothers have husbands who supply the family with income, companionship, leadership, and maybe even love." The Hill paper provides ample documentation that such a stereotype is not a description of reality for a large share of the nation's families. And this fact "has major implications for women's well-being, children's well-being, and women's ability to succeed in the marketplace."

First, mothers' earnings provide an important share of the earnings of most female-headed families. If female wage rates were closer to those of men, indeed, the gap between the family income of one-parent and two-parent families would narrow substantially. But when women, either in training for a career or working full time, add 25 hours a week to their workload, it should not be surprising to find that their competitive position in the marketplace is impaired. Indeed, a study of Chicanos in higher education in California shows that the number of hours of housework these women have to do every week turns out to be one of the most important determinants of whether they drop out of school or not. To this was added the point that recent policy initiatives have increased the reward for working outside the homes for middle income women—by reducing the marriage penalty and increasing the child care tax credit—while the cutbacks in the AFDC earnings disregard and the cap on the child care expenses of AFDC women who are working have further reduced the incentive to work for poorer mothers in society. Second, the more a mother works outside the home, the less time by definition she will be with her children. During the time she is unavailable, the children will be with other adults, by themselves, or in some kind of day care. So an important question is: Who is taking care of the children, and what effect does the current patchwork of child care have on them? On both issues an imperative need is for more information.

With respect to housework, which often includes child care, Strober's plea was for more and better time use data.

Housework is complex because it often involves doing several things at the same time. Interestingly, there is a known bias with respect to our current data. If a well-educated woman is doing several things in the house, one of which is looking after her children, she will tend to give that as the answer to a question about what she is doing. Less well-educated women, in contrast, who may be doing the same package of things, are likely to choose some other activity (such as ironing) as their answer to the question. Strober suggested that the beeper technology used for executive time use studies is far superior to a diary kept by the respondent at 10-minute intervals, which is the typical method used for time use studies of activities in the home. And to get a better profile of child care, time use data should be collected from the child's perspective, which older children can, in fact, do themselves.

Day care data should also be collected, according to Strober, using a different methodology from the one typically used now—which is to ask a mother, "Are you satisfied with your day care arrangements?" A mother is unlikely to be able to live with herself if she answers "no" to such a question. We should get at potential day care demand another way. We should divide a sample into several similar groups and ask each group how much day care they would use at a certain price (different for each group). From these, day care demand curves could be generated to yield estimates, for example, of the subsidies that would be needed to provide day care of a certain standard. In addition, we need more information on particular types of care—after-school care and sick-child care.

With respect to proposals for improving the income balance between one-parent and two-parent families, two specific ideas were expressed. First, it should be remembered that most children in mother-only families have fathers as well. Many of these fathers have substantial resources. If some way could be found to tap these resources, the economic status of children in single-parent families could be much improved. Isabel Sawhill, for example, quoted a calculation she had made that indicated that if absent fathers contributed according to ability to pay, and if some equitable scheme could be found for redistributing these resources according to need, the whole AFDC program could be eliminated without making any of these children worse off. The second policy suggestion to remedy the income situation for single-parent families was to find some method of calculating the labor market equivalent value of housework and developing a transfer payment system based on that calculation.

3

Youth Employment in the 1970s: The Changing Circumstances of Young Adults

DAVID T. ELLWOOD AND DAVID A. WISE

Virtually all 16-year-old Americans live at home, are supported by one or both of their parents, trudge wearily to school, avoid full-time work, and are intrigued by members of the opposite sex. Within less than 10 years, much of that changes. By age 24 most live independently. With a few exceptions, they have long since left school. Most are married; many have babies.

The transition from teenager to adult includes an almost overwhelming concentration of major events. Two-thirds of first marriages and more than half of first births happen during this period. Less than one-third of 20-year-olds will be living in the same house 4 years later. Teenagers average two jobs per year; by age 24, they are likely to be in one that will last 10 years.

For most youth, the transition from full-time schooling while living at home to independent household formation and labor market participation occurs without great difficulty. For a few, however, the period entails long spells out of school and without work. In the past decade there has been increasing concern about youth employment problems. Indeed, in the 1970s teenage unemployment emerged as a major issue in the public domain. The scope of this paper extends beyond teenage unemployment, however. Our goal is to survey the evidence on recent trends in youth labor market experiences more generally and to explore possible explanations of these trends.

We discuss the labor market experience of youth aged 16-24, focusing primarily on *employment*. Employment rates differ among youth for many reasons. National economic fluctuations, age, military service, household formation, parenting responsibilities, and family background all influence employment. We report differences in employment patterns across groups and trends in these patterns over time, particularly in the 1970s. Where possible we explore causes and effects of these patterns and trends.

The wide variety of critical changes that occur between ages 16 and 24 create particularly extreme heterogeneity in this group. The timing of school leaving, marriage, childbearing, and serious job search differ greatly among youth. Each of these has important labor market consequences and may in turn be influenced by labor market conditions. The diversity also complicates interpretation of labor market statistics.

Virtually all middle-aged adult men are working or looking for work. For them nonemployment is relatively easy to interpret. The situation is slightly more complex for women of a similar age, because the group that is not working is composed of both those actively seeking work and a large number who have other responsibilities that preclude labor market work. These persons are usually termed unemployed and not in the labor force, respectively.

Normally the unemployment rate is defined as the number of unemployed divided by the labor force (those who are working or seeking work). The employment rate is the ratio of employed persons *to the total population* (not just the labor force). In principle the unemployment rate measures the difficulty of getting work, that is, the proportion who are looking for work but can't find it. The employment rate simply captures the proportion of the population who have jobs.

For those who are still in school, work may be sporadic and part time during the school year, full time but temporary during the summer. The ones seeking work will include both persons who want extra spending money and those who need support to continue in school. By contrast, out-of-school youth presumably are interested in longer-term employment, at least eventually. Still, it may be hard to distinguish those who are diligently engaged in job search from those with relatively weak labor market attachment. The unemployed may include some who are not seriously interested in working; those not in the labor force may include some persons who have become discouraged by fruitless job search.

The confusion created by the dynamics of youth schooling and work can be illustrated by considering two measures of unemployment. In early 1976, the official Bureau of Labor Statistics unemployment rate was 20 percent for persons aged 16-19, yet just 4 percent of this group was both out of school and unemployed. The 20 percent figure indicates that one-fifth of those who were in the labor force (employed or seeking work) were unable to find work. Both numerator and denominator include persons enrolled in school along with those who were not. Almost half the teenagers classified as unemployed are also in school. If we confine our attention to those not in school, we still have an unemployment rate of close to 20 percent because we exclude both employed and unemployed persons in school. The 20 percent figure may well reflect the employment difficulty faced by those youngsters who have left school before most of their peers. It does *not* indicate that being out of school and without employment is a serious problem for most teenagers. Most teenagers are in school. What might be regarded as the most serious social ill, being both out of school and unemployed, touches just 4 percent of youth at any one moment. Certainly these figures do not indicate that the bulk of all teenagers are in desperate straits.

We shall concentrate on employment rates (employment to population ratios) in order to avoid for the most part distinctions between the unemployed and those out of the labor force that are so difficult for this age group. Employment is a convenient bottom line, an important indicator to compare across groups and over time.

Employment Patterns

Figure 1 shows the civilian employment rates between 1955 and 1979 for all persons aged 16-24, by sex and race. It is these patterns we seek to understand. Employment rates for the four groups and the changes over time are quite different:

- Employment rates for white males have been highest and have been relatively stable over time, rising slightly in the 1970s.
- Employment rates for black males were comparable to those of whites in 1954, but by 1979 the gap had widened to over 20 percentage points. Moreover, the largest declines came during the 1970s.
- Employment rates for white females rose gradually over the 1960s and jumped quite dramatically during the 1970s.
- Employment rates for black females have remained low and largely unchanged over the period.

For both young men and young women, the gap between blacks and whites widened roughly 14 points between 1969 and 1979. For males the widening reflected primarily a fall in black employment; for females it reflected a rise in white employment.

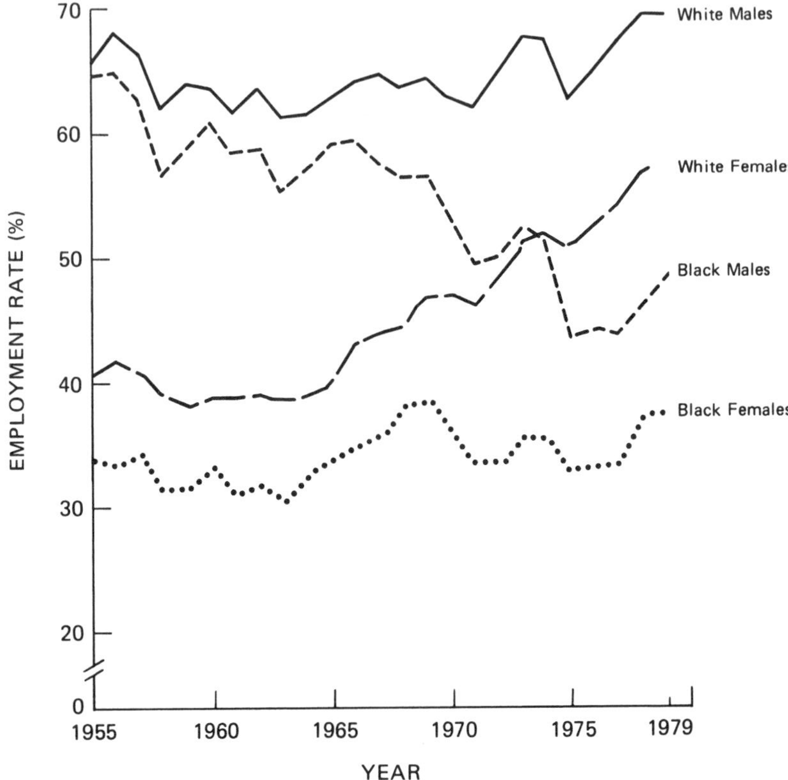

Figure 1 Employment rates for persons aged 16-24 by race and sex, 1955 to 1979. SOURCE: U.S. Department of Labor (1980).

In the remainder of the paper, we explore a wide variety of potential explanations of these differences and trends, paying particular attention to six major issues:

Demography	Household Formation
The Military	Family Background
Schooling	Public Policy

We have made no attempt to disentangle fully the multitude of possible interactions or to review the sometimes large literature surrounding each issue. Instead, we have chosen to rely primarily on published data and simple tabulations of the 1976 Survey of Income and Education and to report the trends and patterns that appear in these data. We seek to decompose the overall changes into the effects of the six individual influences by asking for each factor the hypothetical question: How much would employment rates have changed had that variable alone changed? It should be kept in mind that, inevitably, this sort of calculation ignores interactions and often raises issues of causality.

Demography

The baby boom has come of age. Between 1960 and 1980 the number of youth aged 15-24 rose from 12 percent of the population to more than 17 percent. The sudden expansion in the supply of young workers over this period and the absence of a commensurate increase in demand might be put forth as an explanation for the declining employment rates of some youth groups. Some economic reasoning would suggest, indeed, that the relatively greater number of young workers could be employed only if their wage rates fell relative to the wage rates of adult workers.

This large demographic bulge surely had an impact on the youth labor market. Relative wage rates of young white workers did fall; and quite possibly the occupational choices of young workers were affected. However, we do not believe the data support a hypothesis linking the bulk of the changing employment patterns described in Figure 2 with the bulge in the relative number of youth. Our conclusions rest on three facts.

First, the employment patterns over this period differ dramatically by demographic group. Throughout the 1960s and 1970s, the employment rates for young whites, particularly women, were moving upward. The rates for these groups rose particularly rapidly in the 1970s, just when

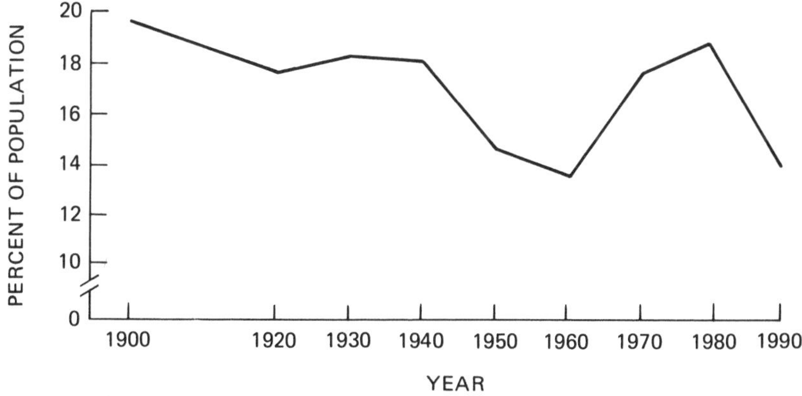

Figure 2 Youth aged 15-24 as a percent of total population.

the rate for black men was beginning to fall most sharply. If a sudden excess supply of young workers had appeared, we should have expected all groups to suffer at least to some degree. Instead, we see opposite trends for whites and blacks in the 1970s.

Second, the timing of the boom does not coincide with the most rapid falls in minority employment. We still might be tempted to turn to the baby boom as a primary explanation of black employment problems were it not that the bulk of the baby boom bulge was absorbed in the 1960s, while the worst problems for minorities occurred in the 1970s. Between 1961 and 1971 youth increased from 12 to 16 percent of the population. By contrast, over the decade of the 1970s the proportion of the population aged 15-24 rose just 1 more percentage point. Even so, both comparatively and absolutely, minority youth fared far better in the 1960s than in the 1970s.

Finally, the market has shown a remarkable ability to adjust to changing supplies of youth during the summer. In March of 1976 there were 3.8 million teenagers in the full-time labor force, 3.0 million of whom had jobs. In July of that same year, when youngsters were on summer vacation, the ranks had swelled to 8.3 million workers. Of the additional 4.5 million new entrants to the labor force, 4.0 million had found jobs. Indeed, the unemployment rate among youth is typically lower in July than during the school year. If the market can adjust to a nearly threefold increase in teenage labor supply each summer, it is hard to believe it could not adjust to the gradual increase in the teenage labor force that has occurred over several decades.

Nonetheless, several authors, notably Wachter (1978), have argued that the supply effects have interacted with institutional rigidities in the labor market to worsen the position of youth, especially black youth. We cannot rule out the possibility that the baby boom was an important contributing factor, but we cannot assess with much precision its independent contribution to the growing racial employment gap.

We turn now to an issue about which we can say a good deal more: the impact of the fluctuating level of military manpower on youth employment.

The Military

One of the most dramatic changes in the 1970s was a substantial reduction in the size and composition of the military. While these changes have been widely noted in popular discussion, they have received surprisingly little attention in the youth employment literature, one notable exception being Cooper (1978). The silence may, in part, reflect uncertainty about how to treat the military. Most authors are interested primarily in assessing the performance of the civilian labor market, and data are almost always collected only for those in the civilian population.

The military is a major employer of men between the ages of 18 and 24. Obviously the need for military personnel serves as additional labor demand for young men. At the same time, military employment is often regarded as very different from civilian employment. The working conditions, the skills, the commitment, and the risks may indeed differ enormously between the sectors; and the working conditions within the military obviously vary depending on whether or not the country is fighting a war. Moreover, the nature of the selection process changes from year to year. In draft years, the proportion of the eligible population inducted and the rules for deferral or avoidance are quite variable. With the volunteer army, rigid pay rules and working conditions seem to deter many of the more able or educated young men, while the military may reject those with comparatively low skills. The vast complexity of the whole issue, coupled with poor data, probably has led most authors to ignore the entire issue (it certainly has for us until now).

Yet the changes in the military over the past several decades have been dramatic and may have had a serious impact on the youth labor market. Three findings are particularly worthy of note.

First, there has been a sizable long-term decline in the relative number of young men in the military over the last three decades, interrupted by the Vietnam war. The decline in military manpower in the 1970s effectively increased the civilian 18- to 24-year-old labor force at least as much as the baby boom did during this decade. Figure 3 shows that in 1952 nearly one-third of all young men aged 18-24 were serving in the military. By 1964 the proportion had fallen to 15 percent. Five years later, the Vietnam war had boosted the proportion in the military back up to 20 percent. But by 1979, the figure had dropped to only 7 percent. The possible impact of these declines can be gleaned by contrasting them with the effect of the baby boom of the 1970s. Between 1969 and 1979, the total male population aged 18-24 rose 25 percent. However, the total male *civilian* population jumped by more than 50 percent. Thus, at least one-half of the rise could be traced directly to the decline in the role of the military. By contrast, in the previous decade the total population had risen 50 percent but the civilian population had grown by slightly more than 40 percent. Thus, although the baby boom occurred primarily during the 1960s, the growth in the civilian labor force of persons aged 16-24 was actually slightly greater in the 1970s.

Second, between 1969 and 1978, the proportion of young whites in the military fell precipitously, while the proportion of young blacks

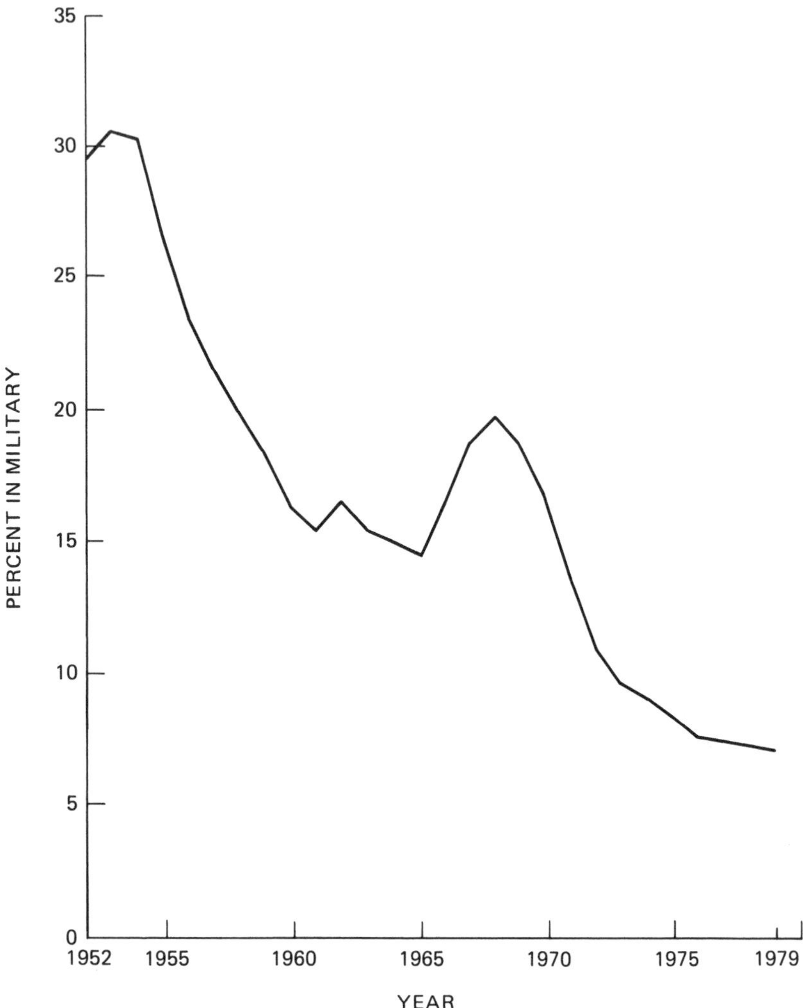

Figure 3 Percent of all men aged 18-24 in the military. SOURCE: U.S. Department of Labor (1980).

remained relatively constant. Figure 4 shows that after the Vietnam war the proportion of young whites aged 18-24 doing military service fell sharply. After peaking at roughly 20 percent, the proportion fell to less than 7 percent in 1978. Somewhat to our surprise, at the military peak in the late 1960s, whites were actually proportionately more common than blacks—with only 16 percent of blacks and 20 percent of whites

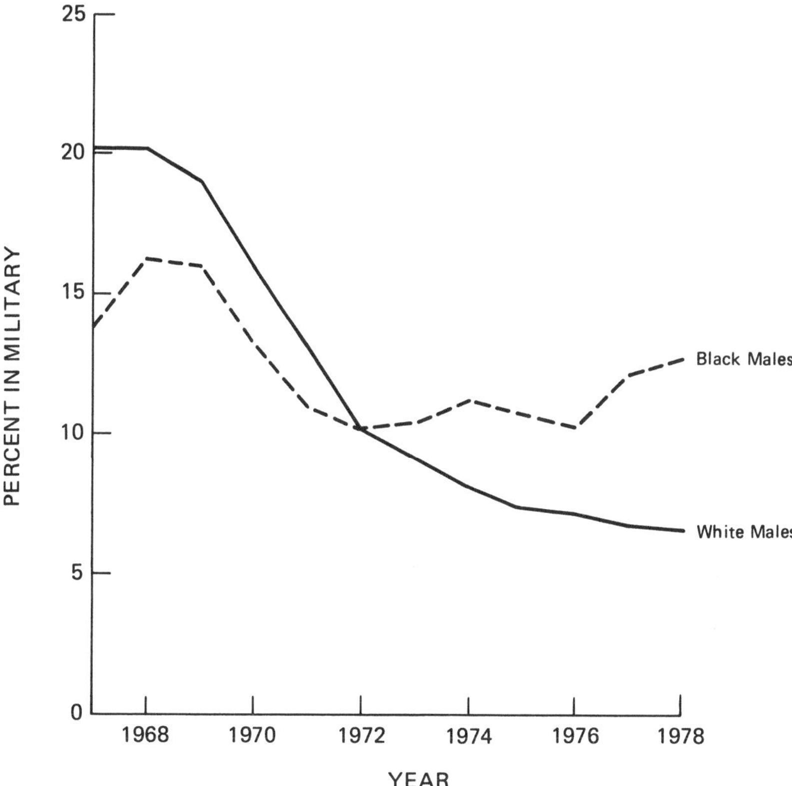

Figure 4 Percent of men aged 18-24 in the military, by race. SOURCE: U.S. Department of Labor (1980).

serving. But the fall off in service for blacks was much smaller in the 1970s. Indeed, after a low of 10 percent in 1972, black participation rose during the 1970s. Beginning in 1973, young blacks have been disproportionately in the military. By 1978, blacks were twice as likely as whites to have enlisted.

Third, if those in the military are treated as employed, the black/white employment gap grew 11 points rather than 14 points during the 1970s. Moreover, if we take account of the likelihood that draft avoidance induced many young whites to remain in school longer than they otherwise would have, the gap narrows another 2 points. It is unclear what is the proper way to treat the military. One logical treatment would be to include military personnel as employed and calculate employment to population ratios for the entire population (civilian and military). Such a calculation leads to less growth in the black/white employment gap over the 1970s than the employment rates based only on the civilian population show. Since whites were disproportionately serving in the military in 1969, their employment rates are thus boosted more than those for blacks. Conversely, blacks were overrepresented in the later years, so their employment rates are pushed up relatively more in 1979. The net effect is that the racial employment gap grows by 2 to 3 points less if serving in the military is treated as employment.

The Vietnam war buildup also depressed employment rates for another reason. It induced persons to remain in school longer to avoid the draft. We shall see later that enrollment rates for men bulged in the late 1960s while those for women did not. This is important because persons enrolled in school tend to work much less than those out of school. We are not aware of any studies of this military impact on enrollment. A rough calculation based on the assumption that enrollment patterns would have followed a straight line for both races between 1964 and 1974 in the absence of the war indicates that the enrollment effect was much larger for whites. We shall discuss the importance of school enrollment in a later section. But it appears that some of the growth in employment rates for whites over the 1970s was spurious, caused by the artifically high school-attendance rates in the late 1960s. A rough estimate is that another 2 points of the widening black/white employment gap can be traced to this enrollment effect.

Thus, as much as 4-5 points of the original 14-point gap for men might be eliminated by including those in the military as employed and by controlling for draft-induced school enrollment. These calculations, however, take no account of the possible additional impact that the rapid increase in the civilian labor force might have had. Let us turn now to the impact of the rapid fluctuations in the short-term demand for labor.

Macroeconomic Conditions

Macroeconomic conditions have a sizable impact on both employment and unemployment rates of youth. A common indicator of the strength of the economy is the adult unemployment rate. According to recent estimates, for every 1 percentage point rise in the unemployment rate for adult males there is a 2-point fall in the employment rate for white teenagers, and a 3-point fall in the rate for blacks. For youth aged 20-24, the figures are slightly higher (Freeman, 1978). The unemployment rate for adult males varied greatly over the late 1960s and early 1970s. In the boom of 1968 and 1969, this rate reached 1.5 percent, the lowest in many decades. During the recession of 1970-1971 the rate rose to 3.1 percent, and in the recession of 1975-1976 it topped 4.9 percent.

Unemployment rates, which may capture job availability more precisely than employment rates, show the influence of macroeconomic conditions quite dramatically. Figure 5 displays unemployment rates for black and white teenagers, for persons in their early twenties, and for men over 20.

We can draw several important conclusions. The youth unemployment (and employment) rates are very sensitive to macroeconomic conditions. During the recessions of 1958, 1961, 1970-1971, and 1975-1976, youth unemployment rates rose very sharply. During the most serious postwar recession in 1975-1976, the black teenage unemployment rate was over 35 percent, and for whites the figure exceeded 15 percent. By contrast, during the late 1960s when the economy was heated to its highest (and most inflationary) postwar level, black teenage unemployment rates fell below 25 percent, and white rates were close to 10 percent.

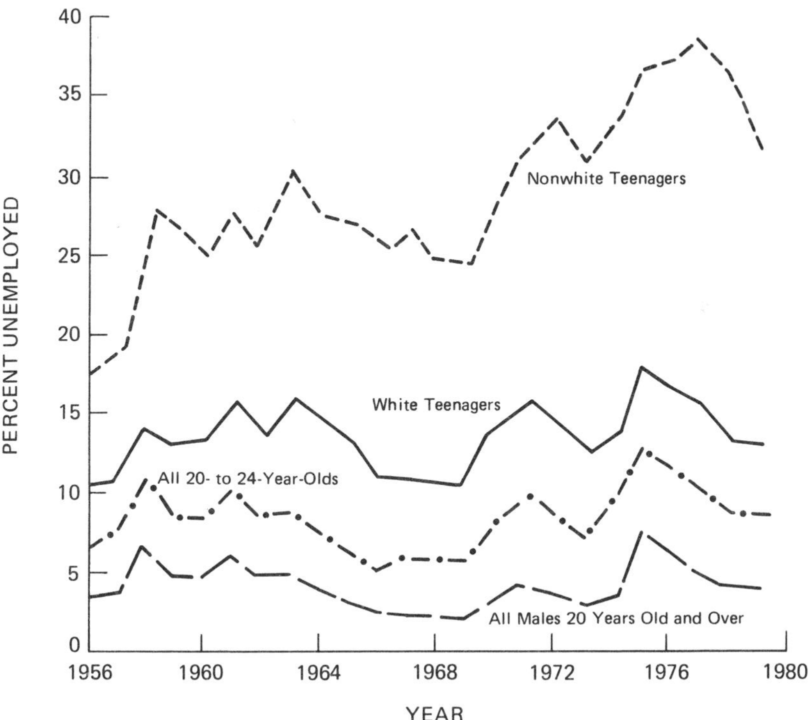

Figure 5 Unemployment rates for selected groups. SOURCE: U.S. Department of Labor (1980).

About one-third to one-half of the decline in male black employment rates between 1969 and 1979 could be traced to weaker economic conditions. But only about 14 percent of the increase in the disparity between black and white employment rates could be so attributed. The 1970s were a period of much weaker economic performance than the 1960s. The average unemployment rate for all persons was below 5 percent in the 1960s; in the 1970s it rose to 7 percent. Between 1969 and 1979, the adult male unemployment rate rose by 1.4 percentage points. Using the cyclical sensitivity figures quoted earlier, we would have predicted a 4-5 percent drop in the employment rate for black youth during that period and an additional 3 percent drop for whites, all else the same. In fact, during that period the overall employment rate of black males fell almost 10 points, while it *rose* about 4 points for whites. About one-third to one-half of the 10-point decline for blacks would be accounted for by the decline attributable to weaker aggregate demand. But the difference between the rates for blacks and whites increased by 14 points between these 2 years, only 2 points of which (14 percent) could be attributed to economic conditions. We have not seen separate estimates of the cyclical sensitivity of women's employment rates. But we presume the results would be similar to those for men.

Even when the economy is booming, extreme black/white differences remain. While macroeconomic conditions help to explain the employment patterns of different groups over time, they provide little help in understanding the differences between them at any given time. In 1969 the economy was extremely tight, the military buildup had reached its peak, and many white youngsters were staying in school. Yet sizable differences in employment and unemployment rates remained. For example, the teenage unemployment rates for blacks was still 25 percent, but the white rate had fallen almost to 10 percent.

In combination, then, the changing military and macroeconomic conditions can explain up to half (7 points) of the 14-point growth in the racial employment gap for young men, though possible interactions between the two have not been considered. For women, only the macroeconomic effects can be used, of course, so much more remains unexplained. Recall that a portion of the military effect was related to reduced school enrollment. We now explore the importance of schooling more directly.

Schooling

Schooling plays a major role in the labor market experiences of youth. The influence is twofold. First, while young people are in school they often do not work. When they do, their jobs typically involve short-term part-time work. During the summers, as we have already seen, teenage employment represents a massive influx into the full-time labor force. Second, after young people complete their schooling, their level of education is highly correlated with their labor market employment experiences. In the language of human capital, youngsters who have accumulated more capital reap larger rewards.

We begin by looking at the differing patterns of schooling over time for men and women, and blacks and whites. We then consider changes in the employment rates of youth in and out of school. Finally, we explore the impacts of changes in enrollment, together with increase in the employment of students, on the overall employment rates we seek to understand.

There are several statistics that might be used as indicators of school attainment. An appealing one is the enrollment rate for persons aged 16-24, which captures the proportion of that age-group enrolled in school. It also is ideal for understanding how employment patterns for those enrolled in school differ from the patterns of those who have left school.

Figure 6 shows enrollment rates for men and women between 1954 and 1978. Enrollment rates, which rose steadily through the 1950s and 1960s, leveled off during the 1970s for young women and actually fell for young men. In 1954, only 25 percent of women aged 16-24 were enrolled in school. By 1970, more than 40 percent were. The pattern was rather different for men. Enrollment rates for men moved from 43 to 55 percent in the 1960s. But in the 1970s this trend halted abruptly. Male enrollment rates fell rather dramatically over this period. We have already suggested that this pattern may reflect a surge in enrollment to avoid the draft in the late 1960s. The labor market effects of all of these enrollment changes are likely to be profound, since those enrolled in school typically are employed far less than those out of school.

Enrollment rates by race have been published since 1964. Table 1 reports these rates by sex and race in selected years. During the 1960s and 1970s, the enrollment gap between blacks and whites was largely eliminated. Enrollment rates for blacks continued to rise slowly over the 1970s for both men and women. In 1964, some 51 percent of white men were enrolled in school compared with only 39 percent of black men. By 1979, a larger proportion of black men than white men were actually enrolled. Similarly, for women, black women now remain enrolled as long as white women.

The median black, as well as the median white, now completes high school. But other measures show a continuing gap in total educational

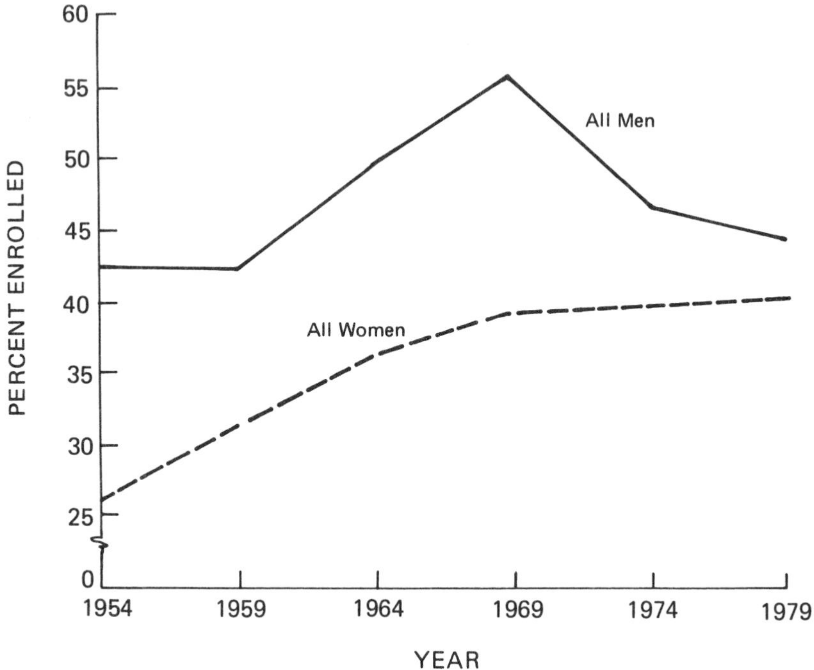

Figure 6 Percent enrolled in school by sex for persons aged 16-24. SOURCE: U.S. Department of Labor (1980).

achievement. The dropout rate for blacks continues to exceed that for whites: 13 percent of whites ages 16-24 are high school dropouts while 20 percent of blacks in this age-group have not completed high school. Black youth apparently pass through fewer grades per year of enrollment. In addition, for any number of grades completed, achievement test scores typically are lower for blacks than for whites. Thus, while blacks remain in school almost as long as whites, the educational outcomes may continue to be very different.

TABLE 1 Percent of Persons Aged 16–24 Enrolled in School, by Race and Sex

	1964	1969	1974	1979
White male	51.1	56.4	45.9	43.9
Black male	39.4	47.2	49.0	47.1
White female	36.5	39.2	39.2	40.2
Black female	34.2	38.4	41.8	40.2

SOURCE: Data provided by the Bureau of Labor Statistics.

Fewer blacks go on to college. According to a 1972 survey of high school graduates, about 54 percent of whites upon graduation from high school attend a postsecondary school full time, while about 42 percent of blacks do so. However, after controlling for individual and family background attributes—including parents' education and income, high school class rank, and scholastic test scores—blacks are much more likely than whites to attend a postsecondary school. For example, the probabilities of attendance evaluated at the mean of attributes of white and at the mean of attributes of nonwhite high school graduates are as follows:

Evaluated at	White	Nonwhite
Mean of white attributes	0.68	0.83
Mean of nonwhite attributes	0.36	0.58

By these measures, there is a substantial *positive* race effect on postsecondary school attendance even as early as 1972 (Meyer and Wise, 1981b).

The changing enrollment patterns clearly influence labor markets. Persons in school are less likely to work. Thus, all else the same, we would expect to see falling employment rates for blacks and whites over the 1950s and 1960s as enrollment rates rose, since fewer students than nonstudents work. In 1954, when 33 percent of all youth aged 16-24 were enrolled in school, the employment rate for students was roughly 25 percent; for nonstudents, it was 65 percent. The overall employment rate was 52 percent. Therefore, when enrollment had risen to 47 percent, as in 1970, we would expect the employment rate to have fallen to 49 percent if nothing else changed, and, for men and women calculated separately, we would expect the rate to have fallen 2 points for men and 3 points for women. That they did not, in fact, fall indicates that one of two things happened. The employment rate rose for either in-school youth, or out-of-school youth, or both.

To discover which, Figure 7 shows, by sex, the employment rates for youths aged 16-24 who were enrolled and not enrolled in school:

- For both men and women, employment rates for those in school have risen sharply since 1954.

- For men out of school, there has been relatively little change in employment rates. For out-of-school women, on the other hand, work has become increasingly common.

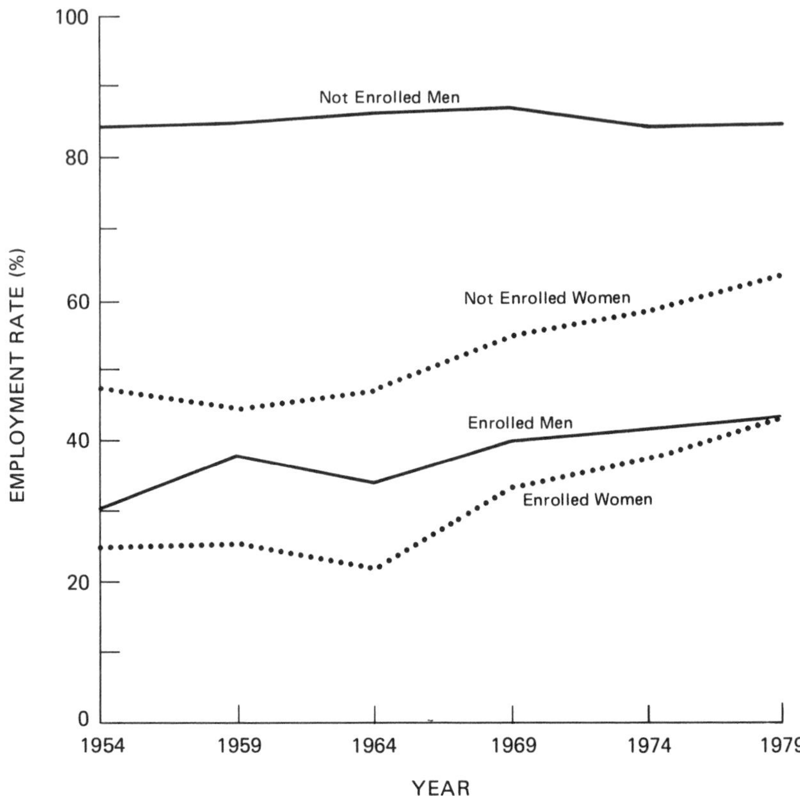

Figure 7 Employment rates by sex for persons enrolled in school and not enrolled in school. SOURCE: U.S. Department of Labor (1980).

Of all persons aged 16-24 enrolled in school, more than 40 percent are now working in October of the school year. Presumably, a much higher proportion work at some time during the school year. Work while in school became increasingly common throughout the 1970s. Obviously, the increased work may have important implications for education practices and, indeed, for the effects of education. For example, it raises questions about the impact of outside work on the quality of education received and the longer-term prospects for jobs. Meyer and Wise (1982) found that young persons who work while in high school are employed substantially more weeks per year after graduation than youth who do not work while in high school.

The racial patterns in employment by school enrollment status are even more startling. As Table 2 shows, in spite of similar enrollment

TABLE 2 Employment Rates for Persons Aged 16–24 Enrolled in School and Not Enrolled, by Race and Sex, Selected Years

	1964	1969	1974	1979
Enrolled				
White male	34.1	41.4	43.8	45.4
Black male	30.1	29.4	26.4	23.4
White female	23.3	34.7	40.4	45.4
Black female	15.4	22.3	18.2	20.6
Not enrolled				
White male	86.7	88.1	85.4	85.7
Black male	80.5	82.4	72.1	69.8
White female	47.3	55.1	60.2	66.0
Black female	48.0	50.7	46.9	43.1

SOURCE: Data provided by the Bureau of Labor Statistics.

rates, blacks are far less likely to work whether in or out of school. While employment rates were rising for whites in school and white women out of school, employment rates were stagnant or falling for black men and women, whether in or out of school. Employment rates for in-school blacks are half those of whites. Moreover, blacks lost ground over the 1970s. For example, between 1969 and 1979, employment of white women in school rose from 35 to 45 percent, in spite of the fact that general economic conditions worsened. Black women in school, in contrast, experienced a small decline in employment rates. Jobs while in school are now of major significance for white youth, but they are far less common for blacks. The stagnant job picture for blacks transcends school enrollment. Whereas white women out of school worked much more in 1979 than in 1969, black women were actually working a lot less.

Summary of School Enrollment Impacts

Let us now summarize the labor market impact of the changing enrollment patterns for blacks and whites. We treat each group separately.

For white men, the rising employment rates over the 1970s reflect a falling enrollment rate and a rising employment rate for those in school. Virtually the entire change in employment rates for white men over the past three decades might be traced to the combination of schooling and macroeconomic effects. In the 1960s when the economy was strong, increased enrollments were offset by increased work in school, and overall employment rose somewhat. In the 1970s, enrollment rates started to fall. Together with rising employment of school enrollees, these forces would have pushed overall employment rates up considerably, other things equal, but macroeconomic conditions dampened the increase.

For black men, the falling employment rates transcend school boundaries. In school or out, black male employment rates declined over the 1970s. Since school enrollment for black men was the same in 1979 as it was in 1969, very little of the decline in employment can be traced to changing enrollment patterns. Blacks are very unlikely to work while in school, and the proportion who do is falling rapidly.

For men, changing enrollment rates seem to account for as much as 3 points of the 14-point growth in the racial employment gap. We have already accounted for the bulk of this impact when we described the effects of induced enrollment in the Vietnam era. Thus, we have "explained" slightly more than half the gap so far, using the military, macroeconomic, and schooling effects. We shall have to look to other forces, such as family background and family formation, for futher explanation.

For women, on top of rising employment rates for those in school, there were rapidly rising rates for those out of school. Employment rates for white women both in school and out rose more than 10 points during the 1970s, even though the economy was weaker than in the 1960s. Only half the rise for women over this period can be linked to the employment patterns of those in school. The rapidly changing behavior of those out of school must also be considered.

For black women, enrollment and employment patterns were virtually identical in 1969 and 1979. Black women are by far the most stable group along these dimensions. Enrollment rates changed little, and employment rates for those in school and out fell only slightly. The widening racial employment gap for women thus reflects rapidly changing employment patterns for white women.

We will seek clearer answers as we explore household formation and family background influences below. Before proceeding to these issues, however, let us analyze in a little more detail employment patterns of whites and blacks in school and out, using a special tabulation of the Survey of Income and Education for 1976. Employment and enrollment patterns from this special tabulation are shown in Table 3.

The racial differences are dramatic. Once again we see that, although blacks and whites have relatively similar enrollment rates, employment rates both for school enrollees and school leavers are vastly lower for blacks. For younger age-groups, enrollment rates by race were quite similar by 1976, although some differences remain for the older ones. The critical racial difference lies in employment. Whether in school or

TABLE 3 Percent Enrolled and Employment Rates for Persons Aged 16-24 Enrolled in School and Not Enrolled, by Age, Race, and Sex, 1976

	Percent Enrolled in School		Employment Rate for Those in School		Employment Rate for Those Not in School	
	White	Black	White	Black	White	Black
Males						
16–19	82.0	80.1	0.471	0.177	0.708	0.376
20–24	42.7	33.9	0.493	0.344	0.793	0.639
Females						
16–19	84.0	79.3	0.394	0.171	0.624	0.334
20–24	44.1	35.8	0.316	0.354	0.777	0.536

SOURCE: Tabulations of the 1976 Survey of Income and Education.

out, blacks work much less. Whereas nearly half of white male teenagers work while in school, less than one-fifth of comparable blacks do. Similar patterns emerge for white women. We again conclude that school enrollment cannot explain the bulk of the black employment declines in the 1970s. Indeed, the employment rates for out-of-school teenage blacks are now so low that they approach the rates for those in school. These results are troubling indeed, for they suggest that either more years in school has done little to improve the employment prospects of young blacks or that other forces have swamped these benefits.

We noted that school also affects employment for those who are out of school, because employment rates are strongly correlated with level of schooling. We turn to that issue next.

Employment of Out-of-School Youth

Once a youngster leaves school, level of education is strongly associated with employment. Persons with college diplomas work more than high school graduates, who in turn work more than high school dropouts. The pattern applies equally to whites and blacks, and men and women, and the differences persist as people age.

Figure 8 displays employment rates for out-of-school men by race, age, and years of schooling. Figure 9 displays similar figures for women. Race, age, sex, and schooling are all highly correlated with employment. For black dropouts the picture is particularly bleak. Less than 20 percent of 17-year-old black male high school dropouts work; virtually none of the comparable women work. Even 7 years later, at age 24, only 67

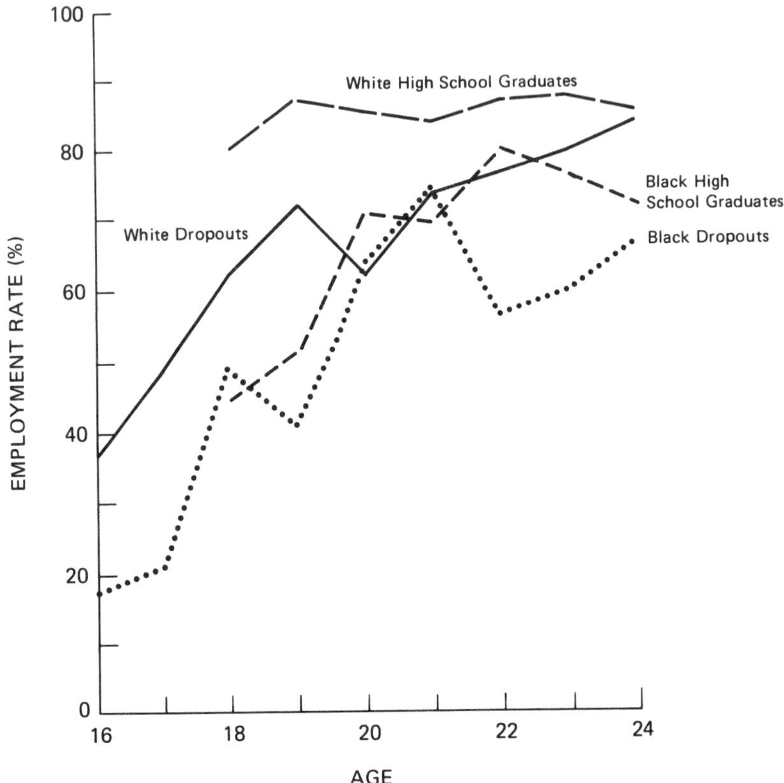

Figure 8 Employment rates for out-of-school males by age, race, and level of education, 1976. NOTE: Results for black dropouts have low precision. SOURCE: Tabulations of 1976 Survey of Income and Education.

percent of black men and 35 percent of black women high school dropouts work. Fortunately, less than one-quarter of all blacks can be found in this category. Still, the low levels of work are distressing. Increasing education raises the employment rates quite dramatically; yet, for men, black high school graduates still fare worse than white high school dropouts.

It is obvious that schooling level and employment are closely related. Higher levels of schooling are associated with distinctly higher employment for all groups. And, at the high school level at least, blacks and whites of equal age and education have quite different employment levels.

This concludes our discussion of the relationship between schooling and employment. Emerging already is a picture of an employment pattern for white men that is stable and easy to explain on the basis of

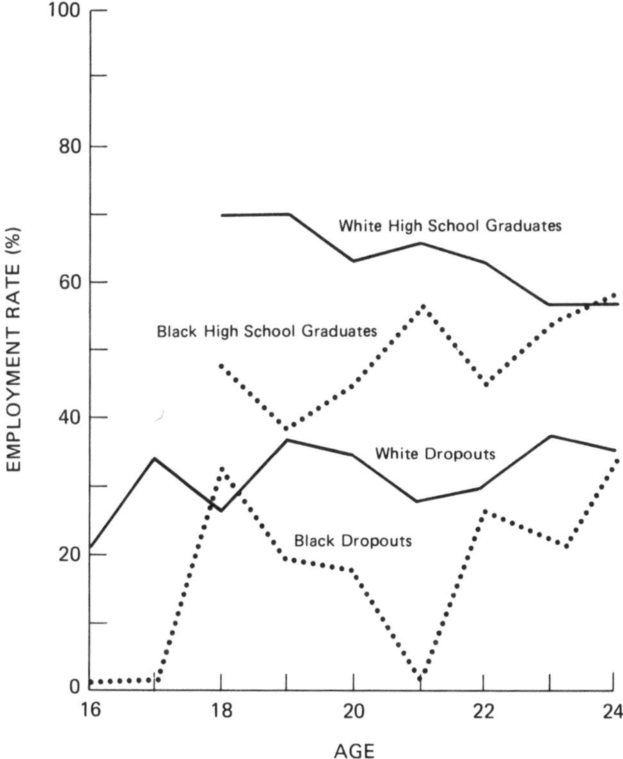

Figure 9 Employment rates for out-of-school women by age, race, and level of education, 1976. NOTE: Results for black dropouts have low precision. SOURCE: Tabulations of 1976 Survey of Income and Education.

traditional economic determinants like schooling and macroeconomic conditions. Employment for white women rose faster over the 1970s than we might have expected based on these factors alone. The employment patterns for blacks are deteriorating very rapidly, for reasons that are not easy to explain. We have explained slightly more than half of the worsening position for men thus far, but much less for women. In an effort to understand more, we turn to issues of household formation.

Household Formation

Perhaps the most significant of the events that occur during the late teenage and early adult years involves household formation. As noted, more than 98 percent of 16-year-olds live at home, and almost none are married or have children. By age 24, all but a quarter have left home, half are married, and one-third are living with children of their own. The labor market implications and complications of family formation are far reaching. Married women work less; married men work more. Women with children rarely attend school and are far less likely than childless women to work. Labor market outcomes undoubtedly influence family formation too. Couples may not want to marry or have children until one or both are "established" in their jobs. In this section we shall discuss the association between household formation and employment. We begin with a description of such associations in 1976 and then consider the implications that changing family formation had for the 1970s. It is exceptionally difficult to disentangle cause and effect here.

Youth between 16 and 24 are far too heterogeneous to be analyzed as one group. Thus, we concentrate on family formation variables for persons of two ages—18 and 24—and break each age-group into three categories: married and not living in a parent's home (independent married), single and not living in a parent's home (independent single), and living at home (dependent). More than 95 percent of those living in their parent's home are unmarried. Within each group we distinguish persons with no children from those with children. Tables 4, 5, and 6 describe the distribution, the school enrollment, and employment patterns of those not enrolled in school for 18-year-olds and 24-year-olds by race and sex.

A wide variety of patterns emerge. The overwhelming majority of 18-year-olds still live at home. Some 80 percent of women and nearly 95 percent of men live at home at this age. By age 24 most persons have left home.

Table 4 makes clear that household formation has hardly begun by age 18, particularly for men. Whether in school or not, working or not, the vast majority of men still live with their parents. Indeed, another tabulation shows that 84 percent of out-of-school *employed* 18-year-old men are still living at home. Marriage pulls a larger percentage of women out of the household. Some 12 percent of white women are married and living separately; 6.3 percent of black women are.

This finding may be important as we consider the significance of early employment problems. Since virtually all teenagers live at home, there may be less pressure for them to work, and the short-term financial consequences of being out of work may be less severe than for older independent persons. It is possible that a fraction of these make important contributions to family income. Yet even out-of-school youth living with families in poverty or near poverty provide on average only

TABLE 4 Percent Distribution of 18- and 24-Year-Olds, by Race and Sex

	Age 18		Age 24	
	White	Black	White	Black
Males				
Not living independently				
Without child	93.2	95.1	27.2	34.7
With child	0.4	0.0	0.7	0.4
Living independently				
Married without child	1.6	0.6	22.3	10.6
Married with child	1.1	0.1	27.7	29.0
Single without child	3.6	3.0	21.5	25.0
Single with child	0.1	1.1	0.7	0.2
Females				
Not living independently				
Without child	80.4	78.2	15.1	20.1
With child	0.8	6.9	1.6	5.8
Living independently				
Married without child	6.1	3.3	25.8	12.3
Married with child	5.4	3.0	38.3	32.2
Single without child	6.4	4.8	15.1	9.2
Single with child	0.8	3.9	4.2	20.5

SOURCE: Tabulations of 1976 Survey of Income and Education.

10 percent of family income. Some teenagers may face serious financial hardships when they are unemployed, but most probably do not.

By age 24, however, things have changed rather drastically. Only one-quarter of white men and just 16 percent of white women are still at home. One-third of black men and one-fifth of black women are. Moreover, for those who have not left home, lack of a job may prevent exit. By this age, employment has become far more important.

Marriage and childbearing sharply reduce school enrollment and employment rates for women. For men, school enrollment also is lower for those who are married, but employment is higher.

At age 18, the enrollment rate among married white women with no children is 31 percent, as compared to 77 percent for those who are unmarried and living at home. If the woman has a child and lives away from home, chances are 9 out of 10 that she is out of school. If she has a child but lives with her parents, she is more likely to remain in school, but even then only 20 percent are enrolled.

For married black women, the situation is perhaps worse, but for those who are unmarried and have children the enrollment effects are much less pronounced than for white women. Virtually none of the 18-

TABLE 5 Percent of 18- and 24-Year-Olds Enrolled in School, by Race and Sex

	Age 18		Age 24	
	White	Black	White	Black
Males				
Not living independently				
Without child	75.8	75.4	25.3	22.9
With child	NA	NA	NA	NA
Living independently				
Married without child	16.9	NA	27.0	13.2
Married with child	13.9	NA	11.7	14.8
Single without child	45.3	76.5	27.0	22.9
Single with child	NA	NA	NA	NA
Females				
Not living independently				
Without child	77.3	77.3	21.3	34.5
With child	17.6	42.9	22.9	16.5
Living independently				
Married without child	31.4	0.0	18.7	35.3[a]
Married with child	10.5	9.3	5.6	16.9
Single without child	51.5	48.1	28.0	28.5
Single with child	9.6	51.8	2.9	21.2

NOTE: NA = not applicable.

[a] This figure appears to be a statistical artifact. At all other ages less than 5 percent of married black women without children are enrolled in school.

SOURCE: Tabulations of 1976 Survey of Income and Education.

year-old married black women in our sample are enrolled in school. However, for unmarried black women, childbearing seems to have smaller effects on enrollment than it does for whites. Some 42 percent of unmarried black women who have children and live independently are still enrolled in school. More than half of those who are single parents living with their parents go to school. These figures are lower than those for women without children, but the differences are not so great as they are for whites.

Employment is also lower among mothers. White teenage mothers who have left school are half as likely to work as their out-of-school peers without children. For black mothers, however, the employment effects of children are not nearly so strong as for whites, whether living with parents or a husband. It is not that black mothers are so likely to work; rather, their unencumbered peers are so unlikely to be employed that both groups look similar.

The living situation of unwed mothers sharply influences the likelihood of their working. A mother living with her parents is much more

TABLE 6 Employment Rate for Persons Aged 18 and 24 Who Are Not Enrolled in School, by Race and Sex

	Age 18		Age 24	
	White	Black	White	Black
Males				
Not living independently				
Without child	0.727	0.428	0.776	0.561
With child	NA	NA	NA	NA
Living independently				
Married without child	0.964	NA	0.912	0.842
Married with child	0.682	NA	0.957	0.851
Single without child	0.708	0.390	0.875	0.918
Single with child	NA	NA	NA	NA
Females				
Not living independently				
Without child	0.681	0.449	0.795	0.814
With child	0.397	0.378	0.742	0.158[a]
Living independently				
Married without child	0.315	0.227	0.798	0.552
Married with child	0.218	0.289	0.379	0.513
Single without child	0.759	0.245	0.918	0.784
Single with child	0.215	0.112	0.603	0.394

NOTE: NA = not applicable.
[a] This figure appears to be a statistical artifact; employment rates are typically 0.4 for all other ages.
SOURCE: Tabulations of 1976 Survey of Income and Education.

likely to work than one who is married or living singly. For black teenagers, the effects are particularly pronounced. An unwed teenage black mother living with her parents is four times as likely to work as an unwed mother living alone.

Although the effects of childbirth and marriage are particularly strong for the teenager who marries, it is important to keep in mind that only 13 percent of white and 14 percent of black 18-year-olds in our sample are married, have children, or both. The 24-year-old age-group is the one most affected by marital and family status.

By age 24, only 30 percent of women of either race are both unmarried and childless. Some 85 percent of the whites and 80 percent of the blacks in this category who are out of school are working. For women who marry but do not yet have children, employment rates fall to 80 percent for whites and 55 percent for blacks. Obviously, for whites, at least, marriage alone has ceased to be strongly related to labor market activity. Children have the most significant influence. Mothers, black or white, work less than half the time.

Men are affected differently by marriage. Married men, like married women, are unlikely to be enrolled in school. But they are more likely to work than their unmarried peers. Married men may feel more financial pressure. Or marriage may be postponed until employment is obtained. Whatever the direction of causality, according to recent Current Population Survey data, once marital status, schooling, and race are controlled for, there is no relationship between the age of youth and their employment status (Meyer and Wise, 1981b). It may be that changing family status accounts for much of the apparent rise in employment as youths age.

How has childbearing affected employment? One of the most dramatic trends of the 1960s and 1970s was a substantial decline in the fertility rate for young white women (see Figure 10). Over the same

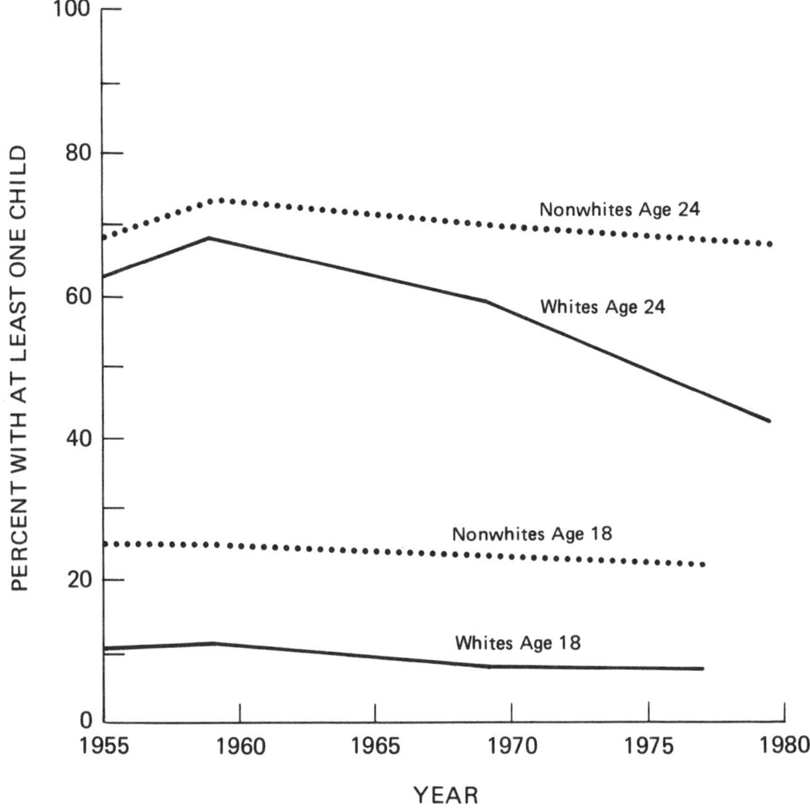

Figure 10 Percent of women aged 18 and 24 with at least one child, by race.

period, fertility rates were essentially level for black women. Marriage rates declined for both groups. It seems likely that the changing patterns of family formation have affected the employment rates of women. We conclude that the changing family structures between 1970 and 1980 could have been associated with as much as a 2 percentage point increase in the employment rate for white women aged 16-24 and a 1-point decrease in the employment rates for black women. As much as 3 points of the widening employment gap between black and white women during the 1970s might be traced to changes in family structure. Changing household formation seems to explain little for men.

In performing these calculations, we compared what the 1980 employment rates would have been had family structures been the same as in 1970 with what they would have been had employment rates by family type been identical to those in 1976. One reason that the net effects of changing fertility are so small is that some mothers actually work more than nonmothers because they also are not enrolled in school. It should be noted that these simple calculations do not indicate the direction of causality. Household formation decisions may be influenced by labor market conditions. If childbirth and marriage are more likely when conditions are bad, our calculations would exaggerate the impact of changing household formation and vice versa.

For women, the widening racial employment gap can be traced largely to rising employment rates of white women. Thus far, we have explained 2 points of the 14-point gap for women by the worsening macroeconomicconditions and 3 points by changing family structure. Changing enrollment patterns offer little explanatory power. The remaining differences must be traced to rising employment for women (both in school and out) within a family structure category. The labor force participation of married women, particularly those with children, rose dramatically over the 1970s. Young married women between 20 and 24 had participation rates of 43 percent in 1968. Ten years later, 59 percent of married women were in the labor force. Some of this increase can be traced to reduced childbearing, which we have already accounted for. But much of the rise reflected increased work by mothers. During the 1970s the labor-force-participation rates for married mothers with young children shot up 10 points. The forces we have explored offer little power in explaining these increases. It is clear, however, that for white women the increased employment in the 1970s must be traced in large part to this last fact. We have yet to explain why employment patterns for black women did not follow suit.

For men, the family structure variables seem far less potent. We have already noted that the bulk of the changes in white employment rates can be traced to changing military composition, macroeconomic conditions, and school enrollment; and some of the fall in employment for blacks can be traced to these same causes. Overall, these factors explain roughly 8 of the 14-point increase in the employment gap. In the next section we explore yet another possible influence, family background.

Family Background

One of the most obvious differences between blacks and whites is family background. Whereas 85 percent of white teenagers live in two-parent households, nearly half (45 percent) of blacks live with one parent. Moreover, while only 7 percent of white teens living at home live in households with incomes below the poverty line, 35 percent of black teens do. In this section we explore whether these differences and the dramatic changes in family structures over the 1970s might have influenced employment patterns.

It is difficult to trace family background for youngsters who have already left home. Virtually all teenagers live at home, but a substantial portion of persons aged 20-24 have moved out. Thus, we will concentrate only on teenagers in this discussion, then seek to generalize the results to the older age-group. In our analysis we have divided all families into two types, single-parent and two-parent. Within each type we have further subdivided these families into three income categories: below the poverty line, 100-200 percent of the poverty line, and over 200 percent of the poverty line. This makes six family type and income categories.

Tables 7 and 8 give the percent distribution by category and the percent enrolled in school, by race and sex, for teenagers living at home. Here we see that school enrollment is strongly related to both family type and income for both races and both sexes. Teenagers from poor and single-parent families are less likely to enroll in school. Less than 70 percent of white males in poor single-parent families are enrolled in school. Some 77 percent of white males in single-parent families with income more than twice the poverty line are enrolled. And fully 85 percent of persons in two-parent families with this higher level of income are enrolled. Similar figures apply to all three other sex and race combinations.

As is well known, blacks are heavily concentrated in single-parent and low-income families. Some 60 percent of white teenagers are in moderate- to high-income, two-parent families; only 15 percent of blacks are. Only 3 percent of whites are in poor single-parent families; nearly one quarter of black teenagers are. Black school enrollment is as high as or higher than white enrollment within virtually every family type

TABLE 7 Percent Distribution and Enrollment Rates for Males Aged 16–19, by Race, Family Type, and Income Level

	Percent Distribution		Percent Enrolled in School	
	White	Black	White	Black
Single parent				
Family income				
Below poverty line	2.5	22.3	68.4	78.6
100–199 percent of poverty line	6.7	18.7	74.9	74.6
200 percent of poverty line and over	5.3	2.9	77.4	71.1
All incomes	14.5	43.9	74.7	76.4
Two parent				
Family income				
Below poverty line	4.0	11.5	71.1	71.6
100–199 percent of poverty line	24.0	29.5	81.1	85.4
200 percent of poverty line and over	57.6	15.6	84.7	86.6
All incomes	85.5	56.1	83.1	82.9

SOURCE: Tabulations of 1976 Survey of Income and Education.

and income category. Lower enrollment rates for blacks thus can be completely accounted for by family background differences.

Sample sizes in many cells are small, but in general black and white enrollment rates look remarkably similar within family type and income groupings. In many cases, black enrollment rates are actually higher. Thus, the lower enrollment rates for blacks overall can be attributed to their concentration in lower-income and single-parent families. As mentioned above, analysis of postsecondary school attendance patterns show that, when family background and other individual attributes are controlled, blacks are much *more* likely than whites to attend a postsecondary school and, in particular, to attend a 4-year college or university.

Tables 9 and 10 display employment rates for those in school and out of school for the various family type and income groups. The results are dramatic. For males and females, blacks and whites, enrolled or not, from single-parent or two-parent families, rising family income is associated with rising levels of employment.

One out of every four white males in poor single-parent families who is enrolled in school is also working. If his family has income over twice

TABLE 8 Percent Distribution and Enrollment Rates for Females Aged 16–19, by Race, Family Type, and Income Level

	Percent Distribution		Percent Enrolled in School	
	White	Black	White	Black
Single parent				
Family income				
Below poverty line	3.0	25.4	60.5	73.3
100–199 percent of poverty line	5.7	17.8	81.9	75.3
200 percent of poverty line and over	5.7	2.7	81.0	91.9
All incomes	14.4	45.9	77.1	76.4
Two parent				
Family income				
Below poverty line	4.1	12.3	71.4	79.2
100–199 percent of poverty line	24.3	26.9	83.4	80.8
200 percent of poverty line and over	57.1	15.1	87.0	89.2
All incomes	85.6	54.1	85.5	82.9

SOURCE: Tabulations of 1976 Survey of Income and Education.

the poverty line, he is twice as likely to be working. Astonishingly, only 30 percent of *out-of-school* black males living in poor single-parent households work. Some 55 percent of those in higher-income families are working. In each category, we see rising family income associated with higher levels of employment. This may be in small part a statistical artifact: Families with working teenagers are not as likely to be poor. However, since (as we have noted) in virtually none of the household groupings do the youngsters contribute more than 10-15 percent of family income on average, we believe this effect is small.

For persons out of school, family type is strongly associated with employment rates. Teenagers from two-parent families are far more likely to be working. For those enrolled in school, family type shows a less dramatic but still substantial relationship to employment for whites and very little relationship for blacks.

For both races and both sexes, coming from a single-parent family substantially diminishes the likelihood that a youngster out of school will be working. Some 40-45 percent of out-of-school blacks of either sex in

TABLE 9 Employment Rates for Males Aged 16–19, by School Attendance, Rate, Family Type, and Income Level: Males

	Persons Enrolled in School		Persons Not Enrolled in School		Total	
	White	Black	White	Black	White	Black
Single parent						
Family income						
Below poverty line	0.248	0.129	0.456	0.288	0.314	0.163
100–199 percent of poverty line	0.376	0.200	0.615	0.299	0.436	0.225
200 percent of poverty line and over	0.522	0.336	0.705	0.545	0.563	0.395
All incomes	0.410	0.172	0.611	0.313	0.461	0.205
Two parent						
Family income						
Below poverty line	0.358	0.116	0.614	0.422	0.432	0.203
100–199 percent of poverty line	0.449	0.190	0.645	0.327	0.486	0.210
200 percent of poverty line and over	0.501	0.204	0.791	0.718	0.545	0.273
All incomes	0.480	0.181	0.732	0.444	0.523	0.226

SOURCE: Tabulations of 1976 Survey of Income and Education.

two-parent families are employed; roughly 30 percent of those from single-parent families are employed. For white women living with two parents, the employment rate is 67 percent; for those living with only one, the employment rate is 45 percent. The pattern applies for all income groups, though there is a hint in the data that the negative relationship is less severe for higher-income single-parent families. Family type seems to alter behavior most for white women and least for white men, but in all cases the impact is large. It is unclear from these data whether the family type effects are direct or indirect via level of schooling achieved or household formation decisions. In any case, family structure seems to be strongly correlated with labor market outcomes, particularly for women.

We can only speculate about the reasons for these findings. Possibly youth from poor families have less access to networks or contacts and information that help in finding jobs. Alternatively, persons from poor or single-parent families may be less likely to have working role models.

TABLE 10 Employment Rates for Females Aged 16–19, by School Attendance, Rate, Family Type, and Income Level

	Persons Enrolled in School		Persons Not Enrolled in School		Total	
	White	Black	White	Black	White	Black
Single parent						
Family income						
Below poverty line	0.189	0.084	0.204	0.227	0.195	0.122
100–199 percent of poverty line	0.330	0.204	0.507	0.330	0.362	0.235
200 percent of poverty line and over	0.381	0.318	0.687	0.392	0.439	0.324
All incomes	0.329	0.147	0.457	0.270	0.358	0.178
Two parent						
Family income						
Below poverty line	0.258	0.104	0.307	0.163	0.272	0.116
100–199 percent of poverty line	0.355	0.177	0.631	0.456	0.401	0.230
200 percent of poverty line and over	0.432	0.272	0.745	0.671	0.473	0.315
All incomes	0.405	0.189	0.668	0.418	0.443	0.228

SOURCE: Tabulations of 1976 Survey of Income and Education.

Perhaps they are more likely to be rejected when they apply, making their discouragement from applying a response to reality. It is possible that welfare rules offer substantial disincentives to work for youth in poor families. And (as Chapter 5 discusses) they may be working in the irregular economy.

For those in school, the effects are less strong. White employment rates for youngsters in two-parent families are still somewhat higher than those for persons in single-parent families. But for blacks, family type has only a small impact. Only a small fraction of young blacks work while in school, regardless of their family type. (The proportion who work does rise somewhat with income.)

These results suggest that the rapidly changing family structures of the 1970s may indeed have had profound labor market impacts. We will consider that issue in a moment. It is important to recognize, however, that in every family type and income classification, blacks always fare much worse than whites. Even if family structures and income levels for blacks were identical to those of whites, the overall employment rate for black teenagers living at home would rise only from 21 to 27 percent. The overall rate for whites is 48 percent. Thus, the black-white gap cannot be attributed primarily to family background differences.

The sample sizes are probably too small to perform such a calculation for out-of-school youth only and get a very reliable result. When the calculation is performed, for what it is worth, we find that roughly half the difference can be traced to these characteristics. The result follows from the substantial impact of family income and structure on the employment of out-of-school blacks.

We turn at last to the changing family patterns of the 1970s and their possible influence on employment rates. Figure 11 documents a trend that has been widely discussed elsewhere. There was a sudden and sharp

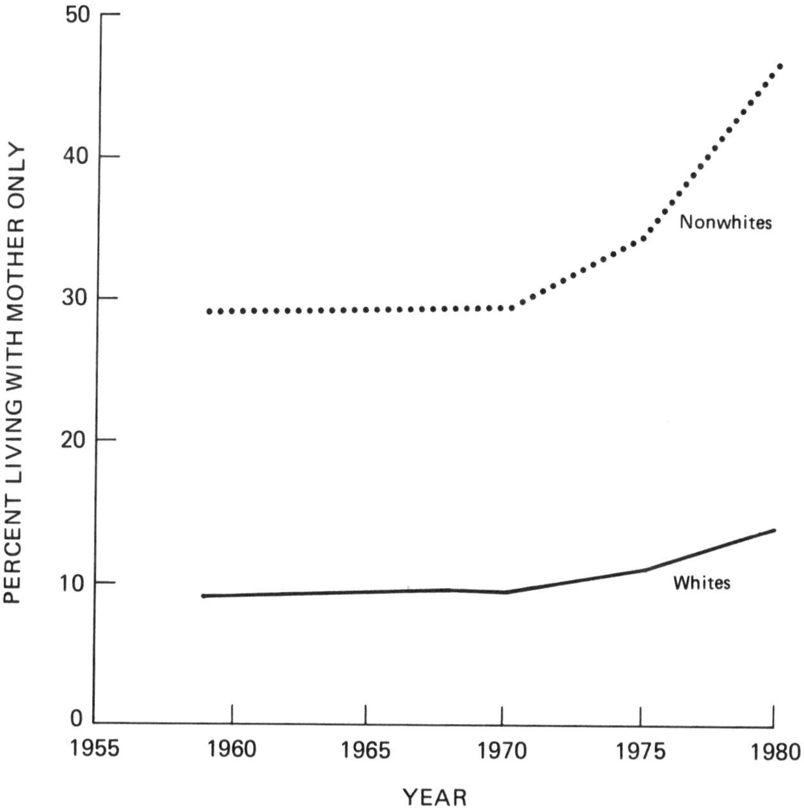

Figure 11 Percent of persons aged 14-19 living with mother only, by race.

increase in the number of single-parent families during the 1970s. For blacks the changes were enormous. Whereas 30 percent of black teens were found in single-parent households in 1970, this figure rose to nearly 50 percent by 1980. During the same period, the percentage of white teenagers in single parent households rose from 9.1 to 14.4 percent. It is instructive to consider the possible impacts of these changes on employment.

For out-of-school teenagers, the changing family structure may have been associated with a decline in the overall employment rate of as much as 3 points for black males and females; it had no influence on whites. For in-school teens, impacts for all groups were negligible. Since most teens are in school, overall the changing family structure lowered employment rates for minority teenagers by 1 point. However, since most 20- to 24-year-olds are out of school, impacts could be larger for that group. Perhaps 2 points of the 12-point increase in the black-white employment gap could be traced to family structure changes.

The nearly 20 percent increase in single-parent black families might have been expected to be associated with lower employment rates, particularly for those out of school. If the differences in employment patterns between youngsters for single-parent and two-parent families had held at the 1976 level (roughly 0.15 points) throughout the period, and if we treat the changes as exogenous, then overall employment rates for those out of school would have fallen 3 points. Between 1970 and 1980, however, the impacts of the altered family structure on those in school would be negligible, since family structure is so weakly related to employment rates for blacks in school. Since most persons are in school, the overall impact for black teenagers is small, perhaps lowering employment by 1 point.

Recall, however, that most 20- to 24-year-olds are out of school, so they may be more heavily affected by family background. But it is also true that many left home before the full change of the 1970s had occurred. At most we might believe the changing family structure caused a 2- to 3-point fall in minority employment for those in their early twenties. Averaging the effects for the teenagers with that for 20- to 24-year-olds, at most 2 points of the 12-point fall in minority employment might be traced directly to changing family structure and then only if such changes are treated as exogenous.

In short, family structure and family income are critical determinants of employment patterns. For males, then, we have now explained as much as 9 or 10 points of the 14-point growth in the gap. For females, we have accounted for perhaps 6 or 7 points. Nonetheless, we still are unable to explain all the changes in minority employment patterns relative to whites over the 1970s. Now we turn to our final topic: government programs.

Public Programs

Many government programs may have had an influence on the employment and related experiences of youth over the 1970s. We shall focus on three: youth employment programs, minimum wage legislation, and the Basic Educational Opportunity Grant (BEOG) program.

Youth Employment Programs

The rising interest in the labor market problems of youth was matched in the late 1960s and 1970s by a rapid increase in public training and employment programs for youth. In 1964, fewer than 50,000 youth under age 22 were served by federal employment and training programs. By 1969, perhaps 750,000 participated in some program. In 1979, nearly 2 million youth received federally sponsored labor market aid. During the Carter years, a diverse set of programs, many experimental, were created or expanded to help youth. These ranged from the Young Adult Conservation Corps, where youth are employed in conservation or other public projects, to the Youth Incentive Entitlement Projects—experimental programs where youth are guaranteed part-time work while in school and full-time summer jobs if they return to school.

The largest single program was the Summer Youth Employment Program (SYEP), which provides employment for disadvantaged youth aged 14-21 during the summer months. The program grew from roughly 400,000 persons in 1969 to more than 1 million in 1978. The vastness of the program can be illustrated by the fact that nearly 45 percent of all summer jobs held by nonwhite youth aged 14-19 in July 1978 were provided under SYEP. In contrast, just 3 percent of jobs for whites during the same period were similarly provided. As shown in Figure 12, some 50 percent of white youth (aged 14-19) had private sector jobs outside the program, but only 18 percent of nonwhite youth did. The program provided jobs for another 2 percent of whites and 14 percent of nonwhites. Those figures must be interpreted carefully. Fully 40 percent of all SYEP jobs go to very young teenagers aged 14 and 15, so the contribution for older youth may be smaller. Still, the size of the public sector role in the labor market for nonwhite teenagers is astonishing.

It is impossible to know the extent to which summer jobs displaced some youth from unsubsidized private sector jobs. It is worth noting

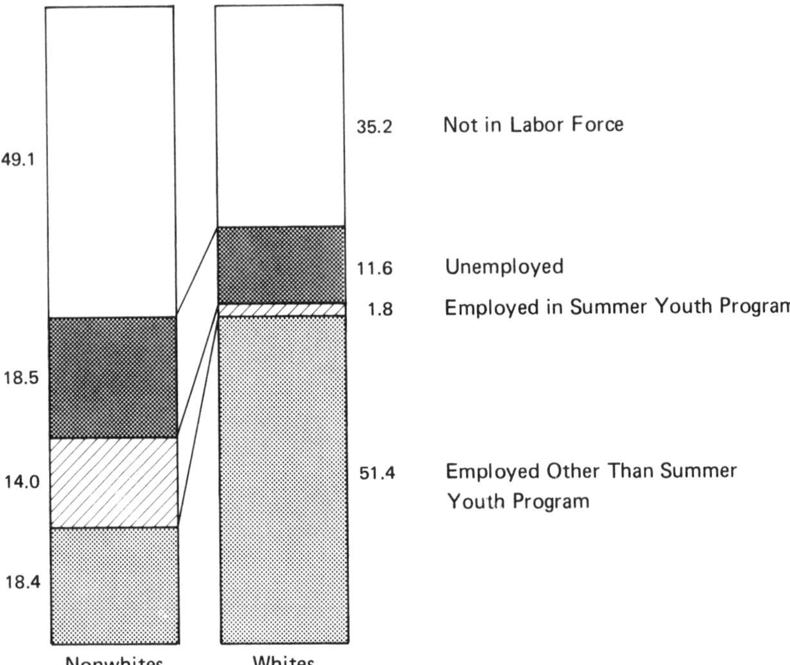

Figure 12 Employment status of 14- to 19-year-old whites and nonwhites, July 1978. SOURCE: U.S. Department of Labor (1979).

that employment rates for nonwhite teenagers as shown in Figure 13 may not have fallen as much over the 1970s in the summer months as they did during the school year, suggesting perhaps that these programs mitigated the problems of nonwhite youth. On the other hand, it is possible that these public sector jobs do not provide the kind of work experience and job networks that private employment might.

The Minimum Wage

Since its inception in 1938, the scope of the minimum wage has been continuously expanded, primarily through extended coverage. Perhaps 90 percent of nonsupervisory workers are now subject to the minimum, either through the federal legislation itself or through state extensions. In real terms, the minimum wage was about the same in 1970 as in 1980, both of which were about 15 percent higher than the 1973 level, the lowest level in real terms during the 1970s.

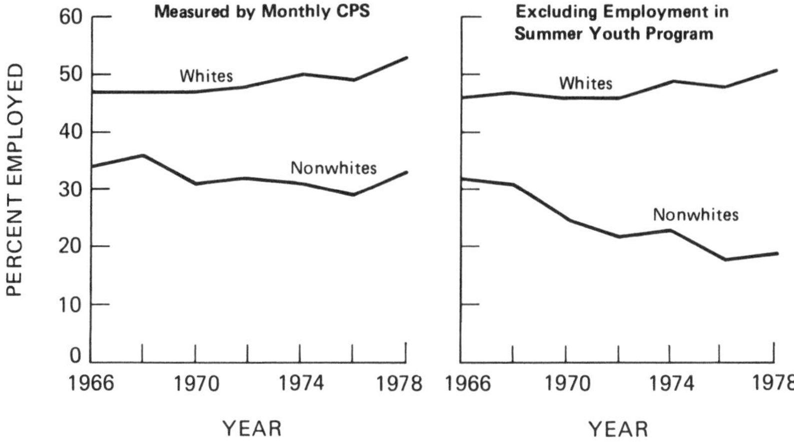

Figure 13 July employment/population ratios for 14- to 16-year-old whites and nonwhites. SOURCE: U.S. Department of Labor (1979).

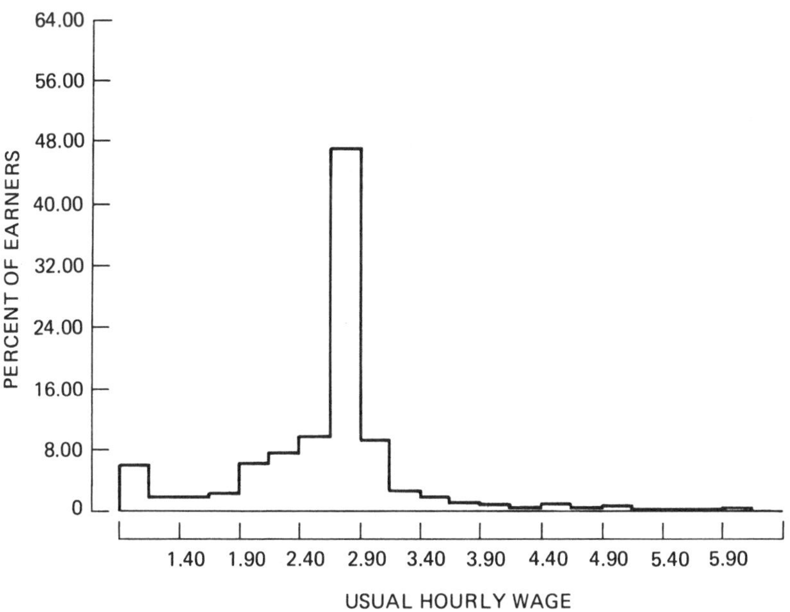

Figure 14 Wage distribution for 16- and 17-year-olds. SOURCE: Current Population Survey (May 1978).

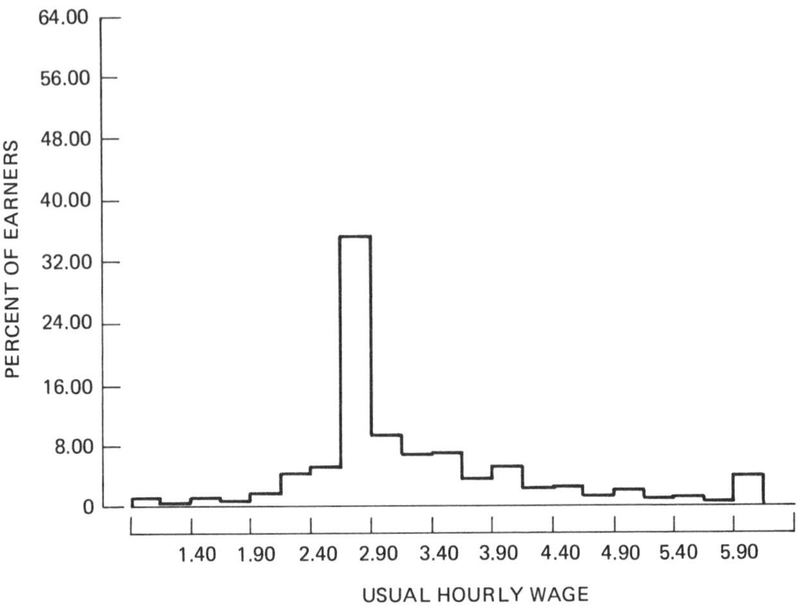

Figure 15 Wage distribution for 18- and 19-year-olds. SOURCE: Current Population Survey (May 1978).

What has been the effect of the minimum wage on the employment and earnings of youth? Figures 14 through 16 show the distribution of youth wage rates for selected age-groups in 1978, when the minimum was set at $2.65. The figures make clear that the minimum has a dramatic effect on youth wage rates. A large proportion of the age-groups under 20 are paid at the minimum. A substantial proportion of teenagers are also paid below the minimum.

The employment impact of the minimum wage has been the subject of a long list of studies that we shall not attempt to summarize here. Rather, we shall report results from a recent simulation analysis by Meyer and Wise (1981a) of the earnings and employment effects of the minimum wage. Their study concentrates on youth aged 16-24 during the 1970s. According to their estimates,

> Without the minimum wage, employment of youth would have been 3.9 percent higher than it was. Employment of those aged 16-19 would have been 7.1 percent higher, and among those aged 20-24, it would have been 2.2 percent higher. The effect among blacks was considerably larger than among whites, 5.6 versus 3.7 percent.

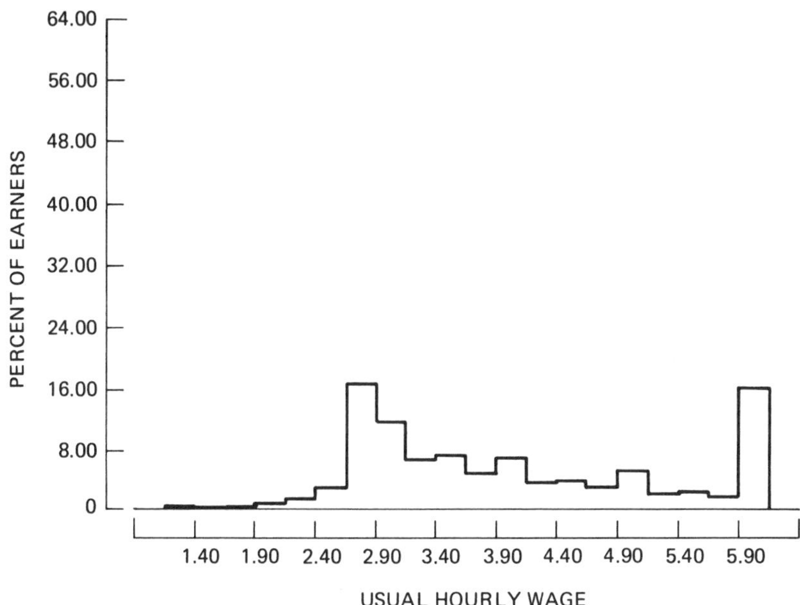

Figure 16 Wage distribution for 20- to 24-year-olds. SOURCE: Current Population Survey (May 1978).

Their employment results (shown in Table 11 by race and age-group) thus reveal a rather substantial employment effect. The minimum wage also affects youth earnings. It increases the average wage of those employed but reduces the number of persons employed. Results not shown here show that the two effects almost exactly offset one another. Total youth earnings are about the same with the minimum as they would be without it. It is not surprising that the minimum should have a relatively large effect on teenage employment. Over the 1970s, the minimum stayed very close to the *average* wage rate 16- to 17-year-olds would have had in the absence of the minimum.

TABLE 11 Employment Effects of the Minimum Wage, by Race and Age

Age-Group	Total	White	Black
16–24	3.9	3.7	5.6
20–24	2.2	2.1	3.5
16–19	7.1	6.9	10.1
16–17	8.7	8.6	10.1

SOURCE: Meyer and Wise (1981a).

As we have shown above, many employed youth, especially nonwhite youngsters, have government-provided jobs that pay the minimum—more than some would otherwise receive. If it were not for these jobs, the observed effect of the minimum would presumably have been somewhat greater.

Aid for Postsecondary Education: The BEOG Program

The role and scope of federal student financial aid activities has been periodically debated and revised. In the middle 1960s a desire to equalize educational opportunities across income classes became prominent. The Basic Educational Opportunity Grant (BEOG) Program initiated in 1973 gave fullest expression to this policy goal. Over the 1970s, programs became the dominant aid instrument as, over time, benefits under the program were extended to higher-income groups.

We know of only one analysis of the program's impact (Fuller et al., 1980). It reveals that:

> Without BEOG awards, postsecondary enrollment of low income youth would be about 37 percent lower than it is. Enrollment of middle and upper income youth would be only 6 percent lower although, by 1979, 40 percent of BEOG aid went to middle and upper income youth.
>
> Without the BEOG grants, enrollment in two-year colleges and in vocational-technical schools would be about 31 percent lower. Enrollment in four-year colleges and universities is virtually unaffected by the program.

Awards to upper- and middle-income youth have very little effect on their enrollment patterns, whereas awards to low-income students have a substantial effect on the postsecondary enrollment of this group. In addition, the awards have virtually no effect on enrollment in 4-year colleges for any income group. The effect of the awards is, therefore, to increase enrollment by low-income students in 2-year colleges and in vocational-technical schools. Predicted enrollments (in thousands) by school type and by income group, with and without BEOG awards, were as follows in 1979:

	All Schools		Four-Year Schools		Two-Year and Voc-Tech Schools	
Income Group	With BEOG	Without BEOG	With BEOG	Without BEOG	With BEOG	Without BEOG
Lower	590	370	128	137	462	233
Middle	398	354	162	164	238	190
Upper	615	600	377	378	238	222
Total	1,603	1,324	668	679	935	645

Total enrollment would have been 17 percent lower without the BEOG awards according to these estimates: 37 percent lower among low-income youth, 11 percent lower among middle-income youth, and 2 percent lower among upper-income youth. While for many low income students the awards seem to tip the balance in favor of junior colleges and vocational schools versus full-time entry into the labor force, attendance at 4-year colleges and universities is not affected greatly by the awards. Apparently, 2-year schools, vocational schools, and work are much closer substitutes for one another than 4-year college programs are for any of the other three.

We end this section by emphasizing that these three programs apparently have countervailing influences on employment of young people. Youth employment programs are intended to increase employment, especially among the disadvantaged. The BEOG program reflects a different approach to aiding the disadvantaged. The grants are designed to increase education and therefore improve labor market opportunity later. But since these programs increase the enrollment of low-income youth, they reduce their measured employment while they remain in school, since persons in school work less than persons out of school. At the same time, the minimum wage reduces employment for these same groups.

Conclusions

We have examined employment patterns across groups and over time. Our basic focus has been on understanding the widening racial employment gap. For both men and women, this gap grew by roughly 14 points over the 1970s. For men, this reflected a roughly 4-point rise in employment rates for whites and a 10-point fall for blacks. For women, virtually all the change came from rising employment of white women. We have explored a wide variety of possible explanations for these changes. Our findings are:

- The changing structure of the military may have had a significant influence on employment patterns of youth. If persons in the military are treated as employed, we reduce the unexplained growth in the employment gap by 2-3 points for men.
- The macroeconomic state of the economy continued to have a substantial influence on the employment of young people. The general economic weakness of the 1970s hurt the young, particularly blacks, disproportionately—a factor that may have added 2 points to the gap for both men and women.

• Enrollment rates for blacks rose slightly over the 1970s. For white males rates fell sharply (perhaps due to the elimination of draft-induced enrollment in the late 1960s), while for females employment was stable. These changes can explain perhaps 3 points of the gap for males and none of the gap for females.

• The median black is now receiving almost as much education, measured by years of schooling, as the median white. Yet employment rates for blacks vis-a-vis whites have not increased correspondingly.

• Employment for whites enrolled in school grew considerably in recent years and now encompasses almost half of all youngsters in a given month. For blacks, work while in school remains uncommon.

• Household formation decisions are highly correlated with schooling and employment patterns. Women with children are far less likely to work or attend school than their childless peers. Unwed whites are almost always out of school and rarely work. For unwed blacks, the influence of childbirth on school enrollment is less severe, but still substantial. In general, employment rates are higher for unwed mothers if they live in a parent's home than if they live independently. The sharply reduced birthrate of the 1970s for white women seems to have pushed up school enrollment and work when out of school. Moreover, the labor force participation of mothers and childless married women rose sharply over the decade. Perhaps 3 points of the rise in the employment gap for women can be traced to these influences.

• Family type (single-parent versus two-parent) and family income bear a strong relationship to employment and school enrollment. Children from intact and wealthier families work more and attend school more. Between one-fourth and one-half of the difference in employment rates between blacks and whites can be traced to these factors. The trend toward single-parent families in the black community may have negative consequences for the labor market performance of young blacks. But at most only 2 points can be accounted for by these forces for both men and women.

• Policies of the 1970s simultaneously increased and diminished demand for youthful workers. Youth programs grew enormously over the decade. At the same time, the minimum wage remained a deterrent to hiring unskilled youth, and BEOG grants increased postsecondary enrollment for youth from low-income families. Overall, there was an enormous increase in youth employment programs during the late 1960s and 1970s. Unfortunately, the employment picture for black youth looks even worse today than it did in the 1970s.

The one area where we remain somewhat uncertain involves the large supply changes affecting the labor market. While we believe the baby boom alone cannot explain very much, coupled with the sharply reduced military manpower needs in the 1970s the increase in the supply of civilian manpower was quite sizable. Moreover, the steep rise in labor force participation of white women, both young and old, may have further crowded the labor market. Black workers may have been displaced.

The changing employment patterns for whites can be traced almost entirely to the factors we could measure. White men attend school somewhat less and work more when they are in school than they did in the 1960s. As a result, employment rates have risen, even though dampened somewhat by worsening economic conditions and the minimum wage. White women work more in school, are less likely to be married or have children, and, if they are married or have children, they are more likely to work now than in the 1960s. These trends collectively overpowered negative macroeconomic forces.

For blacks, the patterns are somewhat more perplexing. Changing military structure, worsening macroeconomic conditions, changing family structure, and increased school enrollment all contributed to the decline in civilian employment of blacks relative to whites. Still, many of these results simply push questions back one level further. Why are blacks more likely to be in the military, why are they strongly influenced by macroeconomic fluctuations, why are family structures changing? Perhaps the answers to these questions would also shed light on the large residual gap we have been unable to explain.

References

Anderson, Bernard E., and Isabel V. Sawhill,
1978 *Youth Employment and Public Policy.* Englewood Cliffs, N.J.: Prentice-Hall, Inc.

Bureau of Labor Statistics
1980 *Handbook of Labor Statistics.* Bulletin 2070. Washington, D.C.: U.S. Department of Labor, December.

Cooper, Richard V. L.
1978 Youth Labor Markets and the Military. Paper presented at the Policy Conference on Employment Statistics of Youth, University of California at Los Angeles, February.

Freeman, Richard
1978 Why is there a youth labor market problem? In Anderson and Sawhill (1978).

Freeman, Richard B., and David A. Wise, eds.
1982 *The Youth Employment Problem: Its Nature, Causes, and Consequences.* Chicago: University of Chicago Press.

Fuller, Winship C., Charles F. Manski, and David A. Wise
1982 The impact of the Basic Educational Opportunity Grant Program on college enrollments. *Journal of Human Resources.*

Meyer, Robert H., and David A. Wise
1981a The Effects of the Minimum Wage on the Employment and Earnings of Youth. Working Paper, November.
1981b The Transition From School to Work: The Experiences of Blacks and Whites. Working Paper, July.
1982 High school preparation and early labor force experience. In Freeman and Wise (1982).
U.S. Department of Labor
1979 *The Summer Youth Employment Program: A Report on Progress, Problems, and Prospects.* Office of Youth Programs. Washington, D.C.: U.S. Department of Labor, February.
1980 *Youth Knowledge Development Report 25, Factbook on Youth.* Office of the Assistant Secretary of Policy Evaluation and Research. Washington, D.C.: U.S. Department of Labor, May.
Venti, Steven F., and David A. Wise
1981 Individual Attributes and Self-Selection of Higher Education: College Attendance Versus College Completion. Working Paper, October.
Wachter, Michael L.
1978 The dimensions and complexities of the youth employment problem. In Anderson and Sawhill (1978).

DISCUSSION

The general sense of both the formal discussants and the participants from the floor was that the Ellwood and Wise paper did an excellent job of documenting the major deterioration over the last decade in the labor market position of black youth, both men and women, relative to their white counterparts. They were less successful, however, in identifying why the relative position of black youth should have deteriorated so much.

Two kinds of problems surfaced. The first was the methodological problem of estimating the effect of one factor independently of the others. As the first formal discussant, Ellen Greenberger, put it: "You run these variables about singly as if their effects are not interactive. What I miss is a multivariate analysis and a model that talks about how these and other variables might be related to one another and how, together, they might affect employment." The second problem was the view expressed by several that there could well be other important variables, as well as interactions of variables, that were not discussed in the paper.

The most important findings were generally agreed to be the major influence of military manpower needs on the civilian labor market, the enormous proportion of black youth employment that was provided by public sector employment programs (of the 45 percent of black youth employed in the summer of 1978, one-third were in summer youth programs), and the not always favorable interaction between different types of policy designed with the same goal—increased youth employment.

The conference discussion focused on identifying other possibly important explanatory factors.

Greenberger opened the discussion by raising the question of whether the 16- to 24-year-old group may be too heterogeneous to make it a good aggregation for analysis. For example, 6- to 10-year-olds are strikingly similar as a group, both in terms of their stage of development and in terms of their life-style. The 40- to 49-year-old group is also rather homogeneous, in that they face similar kinds of life-cycle issues. The 16- to 24-year-old group, in contrast, is "so diverse in terms of life issues that the record keepers of the world and the analysts of employment and unemployment problems might benefit from making finer distinctions the rule rather than the exception." This point was brought home by Isabel Sawhill, who emphasized how struck she was by the findings in the Ellwood and Wise paper about the enormous amount of family formation that is going on. "Two-thirds of the marriages and half the first births occur between the ages of 16 and 24."

The second major point raised by Greenberger and reiterated by other conference participants was that other data indicate that teenagers work much more than was reflected in the data base used by Ellwood and Wise. According to the National Center for Educational Statistics, which surveys a nationally representative sample of 60,000 high school sophomores and seniors, in 1980 about 74 percent of 17-year-olds (both male and female) were working at some point during the school year, 60 percent of 16-year-olds, and 53 percent of 15-year-olds. And these are typically jobs that involve a considerable amount of work. According to the NCES data, for example, sophomore boys who have a job work an average of just under 15 hours a week, but 23 percent are actually working 22 hours or more, and 8 percent are working 34 hours or more while attending school. These findings represent a revolution since the 1940s, when only 4 percent of males and 1 percent of females worked while in high school. The NCES data support the Ellwood and Wise finding in that white high schoolers are more likely to be employed than their black counterparts—although this difference narrows by the senior year in the NCES data, for reasons that are not clear. Another relevant finding from the NCES data is that high schoolers from the economically more advantaged families are somewhat *more* likely to hold jobs than the students from poorer families. Finally, also in contrast to the past, only a relatively small proportion of these working children (18 percent according to one study) hand their earnings over to their families or save it for future family formation, education, or whatever. They typically spend it for their own consumption.

Greenberger also pointed out, a finding confirmed by Ellwood and Wise during the general discussion, that whether youths are working when they are 18 does not seem to be related to how much they are employed later on. It does, however, have a bearing on what they earn later on. That is, if a person is working at 18, his or her wage rate will be higher at 25 than if that person is not working at 18.

Why are these data so discrepant? The likely answer seemed to be that the CPS questions are not answered by the youths themselves, but by the relevant heads of household. There are several fairly obvious reasons why this might lead to downwardly biased estimates, ranging from ignorance about what their children are doing, to not wanting to include children's earnings in family income for purposes of taxation—a lively possibility to the extent that the earnings come from the underground economy (see Chapter 5 and associated discussion).

Sawhill, the second formal discussant, led the discussion away from the issue of how much youth actually work to the issue of why there has been such a drastic deterioration in the relative position of black youth. She started off by listing the major speculations in the literature: (1) Relative wages for black youth have risen over the last decade. (2) Industrial structure has been changing in ways that may have had adverse effects on the employability of black youth. (3) Over the last 10 years businesses, where the jobs are, have been moving out to the suburbs, away from the central city areas where many of the black youth are. (4) The quality of schooling received by blacks may not have increased commensurately with the quantity of schooling. (5) There may be alternative income sources for these youth, whether from welfare, their own families, or the irregular economy. (6) The attitudes of employers or the youths themselves may have been changing in ways that reduce the proportion who want or can get jobs.

Sawhill's own preferred combination of these possible explanations into one coherent story sees the large increases in supply of labor since 1970 as the primary villain, leading to a serious deterioration in job opportunities and a situation in which the blacks were behind in the queue for those jobs. Her argument goes as follows: "There were large increases in the size of the labor force during the 1970s: from the baby boom, from the military developments already mentioned, and from the increase in female labor force participation. Job growth over this period did not keep pace with these developments. The average unemployment rate between 1965 and 1970 was about 4 percent. Between

1975 and 1980, it was about 7 percent. So, we really are talking about a serious deterioration in job opportunities.

"Now, suppose you have a model that assumes employers select workers from a queue in which people are lined up depending on their relative attractiveness to employers, and relative attractiveness depends both on your employability or your qualifications and the wage level at which you can be hired.

"Next, assume that black youth are at the end of this queue, especially black youth from low-income families. Why are they at the end of the queue? Partly, it seems to be quality of education. (It certainly isn't quantity or doesn't seem to be from the analysis contained in the Ellwood and Wise paper and others.) Partly it seems to be continuing discrimination (stereotyping) based on race and class. Some of it may be an unwillingness on the part of these youth to take menial jobs when they have alternative sources of income. Some small part of it may be the minimum wage."

Her conclusion, which was shared by others and is discussed further below, was that to get any further in identifying why the black youth are at the end of the queue requires more research of an anthropological character that looks at history and life-style issues, rather than more analysis of statistical categories. Her final policy recommendation, however, was independent of the reasons for the queue:

"Most policies are designed to move minority youth up in the queue by making them more employable or by introducing a subminimum wage for youth or by using affirmative action to put them ahead of whites. But if the length of the job queue itself does not change, you are simply reshuffling people; for every disadvantaged youth that you move up in the queue, somebody else has to go to the back of the line. I conclude, then, that faster growth and a higher-employment economy is a prerequisite to solving these problems in both a political and economic sense. That does not mean that macroeconomic policy will necessarily solve all the problems. We know that even in the very tight labor markets of the late 1960s there were still high unemployment rates for some groups. But I think it is the key, and that without it nothing else will be effective."

Diana Slaughter, the third formal discussant, pursued the historical and life-style issues that Sawhill was searching for, and the rest of the floor discussion followed her.

She framed her remarks around four implicit hypotheses underlying the Ellwood and Wise analysis, which she regarded as misplaced and which, in her words, "led to the relatively inconclusive nature of their findings with respect to the causes and consequences of the black employment problem."

The first assumption is that comparing labor force participation of blacks and whites over the years 1955-1979 has any meaning independent of historical or contextual factors. Blacks, as a group, did not live in predominantly urban areas until around 1955 (the beginning point of the comparison), while whites, as a group, had lived in urban, industrialized areas for at least 20 years before. The blacks who were used to the city had labor market experience comparable to whites. But, as increasing numbers of blacks moved to the city, away from agricultural work opportunities to which they were accustomed, black labor force participation went down—the point being that labor-force-participation rates should not be examined independent of the type of work typically done by different groups. "The meaning of color needs to be interpreted from the perspective of the history of the respective generations in the urban economy; that is best done by an analysis of the types of work done by the groups as a whole, both before and certainly during the period under consideration."

Christopher Winship has recently shown, for example, that when blacks shifted from an agricultural economy to an urban one their rates of labor force participation as a group began to decline. Such a view, as pointed out in the floor discussion, is consistent with research by John Cogan to the effect that the South in 1970 was very different in the unemployment and employment differentials by race from the rest of the country. The explanation seems to have to do both with agricultural origin and the fact that a much larger share of the young labor force was in the South. Since the South is still such a different economy from the North, the nationwide minimum wage, for example, probably has very different effects on work incentives in the South. Ellwood and Wise agreed with this assessment of the Cogan research, but said that the regional migrations and differences he looked at to explain the patterns up to 1970 had largely ended by the 1970s. Their view was, therefore, that geography could not explain the big changes since 1970. They had not done the analysis, however, and to the extent that Slaughter's explanation works itself out *after* migration, the fact that the big movements had occurred by 1970 does not disprove her argument.

The second implicit assumption that Slaughter took issue with is that the behavioral patterns of youth can be understood irrespective of the lives they lead. The lives of black families have, of necessity, changed dramatically over the past 50 years. Not only have the kinds of work (for men, though not so much for women) changed, but life-styles have changed. Certain kinds of familial life-styles supported and contributed to the southern agricultural economy: extended, large families; teamwork and sharing; large numbers of children; a dissociation between early childbearing and later marriage; and so on. Every hand was needed, and youth were expected to contribute substantively to the economic and social life of their families of origin. These life-styles have their own intrinsic sources of satisfaction, which may only reluctantly be abandoned in the face of newer labor/work demands. They were supported by basic religious values and an essentially patriarchal family structure. The pressure of accommodating newer labor force demands to these traditional, cultural life-styles is one of the major issues confronted by many urban black youth—their worsening participation in the labor force reflects the hiatus between preferred life-styles, well-rationalized in terms of a now largely extinct economy, and the demands of educational institutions and urban occupational settings that they leave their "culture" outside.

Even more important, of course, is the current shift to an essentially service economy; black youth were latecomers to the urban scene because their families were latecomers, and the adjustment some families have been able to make to industrial, factory work have been undercut by a second shift in the type of work available: delivery of services, for which their parents in turn have had little direct, continuous preparation. When generations cannot transmit stable work patterns, relative to the informal, socialization norms and skills involved in particular types of work, then it is difficult for the family to assume a role as educator.

The third assumption questioned by Slaughter was that working, or actively seeking work, bears the same relation to schooling irrespective of color or sex. When we as a society decided to use schools to engender educational equity—that is, to attempt to give every student regardless of social background a *chance* at the best this nation had to offer—we perhaps unknowingly committed ourselves to dealing with the questions of class, race, and sex, because these are the major parameters under which people's lives differ in our society. "Here is the dilemma: equal treatment produces unequal outcomes precisely because of initial and sustaining differences. Youth do not, as Ogbu (1974) has documented in his research, perceive the world in terms of American society as a whole such that *any* individual is a potential role model. Rather, role models are chosen in accordance with one's own class, race, and sex. Black males from poor communities thus estimate their potential in the labor force in accordance with what they perceive other older, black males like them to be doing. If education has no direct linkage to occupational success, as some like Jencks (1972) have argued, this may well be because what is learned in school is evaluated against how and what the children know the relationship to be between school and the types of work and associated costs and benefits to members of the immediate adult community. An important, frequently overlooked, dimension of education or schooling is the real material relationship it bears to the work roles assumed by adult members of the youth's own class, race, and sex group."

The last implicit assumption is that any group of youth (black, white, male, female) can search for its place in society in a similar way vis-a-vis the larger institutions. "The essential psychological task of youth in a society is to begin to establish a commitment to a life pattern, to lay down the basis for identity as an adult, along at least two dimensions: work and close personal relationships. Many studies have stressed that the work environment, the capacity to see oneself as engaged in productive, useful work, is as important as the income from that work itself. Putting youth to work simply to give them something to do by reducing or eliminating the minimum wage, for example, will not solve the problem of the longer-term commitment to work as an aspect of individual identity formation. In this society, meaningful work is associated with meaningful human relationships generated within the work environment that have visible, tangible rewards and status in the worker's community at large. A solution to the problem of black youth unemployment, as well as the increasing likelihood of unemployment among white youth, in a modern civilized society requires attention to the meaningfulness of work in the context of the youths' overall identity formation, for we want, ultimately, not just workers but citizens who work with commitment to our nation's values and goals."

John Ogbu added one more implicit assumption to Slaughter's list—the assumption that different groups have equal access in this society. "This is a stratified society, and social stratification has consequences that are not in fact explained by looking at individual differences, because it means impairment of access to the goods and services in society for those who are subordinate. The factors we have been discussing would not in my judgment be so significant if it were not for the underlying reality of stratification. If you compare U.S. experience with that of other stratified societies, you find the same things happening. In Japan, for example, the social outcasts have difficulties in school and in getting jobs. But when they come to this country, where they are not treated any differently from other more highly placed Japanese who also come here, their performance is indistinguishable."

4

Trends in Public Spending on Children and Their Families

MARY JO BANE, JULIE BOATRIGHT WILSON, AND NEAL BAER

Few topics have generated as extensive or intense discussion over the last year as that of government spending. The federal budget dominates the agenda of the President and Congress, as well as the front pages of the newspapers. State and local tax and expenditure limitations preoccupy state legislatures, city councils, town meetings, and citizens' groups.

Questions of the level, direction, and future growth of public spending on all population groups, including families and children, are thus very much on the public agenda. This paper examines trends in public spending on income transfers and services for families with children over the last two decades. It compares levels and trends in public spending on children with those of spending on the elderly. Although there are other groups with claims on public resources with which children could be compared, like the handicapped and disabled, the elderly are particularly important. The elderly continue to be an increasingly large proportion of the population. Moreover, the elderly are increasingly powerful politically and, in times of scarce resources, the relative political strengths of various claimant groups are likely to be decisive in affecting the allocation of public goods.

The patterns of public welfare spending for different groups over the last few decades suggest the shape of policy and political battles of the next few years and the lines on which those battles may be won or lost. A review of this recent history raises some fundamental questions about the effectiveness and appropriateness of the government's roles in regard to families with children vis-a-vis other groups.

Three important trends (examined in more detail below) emerge from our analysis of public spending between 1960 and 1980:

- Aggregate public spending on all functions and on social welfare functions has grown steadily in real terms over the period. This spending grew rapidly during the 1960s, slowed somewhat during the 1970s, and began dropping only in FY 1980. Spending on programs for children and their families generally shared this pattern of overall growth.
- The programs serving children and their families grew relatively more slowly and less steadily than other programs, especially those benefiting the elderly. Per capita public spending on the elderly was three times as high as spending on children in 1960 and remained three times as high in 1979. The patterns of spending cuts now emerging at all levels of government are likely to increase substantially the differential between spending on children and spending on the elderly over the next few years.
- Relative to programs for the elderly, programs for children and their families tend less often to be: universal rather than means-tested (e.g., income support programs, services); adequate, and indexed to inflation (e.g., AFDC versus SSI; Medicaid versus Medicare); uniform across the nation (e.g., public education, AFDC versus SSI, Medicaid eligibility).

To note these trends is not to imply that increased public spending is necessarily a good thing, or that differentiated spending for different groups is necessarily a bad thing. It does seem worth inquiring into why the spending patterns have developed the way they have, and what those patterns suggest about the logic and the politics of future spending decisions. For it is not completely obvious that it was either inevitable or right that public spending, especially at the federal level, came to be focused as much as it now is on the elderly. Children and the elderly are both vulnerable groups, dependent on the working population for care and support. Until recently their families have been considered to bear the major responsibility for care and support of both children and the elderly. For both groups, government has long shared this responsibility, most notably (and with the longest historical antecedents) for educating children. Both children and the elderly are vulnerable to problems not of their own making—poverty, ill-health, and lack of care; but children are, if anything, more vulnerable and more blameless than the elderly.

This paper can only explore a few possible explanations for why, despite some similarities between children and the elderly, patterns of public spending on the two groups have been so different. The possibilities we look at include:

- differences in the "needs" of the two groups;
- differences in the effectiveness of government programs vis-a-vis other institutions in meeting these needs;
- differences in politics and historical accidents; and
- differences in the difficulty of solving the problems of each group.

Not surprisingly, even our cursory analysis reveals that all four explanations have some plausibility. We do not believe that either differences in needs or differences in effectiveness of government programs satisfactorily explains the trends. Politics and history go further and will undoubtedly be crucial in determining what happens over the next few years.

We also believe that the policy problems in areas dealing with children and families are very difficult, both analytically and practically. The difficulty of the problems is probably one reason they have not been solved and will continue to plague—and challenge—political efforts.

The Aggregate Trends

Data on public social welfare spending are published periodically by the Social Security Administration, most recently for the fiscal years 1960 to 1979. These are the source of the statistics used in our analysis. (To illustrate the orders of magnitude, Figure 1 shows spending in current dollars by type of program for selected years during that period.) We used these data to estimate total and per capita public spending on children and their families and on the elderly.

Allocating spending to population groups requires using a variety of procedures and assumptions, not all of which are completely straightforward or noncontroversial.[1] The bases for our allocation, by program are presented in Figure 2. In general, we allocated as follows:

- Spending on programs serving only one population group, like public education and child nutrition, was allocated to that group.

[1] Others have used more refined allocation techniques for estimating children's budgets, but only for a subset of government spending. See, for example, Rose (unpublished) on the federal budget. Charles Brecher and Raymond Horton, Columbia University, are developing a children's budget for New York City. A children's budget has also been prepared for the state of North Carolina; others may exist as well.

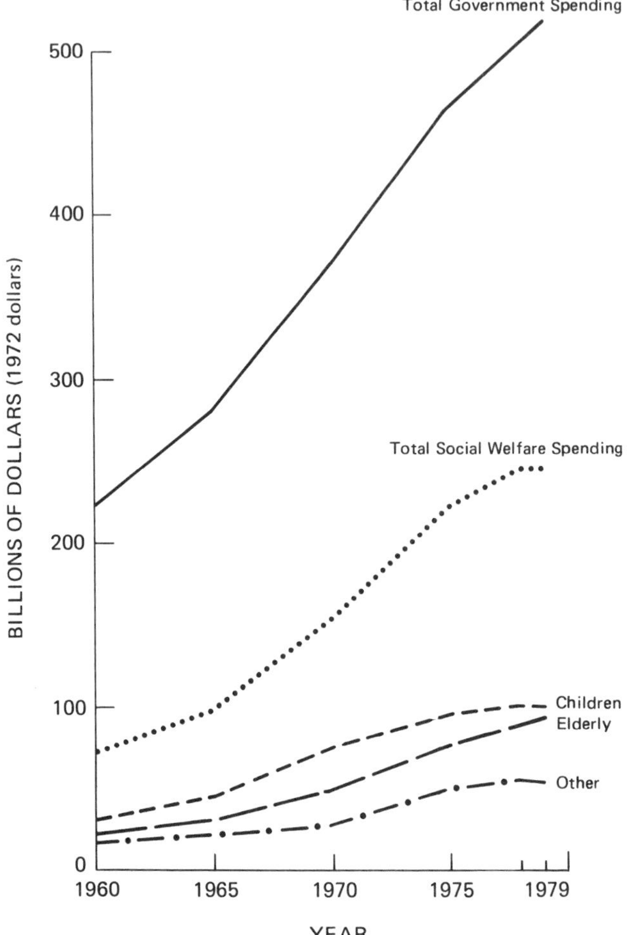

Figure 1 Public spending in 1972 dollars, fiscal years 1960-1979.

• Spending on programs serving more than one group, such as Social Security (aged, blind, and disabled) and food stamps, was allocated according to available data on the characteristics of program participants and the proportion of benefits various groups received. In some cases, these data were excellent (e.g., Social Security); in others, very poor.

• Programs directed at children and their families, most notably AFDC, were allocated to that group. Programs with more general coverage but tied loosely to AFDC, most notably food stamps and Medicaid, were allocated according to participant characteristics. Programs directed at

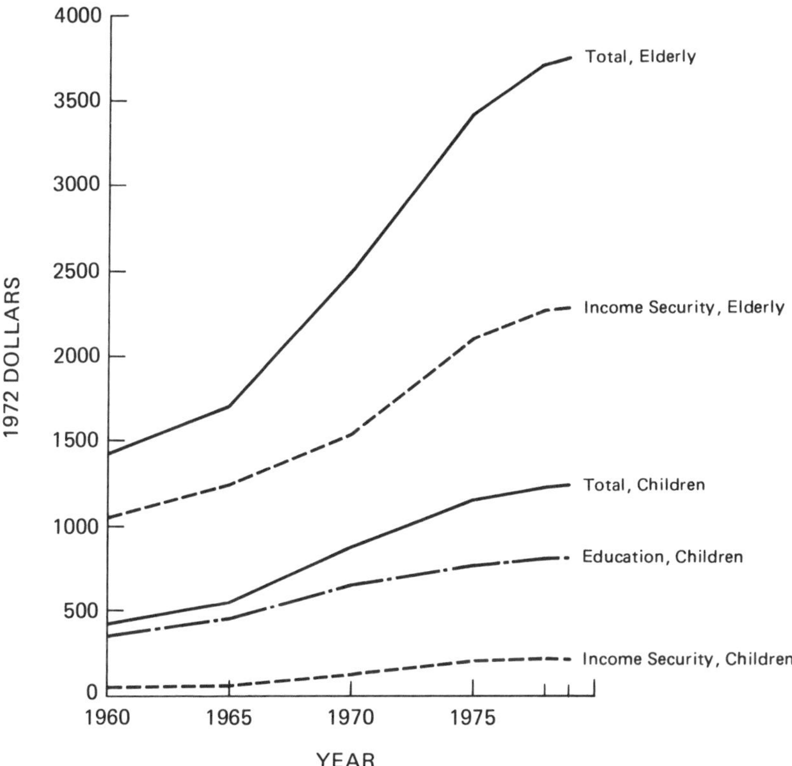

Figure 2 Per capita public spending, children and elderly.

adults, specifically unemployment insurance, workman's compensation, and disability insurance under OASDI and SSI, were allocated to "other," even though children in recipient families benefit indirectly. (This was the most troubling of our allocation decisions.)

Most of the numbers we are dealing with are so large, the allocation decisions so clear, and the trends so strong that we have considerable confidence in our estimates. We will note in the text where different allocation procedures or assumptions would affect our interpretations of the data.

Total Spending

Figure 1 shows the trend in total government spending, total social welfare spending, and spending on children, the elderly, and others, from 1960 to 1979, in constant 1972 dollars. Social welfare spending grew dramatically over this period, most rapidly in the early and middle 1970s. Since 1975, spending has grown more slowly, leveling off by fiscal years 1978 and 1979. Spending on children and their families has followed the same pattern. Spending on the elderly, however, has grown more rapidly over the period than spending on children and their families or on "others" and does not appear to be leveling off.

These overall trends obscure changes in spending patterns by various levels of government. In FY 1979, 62 percent of all social welfare spending was federal, and 38 percent was state and local (Bixby, 1981). Federal social welfare spending continued to increase, in real terms, through FY 1981, primarily because of continued growth in Social Security and Medicare. Real spending on the major federal programs affecting families and children, however, peaked in FY 1979 and is projected to fall sharply during the 1980s.[2]

Most state and local social welfare spending is allocated to programs serving children and their families. By far the largest is public education, which absorbed 59 percent of state and local social welfare budgets in FY 1979. Total nonfederal social welfare expenditures have been declining in real terms for several years. Real spending on public education peaked in FY 1978 and fell in FY 1979 and FY 1980.[3]

These trends, in federal spending and in state and local spending, suggest that both total social welfare spending and spending on children and their families reached a peak in FY 1979 and are now beginning to fall. Spending on the main programs affecting the elderly, however, is projected to continue increasing.

Per Capita Spending

To get a better sense of the spending trends, we divided total public spending on children and their families by the number of people aged 21 and under and spending on the elderly by the number aged 65 and over. (We defined children as 21 and under, since we include spending on higher education in our allocation to children and their families.) The trends in per capita spending are shown in Figure 2. The number of persons 21 and under rose during the 1960s, reaching 83.8 million in 1970, and fell during the 1970s, to 79.6 million in 1979. The number

[2] See Table 2 and discussions of spending components, below.

[3] Spending percentages from Bixby (1981, Table 1). Data on education spending from National Center for Educational Statistics (1980) and unpublished data from Helen F. Ladd, John F. Kennedy School of Government, Harvard University.

of elderly in the population increased steadily over the period, reaching 24.7 million in 1979. As a result, per capita spending on children leveled off somewhat less noticeably than total spending, and per capita spending on the elderly rose somewhat less sharply. Figure 2 shows that real per capita spending on both groups almost tripled over the two decades, with programs for children and their families growing at a slightly greater rate than those for the elderly. Nonetheless, the striking finding in Figure 2 is that per capita spending on the elderly was three times as high as spending on children and their families in 1960 and remained three times as high in 1979.

Later in this chapter, we examine the components of public spending on children and their families and on the elderly and the possible explanations for the spending disparity. Before turning to that topic, it may be useful to examine some possible explanations for public spending growth more generally.

Explaining Overall Growth

Explaining the enormous growth in social welfare spending between 1965 and 1975 is difficult. Three general explanations, however, seem worth exploring, before we move to explanations based on the characteristics of specific programs:

- economic cycles, with two possible effects—economic growth making more resources available for public spending and economic downturns requiring more public spending on such programs as unemployment compensation and public assistance;
- demographic shifts—increases in the proportions of the population in groups, such as orphans or the elderly, that tend to be recipients of public services; and
- political change—more liberal administrations, or greater consciousness of unmet needs.

Each of these explanations seems to make some contribution toward explaining spending growth over the period, but none of them individually, nor the three taken together, is completely satisfactory.

Economic conditions

Economic conditions, as measured by unemployment rates and GNP growth, were generally very good in the late 1960s and early 1970s, improving from the 1961-1963 period. The mid-1970s saw a fairly severe recession, followed by recovery, followed by the economic downturn occurring now. Real social welfare spending grew from year to year over these two decades. The rate of growth in social welfare spending generally tracked the unemployment rate, growing more rapidly in recession years. These year-to-year fluctuations in the rate of growth seem to be almost entirely accounted for by changes in spending on unemployment insurance and a few smaller means-tested programs, like food stamps (Bixby, 1981; Macmillan and Bixby, 1980).

Economic cycles thus account for some of the fluctuations around the trend. Overall economic growth does not, however, seem to account for the general growth in spending over the period. Public social welfare spending, in fact, grew as a proportion of GNP, from 10.5 percent of GNP in 1960, to a high of 20.4 percent of GNP in 1976. It then began falling and is estimated at 18.5 percent of GNP in FY 1979 (Bixby, 1981).

Demographics

Another possible explanation for the growth in social welfare spending is demographic change, particularly growth in vulnerable population groups. Table 1 shows some of the more interesting trends. The dependency ratio (calculated here as the ratio of those under 22 plus those over 64 to the 22- to 64-year-old population) was relatively high during the early 1960s and fell thereafter. This reflects the change in the number of children as a proportion of the population, which peaked in 1965. The proportion of 18- to 21-year-olds in the population, however, grew

TABLE 1 Demographic Trends

	1960	1965	1970	1975	1978	1979
Dependency ratio (elderly [65+] plus children <21 divided by population 22–64)	1.01	1.07	1.02	0.97	0.92	0.90
Groups as a percent of total population:						
Elderly 65+	9.2	9.5	9.8	10.5	11.0	11.2
Children <21	41.0	42.2	40.6	38.7	36.8	36.1
Children <18	35.7	35.9	33.4	31.0	29.0	28.3
Youth 18–21	5.3	6.3	7.2	7.7	7.8	7.8
Children <18 in single-parent families	3.3	3.7	3.9	5.0	5.3	5.2

SOURCES: Bureau of the Census (1976, 1980a,b).

steadily over most of the period, peaking in 1978 or 1979. This growth in the young adult population may well have focused attention on the educational and service needs of that group and generated some of the spending growth over the period.

Another group that increased as a proportion of the population over most of the 20-year period, starting to turn down only in the last year, is children in single-parent families. Although the total number of children fell, larger proportions of children lived in single-parent families, due largely to rising divorce rates and rising birth rates to unwed mothers (see Chapter 2). Single-parent families are relatively substantial consumers of public resources. Their growth as a proportion of the population, their increased visibility, and their increased participation in the political process may well have generated some of the growth in specific social welfare programs.

Finally, the proportion of elderly in the population grew steadily over the period and is projected to continue growing for the next several decades. This group has also become increasingly visible and increasingly powerful politically, which may well be one of the most important explanations for the growth in social welfare spending.

Politics

The translation of demographic changes into political claims seems to be part of the explanation for growth in social welfare spending. Partisan political explanations do not work very well, however. The greatest growth in social welfare spending took place during the republican administrations of Nixon and Ford, rather than the democratic administrations of Johnson and Carter. The programs of the War on Poverty, Johnson's highly publicized and controversial social welfare initiative, did not grow particularly rapidly during the period and certainly did not spearhead the social welfare expansion. Instead, as we shall see in more detail below, the growth was relatively unnoticed, coming primarily from the expansion of Social Security, the huge expansion of Medicare and Medicaid, and the liberalization of programs such as food stamps.

Thus, it does not appear that the civil rights movement of the middle 1960s was directly responsible for the expansion of social welfare programs, since the programs of greatest interest to the civil rights movement were not those in which the greatest growth took place.[4] To understand where growth did take place, and to begin exploring the reasons

[4] For a discussion of the history of social welfare in the United States, see Patterson (1981).

TABLE 2 Selected Programs: 1979 Budgets, Percent of 1960 Social Welfare Spending and Percent of 1960–1979 Social Welfare Growth

	Children			Elderly			Others		
	1979 Spending ($ billions)	Percent of 1960 Spending	Percent of 1960–1979 Growth	1979 Spending ($ billions)	Percent of 1960 Spending	Percent of 1960–1979 Growth	1979 Spending ($ billions)	Percent of 1960 Spending	Percent of 1960–1979 Growth
Income security									
OASDI	6.4	2.8	2.5	51.4	18.8	21.9	6.6	1.0	3.4
Unemployment and workers comp.							14.0	8.5	4.6
AFDC	6.9	2.1	3.2						
SSI				1.7	0	1.0	3.1	0	1.8
Food stamps	3.2	0	1.9	0.6	0	0.4	0.2	0	0.1
Other				2.7	5.6	−0.8	2.8	1.5	0.5
Health and medical									
Medicare				16.0	0	9.2	2.3	0	1.3
Medicaid	5.1	0.1	2.9	5.9	0.6	3.1	3.7	0.3	2.0
Other	4.9	1.3	2.3	4.8	3.9	1.2	3.0	2.1	0.9
Veterans				7.1	3.9	2.5	5.7	7.3	0.3
Education									
Elem. and secondary	48.4	31.0	15.2						
Higher	15.1	4.5	6.9						
Voc. adult, voc. rehab.							10.6	1.8	5.4
Housing	2.0	0.2	1.1	1.4	0.1	0.7	0.6	0	0.3
Child nutrition and social services	6.9	1.3	3.4	1.1	0	0.6			
Total	98.9	43.3	39.4	92.7	32.9	39.8	52.6	22.5	20.6

for the differentials between children and the elderly, we need to look at the specific programs that make up the social welfare budget.

The Components of Social Welfare Spending

The total public social welfare budget is made up of specific federal, state, and local programs in the areas of income security, health and medical care, veterans benefits and services, education, housing, nutrition, and social services. The programs are different in many ways: in the groups they serve; the amount of resources they require; their eligibility criteria, benefit levels, and participation rates; the level of government that funds and administers them; and the extent to which they contributed to the overall growth of social welfare spending between 1960 and 1980. In this section, we examine the characteristics of the most important social welfare programs serving children and their families, the elderly, and others, with a view toward answering three questions:

- Which programs contributed disproportionately to the growth of social welfare spending?
- What are the characteristics of the programs that expanded the most? Do they serve particular groups, meet particular needs, or have other identifiable characteristics?
- What program characteristics differentiate programs serving children and their families from those serving other population groups?

Table 2 shows the major public social welfare programs, with their 1979 real dollar budget levels, their shares of the total social welfare budget in 1960, and their shares of the 1960 to 1979 social welfare spending growth. An examination of the table, comparing shares of the 1960 to 1979 spending growth with shares of 1960 total social welfare spending, reveals the major trends:

- Social Security, which accounted for 26 percent of social welfare spending in 1979, accounted for the largest share of 1960-1979 spending growth (21.9 percent). This share of the spending growth was 16 percent larger than its share of the 1960 social welfare budget.
- Elementary and secondary education, which accounted for 20 percent of 1979 spending, accounted for the next largest share of spending growth (15.2 percent). Its share of spending growth was 50 percent smaller than its share of the 1960 social welfare budget. Higher education grew proportionately more rapidly.

• Health and medical programs, especially Medicare, grew rapidly in comparison to their 1960 levels. They accounted for 19 percent of 1979 social welfare spending.

• Means-tested income security programs (AFDC, SSI, and food stamps) and social services programs grew very rapidly, to 9 percent of 1979 social welfare spending, from a very small base.

• Spending on the elderly, 38 percent of 1979 spending, accounted for about 40 percent of the total 1960-1979 spending growth, a share 21 percent larger than its share of the 1960 budget.

• Spending on children and their families, 40 percent of 1979 spending, accounted for about 39 percent of total spending growth, a share 9 percent smaller than its share of the 1960 budget.

The characteristics of the major programs that contributed to this 1960-1979 spending growth suggest some plausible explanations for the differentials in per capita spending levels and in patterns of growth between programs serving families and children and those serving the elderly:[5]

• Elementary and secondary education is financed and controlled almost entirely at the state and local levels. Public higher education is financed almost entirely at the state level. This leads to large state-to-state variations in services and spending and to spending patterns that are very responsive to local economic and fiscal conditions.

• Social services programs for both children and the elderly are occasionally universal, but primarily means-tested. The services offered, and the extent of emphasis on children vis-a-vis the elderly, vary enormously from state to state.

• The most important health insurance program for children and their families, Medicaid, is means-tested, is limited in many states to female-headed families, and varies widely from state to state in eligibility criteria and benefit levels. The basic hospital and physician insurance program for the elderly, Medicare, is not means-tested, is tied to Social Security, and is uniform throughout the country.

• The major income security program for the elderly, Social Security, is conceived as insurance, is related to previous work experience and earnings, and is not means tested. It operates uniformly nationwide, administered at the federal level. No comparable income security program under social insurance exists for families with children.

[5] Program characteristics were obtained from a variety of sources, including the authorizing legislation, Office of Management and Budget (1980, 1981a).

• The most important means-tested income security program for the elderly, SSI, has a uniform national floor, is indexed to the CPI, and, in conjunction with food stamps, is adequate to raise household income to the poverty level. The largest means-tested income security program for families with children, AFDC, is primarily limited to single-parent families. It is administered by the states, with benefit levels widely varying and in most cases inadequate.

These five program areas raise most of the issues relevant to both explanations of past trends and future projections. We will discuss each of them, first elaborating on the facts summarized above, and then looking at the major issues in each program area.

Education

Total real spending on elementary and secondary education grew through the 1960s and early 1970s and began declining around 1975. Total real public spending on higher education grew steadily throughout the period. These trends only partly reflect population changes. As Table 3 shows, per child (0-17) spending on elementary and secondary education rose through almost the entire period, falling only in 1979. Public spending on higher education per youth (18-21) rose through the entire period.

These aggregates conceal considerable state-to-state variation. Table 4 gives some indication of the variation, with data for five states selected

TABLE 3 Education Spending (1972 Dollars)

	1960	1965	1970	1975	1978	1979
Elementary and secondary						
Total real public spending (billions of dollars)	22.1	30.4	43.4	49.7	49.6	48.4
Spending per child (0–18) (dollars)	343	461	622	751	783	774
Higher						
Total real public spending (billions of dollars)	3.2	6.6	11.1	13.6	14.8	15.1
Spending per youth (18–21) (dollars)	336	537	756	827	867	881
Spending per enrolled student (dollars)	897	1108	1296	1219	1317	1314

SOURCES: Spending from Figure 1; population data from Bureau of the Census (1980c) and National Center for Educational Statistics (1980).

TABLE 4 Education Spending: Five States (in 1972 Dollars)

	Arkansas	Illinois	Massa-chusetts	Texas	Virginia	United States
Per capita income, 1975	3,958	5,341	4,829	4,401	4,550	4,639
Per child spending on schools, 1975	847	1,276	1,172	836	959	1,115
Per capita public spending, higher education, 1977–1978	41	45	29	58	41	50
Spending per student in public higher education, 1978	1,420	1,087	993	1,298	938	

SOURCES: Bureau of the Census (1980c); National Center for Educational Statistics (1980).

to illustrate a range of situations. (We will use these states as illustrations in other program areas as well.) In general, spending levels are closely associated with state per capita income and spending growth with income growth. Spending on higher education also reflects differences in the states' historic commitments to public or private higher education, as illustrated by the relatively low spending in Massachusetts—a state high on most other indicators.

What is perhaps most surprising in these data is neither the recent downturn in spending on elementary and secondary education nor the state-to-state variations, but two other facts:

- the large growth in real per child spending on elementary and secondary education up to 1978; and
- the large and continuing growth of spending on higher education.

These facts are especially surprising in light both of current allegations in the popular press that public education is in a state of crisis and of widespread perceptions that education is relatively ineffective.

Elementary and Secondary Education

Part of the trend in elementary and secondary education is undoubtedly due to the process of adjusting to declining enrollments: Since some costs are fixed and others hard to adjust, costs cannot go down at the same rate as enrollment, and per pupil expenditure thus goes up. Another possibility is that some elements of the cost of elementary and secondary education have gone up particularly rapidly. This is surely true of energy costs. It does not seem to be true, however, of salaries for instructional staff, which have not risen, on average, since the early 1970s (National Center for Educational Statistics, 1980, Table 52).

It is also possible that services have been expanded. The ratio of enrolled students to instructional staff fell quite dramatically, from 24.6 in school year 1959-1960 to 19.4 in 1978-1979 (National Center for Educational Statistics, 1980, Tables 29 and 45). That ratio may have risen slightly in 1979-1980, but nonetheless remains at a historic low. Services other than basic instruction have certainly expanded. For example, the number of high school student enrollments in one or another vocational education course rose from 3.8 million in 1968 to 11.0 million in 1978 (National Center for Educational Statistics, 1980, Table 151).[6] The number of handicapped students receiving special education services was about 3.4 million in 1978, a vast increase over the decade (National Center for Educational Statistics, 1981, Table 6.1).[7]

All this growth in both spending and services was occurring during a period when researchers were raising serious questions about the relationship between spending levels, the quality of instruction, and educational outcomes. Indeed, the new conventional wisdom in education is that leadership, time spent on instruction, and the maintenance of an orderly and motivating environment are far more important to educational effectiveness than levels of spending or numbers of staff (Coleman et al., 1966, 1981; Rutter, 1979).

It would not be surprising, therefore, if per pupil expenditures slowed their growth or began to fall independent of fiscal constraints on state and local government—which of course do exist. Elementary and secondary education is a good example of a very hard problem. It is now clear that more money is no longer the simple solution to educational problems; but what the solution is, and how funds should be spent to bring the solution about is not at all obvious. This is not to suggest that problems have all been solved or that "need" no longer exists. Nor is it to suggest that expensive programs such as compensatory education or special education are completely ineffective. It does suggest, though, that the combination of political pressures at the state and local levels and the difficulty of the problems is likely to bring about a slowdown in spending for public education over the next few years. This may explain the decline in real per capita spending in public education between 1978 and 1979.

[6] It should be noted, however, that statistics on vocational education are notoriously unreliable.

[7] Statistics on the handicapped are also poor.

Higher Education

The story of public spending on higher education has been somewhat different. We can think of total public spending on a program as depending on the number of people eligible for the program, the rate at which eligible people actually participate in the program, and spending per participant. Variations in spending on elementary and secondary education depend almost entirely on the first and third elements: changes in the number of 6- to 18-year-olds and changes in per pupil expenditure. The participation rate is nearly irrelevant, since for 6- to 16-year-olds participation is almost 100 percent, and for 17- to 18-year-olds the dropout rate has stayed at about 20 percent for almost a decade.

Spending on higher education, in contrast, is very much a story of increased participation. Since 1960, as Figure 3 shows, enrollment in public higher education has increased enormously. This is the result of two trends. First, the proportion of high school graduates going on to higher education has increased, particularly the proportion of women and minorities. Second, there has been a shift from private to public. In 1978, 78 percent of postsecondary students were in public institutions, up from 64 percent in 1963. Public community colleges have been by far the fastest growing sector of higher education (National Center for Educational Statistics, 1980, Table 79).[8]

State and federal spending on higher education has presumably been both a cause and a result of this dramatic expansion in participation. Although (as Table 4 shows) there is considerable state-to-state variation in both the ratio of public higher education slots to the youth population and the amount of state subsidy per enrolled student, all states expanded their college and university systems during the 1960s and 1970s. In addition, substantial student assistance programs were established at the federal level during the late 1960s and expanded dramatically during the 1970s. The Basic Educational Opportunity Grants (now Pell Grants) Program began in the mid-1960s and reached a spending level of $2.0 billion in FY 1980. The Guaranteed Student Loan Program spent an additional $1.6 billion in FY 1980 (Office of Management and Budget, 1981a). The basic grants program seems to be at least partly responsible for the increased enrollment of poor and minority students and, indirectly, for the growth of public community colleges. Both programs represented a substantial influx of public funds into higher education.

The future of public spending in higher education is not completely clear, but can probably be seen in terms of the same issues shaping

[8] For a fuller discussion of enrollment patterns, see Bane and Winston (1980).

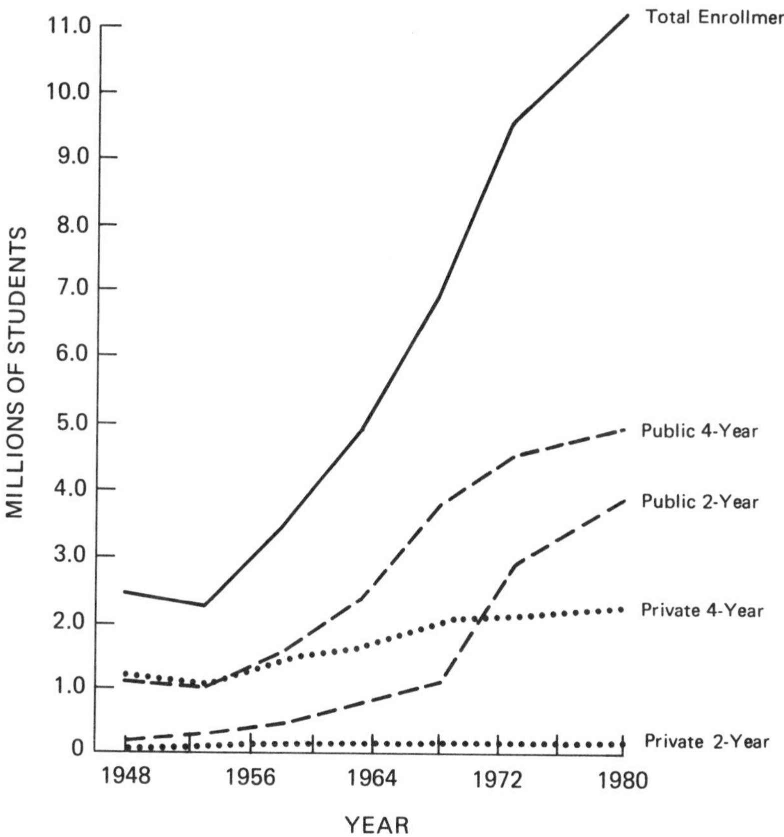

Figure 3 Growth in student enrollment, 1948-1978. SOURCE: National Center for Educational Statistics (1980).

elementary and secondary education: not so much need or effectiveness, but politics and hard problems. Participation in higher education, at least by students of traditional college age, now seems to have leveled off. The public versus private share of enrollment seems also to have stabilized. Both private and public institutions are experiencing at least a perceived falloff in demand.

At the same time, serious questions are being raised not so much about the effectiveness of higher education (though those are there, and may become more important) as about the appropriate role of government in the enterprise. Federal funding for student assistance is budgeted to fall dramatically, presumably on the assumption that families, student self-support, and other private sources can make up the difference. Many states seem to be not only curtailing expansion of facilities but also raising or considering raising tuition charges. Since higher education clearly confers both public and private benefits, questions about the allocation of the costs seem entirely appropriate, if not easy to answer.[9] With tight resources at the state level (at least in most states), the politics of competing groups may well lead to different spending patterns over the next few years.

Social Services

For purposes of thinking about people's needs and about devising programs and institutions to meet them, the categories of education, social services, health, and income security may, as many commentators have pointed out, be both arbitrary and misleading. For handicapped children, whether such services as counseling or physical therapy are delivered through school systems, health services, or social services agencies, is less important than whether or not they are delivered. For noninstitutionalized elderly who need some help with the tasks of daily living, the question is whether that help comes, not whether it is paid for by Medicaid, Title XX, or their own Social Security income. In looking at programs and funding, though, it is necessary to include that group of programs that go somewhat arbitrarily by the name social services.

The major activities that fall under this category, as we have defined it here, include day care, Head Start, home care services, child welfare services, foster care and adoption services, counseling, shelters for runaways and battered women, and so on. Funding for these services is shared by the states and the federal government, usually through federal-state matching programs. The major funding source at the federal level is Title XX of the Social Security Act, supplemented to a lesser extent by the Older Americans Act, the Economic Opportunity Act, Title IV-B of the Social Security Act, and other legislation administered by the Department of Health and Human Services' Office of Human Development.

The quantity of social services legislation, the number of programs, and the level of public funding for social services (as shown earlier in Table 2) grew very rapidly between 1960 and 1979. What is striking about this set of programs, however, are two facts:

- Relative to other countries, to other areas of social welfare expenditure, and to what many perceive as need, spending levels are and remain very low.

[9] See Bane and Winston (1980) for further discussion of these issues.

• The programs are fragmented, the logic of whom they serve and what they provide is virtually incomprehensible, and they vary enormously from state to state.

Title XX is the major federal social services program. Decisions about services to be offered and people to be served under Title XX are made by the states, within very broad federal guidelines. States are reimbursed for 75 percent of expenditures, up to a certain limit. The purpose of the program is to provide services to past, present, and prospective welfare recipients to help them achieve independence. Although states are allowed to extend eligibility for services to those not on welfare with sliding fee scales, in practice Title XX services are means tested and used primarily by AFDC and SSI recipients. States allocate their money, though in very different proportions, primarily to some combination of day care, foster care and other child welfare services, and home care for the elderly. In some states the elderly seem to benefit disproportionately from Title XX services; in other states children receive the bulk of the spending.

The federal Title XX budget grew in real (1972) dollars from $600 million in FY 1970 to $1.9 billion in FY 1978. But funding for social services is almost certain to decline dramatically over the next few years. Federal social services spending was budgeted in the March 1981 budget revisions to fall to $1.5 billion in real dollars in FY 1982 (Office of Management and Budget, 1981a).[10] The FY 1983 budget includes only $900 million in real dollars for the social services block grants.

It seems inconceivable that the states will make up for the federal cutbacks. Indeed, many states seem to be cutting back on their own social services budgets, pressed by revenue losses and by pressures to protect more popular and more seemingly necessary programs. Certainly there are no indications in the present climate of any movement toward expanding services, toward rationalizing them, or toward making them available more universally.[11]

Why is this the case? Probably all the categories of explanations noted above come into play. It is hard to know what "need" is or how much "unmet" need exists. There is no persuasive evidence of real effectiveness in many areas. There are serious questions about the appropriate role of government. But politics, of course, may be decisive. The constit-

[10] Budget data from the Budget Appendix and the March 1981 Budget Revisions.

[11] For an excellent summary of changes made by the 1981 Omnibus Budget Reconciliation Act, see Sugarman (1981). For a discussion of many of the issues in delivering services to children, see Committee on Child Development Research and Public Policy (1981).

uencies that do exist for social service programs, mainly constituencies of providers and professionals, have not built effective coalitions. Other claims, for education, health, and income security, not to mention public safety, seem much more pressing. Social services programs are relatively easy to cut, and that is what is happening.

Health

As noted earlier, public spending on health increased dramatically between 1960 and 1980 and now makes up a substantial and growing proportion of public social welfare expenditures. The programs, extent of coverage, and per capita spending levels for health are very different for children and the elderly. Indeed, differential levels of spending on health are quite important components of the overall spending differential shown in Figure 2.

The most important health programs are Medicare and Medicaid. "Other" spending on health includes state and city hospitals and clinics, public health services, health research, and other programs. Although these other programs are substantial and growing in the aggregate, they are not as important to an understanding of trends in social welfare expenditures as Medicare and Medicaid.

Both Medicare and Medicaid came into being through amendments to the Social Security Act of 1965. Medicare provides hospital insurance and pays part of the cost of supplemental medical insurance for the aged, blind, and disabled. It is basically a federal program. Participation in Medicare is almost universal among those eligible. Medicare spending in FY 1979 amounted to about $1,031 per elderly person. No national health insurance program comparable to Medicare exists for children or for other nonelderly (except the covered disabled).

Medicaid was established to provide medical assistance to certain low-income families and individuals. Medicaid is a federal-state matching program, administered by the states. States are required to provide coverage to recipients of AFDC and SSI and have the option of extending coverage to the "medically needy" and to nonwelfare children in poor families. States have some discretion over eligibility, services covered, and rates of reimbursement. In 1979, 20 states covered all poor children under Medicaid. Spending per Medicaid recipient also ranged widely, from $1,188 in Minnesota in FY 1976 to $306 in Pennsylvania.[12] Participation in Medicaid is hard to estimate, since eligibility rules vary. A Census Bureau survey on noncash benefits in 1980 found that 37

[12] Data on Medicaid primarily from Health Care Financing Administration (1979).

percent of poor elderly households and 52 percent of poor households with children reported being covered by Medicaid (Bureau of the Census, 1981).

Per capita Medicaid spending, whether measured on the basis of eligibility, participation, or use, is much higher for the elderly than for families with children. (Table 5 shows the differences in per recipient expenditures in five states, for different groups.) This is primarily because Medicaid has increasingly become a program that funds long-term nursing home care. In 1976, 38 percent of the Medicaid budget went for long-term care. In contrast, 35 percent of the Medicaid budget was spent on children and their families. Despite these relatively low per capita spending levels, however, Medicaid and other health programs do seem to have brought about much greater equality in the use of health services between poor and better-off children (Health Care Financing Administration, 1979).

The huge growth of Medicare and Medicaid over the last 15 years has focused attention on the two programs and resulted in any number of proposals for capping or otherwise containing them. The most vexing problem is long-term care, an issue the outcome of which cannot really be predicted at this time. Other issues in both explaining the growth and projecting the future of Medicare and Medicaid are closely tied to the income security programs with which they are associated:

- Medicare and Social Security have both grown very rapidly but are seen as social insurance and perceived as relatively benign. The future of both programs is likely to revolve around specific financing issues.
- Even though the bulk of Medicaid expenditures goes for the elderly, and even more specifically for long-term care, it is widely perceived as a program serving welfare mothers. The issues thus tend to be defined

TABLE 5 Average Medicaid Payment per Recipient, FY 1976

	Total	Aged	Children Under 21	Adults in AFDC Families
United States	582	1,363	221	429
Arkansas	527	823	164	354
Illinois	509	1,695	237	402
Massachusetts	627	1,656	291	298
Texas	815	1,294	195	549
Virginia	560	1,184	198	447

SOURCE: Health Care Financing Administration (1979).

in the same terms, and to be as controversial, as the issues surrounding AFDC.

We therefore turn to the programs and issues of income security.

Income Security

The income security component of public social welfare spending accounts for the largest portion of spending growth between 1960 and 1979, is the crucial source of spending differentials between children and the elderly, and raises the most difficult issues for the future. The patterns are somewhat different for three types of programs, which will be looked at separately:

- Social security spending grew enormously over the two decades, with expansion in both coverage and benefit levels, as well as in the sheer size of the retired population.
- The two major means-tested cash assistance programs, SSI and AFDC, grew rapidly during the 1960s and early 1970s and then leveled off—but for different reasons.
- The two major quasi-cash programs, food stamps and housing assistance, like Medicaid (which should perhaps also be considered here), grew rapidly over the entire period, but are now budgeted to level off.

A short review paper can obviously not go into detail on either the programs or the issues. Instead, we try to sketch some background and raise some issues for thinking about both explanations of the past and projections for the future.

Social Security

The importance of Social Security is apparent not only in its sheer size (20 percent of the federal budget in FY 1980; 26 percent of total social welfare spending in FY 1979), but also in its contribution to the income of the elderly. In 1979, 92 percent of all elderly households received some income from Social Security or railroad retirement. Social Security made up 32 percent of the total income of elderly families in 1978 and 46 percent of the income of elderly living alone (Bureau of the Census, 1978, 1980b).

Coverage and benefit levels under Social Security have expanded steadily since the program began. In 1979, about 85 percent of all workers were in covered employment. Monthly Social Security benefits for couples including a worker retiring in 1978, were, $361 or 109.9 percent of the poverty level for a minimum wage worker, $553 or 168.4 percent of the poverty level for an average wage worker; and $690 or 209.8 percent of the poverty level for a maximum wage worker.[13] Because of Social Security, most elderly households now have incomes above the poverty line. In 1978, 32 percent of elderly families and 71 percent of elderly individuals would have been poor without transfer, mostly Social Security, income; with that income, only 8 percent of elderly families and 27 percent of elderly individuals were poor (Bureau of the Census, 1978, Table 41).

Cash Assistance

The two major public, means-tested cash assistance programs are Supplemental Security Income (SSI) for the aged, blind, and disabled, and AFDC, for dependent children and their caretakers. The two programs are quite different in the way they operate and in the levels of benefits they provide.

SSI was established in 1965, through amendments to the Social Security Act, to replace the original act's state-administered program of assistance to the aged, blind, and disabled. SSI established a federally funded floor for benefits to low-income members of these three groups and national standards for eligibility and benefit levels. Recipients are allowed to keep the first $85 per month of earned income and 50 percent of income above that. Benefits are indexed to the CPI and adjusted annually.

In 1979, about half of SSI benefits went to the elderly, about 8 percent of whom received benefits under the program. The basic benefit level was $208 per month (or 72 percent of the poverty line) for an elderly individual and $312 per month (or 86 percent of the poverty line) for an elderly couple (Social Security Administration, 1980).

SSI expenditures grew rapidly until 1975 but have declined in real terms since then. It seems that as more and more elderly and disabled are covered by Social Security, the need for SSI has decreased. Expenditures are not expected to increase greatly in the future, and there seems to be no particular pressure to curtail the program.

AFDC was established as Title IV of the original Social Security Act to provide income for children deprived of the support of a parent. The program began as a federal-state matching program administered

[13] Coverage data from Social Security Administration (1980, Table 46). Data on benefits from Ball (1978).

TABLE 6 AFDC Basic Monthly Benefit Levels

	Monthly Benefit (dollars)	Percent of Poverty
Arkansas	273	44
Illinois	331	54
Massachusetts	445	72
Texas	140	23
Virginia	283	46

SOURCE: U.S. Department of Health and Human Services (1981).

by the states and remains so. Eligibility is defined federally, with some state options—whether to cover unborn children, children aged 18-21, and children with unemployed parents. Benefit calculation rules, deductions, and disregards are also set federally. In contrast to the rules on earned income for SSI, families on AFDC are allowed to keep only the first $30 per month of income plus 33 percent of any additional income. Under the provisions of the August 1981 omnibus reconciliation bill, even this 30-and-one-third rule applies only to earnings during the first 4 months families are on the program.[14]

Basic benefit levels are set by the states and vary widely. For example, in the five states we have been using as illustrations, basic monthly benefits in 1980 for a family of four with no other income are shown in Table 6.

AFDC expenditures increased rapidly in real terms during the late 1960s and very early 1970s and then began to level off. Figure 4 shows the components of the pattern: total real expenditures, number of participants, and average monthly benefit. Participation grew dramatically between 1965 and 1975, due both to an increase in the number of eligible families and, more importantly, to an increase in participation rates. Currently, the participation rate among eligibles is estimated at almost 95 percent. Average monthly benefit levels rose in real terms from 1960 to 1976 and have fallen since then. This fall may be partly due to increased income from other sources among participants but also results from the fact that no state automatically adjusts benefits for inflation, and few have raised benefits so as to keep up.

Federal spending on AFDC is budgeted to fall from $4.2 billion in real (1972) dollars in 1980 to $3.7 billion in 1982. Further cuts are being proposed, and a program to turn all responsibility over to the states is being considered. Although, as noted earlier, the proportion of the

[14] Data on AFDC from Social Security Administration (1980).

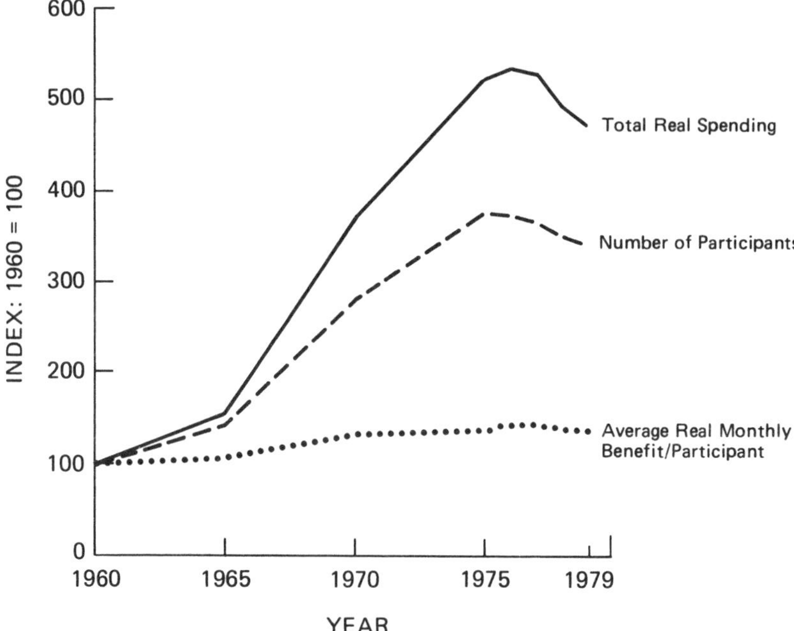

Figure 4 Indices of AFDC growth.

population that consists of children in single-parent families has started to decline (because of falling birth rates), continuing high rates of divorces and births to unmarried mothers suggest that the number of poor children in single-parent families is not likely to decrease appreciably. AFDC cuts seem likely to be made, therefore, by limiting eligibility or decreasing benefits.

Quasi-Cash Programs

Two federally funded quasi-cash programs are important parts of the public income security system: food stamps, which cost $9 billion in FY 1980, and housing assistance, which cost $5.5 billion. Food stamps are available to low-income households regardless of age or household structure. Housing assistance is available to low-income families, the elderly, and disabled individuals. Both programs provide substantial benefits to both the elderly and children and their families.

In 1980, about 8 million households, or 10 percent of the population, received food stamps, with an average value of $89 per month. About 60 percent of recipient households included children (approximately 60 percent of poor households with children), while about 23 percent included an elderly member (about 26 percent of the elderly poor).[15] Participation seems to be higher among eligible households with children than among eligible elderly, though participation among the elderly grew rapidly after the elimination of the purchase requirement in 1979. The food stamp program guarantees recipient households stamps sufficient to purchase the "thrifty food plan," which is set at about one-third of the poverty line and adjusted periodically for inflation.

The subsidized housing programs, both public housing and "Section 8" housing assistance, provided assistance to about 2.5 million households in 1977 (Congressional Budget Office, 1978). The level of subsidy per household is high, amounting to the difference between reasonable rents and a set percentage of household income, between 10 percent and 30 percent. However, only a fraction of eligible households receive housing assistance. In 1980, 25 percent of poor renter families with children and 33 percent of poor elderly renter households reported receiving housing assistance (Bureau of the Census, 1981).

Levels of Support and Poverty

Table 7 shows the levels of support available under public programs in 1978-1980, excluding housing assistance, and compares these levels to the official poverty line. The combination of cash assistance and food stamps is enough to bring SSI and Social Security recipients close to or above the poverty line but not enough in any state to bring AFDC recipients above the poverty line. Public income-support programs seem generally to be more adequate for the elderly than for families with children.

The effects of public programs on the two groups can also be seen, though indirectly, in the trends in poverty rates for the elderly and for children. These trends can be seen in Figure 5. They are calculated on the basis of cash income only and do not include the value of food stamps or housing assistance. Inclusion of these benefits would reduce poverty rates by approximately a third. Since 1959, the poverty rate for the elderly has declined dramatically. In contrast, the poverty rate for children has remained at about 15 percent since about 1970. While the explanations for these trends are complex, they do reinforce the per-

[15] Data on food stamp recipients from U.S. Department of Agriculture (1981). The percentage of the poor receiving food stamps was calculated from Bureau of the Census (1981). The latter numbers are almost certainly underestimates.

TABLE 7 Levels of Support from Public Programs

	Monthly Benefit (dollars)	Percent of Poverty
Texas: AFDC plus food stamps, family of four, 1980	341	54.9
Arkansas: AFDC plus food stamps, family of four, 1980	389	62.6
Virginia: AFDC plus food stamps, family of four, 1980	459	73.9
Illinois: AFDC plus food stamps, family of four, 1980	478	77.0
Massachusetts: AFDC plus food stamps, family of four 1980	561	90.3
SSI plus food stamps, elderly couple, 1979	353	97.1
Social Security benefit, minimum wage worker retiring in 1978	361	109.9
Social Security benefit, average wage worker retiring in 1978	553	168.4

SOURCES: Ball (1978), Social Security Administration (1980), U.S. Department of Agriculture (1981b), and U.S. Department of Health and Human Services (1981).

ception that public programs have done better in supporting the elderly than they have in supporting children.

Issues

A number of interesting questions can be raised about the income support programs, with relevance for both explaining the past and projecting the future:

- Why is there no large-scale social insurance program for children in the United States, comparable to the children's allowances and child benefits of other countries, analogous to social security for the elderly and disabled?
- Why do cash and quasi-cash assistance programs for children and their families tend to be less adequate, and more subject to state and local discretion, than assistance programs for the elderly?

It is hard to argue that the answer to those questions lies primarily in the greater needs of the elderly population. Both children and the elderly are dependent on the working age population for care and

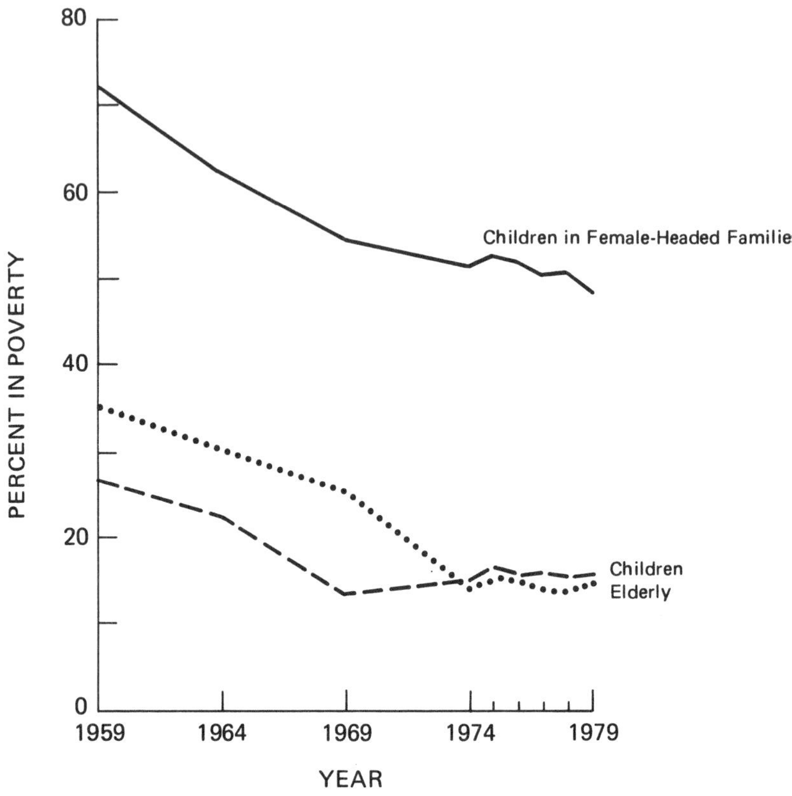

Figure 5 Poverty rates: elderly, children, and children in female-headed families, 1959-1979. SOURCE: Bureau of the Census (1980b).

support. Both children and the elderly have high poverty rates. Neither group would seem to be very well able to get along on income below the poverty level. Neither group is considered to be responsible for working to support themselves, though self-support may seem appropriate for some older youth and some elderly.

There are, however, important differences between children and the elderly in three important and related areas:

- the extent to which transfer programs include an intraperson transfer in addition to interperson transfers;
- in addition to interperson transfers, the extent to which families are considered responsible for basic support; and

• the extent to which serious "moral hazard" issues complicate the design of assistance programs.

The Social Security program is an interesting combination of forced savings and intergenerational transfers. Set up from the beginning as a pay-as-you-go program, it has never operated with a strict actuarial equivalence of individual contributions to the system and expected benefits from it. Nonetheless, a portion of Social Security spending is rightly thought of as an intrapersonal transfer. Moreover the system as a whole was originally sold as, and continues to be perceived as, a retirement insurance system: Retired people are entitled to their benefits as a result of the contributions they made during their working life.

Strictly speaking, the portion of Social Security spending that represents intrapersonal transfers should probably be excluded from the kind of spending calculations made in this paper. Even after such an exclusion, however, a substantial proportion of Social Security spending remains. Most recipients now receive far more than they paid in contributions, even after a normal rate of return is imputed—a situation that is likely to continue at least in the near term.

Even interpersonal transfers are thought about differently for the elderly than for children. One difference has to do with family responsibility. It is no longer the case, if indeed it ever was, that children are considered primarily responsible for the financial support of their elderly parents. Instead, a public opinion poll in 1974 found the following perceived division of responsibility among sources considered responsible for income support of the retired elderly:[16]

	Percent
self	33.8
children	10.3
pension (private)	45.5
government (nonspecific)	27.6
Social Security	67.3

In contrast, we would expect to find near unanimity on the principle that parents are primarily responsible for the financial support of their children.

[16] Data reported in Steven Crystal, unpublished Ph.D. dissertation, Harvard University (1980).

Because parents are considered primarily responsible for children, and because assistance cannot be given directly to children independent of their parents, the issue of how programs affect the ability and willingness of parents to exercise their responsibility has to be contended with. Welfare reform efforts over the years have foundered on this issue of incentives: how to design a program that provides incentives for parents to work to support their children. Neither Nixon's Family Assistance Plan nor Carter's Program for Better Jobs and Income was able to deal with these issues to the satisfaction of Congress or the public.[17]

In contrast, programs for the elderly do not seem to stumble so seriously over issues of incentives. Since people have no control over whether they turn 65 or not, the issue of choosing to become eligible for benefits does not arise, as it does when parents can split up or stop working in order to establish eligibility for cash assistance. Since children are not considered responsible for the financial support of their elderly parents, the issue of work incentives for them does not arise. Since it seems to be considered entirely appropriate for elderly couples and individuals to live independently of their children if they wish, the issue of incentives for households to split up does not arise in any serious way. And since the retired elderly are not expected to work (indeed, not always wanted in the labor market), issues of work incentives for the elderly themselves do not arise either.

Thus, the issues of defining an appropriate role for government and designing a program with sensible incentives are much more difficult for programs directed at children and their families than for programs directed at the elderly. In addition, of course, the elderly are a far stronger political force than children and families. The strength of elderly interests was perhaps best illustrated by their success this year in opposing even minor changes in Social Security. The combination of relatively greater political strength and relatively easier problems probably goes a long way toward explaining the better treatment of the elderly under our income security programs.

Implications

The programs that make up social welfare expenditures in the United States have developed in ways that reflect their history, the seriousness and difficulty of the problems they seek to address, and the relative political strengths of competing groups. The programs have developed in ways that have resulted in rather different patterns of services and

[17] For descriptions of these efforts, see Moynihan (1973) and Lynn and Whitman (1981).

spending for families with children and for the elderly. Spending on the elderly is higher, per capita, than spending for children and their families, and has grown more rapidly. There are obviously large programs (like education and, to some extent, Social Security), for which comparisons between children and the elderly are not appropriate. In the income security and health areas though, where comparisons do seem relevant, there are many cases where the elderly seem to be treated more generously, more uniformly, and with less stigma than families with children.

There are some good reasons why this has turned out to be the case. Designing programs that appropriately recognize the responsibilities of families, avoid perverse incentives, and operate effectively is indeed difficult. The claims of the elderly are often persuasive and backed up with political strength. Nonetheless, our current very strong focus on the elderly seems to have developed almost haphazardly. As the programs developed, there was no explicit competition between children and the elderly and no sense that resources needed to be taken away from one group to meet the needs of the other. The programs were set up and developed in ways that seemed most appropriate at that time. The decisions that were made, however, led to quite different patterns of development: toward uniform entitlement programs for the elderly and state and locally controlled service programs for children. This in turn led to differences in spending levels and in growth and to quite different prospects for the future. Our guess is that most Americans would be surprised by the picture painted in this paper. Recognizing the patterns is especially important, however, as we move into the resource allocation debates of the next few years. All the current indications are that the spending differentials will widen considerably as a result of current budget battles. Social Security and Medicare seem almost immune from serious spending cuts, while services and cash transfer programs at the federal level that serve poor families with children are being cut dramatically. State and local spending cuts, while harder to predict since they vary so widely, seem also to be hitting hardest at education, services, health, and income security programs for families with children.

All this is not necessarily a bad thing. It may well be that public spending patterns indeed reflect national priorities and that, if we collectively thought hard about it, we would come out in the same place. It does not appear, however, that there has been hard thought about priorities. Children and families may be losing out by default rather than by plan. If things go the way they seem to be going, the relative situation of children and families may become even worse over the next decade. The time to start thinking about this prospect is now.

References

Ball, Robert

1978 *Social Security Today and Tomorrow*. New York: Columbia University Press.

Bane, Mary Jo, and Kenneth I. Winston

1980 Equity in Higher Education. Unpublished report to the National Institute of Higher Education.

Bixby, Ann Kallman

1981 Social welfare expenditures, Fiscal Year 1979. *Social Security Bulletin* (44):3-12.

Bureau of the Census

1976 Current Population Reports, Series P-25, No. 619. *Estimates of the Population of States, by Age*. Washington, D.C.: U.S. Government Printing Office.

1978 Current Population Reports, Series P-60. *Characteristics of the Population Below the Poverty Level*. Washington, D.C.: U.S. Government Printing Office.

1980a Current Population Reports, Series P-25, No. 875. *Estimates of the Population of States, by Age*. Washington, D.C.: U.S. Government Printing Office.

1980b Current Population Reports, Series P-60, No. 125. *Money Income and Poverty Status of Families and Persons in the United States: 1979*. (Advance Report). Washington, D.C.: U.S. Government Printing Office.

1980c *Statistical Abstract of the United States: 1980* (100th edition). Washington, D.C.: U.S. Government Printing Office.

1981 Current Population Reports, Series P-23, No. 110, *Characteristics of Households and Persons Receiving Noncash Benefits: 1979*. Washington, D.C.: U.S. Government Printing Office.

Coleman, James, Ernest Q. Campbell, Carol J. Hobson, James McPartland, Alexander M. Mood, Frederick D. Weinfeld, and Robert L. York

1966 *Equality of Educational Opportunity*. Washington, D.C.: U.S. Government Printing Office.

Coleman, James, Thomas Haffer, and Sally Kilgore

1981 *Public and Private Schools*. Draft report submitted to the National Center for Educational Statistics by National Opinion Research Center, Chicago.

Committee on Child Development Research and Public Policy

1981 *Services for Children: An Agenda for Research*. Washington, D.C.: National Academy Press.

Congressional Budget Office

1978 *Federal Housing Policy: Current Programs and Recurring Issues*. Washington, D.C.: Congressional Budget Office.

Health Care Financing Administration

1979 *Data on the Medicaid Program: Eligibility, Services, Expenditures*. Washington, D.C.: U.S. Department of Health, Education, and Welfare.

Lynn, Laurence E., Jr., and David deF. Whitman

1981 *The President as Policy Maker*. Philadelphia: Temple University Press.

MacMillan, Alma W., and Ann Kallman Bixby

1980 Social welfare expenditures, fiscal year 1978. *Social Security Bulletin* 43 (May):3-17.

Moynihan, Daniel P.

1973 *The Politics of a Guaranteed Income*. New York: Vantage.

National Center for Educational Statistics

1980 *Digest of Educational Statistics: 1980*. Washington, D.C.: U.S. Government Printing Office.

1981 *The Condition of Education.* Washington, D.C.: U.S. Government Printing Office.

Office of Management and Budget

1980 *Catalog of Federal Domestic Assistance.* Washington, D.C.: U.S. Government Printing Office.

1981a *Budget of the United States Government, Fiscal Year 1982. Appendix.* Washington, D.C.: U.S. Government Printing Office.

1981b *Fiscal Year 1982 Budget Revisions, March 1981.* Washington, D.C.: U.S. Government Printing Office.

Patterson, James T.

1981 *America's Struggle Against Poverty: 1900-1980.* Cambridge, Mass.: Harvard University Press.

Rose, Ruth

1976 Government programs affecting children: The federal budget FY 1974-76. Part of *A Study of Research and Development Needs for the Making of Social Policy Toward Young Children, Volume VII.* Unpublished paper prepared for the National Science Foundation.

Rutter, Michael, et al.

1979 *Fifteen Thousand Hours: Secondary Schools and Their Effects on Children.* Cambridge, Mass.: Harvard University Press.

Social Security Administration

1980 *Social Security Bulletin Annual Statistical Supplement 1977-79.* Washington, D.C.: U.S. Department of Health, Education, and Welfare.

Sugarman, Jule M.

1981 *Citizen's Guide to Changes in Human Services Programs.* Washington, D.C.: Human Services Information Center.

U.S. Department of Agriculture, Food and Nutrition Service.

1981 *Effects of the 1977 Food Stamp Act.* Second Annual Report to Congress.

U.S. Department of Health and Human Services.

1981 *Characteristics of State Plans for Aid to Families with Dependent Children.* Washington, D.C.: U.S. Government Printing Office.

DISCUSSION

The discussion of the Bane-Wilson-Baer paper fell into two major parts: What do the numbers really mean? And what should be done about the situation politically and programmatically?

No one doubted the authors' evidence that roughly three times as many federal dollars were being spent on the elderly as on children and that this situation had prevailed throughout the decade of the 1970s. It was pointed out that the gap did not actually widen during the period (and in fact narrowed a little bit), but it was certainly agreed that preserving the differential over that period involved an enormously greater absolute amount going to the elderly. The doubts expressed by conference participants concerned whether relative expenditures was the appropriate comparison to make.

It was pointed out by Bane herself that the numbers in the paper treat the full amount of Social Security benefits as a transfer, whereas, in fact, the appropriate number would be the amount that constitutes a transfer among people, leaving out the amount that is a transfer over time (which people pay in during their working life and which comes back to them when they retire). Doing the calculation that way would reduce the differential but certainly not eliminate it.

The other two points raised with respect to the appropriateness of the calculation were more fundamental. Both were raised by John Palmer. First, looking at expenditures alone did not tell one much about who was really gaining at the expense of whom. One should also include what the different groups paid in taxes in order to get the true incidence of government policy. Second, *transfer* payments should be kept quite distinct from expenditures that involve the use of real resources. "Most of the expenditures for children are going to education. These are real resources. Most of the payments to the elderly are social security. These are simply transfers, which tells us nothing about whether resources are really being used up that could otherwise be used for a different purpose. It may make a lot of sense to have massive transfer payments to the elderly and to concentrate real resource commitments on children, as investments in the future."

This point was developed further by Harold Watts. Twenty-five years from now what is going to be available to be divided up among the different groups in society will depend on the productive effort of those who are now growing up. "If the importance of investing in our children now—because their skills and effort are going to determine the size of the pie later—can be brought to the forefront of public discussion, perhaps constituencies can be expanded to support real investment in children." The formal discussant, John Calhoun, quoted Alan Pifer on this point:

> The nation must do everything in its power to see that today's children, the prime age workers of 20 years from now, get off to the best possible start in life. . . . If they become casualties, the loss is twofold; they fail to become productive citizens and they become an additional burden on what will already be an overtaxed generation.[18]

[18] Speech at the annual meeting of the Citizens Committee for Children, April 2, 1981.

In recognition that the essential policy issue was to find ways to ensure that the resources available for children are increased over the next decade rather than reduced, as seems to be the current danger, the discussion turned to the question of what should be done.

The first major point raised in this connection was that the issue should not be phrased as children *versus* the elderly. For one thing, as John Modell noted, it is a *post hoc ergo propter hoc* fallacy to conclude that because the elderly got more than the children, it in fact happened because of a rivalry. "We may very well be talking about two phenomena that just happened to happen at the same time." For another thing, even though the proportion of the population who are old will increase, the total dependency ratio (those who are in the labor force relative to those who are not) peaked in the 1960s and is now going down. So the same tax burden will allow us to distribute more to the elderly *and* children in total than is now the case. In addition, an efficient use of government funds suggests that programs be developed for the combined benefit of the aged and children. Calhoun quoted several examples of congregate eating facilities and day care centers established within an old age home that have been not only economically efficient but have had extraordinarily positive results on the lives of the elderly involved.

With respect to how to build constituencies for the support of children, great enthusiasm was expressed for examining how our society managed to decouple the responsibility for support of the elderly from their individual family with an eye to how such a decoupling could be achieved with respect to children—in the face of the incentive and moral hazard difficulties noted by Bane. The sense of the conference on this was captured by Alfred Kahn, who drew an analogy between AFDC and Social Security, both developed and established back in the 1930s. "Just as we need a new program strategy to preserve the solvency and public support for Social Security as we know it, we also need a new rationale for defending children's budgets. AFDC was modeled in an era in which middle-class mothers stayed home and took care of their (more than one or two) children; the aim was to help poor mothers do the same thing. We are now in a world where middle-class mothers have one or two children and go out to work, and we should be thinking of how to help poor mothers do the same. We will be matching the current ethical and cultural patterns of society better if we think in terms of making available for low-income mothers the sort of child subsidies now available to the middle- and upper-income mothers. Maybe we ought to talk about child credits in which for upper-income people we turn a larger child exemption into a tax deduction and for lower-income people we make it a refundable credit. If you spend money that way, you have not created the same kind of work disincentive as is now created by AFDC, because labor force status has nothing to do with whether or not you collect a child benefit."

Although most of the discussion talked about longer-range problems and solutions, one major short-term policy problem was noted. If the New Federalism turns programs for children over to the states, food stamp benefits will no longer equalize total public assistance benefits across the country. As long as food stamps have national uniform benefits levels, the AFDC benefit calculation is such that the existence of the food stamps program has served to mute the regional differences in AFDC benefits. If that money moves into the states without safeguards, income inequity will get a double boost. No longer will food stamp benefits counteract AFDC benefit differences. They will tend to go in the other direction, as generous states have generous benefits in both programs and and other states do the reverse.

5

The Impact of Unrecorded Economic Activity on American Families

ANN D. WITTE AND CARL P. SIMON

Every week of the year the U.S. government compiles and publishes economic statistics that describe our country's economic health—from the gross national product (GNP) and the productivity rate, to the consumer price index (CPI) and the unemployment rate. At the same time, economists and government officials are beginning to realize that these official statistics fail to include a significant amount of economic activity in the United States—activity that has been named the underground or subterranean economy. Such activity includes babysitting and garage sales and the income earned from hobbies or part-time jobs, when such income is not reported to the Internal Revenue Service (IRS) and is not picked up by any other monitoring agencies of the U.S. government. It also includes unreported income earned by illegal aliens and the income earned by criminal organizations supplying goods or services on the black market. The largest segment of the underground economy is composed of otherwise law-abiding citizens who fail to report some of the income from their regular job or all of their income from a second job. We include in the underground economy all economic activities and transactions not reported in official government economic statistics, such as taxable income and GNP, which involve payment in money or in goods or services of equivalent value.

There are basically three types of activities in the underground economy. The first, which we designate "pure tax evasion," involves individuals employed in legal, properly registered businesses who fail to report all their taxable income. An example might be small business owners who record and report only a portion of their sales, or elderly persons who fail to report income from "bearer" securities or from renting a room in their homes. The other two types of activities are quite different; although incomes earned in these activities generally avoid taxes, the avoidance of taxes is not the primary reason for the conduct of these activities underground. The second type of activity is often referred to as the "irregular" economy, involving the production of legal goods and services in unregistered and, thus, unrecorded establishments. This has both a domestic and an international sector. The domestic sector supplies primarily personal (e.g., hairdressing, babysitting) and household services (e.g., painting); the international sector employs many of the illegal aliens in our country. The final type of activity violates our criminal laws, involving either the production and distribution of illegal goods and services (e.g., traffic in certain drugs) or the illegal transfer of money and goods (e.g., robbery, fraud).

Unfortunately, the very nature of this economy makes estimates of both size and structure difficult and subject to large errors. However, most researchers now agree that the economy is surprisingly large (say 10 to 15 percent of reported national income) and that the structure of the economy is diverse. The existence of a hidden economy of this size has both direct and indirect effects on families with children. Directly this economy provides employment (in the majority of cases part-time employment) and income for many families. The employment provided often differs substantially from employment in the large, impersonal, bureaucratic, but secure organizations that dominate our regular economy. On the positive side, hours tend to be flexible; much work can be carried out at home; leisure, home, and work activities are often quite easily combined; individual initiative and ingenuity tend to be quite highly rewarded; paperwork, structure, and direct supervision tend to be lower than in the regular economy; and formal credentials are generally not required for entry. On the negative side, working conditions can be physically dangerous and economically very insecure. This type of employment is quite attractive to those of us who cannot conform (for example, those who are physically or mentally handicapped) or would rather not conform. The flexibility of the underground economy allows it to provide many part-time jobs and allows those receiving benefits that require a certain labor market status (e.g., unemployment compensation) or level of income (e.g., AFDC) to retain their benefits while supplementing their incomes.

It is important to realize that this economy is also an employer of last resort for those with few labor market skills and credentials and for those who have been displaced by a cyclical downturn in our regular economy. Many of these will find a work environment that ignores federal guidelines and that may be a much less pleasant or safe place to work than the heavily regulated alternatives in the regular economy.

The underground economy also provides goods and services to many families. Goods and services produced in the irregular economy *tend* to be cheaper and more convenient than those in the regular economy. However, the quality of such goods is much more variable than in the regular economy. Still, on balance, families appear to benefit from the availability of goods and services in the irregular economy. The effect on families of the availability of illegal goods and services is, of course, more problematic. Indirectly, the underground economy affects families with children because it affects not only government revenues and expenditures, but also official statistics on which macroeconomic, social, and political policies are based. The unemployment rate, labor-force-participation rate, and productivity rate are the official statistics that appear to be most biased by the existence of the underground economy. Finally, the underground economy is a major factor in the economic and family life in inner-city ghettos.

In this paper, we do two things. First, we discuss briefly how one obtains estimates of the size, growth, and structure of the underground economy and present results of our efforts in this regard. Using this description as a base, we then discuss the impact of the underground economy on families with children. We also discuss the type of distortion in national statistics and the loss of tax revenue that the existence of this economy is likely to lead to. In the final section, we summarize our earlier discussions, consider the income redistribution that results from the existence of a large underground economy, and discuss the options available to federal, state, and local governments who may want to correct any inequities that arise from this income redistribution.

The Size and Structure of the Underground Economy and Its Impact on American Families

Two basic approaches have been used to estimate the size and trends in the underground economy. The first approach is macroeconomic in nature and relies on coincident aggregate indicators or related series to obtain indirect estimates. An example of this approach is the work of Peter Gutmann (1977) and Edgar Feige (1979), who see the growth of the underground economy as related to the growth of currency holdings. This approach was very useful early on and served to alert us to the existence and surprising extent of unreported activity. However, most serious researchers today believe that detailed microeconomic studies of the various sectors of the underground economy are required if we are to understand its nature and impact.[1] Such microeconomic studies require that we first identify the types of activities in the underground economy and then estimate their size and describe their nature. Table 1 provides our listing of the major activities undertaken in this economy along with our estimates of the "National Income" of each sector and its rate of growth during the last decade (1970-1980). The estimates contained in this table were obtained in many and sometimes unusual ways. For example, the estimates of the amount of income avoiding federal income and profit taxes relied on (1) results of IRS's Tax Compliance Measurement Program (TCMP) to estimate the amount of income from regular economic activity that was not reported by those who file federal tax returns, (2) an expenditure approach to estimating incomes from "irregular" economic activity, (3) an exact match file to estimate incomes of those who do not file federal tax returns, and (4) Bureau of Economic Analysis (BEA) estimates of corporate profits.[2] Using similarly diverse sources and techniques, we derived independent estimates for the following additional sectors: (1) excise tax evasion (using a state-by-state expenditure approach), (2) illegal aliens (using an exact match file and labor market information from apprehended illegal aliens), (3) stolen goods (using victimization data, trade publications, ethnographic studies, and criminal justice system records), (4) fraud arson (using information from police departments, fire departments, and insurance companies), (5) heroin (using a value-added approach), (6) cocaine (combining expenditure and supply side estimates), (7) marijuana (using an expenditures approach), (8) illegal gambling (an expenditures and cost of doing business approach), (9) loan sharking (an expenditures approach), and (10) prostitution (an employment and incomes approach).[3] We relied exclusively on the work of others to obtain estimates

[1] This is the conclusion of the IRS, which is likely ultimately to produce the best estimates of size and trends in this economy and to have a major role in dealing with it. This is also the conclusion of a number of researchers, for example, Reuter (1980) and even James Henry (comments at the session on the Underground Economy, meetings of the Southern Economic Association, New Orleans, La., November 1981), who pioneered the coincident indicators approach (Henry, 1976).

[2] Our recent book (Simon and Witte, 1982) provides additional details. See U.S. Department of the Treasury, Internal Revenue Service (1979), for a description of the first three sources, Comptroller General of the United States (1979) for a further description of the third source, and Parker (1980) for a description of the fourth source.

[3] For cocaine, marijuana, and illegal gambling, we used the results of some rather sophisticated household surveys to estimate the expenditures in these sectors. We would certainly know a lot more about the underground economy if such surveys existed for other sectors, such as prostitution, loan sharking, and the irregular economy. The IRS

for all other sectors. These estimates range from quite reliable (counterfeiting) to seriously suspect (other fraud).[4] Below each number in the table, we have noted our subjective evaluation of its reliability.

To determine the effect of the underground economy on families with children, we need more than numbers. We need to know how this economy operates and how it affects national statistics. The underground economy is far too diverse and heterogeneous to be considered as a coherent whole. Some sectors, such as those that produce and distribute illegal goods and services, do appear to have the coherence and interaction of a complex economy. However, their structures are rather diverse—from the monopolies and oligopolies that characterize the heroin and loan shark sectors to the small proprietorships of the marijuana and prostitution industries. Other activities, like tax evasion and the economic life of illegal aliens, are not really industries at all but special types of household activities involving little economic structure or organization. Our discussion of the impact of the underground economy on family life must treat each of the sectors separately. In the next three subsections, we discuss the three major types of activities carried out in this economy and their implications for families with children.

Pure Tax Evasion

We find it natural to divide tax evasion into two basic types. The first type involves U.S. citizens who work in properly registered, legal activities and who purposely underreport their income or overreport their deductions when they file their tax returns. The second type involves the failure to report income or even to file income tax forms by individuals who run or work for businesses that are not generally registered and licensed as required by law and do not generally file required government forms. This type of evasion involves illegal aliens as well as U.S. citizens, with at least 30 percent of the total illegal alien population (1 million persons) falling into this category. It is often not intentional but rather part of the system of unregistered and often informal economic activity that we have been calling the "irregular economy."

---

has commissioned the University of Michigan's Institute for Survey Research to conduct such a survey, and to determine the size and nature of purchases in the irregular economy.

[4] The figures for many types of fraud come from the Chamber of Commerce of the United States (1973). As far as we can discern, the "estimates" are pure guesses from which, indeed, the Chamber of Commerce has recently dissociated themselves. This is an area where much work clearly needs to be done.

TABLE 1 Estimated National Income for the Underground Economy in 1974 and 1980 With Growth Trends (With Reliability Indices)

Sector	Estimated 1974 National Income (in $ billions)	Estimated Average Annual Growth Rate (%) 1970–1975	1975–1980	"Guestimated" 1980 National Income (in $ billions)
I. Tax evasion and avoidance				
Federal income and profits tax	56.7–75.7 (moderate)	5 to 10 (low)	8 to 12 (very low)	98.2–130.9 (very low)
Excise taxes	0.3–0.5 (moderate)	10 to 15 (moderate)	−5 to 5 (moderate)	0.3–0.6 (moderate)
Sales taxes	(no estimates could be found)			
II. Illegal aliens	5.9–7.6 (moderate)	12 to 16 (moderate)	15 to 20 (moderate)	15.1–19.4 (low)
III. Illegal transfers				
Stolen goods	5.4–8.9 (moderate)	10 to 15 (moderate)	10 to 15 (moderate)	10.9–18.0 (low)
Fraud arson	0.2 (moderate)	20 to 30 (moderate)	25 to 35 (moderate)	0.9 (moderate)
Other fraud	2.2–20.1 (very low)	(unknown)		
Counterfeiting	0.001 (moderate)	11	6	0.001
Hijacking	(no estimates could be found)			
Forgery	(no estimates could be found)			
Embezzlement	0.1–1.3 (unknown)	(no estimate found)		
Bribery	6.5–13.0 (unknown)	(no estimate found)		

IV. Production and distribution of illegal goods				
Drugs				
(1) Heroin	3.2–5.0 (moderate)	10–20 (low)	10–20 (low)	7.4–11.6 (very low)
(2) Cocaine	5.6–6.2 (moderately high)	0–5 (moderate)	5–10 (moderate)	8.2–9.1 (moderate)
(3) Marijuana	1.5–2.4 (moderate)	5–10 (moderate)	10–20 (moderate)	3.2–5.2
(4) Other drugs (hashish and synthetic drugs like PCP)	2.8–4.4 (very low)	(no estimate found)		
Smuggling of goods other than drugs	0.2–.3 (unknown)	(no estimate found)		
Pirating records and tapes	(no estimates could be found)			
Pornography	1.3–2.0 (unknown)	(no estimate found)		
Firearms trading	(no estimates could be found)			
V. Production and distribution of illegal services				
Illegal gambling	1.0–2.0 (moderate)	5 to 10 (low)	−5 to 5 (low)	1.1–2.2 (moderate)
Loan sharking	0.2–3.2 (low)	−5 to 5 (low)	−10 to 10 (low)	0.2–3.2 (low)
Prostitution	1.7–14.4 (high)	0 to 5 (low)	−5 to 5 (low)	1.7–14.8 (moderate)
Total national income	94.8–167.2		10	170–300

With regard to the first type of tax evasion, although there are as many distinct types of tax evasion as there are taxes to evade, it is both easier and more profitable to evade some taxes than others. Our survey of the literature on tax evasion leads us to believe that it is sales, profit, income, and excise taxes that are evaded to the greatest degree in this country. In this section, we will consider only evasion of federal personal income taxes, since we know most about this type of tax evasion and since it appears that this type of evasion has the greatest effect on families with children.

In its recent report (U.S. Department of the Treasury, 1979), the IRS estimated that between $75 and $100 billion of taxable personal income earned in legal endeavors was unreported to IRS in 1976. This is between $350 and $500 per year for every man, woman, and child in the country. However, like so many other things in our economy, tax evasion is not evenly distributed throughout our society. It varies markedly with source of income, level of income, and feelings about government.

Studies that ask about the issue, with varying degrees of anonymity, usually find 20-25 percent of people interviewed will admit to noncompliance with tax laws.[5] Needless to say, it is likely that the true percentage of noncompliers is much higher, although it is difficult to estimate *how* much. In a recent study, the General Accounting Office (Comptroller General of the United States, 1979) estimated that about 5 million people (approximately 7 percent of those required to file) did not even bother to *file* federal income tax returns in 1972, although they were required to do so. If we assume that 50 percent of the population fails to comply with federal tax laws, then a tax evader, on average, is failing to report between $700 and $1,000 of income a year. However, there appear to be relatively few average tax evaders. Tax evaders generally fail to report either a very small or a very large portion of their income. The extent of evasion varies markedly with both the source of income and the type of individual involved. For example, voluntary compliance with federal income tax is highest for wage and salary income (97-98 percent of income reported) and is lowest for rents and royalties (50-65 percent reported) and income earned when self-employed (60-64 percent reported) (U.S. Department of the Treasury, 1979). People with very high and very low incomes have more opportunities to avoid taxes than do the middle-income groups; and existing evidence indicates that they often take advantage of these opportunities. The middle-income groups

[5] See the recent study completed by Westat (1980) for the Internal Revenue Service for a recent example of this type of work and a survey of previous work.

are mostly wage and salary workers, for whom the W-2 form leaves a damaging "paper trail."

The family income subsidy provided by tax evasion depends both on the amount of income evading taxes and the marginal tax rate on this income. The subsidy to middle-class wage and salary workers appears to be small, because the amount of income that goes untaxed is small. The subsidy to poor families appeared to be low in the early 1970s, because marginal tax rates were relatively low for this group, but it has increased more recently with the increase in such taxes as Social Security. For example, in 1980 a married couple filing jointly with income below $5,400 paid no federal income tax. Now, if we assume a state and local income tax rate of 5 percent, Social Security deductions of 7 percent, and an income of $5,000,[6] the supplement to a poor family from failure to report any income (i.e., failing to file a return) would be $600 per year. This is a substantial subsidy to those poor families in a position to evade taxes. According to the General Accounting Office (Comptroller General of the United States, 1979), this subsidy is most readily available to those receiving income from agricultural labor, work in private households, and self-employment (e.g., craftspersons).

The subsidy to wealthy families is potentially very large because of both high marginal tax rates and the large amount of income potentially evading taxes. Consider the self-employed professional earning $100,000 per year who succeeds in hiding the last $30,000 of income. If we assume 1980 federal income tax rates and a slightly progressive state income tax, the income supplement for such a taxpayer would be approximately $20,000 per year.[7] This subsidy is most readily available to those receiving income from self-employment or those receiving large amounts of nonlabor income.

The effects of the first type of evasion on families with children are relatively straightforward, although the effects on families that evade are quite different from the effects on those that do not evade.

The major direct effect on families that evade is to raise disposable family income. As we have just noted, it appears that it is the very wealthy and the very poor who are most likely to evade taxes. The income supplement for those who run very small businesses and those who work "off the books" may also be quite large.

[6] GAO estimates that the majority of the nonfiler population had incomes of less than $5,000 in 1972. See Comptroller General of the United States (1979).

[7] Specifically, we assume a state income tax rate of 10 percent, that no social security tax would be owed, and that applicable federal income tax rates were 54 percent on the first $15,600 avoiding taxes and 59 percent on the next $14,400. The total income supplement would be $19,920.

The major direct and predictable effect of tax evasion of this type is the income effect. However, there may be a moral effect as well. If children and other family members are aware of the tax evasion, they may naturally acquire a decreased respect for legal requirements and, indeed, for the law in general. The precise effect on children will depend upon the attitude of their parents toward tax evasion. Parents who enthusiastically refuse to comply with reporting requirements encourage within their children a diminished sense of loyalty and respect for government rules. Thus, as the tax evasion sector of the underground economy grows, each succeeding generation may feel a diminished willingness to comply with tax laws. This situation could pose a serious problem to the Internal Revenue Service, which relies heavily on voluntary compliance for the success of its tax collection system. It could also weaken family members' spirit of compliance with the regulations of other government agencies, including the Social Security system, unemployment, and welfare agencies, even draft registration and civil and criminal justice systems.

The effect on families not evading taxes depends on the reaction of governments to lowered tax revenues. Until quite recently, governments usually reacted to lowered tax revenues by raising tax rates or by allowing an increase in the deficit. The effect of increases in tax rates depends on the type of tax (sale, income, or property); however, these increases have probably had their largest effect on middle-income families. The effects of inflation associated with increased deficits are much more difficult to gauge.

Most recently, shortfalls in revenues are generally being met by decreasing government expenditures, particularly for social programs. Such cuts in expenditures fall quite heavily on families, particularly poor families with children. For example, President Reagan's 1981 program to balance the federal budget included new regulations to cut out 400,000 families from the AFDC program, decrease AFDC benefits for another 279,000 families, drop 875,000 people from food stamp rolls, raise the interest rate and eligibility requirements for loans to families with children in college, and cut back federal subsidies for school lunch programs.

The Irregular Economy

The second type of tax evasion is quite different and may well have more pronounced effects on the families of the individuals who participate in this type of activity. Recall that this type of tax evasion involves people working in unrecorded and unregulated businesses. We will divide this type of activity into a domestic and an illegal alien portion since the two sectors are quite different.

The *domestic sector* of the "irregular" economy appears to flourish in large central cities, particularly ghetto areas, and in rural areas. It tends to be informally organized and to supply primarily services to individuals and households. The IRS report (U.S. Department of the Treasury, 1979) contains a list of services that it believes to be commonly supplied by this economy. A recent study of Detroit by Ferman et al. (1978) provides a more vivid description.[8]

The domestic portion appears to be composed largely of self-employed individuals and very small business establishments. The majority of these businesses operate on a part-time basis. Often the manager/owner is also employed either full or part time in the regular economy. Typical activities include the engineer who does design work on a consulting basis after hours and the carpenter who does odd jobs around the neighborhood. In other cases, particularly in the cases of women with small children and the handicapped, part-time employment in the irregular economy is the only employment. Such individuals generally run small businesses out of their homes. Typical examples might be the mother who provides beautician services to neighbors in her home where she can still care for small children or the handicapped individual who uses a garage to provide repair services. There are some full-time businesses in this irregular economy; they tend, however, to be quite small and quite informally organized.

The IRS estimates that $14-$18 billion of unreported labor income was earned in this economy in 1976. As this income was included in our estimate of tax evasion, we have already discussed the income subsidy effects of this type of activity. However, in contrast to "pure tax evasion," this type of activity appears to generate rather substantial employment. We estimate that perhaps as many as 3 million people worked at least some time in this economy in 1976,[9] the vast majority of whom did so only on a part-time basis. We suspect that only 300,000 to 750,000 found

[8] We have disturbingly little knowledge of the nature of this type of activity. Ferman et al. (1978) used a 1977 survey of households in Detroit to provide the most complete situation of which we are aware. The insights of this report have recently been summarized and extended in Ferman and Berndt (1981). The authors found that the most frequently used services in the irregular economy are lawn care, painting, paneling, carpentry, babysitting, and child care. Dow (1977) provides an interesting anthropological perspective.

[9] We obtain this estimate by using IRS estimates of unreported income earned and assuming that the average income earned in the sector was $5,000.

their primary employment in the irregular economy in that year. However, for these people this economy is very important.

There appear to be three main effects of the domestic portion of the irregular economy on families with children. The first is an income effect for families who participate. It is quite similar, although generally larger, than the effect of the first type of tax evasion. The second effect is a milieu effect. In many cases, irregular economic activity is carried out in the home, and in some instances children are directly involved in the activity. Whether involved or not, children are able to watch adults in productive activities and probably benefit from the exposure. Families who work in the irregular economy may often find themselves in a preindustrial revolution atmosphere. The industrial revolution changed family life dramatically, as it encouraged a separation of the workplace and the family place, an emphasis on specialization, a segmentation of markets, division of labor, and a loss of flexibility in work hours and location. By contrast, persons working in the domestic portion of the irregular economy often do most of their work in their own homes, for example, typists, consultants, income tax accountants, and those involved in child care. In order to minimize their dependence on the regular economy and to keep a low profile, they will often complete an entire task instead of specializing on one segment of it. They will usually be able to set more flexible hours. Sometimes, the family may work together or at least cooperate in these activities. Carrying out economic activity in the home also often allows for greater parental care for children and more hours when parents are readily available to children.

Although many jobs in the irregular economy do present the opportunity for this more informal work environment, there are certainly other irregular-economy jobs where an increased ability to avoid government standards for workplace, comfort, and safety will lead to less desirable working conditions than those in similar jobs in the regular economy. In addition, workers in the irregular economy will often find themselves without the benefits of group life and health insurance, which can be very important for a family's peace of mind and economic stability. The absence of these benefits will provide an impetus for many workers in the irregular economy to look for openings in the regular economy. This is especially true for those workers who joined the irregular economy because it was their employer of last resort or because of either low job skill levels or depressed economic conditions.

The final effect of the domestic portion of the irregular economy is the provision of goods and more generally services to families not themselves employed in the irregular economy. Goods and services provided in the underground economy are generally more convenient, provided on a more personal basis, and *often* cheaper and more diverse than the goods and services of the regular economy.[10] The Detroit study (Ferman and Berndt, 1981) found that some repair jobs, such as chimney sweeping and small appliance repair, were performed *only* in the irregular economy. The quality of goods and services provided by the irregular economy tends, however, to be highly variable, since frequently the only quality controls are word-of-mouth reports. The overall effect of the provision of these items is to increase the real income of the families who purchase them and to increase the sense of community.

IRS estimates that the average U.S. household spent $525 on such goods in 1979 (U.S. Department of the Treasury, 1979). Expenditures on such goods increase with family size but at a rate less rapid than the rate of increase in family size. For example, IRS estimates that an average single person spent $242 on such goods in 1976, while a family of six or more spent $608 on average.

Different income groups fulfill different needs in the irregular economy. The wealthy use it to obtain luxury and specialty items; the middle-income groups call on the irregular economy for savings in home repairs and personal services; the poor often rely on it for day-to-day necessities (Ferman and Berndt, 1981).

A relatively recent development with major tax evasion possibilities is the large-scale reintroduction of barter in the United States. The reintroduction, which goes under the formal name of the "reciprocal trade business," facilitates the exchange of large quantities of goods and services between businesses and individuals. The size of this sector is difficult to determine, but *Purchasing World*, a trade publication, has guestimated that 48 percent of all the purchasing agents in the United States engaged in some form of barter. The service sector is the major user of reciprocal trade services, although manufacturers are increasingly utilizing this sector for stock liquidation purposes. Income received as reciprocal goods and services is just as legally taxable as money income. The IRS is currently completing a study involving a random audit of barter exchange members in the Los Angeles area. Preliminary results indicate that returns with bartering transactions were approximately twice as

[10] Of course, as Professor Ferman reminded us in his comments at the conference, not all prices in the irregular economy are lower than the corresponding prices in the regular economy. Reasons for this include limited information to aid in comparison shopping and the small scale of operation. However, prices are *generally* cheaper for a number of reasons. First, wages are often lower because deductions from pay are either small or nonexistent. Second, many government regulations that tend to increase prices (e.g., regulations of hours and health and safety conditions) are avoided. Third, sales taxes are not generally charged.

likely to require tax changes as were returns without such transactions. In addition, the percentage of individuals with bartering transactions whose returns required tax changes increased from 62 percent in 1976 to 74 percent in 1977 (U.S. House of Representatives, 1980).

Barter between families or individuals is an important component of the irregular economy, yet one whose size seems impossible to measure. As we will discuss in a later section, exchanges of resources, possessions and services play an especially important role in the consumption and survival strategies of lower-income, inner-city communities.

The *international sector* of the irregular economy is made up of foreigners who are in our country illegally—illegal aliens. We estimate that there were roughly 4-6 million illegal aliens in the United States in the mid-1970s with probably about 4 million of this number in the labor force. Approximately 60 percent of the illegal aliens come from Mexico, with another 25 percent coming from the rest of the Western Hemisphere (primarily the Caribbean area) and the remaining 15 percent coming from the Eastern Hemisphere. The illegal alien population grew by approximately 1 million in the 1960-1970 period and by another 1.6 million in the 1970-1975 period. This growth acceleration appears to have continued since then.[11]

We estimate that approximately 30 percent of the working illegal population, 1 million people, found employment in "off-the-books" economic activity, earning $6-$8 billion in 1974.

Off-the-books employment of illegal aliens leads to tax losses for all levels of government, including $500 to $600 million of lost federal income taxes and another $230 to $340 million of lost revenues to state and local governments. Although the loss of this revenue to local governments can be quite important, it is partially offset by the fact that illegal aliens do not make extensive use of locally provided goods and services. Two studies (North and Houston, 1976; Villalpando et al., 1977) estimate that only 30 percent of the illegal alien population use medical services, 4 percent have children in public schools, and less than 1 percent receive food stamps or other welfare services.

The effect of the international portion of the irregular economy on families with children is more difficult to gauge than that of the domestic portion. Some illegal families do quite well by participating in unregistered economic activity and are clearly better off participating in this U.S. activity than they would have been remaining in their own countries. Others are terribly exploited and work in conditions little better, if any,

[11] For estimates of the size of the illegal alien population, see Heer (1979), Robinson (1979), and Lancaster and Scheuren (1977).

than the working conditions in their own countries.[12] Due to fear of expulsion, illegal aliens use very few social services, as mentioned above. Usage is probably even lower for illegal aliens working in unregistered economic activity than for the group as a whole.

Employment of illegal aliens in unregistered economic activity has two basic effects on U.S. families. The first effect is to lower the price of certain types of goods and services. Illegal aliens tend to work in agriculture, services, and light industry, particularly textiles. Thus, their employment at wages below those paid to U.S. citizens means that either the prices of these products are lower, profits are raised, or most likely a little of both. Lowered prices of fresh agricultural produce, restaurant and hotel services, and handmade clothing benefit the U.S. families that purchase these items. Most of these items tend to have high income-elasticities of demand and, thus, probably provide most benefits to wealthier Americans.

The second effect is to lower both the wage and employment opportunities of U.S. citizens (generally citizens in low-wage, low-skill jobs) that compete for jobs with illegal aliens. This negative effect is generally acknowledged but its magnitude is quite controversial. On the one hand, Vallalpando et al. (1977) argue that illegal aliens take jobs that would not be accepted by U.S. citizens. Further, they suggest that these jobs pay sufficiently low wages that U.S. citizens are better off on welfare. On the other hand, Briggs (1976:360) argues that high unemployment, low wages, low per capita income, low union activity, and a high level of welfare assistance in South Texas "are signs of labor surplus which is one indication of the presence of sizable numbers of illegal aliens." Smith and Newman (1977), by gathering data from field survey work, find evidence of differences in real wages between the South Texas border area and Houston farther to the north. They estimated a $719 per year differential (11 percent) for Mexican-Americans and a $580 differential (7 percent) for all other workers. It does appear likely that there is both a detrimental wage and employment effect and that these effects are both geographically and ethnically concentrated—with Spanish Americans in areas of high concentrations of illegal aliens (such as South Florida, South Texas, and Southern California) being most affected.

Taken together, these two effects of the employment of illegal aliens tend to make the distribution of income among American families more

[12] For example, a crew leader for migrant workers and three of his assistants were indicted in October 1981 on charges of kidnapping and enslaving illegal aliens at a North Carolina camp where one potato digger collapsed and died. See *New York Times*, October 9, 1981.

unequal than it otherwise would be. Many of the goods and services that have lower prices as a result of illegal alien employment are consumed by the richer members of our society, while the negative labor market impact of this population falls mainly on low-skilled, low-income U.S. workers.

Illegal Activities

Illegal activities in this country are of two basic types: illegal transfers of goods and money and the production and distribution of illegal goods and services. As they have rather different effects on families with children, we will discuss them separately.

With respect to *illegal transfers*, just as our legitimate economy has developed complex methods of transferring income between individuals, so has our underground economy. However, lacking the force of law, the underground economy makes such transfers by means of force (e.g., robbery, larceny) or subterfuge (e.g., fraud, counterfeiting) rather than through tax and expenditure systems. These illegal transfers are large, running perhaps $30-80 billion in 1974, and thus have potentially large effects on families with children. The most obvious and direct effect is the transfer of income. Some families are made better off and others worse off as a result of these transfers. Overall, thefts of money and goods, whether by strong arm tactics or employees, probably make the distribution of income more equal than it otherwise would be. However, theft is a very arbitrary transfer mechanism and often happens at the expense of the poor as well as businesses and the well off. Other types of transfers (insurance fraud, embezzlement, bribery) appear to benefit more of the richer members of our society and, thus, may actually be regressive.

Like the irregular economy, transferring goods illegally appears to provide mainly part-time employment, although theft and certain types of fraud apparently provide the primary employment for a fairly large number of people. We estimate that anywhere from 3 to 8 million U.S. citizens are involved in carrying out illegal transfers during a typical year in the early 1970s.[13] However, probably fewer than 500,000 find their primary occupation to be that of illegally transferring income.[14]

[13] This figure is a guess based on our income estimates. We estimated that 1-2 million are involved in stolen goods markets (estimated income divided by an estimated average income of $5,000) and that 3-4 times that number are involved in all types of illegal transfers.

[14] This figure is obtained by assuming that 10-25 percent of those involved in stolen goods markets find their primary employment there and that other types of illegal transfer provide very limited primary employment.

The greatest effects of illegal transfers for the vast majority of American families appear to be indirect. These effects include increased prices for goods and services in our regular economy, decreased work incentives, increased expenditures for home security devices, and an atmosphere of fear in many of our cities.

The major goods *produced and distributed illegally* in our country are illegal drugs. Illegal drugs run the gamut from substances believed to have large-scale debilitating effects (e.g., heroin) to those considered by many to have relatively minor effects (e.g., marijuana). We estimate that the illegal drug industry produced incomes of between $13 and $18 billion in 1974. Like illegal transfers, we believe that the sale of illegal drugs provides mostly part-time employment, although a few hundred thousand individuals are probably involved in such activities on a full-time basis.

The major effect of illegal drugs on American families appears to occur because of their use, particularly by young adults. Table 2 summarizes our estimates of the size of the illegal drug industry in the United States in the mid- to late 1970s, in terms of number of users, amount consumed, total retail value, and annual national income. Note that more than 20 million people used marijuana in 1976, of whom 60 percent were regular users. (In 1977, more than 60 percent of the young adults between 18 and 25 admitted that they had used marijuana at least once in their lives; nearly half of these were regular users.) Furthermore, we

TABLE 2 Size and Economics of the Illegal Drug Industry in the United States

	Heroin		Cocaine		Marijuana	
	1974	1976	1974	1976	1974	1976
Number of regular uses (in millions)	0.725	0.725	2.49	2.5–2.85	13.0	14.9
Number of irregular uses (in millions)	3.0	3.0	1.07	1.07–1.22	6.52	6.76
Amount consumed (in metric tons)	6–10	6–10	12–18	13–19	3.14	3.59
Total retail value (in $ billions)	4.9–7.3	8.6	5.86–6.5	7.0	1.76–2.76	2.30–3.59
Annual national income (in $ billions)	3.2–5.0	6.5	5.6–6.2	6.7	1.50–2.35	1.96–3.05
Cost to society (in $ billions)	6.5					

estimate that 400,000-500,000 people were employed in the marijuana distribution network in the late 1970s.

In terms of national income, the cocaine industry appears to be the largest of the drug sectors. The heroin industry is almost as large, but it has a much deeper impact in terms of social costs. Cocaine-related deaths number only about 20 a year, contrasted with more than 2,000 heroin-related deaths. As a further social cost, nearly one-half of the income of the average heroin addict is estimated to come from thievery. It is generally believed that 25-50 percent of all property crime in metropolitan areas (excluding auto theft) is caused by heroin addicts seeking funds to continue their habits.

The major services produced and distributed illegally in our country are gambling, prostitution, and loans at very high interest rates (i.e., loan sharking). These services are illegal because our society has decided (at least implicitly) that they are moral offenses against the common good and, at least in the case of illegal gambling and loan sharking, because they represent efforts to get around the rather stringent regulations our society has placed on the production of certain services. One reason for such regulation is the feeling that the provider of these services can easily take advantage of the consumer. Another is the fear that organized criminal organizations profit from the provision of these services, although it is not clear whether this profit is a cause or an effect of the heavy regulation. The production and distribution of these illegal services generated incomes of between $8 and $30 billion in 1974.

The major positive effects of the illegal sector of the underground economy on American families are the provision of employment and the resulting increase in income, the provision of certain black market goods, and a decrease in the prices of some other goods.

Four popular occupations in the illegal sector of the underground economy are prostitution, bookmaking, numbers running for illegal gambling organizations, and wholesale and retail sales of marijuana and cocaine. Each of these occupations provides at least part-time employment for 200,000 to 500,000 Americans. The incomes earned can be substantial, easily enough to support a family. For example, one of the major enticements for women to become prostitutes is the $20,000-$50,000 that full-time prostitutes can earn, especially when these figures are compared with the $6,000 median annual earnings for full-time, female civilian workers in the United States in the early to mid-1970s (see Simon and Witte, 1982). Other underground occupations earn their high, untaxed incomes while requiring considerably less than the usual eight-hour work day. For example, numbers runners and controllers earned at least $5,000-$7,000 a year in 1967 working just a few hours a day (see Kaplan and Maher, 1970; Rados, 1976). In the late 1970s, a marijuana wholesaler could easily earn $20,000 a year working just 20 hours a month.[15] These flexible hours allow dealers to work at regular jobs too, spend more time with their families, or pursue other activities that interest them.

Of course, by its very definition, the illicit sector of the underground economy also provides families with some goods and services they may not be able to obtain elsewhere. It is certainly possible that some of these goods and services may benefit family life (e.g., relaxation through the careful use of marijuana or gambling services), or increased flexibility through the use of small loans from loan sharks, especially in difficult financial times. Some families may also benefit from the lower prices that prevail on goods available from nearby fencing operations. As we shall see below, the underground economy can have a stabilizing effect on ghetto families.

Of course, the provision of these goods and services can also have a disruptive effect on families. A family member who becomes addicted to heroin or to gambling or who falls behind in payments to a loan shark can bring extraordinary financial and social stresses on his or her family. A son or daughter who becomes a prostitute or a husband who uses the services of a prostitute can destroy the bonds that hold a family together. Finally, a family that loses a breadwinner either to a drug abuse death or to imprisonment because of conviction for black market activities may suddenly find itself without any means of support.

All families undergo some costs because of the existence of the illegal sector of the underground economy. Even families that do not participate in this sector spend money and take precautions to secure their home from thefts and to avoid areas of the city where drugs sales and prostitution thrive.

Role of Family Life in the Growth of Adolescent Prostitution

The connection between the underground economy and families with children is a two-way street. On the one hand, as has been described, they are costs and benefits that participation in the underground economy can bring to such families. On the other hand, family disruptions can lead family members to greater participation. The prostitution industry is a phenomenon that flourishes in large part because of the failures of family life, not only on the demand side, but even more drastically on the supply side. Jennifer James and her colleagues at the

[15] See *Wall Street Journal*, July 16, 1980, and *Ann Arbor Observer*, February 1978.

University of Washington trace the roots of a girl's drift toward prostitution directly to the girl's family life.[16] They classify the young women who see prostitution as an acceptable option into three categories: (1) deprived or disadvantaged, (2) physically and/or sexually abused, and (3) affluent and overindulged. Those in the first class are generally from low social or economic status families and have been denied or inconsistently provided with the physical necessities of life. Using a prostitute mother, sister, or aunt as a role model, they see prostitution as an obvious way to avoid a life of poverty and of a continuing string of personal defeats. Those in the second class, the abused, came from all levels of society. More than 50 percent of adolescent prostitutes are the victims of parental incest who eventually find prostitution as a means of gaining independence from an abusive home situation and of finding the friendships that were missing in their homes or legal placements. Finally, there are unique influences toward prostitution among the affluent, which are distinct from those influencing the deprived or abused. The lifestyle of prostitution appears glamorous to many affluent juveniles who feel bored, spoiled, and resistant to their overly protective life at home, or who were not provided with affection or guidelines by their parents.

The major step occurs when the adolescent girl decides to leave an unacceptable home situation and to run away. Unfortunately, the network of support systems that aided runaways in the Vietnam era barely exists today, even though there are probably more than a million runaways in the United States (mostly teenage girls).[17] In need of food and shelter, the runaway will often find a man who tells the scared and lonely adolescent just what she needs to hear. Soon, the runaway barters sexual access for food, shelter, and companionship; a little later, she can be easily convinced that she can earn a reasonable income through sexual activity. The chain from a family life that promotes a loss of self-esteem to adolescent prostitution is soon complete.

The Underground Economy in the Ghetto

The underground economy is an especially important factor in the economic and social life of poor, inner-city ghetto areas. In interviews with residents of the Watts area of Los Angeles around 1970, Paul Bullock (1973:99) found that "the subeconomy is probably the greatest single source of market income for young men in the central city. The

[16] See, for example, James and Meyerding (1977) or Boyer and James (1981). The latter reference also documents some interesting statistics on runaways.
[17] See Boyer and James (1981).

participants in Watts . . . estimate that they obtain equally as much income from this source as from all government programs." Bullock uses the term "subeconomy" to refer to the illegal sector of the underground economy. However, the legal sector of the underground economy also thrives in ghetto areas since the more intensive social life of the ghetto encourages informal exchanges of goods and services paid with cash or barter. Ogbu (1982) emphasizes this point in his comments by quoting Stack (1974:33):

> The most important form of distribution and exchange of the limited resources available to the poor in The Flats is by means of trading, or what people usually call "swapping." As people swap, the limited supply of finished material goods in the community is redistributed among networks of kinsmen throughout the community.

Furthermore, when incomes are low, the incentives to avoid paying taxes on subsistence levels are increased. Many of the available jobs are service jobs, like car repair or house cleaning, in which one can easily avoid paying taxes.

All the implications of unrecorded activity for families with children that we have discussed in earlier sections also hold for ghetto families. Thus, many ghetto participants in the irregular economy find a lower price for many of the goods distributed in this economy—especially in comparison with the higher prices that some regular economy merchants charge to their ghetto customers. A large number of such participants also find more flexible working arrangements in the underground economy and have increased access to black market goods and services, with its costs and benefits. However, as we have discussed a couple of times earlier in this paper and as Ogbu (1982) emphasizes, these improved working conditions in the underground economy are available mostly to those who are working there by choice. The underground economy is the employer of last resort for a large number of ghetto residents who are unable to find employment in the regular economy because of low levels of job skills, depressed economic conditions, or discrimination. Many of those whose participation in the underground economy is not completely voluntary may find their experiences there especially frustrating and disappointing.

The 1971 Manpower Report to the President[18] describes some of these frustrations and offers an explanation for the importance of the underground economy to ghetto families:

[18] U.S. Department of Labor (1971), as cited by Bullock (1973).

Street economy is the only visible and attainable route to some degree of economic success for many Black youth. Many of the regular jobs, even those that were well-paying, do not promise much of an improvement in life style or chance to move out of the slum or to advance to a more prestigious position. This leaves little incentive to look hard for such jobs or to work hard at them.

Hustling was often regarded as a rational and logical option. The market for gambling, numbers, prostitution, and narcotics is large and highly profitable. The possibility of "being on one's own" competes powerfully with the opportunities available in the regulated middle-class world. . . .

The costs attached to engaging in illegal activities tend to be low. No great social stigma accompanies arrest, so far as the immediate neighborhood is concerned. Job opportunities are already limited by other barriers, so that the effect of an arrest record is not considered important.

In many ways, the underground economy has a stabilizing effect on the economy of inner-city areas, leading to relative peace during periods of severe economic recession. Without the employment opportunities in the underground economy, communities whose young men have an unemployment rate of nearly 50 percent[19] would certainly suffer considerably more turmoil and family stress than they appear to undergo. Conversely, disruptions of the underground economy, such as strong enforcement of tax laws or legalization of current black market goods, could have a major disruptive effect on ghetto families.

This stabilization effect is one reason why official society may feel that it is to its advantage to tolerate the flourishing of the underground economy in ghetto areas. This society may also want to encourage the provision of black market goods and services for itself but in neighborhoods well removed from the homes of its affluent families. It may further appreciate the fact that ghetto employment in the underground economy provides income to poverty groups with minimal direct costs to taxpayers and lessens the incentives for minority groups to compete for jobs in the official labor market. This arrangement undoubtedly has an economic and psychological effect on ghetto youth. "It reinforces his cynicism about law and order and creates the expectation that only through the subeconomy can he meet his economic needs" (Bullock, 1973:135).

[19] As reported in the October 3, 1981, *New York Times*, the unemployment rate for black teenagers was 45.7 percent in August, 1981.

A wide variety of careful econometric studies of cross-sectional data have indicated that the labor supply of black men is more elastic than that of white men See, for example, Cain and Watts (1973). The ready availability of alternative employment in the ghetto underground economy can explain a large part of these observed labor supply patterns.

The impact of the underground economy on family life is particularly striking in American ghettos and deserves more than the single section that we can devote to it in this survey. For a more in-depth discussion of the underground economy in the ghetto, see Ogbu (1982) and the references he cites.

The General Effects of Unrecorded Economic Activity

The underground economy is a source of concern to the general public and to political leaders for three primary reasons: (1) the distortion of economic indicators, (2) the loss of tax revenues, and (3) the possible adverse affects of government laws and regulations.

First of all, unreported economic activity and income distort the major economic indicators upon which we base our policy. Indicators of employment, unemployment, and labor force participation are probably the most distorted indicators. Most of these statistics, such as the unemployment rate, are estimated from data obtained by the Current Population Survey (CPS). We suspect that most individuals who are employed in illegal activities (e.g., drug sales and prostitution), illegal aliens working off the books, and those working in the domestic portion of the irregular economy, will not report such employment to CPS interviewers. To the extent that such individuals do not report, are in the CPS sampling frame (an updated version of the last census), and have no other employment, we will understate both employment and the number of individuals in the labor force and, as a result, understate the labor-force-participation rate and overstate the unemployment rate. Making some reasonable assumptions,[20] we estimate that the labor-force-

[20] We estimate that 2.5 million individuals were actually working in unrecorded "legal" activity or illegal endeavors in 1972 who were estimated by the CPS to be either unemployed or not in the labor force. This is based on an estimate that 1 million illegal aliens are employed off the books or in illegal activities and that 1.5 million U.S. citizens are similarly employed. We assume that neither of these groups will report employment to CPS interviewers. Our estimates for illegal aliens are based on an estimated 4 million illegal aliens in the U.S. labor force with 30 percent of that number employed off the books or in illegal activities. See Simon and Witte (1982) for details. We further estimate that 300,000 to 750,000 individuals had their primary employment in the domestic portion of the underground economy and that approximately 1 million were primarily employed in illegal activities. This gives us an estimate of an unrecorded employed population of approximately 2.5 million in the mid-1970s. Assuming that half these individuals were estimated to have been out of the labor force and half to have been unemployed, the labor-force-participation rate in 1975 was 63 percent rather than 62 percent, and the unemployment rate for that year was 7.5 percent rather than 8.5 percent. We assume that the absolute magnitude of the bias in these two estimates remained unchanged for 1980.

participation rate was underestimated by approximately one percentage point and that the unemployment rate was overstated by a similar amount in 1975. Adjusting 1980 figures using these estimates, we find that the labor-force-participation rate would be 65 rather than 64 percent and the unemployment rate in this year would be 6.1 rather than 7.1 percent.

The estimated bias in the unemployment rate is large but should be treated with considerable caution for a number of reasons. We enumerate only two. First, it is a very crude estimate. Second, as has been noted by the National Commission on Employment and Unemployment Statistics (1979-1980), unemployment statistics are subject to other biases, many of which (for example, counting all part-time workers as employed) cause us to underestimate unemployment. Given these reservations, the bias in the unemployment rate due to the underground economy does seem likely to be large. Others have estimated an even larger bias than we do. For example, Gutmann (1978) estimates that the unemployment rate in April 1978 was overestimated by 1.5 percentage points (estimated to be 6 percent when it actually was only 4.5 percent) due to the underground economy.[21]

Other indicators distorted by the underground economy include the consumer price index, the inflation rate, the gross national product (GNP), and official productivity measures. Since the official statistics will not include the services rendered and goods produced in the underground economy, they will understate the total national output and productivity. Based on the IRS's estimates of unreported "legal" income (illegal income is explicitly excluded from the GNP), the Bureau of Economic Analysis estimates that we understated the GNP by a minimum of $8.3 billion in 1976. This is less than 1 percent of the GNP in that year (U.S. Department of Commerce, 1980). The need for large protection expenditures caused by property crime and the rise in off-the-books activity has led us to understate our level of productivity and its rate of growth. Dennison (1978) has estimated that measured output per unit of input in the nonresidential business sector was 1.8 percent smaller in 1975 than it would have been if 1967 conditions had prevailed.

The purchase of goods and particularly services in the irregular economy means that the consumer price index, particularly the personal and household services portion, is overstated. The effect on the inflation rate is unknown and depends on the rate of growth of irregular sector purchases and prices. We have no reliable information on either.

In addition to its effects on macroeconomic indicators and policies based on them, the existence of unreported legal income may distort

[21] See Berndt (1978) for a critique of the Gutmann's estimates and a thoughtful discussion of the effects of irregular economic activity on labor force indicators.

our measures of the personal, sectoral, and regional distribution of income and, thus, affect our policies toward income redistribution. If, as seems likely, tax evasion is primarily a practice of the poorest and richest members of our society, the personal distribution of income may be quite different than it appears. Middle-class resentment of attempts to redistribute income via taxes may have some foundation in fact since it is their income that is being redistributed to the poor, whose income is understated, and therefore undertaxed, due to underreporting and failure to file tax returns. (We will discuss this issue in more detail in the next section.)

All of the above indicators affect governmental policies, and, thus, the underground economy may provide a partial explanation of the failure of some policies in recent years. We allocate much federal money and social services on the basis of income and unemployment rates. If, as many researchers believe, the irregular economy and off-the-books activities flourish in the ghetto areas of our large cities, on the farm, and among service workers and those receiving social insurance payments (pensions, disability, AFDC, unemployment compensation), then at least some of the funds may not be properly directed.

Some researchers suggest that both the science of macroeconomics and our macroeconomic indices would be much healthier today if figures from the underground economy could be included with those of the regular economy.[22] They claim that the inability to include the irregular economy has led to systematic biases in economic forecasts. As a result, policy-makers are reacting to false economic signals and pushing the economy in wrong directions.

Another obvious effect of the existence of a large underground economy is the loss of public revenue. Indeed, tax evasion appears to be a strong force motivating many of the activities in the irregular economy.

In order to obtain estimates of tax loss due to the underground economy, we require estimates of unreported taxable income. Needless to say, such estimates are very difficult to obtain. We use IRS estimates for individual income tax loss on income from legal activity and Bureau of Economic Analysis estimates for corporate tax loss. For loss due to illegal source income, we combine our estimates of income with IRS estimates of tax and reporting rate. IRS estimates that the $75-$100 billion of unreported taxable income of individuals earned in legal endeavors in 1976 resulted in a loss of between $13 and $17 billion in federal income tax receipts. In addition, using BEA figures, we estimate that failure to report corporate profits accurately and completely resulted in a further federal tax loss of around $5 billion in that year. We estimate that

[22] See, for example, Feige (1980) and Reuter (1982).

incomes earned through illegal transfers and the production and distribution of illegal goods and services amounted to between $40 and $100 billion in 1976.[23] Using the same assumptions as the IRS,[24] we estimate that failure to tax most of these illegal incomes resulted in a federal tax loss of between $8 and $23 billion in 1976. Thus, the total federal revenue loss due to the existence of the underground economy appears to have been between $26 and $45 billion in 1976. These additional funds would have made a substantial dent in the federal deficit or, to look at it slightly differently, could have covered all federal health-related costs for that year. Other levels of governments with income, profit, sales, and excise taxes also lost substantial revenue, although it would be difficult to estimate the exact size of the loss. Our recent book (Simon and Witte, 1982) provides estimates of state and local tax losses due to the illegal alien population and cigarette bootlegging. These losses fall heavily on certain geographic areas (e.g., Texas and California for illegal aliens, and New York and Pennsylvania for cigarette bootlegging).

The growth of the underground economy has led a number of economists and politicians to suggest that the increase in government regulations and reporting requirements has encouraged many people to go off the books and has led to decreased efficiency and lower tax revenues. That government laws, reporting requirements, and regulations cause underreporting is clear. The underground economy would have no illegal sector if we did not declare that the production of some goods and services is illegal. There would be no tax evasion if we had no taxes and no illegal alien problem if we had no immigration laws. The question is: For what laws, regulations, and reporting requirements do the costs outweigh the benefits?

Summary, Conclusions, and Policy Options

The underground economy is a phenomenon that affects a broad spectrum of American life. Its GNP is at least 10 percent of the official reported GNP, and it is growing at least as fast as the reported economy.

[23] We obtain this estimate by moving our 1974 estimate (Simon and Witte, 1982) of the national income of all sectors of the underground economy except federal income and profit tax evasion and illegal aliens forward to 1976. We do this assuming that these incomes grow at 10 percent per annum.

[24] Specifically, we assume that 10-15 percent of these incomes were reported and that the average tax rate was 25 percent. IRS estimates an average tax rate of 25 percent for illegal incomes calculated using the value-added method of National Income Accounting. To obtain our estimates we generally use the incomes approach to National Income Accounting. Neither of the estimates of income includes pure transfer payments, and thus tax loss is underestimated.

Because of its size and growth, officially reported economic statistics—including the GNP, CPI, unemployment rate, and productivity rate—are not presenting an accurate assessment of our country's true economic condition. Policy decisions based on these inadequate official statistics risk moving our economy in wrong directions.

The underground economy affects all segments of American life, especially the American family. Families who participate certainly have more opportunities to raise their spendable income than those who do not. Family members can simply not report some of the income from their regular job or from the rental of some of their property, or they can work at an off-the-books job for which no official records exist. In the latter case, they may be able to work at home near their children in an environment that ignores the industrial revolution's insistence on specialization, separation, segmentation, and inflexibility. Family members who cannot conform or do not wish to conform to the demands of work in the regular economy (e.g., handicapped persons, mothers with young children) may find a more pleasant occupational alternative in the irregular economy.

Those who are willing to work in the illegal sector can find somewhat regular jobs with very high pay, dealing in black market goods and services. The risks of imprisonment for professionals in these occupations are surprisingly low. Like the off-the-books jobs in the legal sector, hours are flexible, permitting more time for family or for a regular job in addition. Those with regular jobs can raise money or obtain supplies through the illicit sector by pilfering at their regular place of employment.

Finally, there are the families of illegal aliens who work in off-the-books activities to minimize their risk of arrest. Many, but certainly not all, of these jobs allow families to work together and provide a better standard of living than that available in their native country. However, such families usually live at minimal subsistence levels by American standards, and typically do not participate in public educational, medical, and social programs. And some end up worse off than they were in their native land.

All families participating in the underground economy face risks of imprisonment, addiction, and emotional and family stress that could seriously disrupt family life. Their participation can also lead to a loss of respect for government regulations and laws by younger family members watching their providers eagerly and easily flaunt these regulations and laws.

Families that do not actively participate in the underground economy are not able to avoid its effects. One the one hand, some families may be able to buy cheaper goods and services through the "irregular economy" or through neighborhood fences. On the other hand, all nonparticipating families will have to pay more than their share of state and federal income taxes or receive government services to make up for the tax evaders in the underground economy. Poorer families are finding that many of the social programs that have supported their family life are being severely cut back as the government reduces spending to make up for lost tax funds. If these poorer families live near areas of intense illegal immigration, they will also find that low-skill jobs are harder to find and are paying relatively lower wages than in other areas.

Many poor families that live in inner-city ghettos may find themselves especially dependent on the underground economy. Some of these families, depressed about the possibilities for advancement in well-paying jobs in the regular economy, or anxious to be "on their own," may turn to "hustling" within the illegal sector of the underground economy to earn a living. In many ways, the underground economy is a source of stability in some of these poorer communities.

Clearly, families that participate in the underground economy increase their disposable income, often at the expense of those families that are conscientiously obeying our country's civil, criminal, and tax laws. Two important questions that must be considered are: (1) How does the underground economy affect the disposable income distribution of American families? and (2) How can federal, state, and local governments correct any inequities that may arise from this income redistribution?

The tax evasion sector of the underground economy is responsible for more income redistribution than any other sector of the underground economy, not only because it is the largest sector, but also because different income groups participate in it to different degrees. As we mentioned earlier, people with very high and very low incomes have more opportunities to avoid taxes than do middle-class wage and salary workers whose compliance is virtually assured by the use of W-2 forms and tax withholding. In addition, people with incomes from rent, royalties, interest, or self-employment avoid taxes most frequently. Tax evasion also appears to rise as the marginal tax rate increases (Clotfelter, 1981). All these facts point to the conclusion that tax evasion shifts income from middle- to upper-income brackets and, to a lesser extent, to lower-income groups.

The employment of illegal aliens also entails a shift upward in disposable income—from lower-income families in high-migration areas who lose jobs or must accept lower wages because of their competition with illegal aliens, to higher-income families who enjoy the lower prices for the goods and services that illegal aliens help produce.

All income classes participate in the irregular economy and in the illegal sector of the underground economy. For example, poor families benefit from these activities by the availability through fences or off-the-books retailers of goods and services at cheaper prices. Some poorer families rely on such businesses for employment and even survival. In many cases, they would not be able to buy these goods and services in the regular economy; so there is little redistribution here. In fact, very frequently in the irregular and illegal sectors, the buyer and seller will belong to the same income class. With our present state of knowledge of just who participates in the irregular and illegal sectors, it is impossible to draw any firm conclusions about the direction of income redistribution that they cause. All one can say is that the families who are benefiting the most from this income redistribution are those who are willing to break or ignore laws and regulations by actively participating in the underground economy.

Of course, governments at all levels would like to counteract the inequities in income distribution that have accompanied the growth of the underground economy. Unfortunately, families that are active in the underground economy are not easily differentiated from their law-abiding neighbors, either by tax reports, economic statistics, or living habits. One possible recourse is to cut back on needs-based social programs, like employment assistance projects in ghettos or other areas where the irregular economy may thrive, on the justification that underground activity in these areas is fulfilling many of the needs that originally motivated these programs. (A similar strategy would be to raise the tax rates of income groups who are more heavily involved in tax evasion.) However, nonselective policies like these, which penalize both guilty and not guilty members of the same group, are likely to be counterproductive. They will send more persons in the group into the underground economy and thus increase the legitimacy, size, and impact of the underground economy, while failing to meet the needs of many for whom these programs were originally established.

At the other end of the spectrum, governments can strive to enforce more effectively the laws and regulations being violated by families participating in the underground economy. In some areas such as tax evasion (the largest sector), more effective enforcement will probably reduce participation in the underground economy. Current evidence indicates that more extensive and effective use of such tools as document-matching programs, withholding-at-source tax forms, and tax law simplification can successfully reduce tax evasion. However, in many areas, the costs of increased enforcement—both fiscal and political—may outweigh the benefits achieved. Do we want IRS agents investigating garage sales or looking over our house-painting or paper-typing arrangements? Are we willing to divert policy resources to increase law enforcement efforts against prostitution, bookmaking, or drug sales? Should businesses in areas of high illegal migration be held responsible for checking the identification papers of workers they hire? Tactics such as these could decrease the size of the underground economy but at a high cost. Before these or other policies are adopted, careful consideration should be given to a broad range of likely effects.

An intermediate government strategy would be to relax some of the laws and regulations that provide incentives for families to join the underground economy. Steps in this direction could range from indexing marginal tax rates so that inflation would not keep pushing families into higher tax brackets (where evasion is more common), to loosening some of the reporting requirements that send frustrated small businesses underground, to legalizing or at least decriminalizing some currently illegal activities (like prostitution, illegal gambling, or marijuana and cocaine use). The goal of the latter policy would be to remove the black market status of certain goods and services—leading possibly to lower prices and better quality supervision for these goods and services and a much greater chance of collecting some taxes from these activities. This policy, however, could have some short-term disruptive effects on communities and families that have become dependent on the high profits that can be earned in the black market. It could also lead to increased use.

As the Detroit study indicates, many participants in the irregular economy are working off the books so that they will not lose their benefits from some government transfer program (e.g., unemployment insurance or AFDC). Officials interested in curtailing the spread of the underground economy would do well to consider ways of offering needs-based programs that minimize incentives to hide earned income.

Many underdeveloped countries, like Brazil, have gone a step further, choosing to support activity in the irregular economy. They find it a valuable source of employment and a place of safety for those who are not able or choose not to cope with a modern technological society. Indeed, many participants in the irregular sector cannot find employment in the formal sector because of unemployment or illegal status; others cannot find jobs in the formal sector with real incomes as high as those in the informal sector. Many of these workers also value the informality and personal contacts involved in their job in the irregular sector; some are ill equipped to cope with life in the formal sector. A policy option open to the United States is one of tolerance or even encouragement of parts of the irregular economy, as some underdeveloped countries have chosen. Such a policy, if carefully constructed, might decrease welfare rolls, allow for more flexibility in family working arrangements, and add color and diversity to a world that at times can be all too homogeneous.

Finally, governments need to be aware of the relationship between macroeconomic instability and growth spurts in the underground economy. There are few sectors of the underground economy for which enough data exist to describe growth trends over the last 20 years. For those areas where it is possible to estimate such trends, activity appears to increase during periods of economic instability. For example, fraud arson increased dramatically during the recessions of 1969-1970 and 1974-1975 (*Business Week*, 1975; Simon and Witte, 1982). Property crime has increased most rapidly in periods of high unemployment (Long and Witte, 1981). Undoubtedly, the use of loan sharks peaks during periods of very high interest rates. Since tax evasion is positively correlated with higher marginal tax rates, it is likely that tax evasion increases during periods of high inflation, when people are being pushed into higher tax brackets. Consequently, any government policy that promotes economic stability should slow the growth of the underground economy to a rate below that of recent years.

As we have tried to illustrate, unrecorded economic activity can have major effects on American family life, not only on families that pursue such activities but even on families that do not. Since concern and information on the American underground economy is relatively recent, most studies of the family have not included these effects in their assessments of the economic and social status of today's families. There is still much that we need to learn and to quantify, not only on the size and structure of the underground economy but also on its impact on the major institutions of American life.

References

Berndt, L. E.
1978 Effects of the Irregular Economy on the Reliability of Estimates of Labor Force Utilization. Paper presented at the annual meeting of the American Sociological Association, San Francisco, Calif.

Boyer, Debra, and Jennifer James
1981 Easy money: Adolescent involvement in prostitution. In K. Weisberg, ed., *Women and the Law: The Interdisciplinary Perspective*. Cambridge: Scheukman.

Briggs, Vernon M., Jr.

1976 Illegal immigration and the American labor force: The use of "soft" data for analysis. *American Behavioral Scientist* (January/February):351-363.

Bullock, Paul

1973 *Aspiration vs. Opportunity: "Careers" in the Inner City*. Ann Arbor, Mich.: Institute of Labor and Industrial Relations.

Business Week

1975 Bad times are good times for the arsonists. February 17.

Cain, Glen, and Harold Watts, eds.

1973 *Income Maintenance and Labor Supply: Econometric Studies*. New York: Academic Press.

Chamber of Commerce of the United States

1973 *White Collar Crime, Everyone's Problem, Everyone's Loss*. Washington, D.C.

Clotfelter, Charles

1981 Tax Rates and Tax Evasion: Analysis of Micro Data. Duke University Discussion Paper, Durham, N.C.

Comptroller General of the United States

1979 *Who's Not Filing Income Tax Returns?: IRS Needs Better Ways to Find Them and Collect Their Taxes*. Washington, D.C.: General Accounting Office.

Dennison, E. F.

1978 Effects of selected changes in the institutional and human environment upon output per unit of input. *Survey of Current Business* 58(January):21-43.

Dow, Leslie M., Jr.

1977 High weeds in Detroit: The irregular economy among a network of Appalachian migrants. *Urban Anthropology* 6(2):111-128.

Feige, Edgar L.

1979 How big is the irregular economy? *Challenge* (November/December):5-13.

1980 A New Perspective on Macroeconomic Phenomena: The Theory and Measurement of the Unobserved Sector of the United States Economy: Causes, Consequences and Implications. Working Paper, Department of Economics, University of Wisconsin at Madison.

Ferman, Louis A., and Louise E. Berndt

1981 The irregular economy. In Stuart Henry, ed., *Can I Have It in Cash*? London: Astragal Books.

Ferman, Louis A., Louise E. Berndt, and Elain Selo.

1978 Analysis of the Irregular Economy: Cash Flow in the Informal Sector. Report to the Bureau of Employment and Training, Michigan Department of Labor.

Gutmann, P. M.

1977 The subterranean economy. *Financial Analysts Journal* 33(January/February):26-27, 34.

1978 Are the unemployed, unemployed? *Financial Analysts Journal* (September/October):26-29.

Heer, David M.

1979 What is the net flow of undocumented Mexican immigrants to the United States? *Demography* 16(August):417-423.

Henry, James

1976 Calling in the big bills. *Washington Monthly* (May):27-33.

James, Jennifer, and Jane Meyerding

1977 Early sexual experience and prostitution. *American Journal of Psychiatry* 134(12):1381-1385.

Kaplan, Lawrence, and J. Maher

1970 The economics of the numbers game. *American Journal of Economics and Sociology* 29(October):391-408.

Lancaster, Claire, and F. Scheuren

1977 Counting and uncountable illegals: Some initial statistical speculations employing the capture-recapture techniques. In American Statistical Association, *Proceedings*, Social Statistics Section, pp, 530-533.

Long, Sharon, and Ann D. Witte

1981 Current economic trends: Implication for crime and criminal justice. In Kevin N. Wright, ed., *Crime and Criminal Justice in a Declining Economy*. Cambridge, Mass.: Oelgeschlager, Gunn, and Hain.

National Commission on Employment and Unemployment Statistics

1979-1980 *Counting the Labor Force*. Washington, D.C.: U.S. Government Printing Office.

North, David S., and Marion Houston

1976 *The Characteristics and Role of Illegal Aliens in the U.S. Labor Market: An Exploratory Study*. Public Document Number PB-252-616., Washington, D.C.: Litton and Co.

Ogbu, John U.

1982 Choice and Economic Reality in Central Cities: Comment on "The Impact of Unrecorded Economic Activity on American Families" by Carl P. Simon and Ann D. Witte. Prepared for the National Academy of Sciences Conference on Families and the Economy, Washington, D.C., January 28-29, 1982.

Parker, Robert

1980 Audit Profits. Working draft, Bureau of Economic Analysis, U.S. Department of Commerce.

Rados, David L.

1976 The numbers game: An economic and competitive analysis. *Quarterly Review of Economics and Business* 16:19-35.

Reuter, Peter

1980 A reading on the irregular economy. *Taxing and Spending* (Spring):65-71.

1982 The irregular economy and the quality of macroeconomic statistics. In V. Tanzi, ed., *The Underground Economy in the U.S. and Other Countries*. Lexington, Mass.: D. C. Heath.

Robinson, J. Gregory

1979 Estimating the Approximate Size of the Illegal Alien Population in the U.S. by Comparative Trend Analysis of Age Specific Death Rates. Paper presented at Population Association of American Annual Meeting, April 26-28.

Simon, Carl P., and Ann D. Witte

1980 The underground economy: Estimates of size, structure and trends. In *Government Regulation: Achieving Social and Economic Balance*, vol. 5. Washington, D.C.: U.S. Government Printing Office.

1982 *Beating the System: The Underground Economy*. Boston: Auburn Publishing Co.

Smith, Barton, and Robert Newman

1977 Depressed wages along the U.S.-Mexico border: An empirical analysis. *Economic Inquiry* 15(January):51-67.

Stack, Carol B.

1974 *All Our Kin: Strategies for Survival in an Urban Black Community*. New York: Harper & Row.

U.S. Department of Commerce
1980 The Understatement of GNP and Charges Against GNP in 1976 Due to Legal Source Income Not Reported on Individual Income Tax Returns. Working paper, Bureau of Economic Analysis, July.

U.S. Department of Labor
1971 *Manpower Report to the President, 1971*. Washington, D.C.: Government Printing Office.

U.S. Department of the Treasury, Internal Revenue Service
1979 *Estimates of Income Unreported on Individual Income Tax Returns*. Publication 1104 (9-79). Washington, D.C.: U.S. Department of the Treasury.

U.S. House of Representatives, Subcommittee on Oversight, Committee on Ways and Means
1980 *Hearings on the Underground Economy*. Washington, D.C.: U.S. Government Printing Office.

Villalpando, Manuel V., Gil Ballow, John Cady, Anthony Pool, Michel Ramirez, Robert Torres-Stanovic, and Spike Steendam
1977 *A Study of the Socioeconomic Impact of Illegal Aliens on the County of San Diego*. Human Resources Agency, County of San Diego, January.

Westat
1980 Self Reported Tax Compliance: A Pilot Survey Report. Unpublished report to the Internal Revenue Service by Westat on Contract No. TIR-78-50.

DISCUSSION

The descriptive material in the Simon and Witte paper as to the size of the underground economy and relative importance of its several components was basically accepted by conference participants with little discussion. The implications of the economy's existence for families with children and for possible policy, however, came in for lively argument—particularly with respect to those families who live in the center city.

Louis Ferman, the first formal discussant, opened the issue by giving his judgment that "a great many value premises and assumptions have been translated into factual statements without any real research basis." The first case in point was the prominence given to tax evasion as a strong motivating force for many of the activities in the irregular economy. Ferman stressed that there are many other functions performed by the irregular economy, the most important of which might be called "social glue." According to his research on the Detroit area, "these economic transactions are really vivifying a whole set of social relationships, creating a community of mutual dependence." The second case in point is the implication—also flowing from the implicit assumption that the participants are largely families of tax evaders—that the moral sense of the children will be undermined and that this will affect successive generations until the whole moral fiber of society and faith in its institutions will be weakened. "Those statements are certainly unwarranted on the basis of any data that exist at the present time." The third case in point is the rather romantic description of the irregular economy as some sort of "neo-cottage work system, like preindustrial societies in some sense." Ferman's research in Detroit indicates that only a small number of such transactions are done in the home and that "to characterize the whole irregular economy that way is totally wrong."

The final point, on which Ferman laid great stress, was that Simon and Witte overlooked the whole plethora of goods and services provided in the ghetto through the regular economy. Income from the irregular economy and income from regular labor market work are complementary rather than mutually exclusive. There is a lot of regular market work done in the ghetto. To advocate policies to cut down on income supplementation programs and massively increase the tax collection machinery in those areas, as some analysts suggest, would run the risk "not only of losing money instead of making it, but also of destroying a social reality that is extremely important in the ghetto."

John Ogbu, the second formal discussant, also focused his comments on the underground economy in the central city—turning from more general considerations to the major and very specific effects of ghetto life and the need to survive on black youth and their labor market aspirations and expectations. His comments thus tie directly back into the issues of youth employment and unemployment (see Chapter 3 and associated discussion).

Ogbu's first point concerned the paper's emphasis on choice with respect to participating in the underground economy or not. Choices about whether to violate rules and regulations, whether to become criminals, cannot be appended to people in the central city in the same way as they may exist with respect to the middle-class and white-collar crime. In some parts of society, and the inner city in particular, such a choice is not always obvious or even possible. People become involved because of social and racial barriers that have traditionally prevented them from working at all or from working at wages sufficient to support themselves and their families. Blacks have responded to this economic reality by developing certain survival strategies, of which the "street economy" is only one. "These survival strategies are various institutionalized ways of gaining subsistence in the central city and elsewhere. They may be irregular from the standpoint of the dominant society, but from the point of view of central city blacks they are more or less normal ways of 'making it.'"

With this as the framework for his argument, Ogbu went on to examine the relationship between the existence of the irregular economy in the inner city and the growth and development of young blacks. The point is not that central city black youths are socialized to be cynical about law and order. "Rather, it is that they are socialized by reality to be disillusioned about their dismal future job opportunities in the regular labor market because of highly consistent pressures and obstacles that selectively assign minorities to jobs at a low level of status, power, dignity, and earnings, while allowing whites to compete more easily and freely for more desirable jobs on the basis of individual training and ability. Central city black parents do not, of course, deliberately encourage their children to become disillusioned about future participation in the labor market or to go into the unrecorded economy. They generally espouse the need for their children to work hard in school to get more education than they themselves did in order to participate in the conventional labor market. However, these parents unwittingly teach their children—through their own life experiences of unemployment, underemployment, and other scars of economic discrimination, as well as through gossip about similar experiences among relatives, neighbors, and friends—that even if the children succeed in school they may not make it as adults in the conventional labor market. Furthermore, these children learn about the same dismal prospects of employment for blacks generally by observing public demonstrations for more jobs and better wages, as well as from reports in the mass media." In this way, even very young central-city black children begin to realize that for black people in America, especially for central-city blacks, the connection between school success and one's ability to get a good job in the regular economy is not good. As they get older and experience personal frustrations in looking for part-time and/or summer jobs, their unfavorable perceptions and interpretations of their future opportunities relative to the opportunities of white youth become even more crystalized and discouraging. Eventually, central-city black children become disillusioned and "give up"; and they learn to blame "the system" for their school failure and for poor future job opportunities, as their parents blame "the system" for their own failure in the conventional labor market.

Ogbu acknowledged the improvements that had occurred in black employment and other economic opportunities structures since the civil rights act of 1964. "But for central-city blacks, these changes have not gone far enough, have not gone on long enough, and have not been consistent enough to change the kind of economic perceptions and expectations which evolved over many generations. It seems unlikely that rising unemployment rates of 17.4 percent among black adults and over 40 percent among black youth will change these perceptions and expectations."

And it is not only the dismal example of their role models' economic and job status reality that has its effect. Learning the survival strategy of the irregular economy requires special kinds of knowledge and competencies for making it that are not necessarily the same as, and may even be inconsistent with, those required for making it in the regular labor market. For example, the skills for making it in the street economy are often those associated with hustling and pimping. Yet there are two features of hustling and pimping that may be incompatible with success in the regular labor market.

One is the reversal of the conventional work ethic. The hustler tends, for instance, to adhere to the principle that one should make it or succeed in getting money, sex, or prestige by not working—i.e., by not holding a conventional job, especially under white employers. The second feature is that to hustlers and pimps, every social interaction is a game, an opportunity to exploit other people for money, power, or sex. And there are only two kinds of people in the game: the exploiters, (i.e., hustlers and pimps) and the exploited or the rest of mankind. Thus, the ethics and world view of hustling and pimping in the street economy may conflict with successful employment adaptation in the regular labor market. Unfortunately, some central-city children begin early to participate in this street economy and thereby acquire perceptions, behaviors, and competencies that make it difficult for them to qualify for and adapt in the conventional labor market.

"I believe that we should make a distinction between people who get involved in the unrecorded economy by real choice (i.e., after considering other options, including conventional employment for which they are eligible) and others like central-city blacks, who may get involved in the unrecorded economic activities because they have no other options. The consequences for families and children may not be the same in the two situations. Nor are the policy implications likely to be the same."

The major addition from the floor was Daniel Yankelovich's question to the discussants about differences between the white and black community in the definition of meaningful work and of preparing for a future stake in society. "At some point one has to develop a cognitive map to get behind the notion of what a meaningful job is, to get a key to the way people construct the path they see for themselves in the future—if we are to break through the vicious cycle of perceiving no good future and, therefore, dropping out of the effort." Both discussants tackled the issue.

In Ferman's view, "meaningful" may not be the appropriate term. A more apposite term might be "secure." According to his research, people leave the irregular economy in favor of the regular economy because the former has no stability. Jobs in the irregular economy do not carry with them Social Security or Unemployment Insurance. Nor, and according to his research this is the most important point of all, do they have health insurance. "Just about everybody I have ever interviewed who was leaving the irregular economy said the one thing that they need, even if it is a dead-end job, is health insurance. That is one of the reasons why I do not think that this country is going to see a permanent cadre of people locked in the irregular economy. It just doesn't work that way."

Ogbu gave a different answer by contrasting interviews he had had with two parents: one was a father, the president of the Bank of America in Stockton; the other was a mother, who has worked in the fields all her life.

"The Bank of America gentleman was telling me how disappointed he was at people in the neighborhood I was studying, who were unwilling to go and work in the fields or do any other work available to them. And he told me about his son, who used to work in the fields every morning. Now, in fact, the son of that gentleman was then overseas training to become a president of one of the branches of the Bank of America. The mother had a son who was finishing high school. People were asking him, she said, why he didn't go and work in the fields. And she said, 'Look at me. I worked in the fields all my life because I had only a second or third grade education, and now my son is finishing high school and they ask him why he won't work in the fields.'

"You see, working in the fields for her son represents no mobility at all. The Bank of America guy knew that working in the field was a temporary thing. He could always move to something else, and this was true of other middle-class people I interviewed. They were willing to take menial jobs because they knew they were not going to stick there and that was probably not what their parents had done. But for people who have grown up with people in that kind of work, it is not meaningful. It represents for them what they have always done, and they don't see much chance of starting there and moving up to where they want to be."

6

The Housing of Families With Children: Basic Trends

JAMES P. ZAIS

Families with children have special housing and financial needs not felt by other household types in the population. They also face special circumstances in the housing market. The most obvious need is for space, because as the size of the household increases, more room—and more bedrooms, in particular—are needed. While it is true that during the childbearing years many households are experiencing growth in income, many others are not. Furthermore, the family budget during this period feels the additional stress of requirements for goods and services other than housing, such as food, clothing, and education. At the same time families with children experience these changes, they may be facing exclusionary practices in the housing market, a phenomenon that has only recently been documented and that will be discussed below.

Introduction

"Families," of course, is not an easy word to define. Some would define it so narrowly as to include only households with a husband and wife present. Others define it broadly, to include all households, whatever their composition. For purposes of this paper, "families with children" are defined as all households with children; it will be clear from much of the discussion that such a universe of households includes wide variety within it. One aim of the paper is to consider whether the presence of children itself is a major factor associated with living in "inadequate" housing, purchasing a home, and other measures of housing circumstances. In addition, I hope to provide some indication of what factors divide families with children who are needy from those who are not.

Many families with children occupy one of several typical life-cycle stages. For the married couple these stages start with childbearing, usually defined as beginning with the birth of the first child and continuing until all children are past infancy. Next, life-cycle analysts have defined a childrearing stage, when children are in their school years. Lastly, "childlaunching" refers to the stage that begins when the first child leaves home and it continues until all children have left (Seaman, 1979).

Each stage has an impact on the housing choices and circumstances of such households. Not only is additional space required, but proximity and quality of schools and recreational facilities become factors in the housing choices as children reach school age. As children become teenagers, the desire for some privacy for them can be expected to increase, making separate sleeping quarters a factor in housing choice. Families, in fact, often choose to own rather than to rent before this point, in part to accommodate the needs of children and in part because of the traditional American dream of raising them in a single-family dwelling.

And yet, not every household with children falls into this neat pattern. Some adults with children never marry, some couples become separated or divorced, some parents become widowed, some remarry, and so forth. The variety of families with children must be taken into account, because, as shown below, it has an important bearing on the answer to the question posed in this paper. Throughout the paper, therefore, an attempt is made to distinguish among families with children on the basis of a number of circumstances, not all of which can be treated in equal detail here.[1]

In recent times, the question of the affordability of housing has been put forward as the most important housing issue facing Americans (Congressional Budget Office, 1968; President's Commission on Housing, 1981). This is not only a result of high mortgage interest rates for homebuyers. It also applies to renters, because many believe the primary, if not the sole, problem facing low-income renters is the high fraction of their income spent on housing. More than a few observers have contended that there has been a dramatic decline in the number of inadequate dwellings since the Second World War. Measures used as a

[1] Although the distinction between one- and two-earner households appears to be increasingly critical in determining housing behavior, it is not treated here (see Roistacher and Young, 1979, for a full discussion of it). We do, however, consider the important differences between single-headed and husband-wife households.

basis for such observations generally have included basic variables that indicate physical inadequacy and crowding.

Although these aggregate patterns are, no doubt, accurate reflections of what has been happening, an important question is how families with children have fared during this period of overall improvement in housing. This topic will be treated below, using a set of standards that include basic structural inadequacy as well as maintenance and operations variables. Throughout the chapter, the important question of the relationship between income and measures of housing circumstances will be considered, and the affordability question will be specifically singled out. Most importantly, we will employ, wherever possible, a breakdown of different household types in the population that will permit comparisons of the housing circumstances of families with children to other household types.

One cautionary note should be made at the outset. The basic purpose of this paper is to present evidence about the housing circumstances of families with children. The housing of various population groups is often analyzed in a way that obscures the distinction between households with children and households without children. Many, for example, concentrate on elderly/nonelderly breakdowns, perhaps because so much of housing policy is related to this basic distinction. Others build their arguments on the prototypical "family of four," with no particular attention paid to additional types of households. One factor contributing to this phenomenon is that data breakdowns reflecting the presence of children require more complex computer programming (when large data sets are used), and the costs of such runs can be prohibitive. This chapter does distinguish among family types and sizes. Resource constraints have, however, limited much of the analysis to bivariate relationships, preventing a completely satisfactory disentanglement of the various housing patterns examined.

The structure of the paper is as follows. The next section reviews some of the basic numbers and trends in household types, particularly to establish the number of households with children. Within that group, basic distinctions are made among single-headed and husband-wife families, small and large families, and on other important demographic characteristics.

Once the magnitude of various household types is established, we have the basis for determining how families with children fare relative to other households. The third section treats several basic indicators of housing circumstances for making these comparisons. First, tenure is discussed, concentrating on the question of whether families with children, relative to other households, are more likely to have become homeowners in recent years. Second, the section analyzes the relationship between household type and "inadequate housing." The issue here is whether families with children are more likely to occupy inadequate housing, therefore deserving some special attention in the formulation of public policy. Inadequate housing will be defined in terms of unit characteristics, for which very good measures have been devised. Unfortunately, suitable measures of neighborhood characteristics—attributes which are important to any concept of adequate housing—are not available. This section also treats the topic of affordability for both renters and homeowners.

The fourth section reviews recent evidence on the extent of exclusionary practices against families with children in the rental market. Until recently, very little was known about this phenomenon. The conclusion notes the main findings.

Families With Children: How Many Are There?

In order to facilitate examination of housing circumstances for families with children, much of this section utilizes the Annual Housing Survey, which, for any particular year, is representative of household types in the United States and can be used to examine the relationship between presence of children and housing phenomena.

Table 1 shows a breakdown of the population in 1977 by household type. It indicates that there is no typical American family. Of the 75.4 million households in the United States, more than half contained no children under 18 years of age.[2] Of the 57 million households with heads under the age of 62 (households accounting for nearly all the children under 18), 27 million contained no children. This represents 36 percent of all households and 47 percent of households with a prime aged head. Although 24 percent of all households in 1977 were headed by an elderly person, the number of these households with children under 18 is small.

Thus, as an approximation, more than 30 million, or 40 percent of all households have children present, constituting "families with children" as defined in this paper. Such households are thus a minority, although they are a sizable minority. The largest subgroup among them are those headed by a husband and a wife between the ages of 30 and

[2] Only children of the household head are represented in these data. Military families living on base are not included in the Annual Housing Survey. The data analysis reported here was undertaken as part of HUD Contract #2882. See Marshall and Zais (1980).

TABLE 1 Distribution of Population, by Household Type

Household Type	Number of Households (millions)	Percent of Total
Nonelderly, with children		
Husband and wife, head's age under 30, less than five children	5.20	6.90
Husband and wife, head's age under 30, five or more children	0.04	0.58
Husband and wife, head's age 30–61, less than five children	18.74	24.86
Husband and wife, head's age 30–61, five or more children	0.79	1.05
Single head, head's age under 62, less than five children	5.09	6.75
Single head, head's age under 62, five or more children	0.22	0.30
SUBTOTAL	30.08	40.44
Nonelderly, no children		
Husband and wife, head's age under 62	13.92	18.47
Single head, head's age under 62	12.95	17.17
SUBTOTAL	26.87	35.64
Elderly		
Husband and wife, head's age 62 or over	8.82	11.69
Other head's age 62 or over	9.62	12.75
SUBTOTAL	18.44	24.44
TOTAL	75.39	100

SOURCE: Special Tabulations, *Annual Housing Survey*, 1977.

61, containing fewer than five children. This group of households numbers nearly 19 million and represents 25 percent of all households and nearly two-thirds of all nonelderly households with children. When larger families are added, husband and wife households constitute about 25 million households, or 82 percent of all nonelderly households with children. Clearly, the dominant type of households in the general population remains the "traditional" household with both parents present. The remaining 18 percent of households with children are headed by single individuals. Such households, 90 percent of which are female-headed, represent 7 percent of all households.

With respect to the number of children present, large families (defined here as having five or more children) represent a very small proportion of all households. Only 3 percent of households with children contained that many children in 1977, and the average size of families continues to go down. The proportion of single-headed families with five or more children is not very different from the proportion of two-parent families that large. In absolute numbers, however, four times as many large families contain two parents as contain one parent, as Table 1 indicates.

Although Table 1 does not indicate historical patterns, we know that the percentage of children living in single-parent households has doubled since 1960 and that the probability of not living with both parents is higher for Hispanics and blacks. In 1977, 43 percent of black children were living with one parent, compared to 13 percent of white children (Wiremain, 1975).[3] Thus, although the number of children in two-parent families still remains high, the growth of one-parent households, especially among minority groups, must be kept in mind when considering the population distribution by household type.

Indeed, such historical trends are very important in anticipating housing needs for Americans in the future. A number of recent trends in family and household formation are directly relevant to how well we are housed. Primary among them is that between 1960 and 1970 the number of households increased by 20 percent and between 1970 and 1979 by another 22 percent. This growth in households held steady over the last two decades despite a slower increase in the population itself. Between 1960 and 1970, the population increased by 13 percent, but between 1970 and 1979 by only about 8 percent (U.S. Department of Housing and Urban Development, 1980). Of course, a large number of these new households do *not* contain children, but they do put pressure on the housing stock that can affect the availability of housing for families with children.

Several other trends are important for the discussion here. On the one hand, there has been a decline in the proportion of husband-wife families with children from 40 percent in 1970 to the 33 percent in 1977 (Table 1). On the other hand, the number of single, never-married people living alone almost doubled between 1970 and 1979. Persons under 35 living alone almost tripled during this period (U.S. Department of Housing and Urban Development, 1980). Marriage is more likely to be postponed until an older age, and the figures demonstrate a dramatic shift in this regard. In 1979, one-half of all women between 20 and 24 years of age had not married compared to 29 percent in 1960. Furthermore, the age of women at the birth of their first child has been increasing. Ultimately, these patterns are reflected in smaller family sizes.

[3] For a general discussion of the growth of female-headed families, see Ross and Sawhill (1975).

The average family size in 1960 was 3.67; in 1970 it was 3.58; and by 1979 it was reduced further to 3.31.

Added to all of this are even more dramatic patterns in marital breakdowns. The ratio of all divorced persons per 1,000 husband and wives in intact marriages rose from 47 to 92 per 1,000 between 1970 and 1979. For blacks, this ratio rose from 83 to 197 per 1,000. For the most part, this accounts for a 50 percent growth in the number of single-parent families between 1970 and 1979. For those with children under 18 years of age, more than 90 percent of such households are headed by women. Put in terms of the number of children affected, this means nearly a 40 percent increase in the number of children with only one parent for the period, even though there was a 10 percent decline in the population below the age of 18. About 12 percent of children lived in such households in 1970 compared to about 18 percent in 1979.

Two other patterns complete the picture of household composition as it bears on housing issues. First, the number of unmarried couples living together—even though they represented only about 3 percent of all couples living together in 1979—doubled over the decade to 1.3 million households. About 25 percent of such couples had one or more children under 14 living with them.

The other significant trend was in the growth of two-earner households. In 1979, more than 50 percent of children in such families had working mothers. The growth of women in the labor force appears to have been a slower process than the other patterns discussed above. In any given year, there has been no more than a 1.5 percent increase. Yet, overall, the change has been extremely significant.[4]

The growth of households is relevant to how well families with children are housed in two ways. First, with more households competing for units, families with children could be more hard-pressed to locate housing of their choice. Second, because of the growth of single-parent households, more children could be finding themselves in a population that suffers additional disadvantages in the housing market. The extent to which this is true is the subject matter of the next two sections of this chapter.

Families With Children and Their Housing

Using these overall figures on household types as a basis for understanding the magnitude of the demographics involved, this section now addresses the key question of this paper: How do families with children

[4] For more detail on this trend, see Smith (1979).

fare compared to other household types in the key dimensions of housing conditions? I consider three important dimensions—tenure, physical adequacy, and affordability.

Tenure

Homeownership has always been the preferred form of tenancy for the majority of American families. Public opinion data suggest that homeownership, more than anything else, is what Americans associate with the "good life." Indeed, public encouragement of homeownership seems to be an irrevocable element of our system, with its centerpiece being income tax deductions for mortgage interest and property tax payments. At various times, political leaders have defended such provisions on the basis of the benefits society derives from homeownership—better maintenance of dwellings, higher rates of savings and investment by homeowners, and even encouraging good citizenship (Struyk, 1977). Recent levels of inflation have made homeownership an even more attractive alternative to renting than in the past. Yet homeownership is becoming more difficult, particularly for low-income, minority, and central-city households. This subsection examines homeownership rates per se, reserving the question of affordability for later.

The majority of American households are homeowners. In 1977, nearly 65 percent of all households owned or were buying their homes. As Table 2 shows, the rate of homeownership has been increasing since 1960, although the annual rates of increase are very small (less than 1 percent). Homeownership rates are lowest inside SMSAs, especially in central cities. Less than half of all central residents were homeowners in 1977, compared to 61 percent of all SMSA residents, and 71 percent of suburban residents. Furthermore, the rate of homeownership inside SMSAs declined very slightly in 1977.

TABLE 2 National Homeownership Rates

Location	1960	1970	1973	1974	1975	1976	1977
National	61.9	62.9	64.4	64.6	64.6	64.7	64.8
Inside SMSAs	58.9	59.5	60.6	61.0	61.2	61.2	61.0
Inside central cities	47.4	48.1	49.3	49.6	49.6	49.5	49.0
Suburbs	72.7	70.3	70.8	70.9	71.0	71.0	70.8
Outside SMSAs	67.1	70.4	72.4	72.6	72.1	72.2	72.9

SOURCE: 1960: *Census of Housing*, Volume 1, Part 1, Table 6; 1973–1977: *Annual Housing Survey*, Part A, Table A–1.

As Table 3 confirms, achieving homeownership is most difficult for households at the lowest end of the income distribution. Households with incomes below $8,000 were the only income group to experience a decline in the rate of homeownership between 1970 and 1977. Their rate of ownership dropped nearly 5 percent during this period. Except for the group of households with 1977 incomes between $8,000 and $11,000, the rate of homeownership increased at an increasing rate as the level of incomes rose. Only 48 percent of households with 1977 incomes of below $8,000 were homeowners, compared to 90 percent of those with 1977 income exceeding $35,000.

The trends in homeownership rates by race are displayed in Table 4. The rate of homeownership for blacks between 1970 and 1977 increased by more than the rate for all households (4.8 percent compared to 3 percent). Despite this gain, the rates of homeownership for both blacks

TABLE 3 Trends in Relationship Between Homeownership and Income

Income Class in 1970	Percent of Total Population, 1970	Homeownership Rates			Home-ownership Rate of Change, 1970–1977
		1970	1975	1977	
Under $5,000 (under $7,000) (under $8,000)	29.4	50.0	48.5	47.6	−4.8
$5,000–$7,000 ($7,000–$10,000) ($8,000–$11,000)	12.0	52.1	56.1	54.7	+4.9
$7,000–$10,000 ($10,000–$15,000) ($11,000–$16,000)	18.8	61.3	65.4	63.7	+3.9
$10,000–$15,000 ($15,000–$20,000) ($16,000–$23,000)	22.6	72.6	76.3	75.3	+3.7
$15,000–$25,000 ($20,000–$35,000) ($23,000–$35,000)	13.2	80.5	84.3	85.0	+5.6
Over $25,000 (over $35,000) (over $35,000)	3.9	84.5	89.3	89.6	+6.0

NOTE: The numbers in the first set of parentheses are roughly the 1975 income values equivalent in real terms to the 1970 income values. The second set represents roughly the 1977 income values. Categories are collapsed at the upper end of the income scale because of the small proportion of cases.

SOURCE: *Annual Housing Survey*, Part A.

TABLE 4 Trends in Homeownership Rates, by Race and Location

Racial Group and Location	Homeownership Rates 1960	1970	1975	1977	Homeownership Rate of Change, 1970–1977
Total					
White	64.4	65.4	67.4	67.7	+3.5
Black[a]	38.4	41.6	43.8	43.6	+4.8
Hispanic	[b]	43.4	43.0	43.1	−0.7
All	61.9	62.9	64.6	64.8	+3.0
Inside central city					
White	50.3	51.3	53.4	52.3	+1.9
Black[a]	31.4	34.8	37.2	36.3	+4.3
Hispanic	[b]	33.0	34.5	34.1	+3.3
All	47.4	48.1	49.6	49.0	+1.8

[a] In 1960, figures for nonwhites are used.
[b] Not available.
SOURCE: 1960: *Census of Housing*, Volume 1, Part 1, Table b; 1973–1977: *Annual Housing Survey*, Part A, Tables A1–A8.

and Hispanics (43 and 44 percent, respectively) were nearly 60 percent lower than that for whites. The rates for blacks and Hispanics living inside central cities were even lower, at 36 and 34 percent, respectively.

What, then, do these trends mean for families with children? Table 5 indicates the rate of homeownership by household type. Between 1970 and 1977, the rate of homeownership increased for nearly all types of households. The largest increase (24 percent) was experienced by young husband and wife households who had a homeownership rate of 39 percent in 1970 and 49 percent in 1977. Older husband and wife households, including those with a head over the age of 65, experienced smaller gains during the period. On the other hand, one-person households under 65 and two-or-more person households other than husband and wife households experienced a decline.

Specifically, the table shows that when children under 18 *are* present, the overall rate of change for the period was about 5 percent, compared to 2 percent when children were not present. Clearly, then, the presence of children did not adversely affect homeownership rates for this period, except for nontraditional households with children. It is not the presence of children but other demographic characteristics—particularly race, income, and single-headedness—which appear to bring homeownership rates down for some households. This is an overall theme in the picture of the housing conditions of families with children that we shall return to later on.

TABLE 5 Trends in the Relationship Between Ownership and Household Types

Household Type	Homeownership Rates 1970	1974	1977	Homeownership Rate of Change, 1970–1977
One-person households				
Head under age 65	33.5	32.4	31.7	−5.4
Head over age 65	54.1	56.2	58.7	+8.5
Two-or-more-person households				
Husband and wife				
Head under age 30	39.4	46.4	49.0	+24.3
Head age 30–44	73.1	77.7	79.4	+8.6
Head age 45–64	80.8	85.2	86.8	+1.3
Other male head under age 65	49.1	44.6	42.9	−12.6
Female head under age 65	42.7	41.9	41.7	−2.3
Head over age 65	76.5	79.8	81.2	+6.1
All households				
No children under age 18 present	59.6	60.7	61.0	+2.3
Children under age 18 present	66.9	70.0	70.3	+5.1

SOURCE: Compiled from *Annual Housing Survey*, 1974–1977, Part A, Table A–1. "Children under 18 present" indicates children of the head of household only.

What about families with children who, for some reason or another, prefer or are forced to remain in the rental market? Some of the current trends in the rental market that face them are well known. For example, throughout the 1970s, the market has been characterized by rapidly increasing costs of operating rental housing and declining tax advantages. At the same time, rents have been rising, although at a relatively sluggish rate. In November of 1979, the Comptroller General (1979) characterized the national vacancy rate as "dangerously low."

What is of particular relevance to families with children is the vacancy rate of units of various sizes. Figure 1 compares these rates for all rental units and rental units with one, two, and three bedrooms. The figure confirms the decline in the vacancy rate as the number of bedrooms increases. Three-bedroom units have a vacancy rate below the rate for all rental units, while one-bedroom units have a vacancy rate above the overall rate. The vacancy rate for two-bedroom units is closest to the overall average.

The vacancy rate for all units did rise from 6.2 percent between 1970 and 1974, from 5.3 to 6.0 percent. By 1977, the overall vacancy rate for rental units fell almost to the 1970 level. The vacancy rates for both

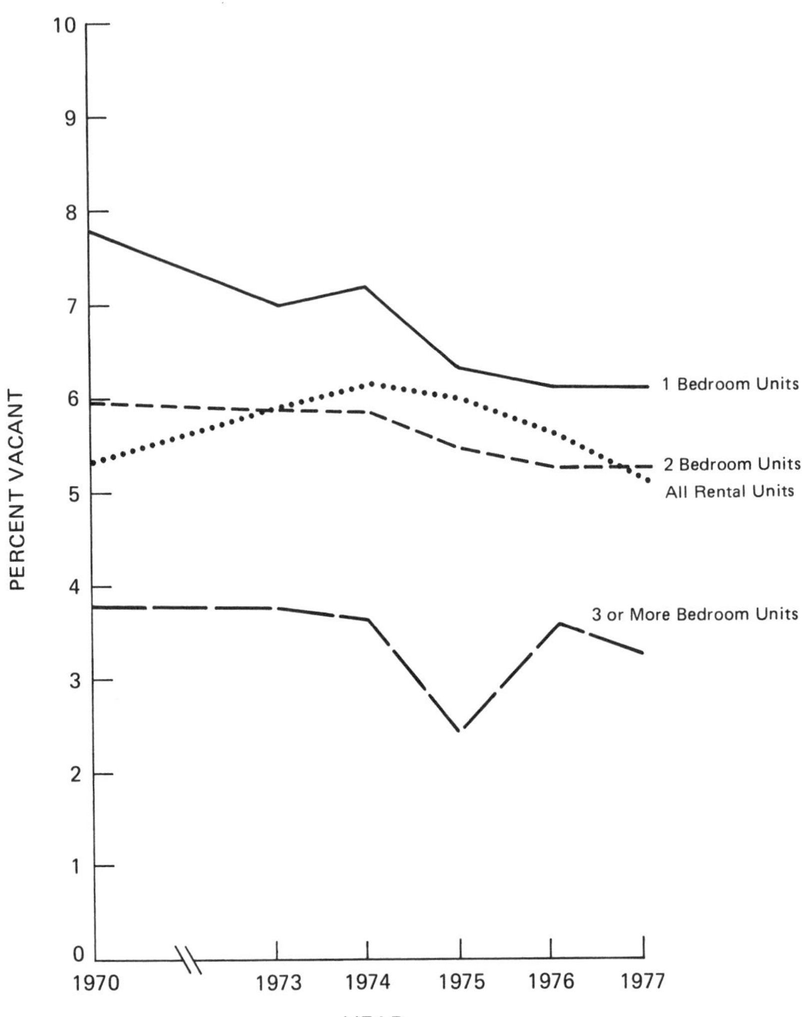

Figure 1 Vacancy rate for rental units by number of bedrooms, 1970, 1973-1977. SOURCES: Bureau of the Census, *Annual Housing Survey,* 1973, 1974, 1975, 1976, and 1977, "General Housing Characteristics" and "Vacancy Rates and Characteristics of Housing in the United States, Annual Statistics."

TABLE 6 Number of Units in Rental Markets, by Structure Type (in Thousands)

	1970	1974	1975	1976	1977	Percent Change, 1970–1977
1 unit	8,530	8,435	8,432	8,477	8,242	− 3
2–4 units	6,218	6,516	6,772	7,116	7,326	18
5–9 units	2,284	2,874	3,028	3,081	3,147	38
10–49 units	4,092	4,377	4,572	4,448	4,683	14
50+ units	2,115	2,299	2,332	2,338	2,460	16
Mobile home	321	545	519	640	657	105

one- and two-bedroom units have declined since 1974, with the rate for one-bedroom units experiencing a 14 percent drop from 1974 to 1975.

There are several other aspects of the vacancy rate problem that are related to families with children. First, low vacancy rates may, in fact, affect families with children more adversely than other households. This was documented (Ashford and Eston, 1979:3) in a study of five California cities, where low vacancy rates appear to have contributed to discrimination against the "less desirable tenant, such as families with children." We return to this topic below. Furthermore, between 1970 and 1977, the number of one-unit structures—those most likely to be of adequate size to serve large families—declined in their actual number in the rental market (Table 6), making matters worse for large households.

Overall, then, rates of homeownership do not appear to have adversely affected families with children in a disproportionate way, except for single-headed and minority households. For those who remained in the rental market, the availability of large units, including single-family houses, appears to have lessened during the 1970s.

Housing Inadequacy

The standards used here to measure inadequacy are based on an earlier study of housing needs, using 1974 and 1976 Annual Housing Survey information (Isler, 1977). The six standards are shown in Table 7, and they include both basic structural inadequacy as well as maintenance and operations variables. The standards used here emphasize physical characteristics. They also indicate the relationship between lower incomes and the probability of living in inadequate housing.

TABLE 7 Six Standards for Measuring Housing Inadequacy

Item	Standard
1. Plumbing	Unit either lacks complete plumbing facilities or shares them
2. Kitchen	Unit either lacks a complete kitchen or shares it
3. Sewage	Services were unavailable or completely unusable for 6 or more hours at least three times during the past 90 days: (a) running water, (b) sewage system, and (c) toilet
4. Heat	The heating system was completely unusable for 6 or more hours at least three times during the past winter
5. Maintenance	Two or more of the following four conditions exist: (a) leaking roof, (b) substantial cracks or holes in exterior walls and ceilings, (c) holes in floors, and (d) broken plaster or peeling paint in areas larger than 1 square foot
6. Public areas	The unit is in a building with public hallways and stairs, and two or more of the following three conditions exist: (a) missing light fixtures, (b) stair railings are missing or poorly attached, and (c) missing, loose, or broken steps

NOTE: A unit is termed "inadequate" if it falls below one or more of these standards.

It is also important to note that these standards apply to the housing unit and the public areas within multiunit structures. They are important aspects of what many would consider inadequate housing, but they are not sufficient because they do not include neighborhood characteristics. Clearly, neighborhood attributes are important aspects of housing, as demonstrated by the role location plays in real estate transactions. But the measurement of neighborhood characteristics lags considerably behind the state of the art in measuring unit attributes, and, despite some gains in our understanding of neighborhoods in recent years, more research is required in this critical area. Using the unit-based definition, Table 8 presents the relevant breakdowns. The following discussion focuses on the most important demographic variables in the table.

TABLE 8 Characteristics of Households in Inadequate Housing

Household Type	Number of Households in Total Population (millions)	Households in Inadequate Housing: Number of Households (millions)	Percent of Household Type	Percent With Income Less 80 Percent Median	Percent With Income 80–120 Percent Median	Percent Black	Percent Hispanic	Percent Other	Percent Homeowners	Percent in Metropolitan Areas
Nonelderly, with children										
Husband and wife, age under 30, less than five children	5.20	0.443	9	75	17	19	13	68	29	57
Husband and wife, age under 30, five or more children	0.04	0.011	25	91	[a]	[a]	64	36	[a]	36
Husband and wife, age 30–61, less than five children	18.74	0.973	5	59	24	19	8	73	57	55
Husband and wife, age 30–61, five or more children	0.79	0.123	16	85	12	22	22	55	53	54
Single head, age under 62, less than five children	5.09	0.662	13	90	7	45	13	41	21	71
Single head, age under 62, five or more children	0.22	0.064	28	97	3	69	14	16	16	66
Nonelderly, no children										
Husband and wife, age under 62	13.92	0.602	4	45	25	20	6	74	46	60
Single head, age under 62	12.95	1.496	12	77	15	28	6	66	17	69
Elderly, age over 62[b]										
Husband and wife	8.82	0.408	5	80	12	24	7	69	67	41
Other	9.62	1.008	11	93	4	26	3	70	42	53
TOTAL	75.39	5.789	8	75	14	27	8	65	36	60

[a] Less than 1 percent.
[b] A small percentage of these households have children under 18.

SOURCE: Special Tabulations, *Annual Housing Survey*, 1977.

Household Type

Table 8 shows that the largest group of households living in inadequate housing are single-headed, nonelderly households with no children—households falling out of the range of those studied in this paper. One and a half million such households, representing about a fourth of households in inadequate shelter, fall within our definition of inadequate housing. The single elderly and the husband and wife families between 30 and 61 with less than five children are the next largest groups of households inadequately housed, at about 1 million (17 percent) each.

Nearly 2.3 million nonelderly households with children were inadequately housed in 1977. Together they represent 39 percent of all such households—again, a minority but a fairly sizable one. Sizable proportions of various subgroups of families with children are poorly housed. For example, 25 percent of households with both husband and wife present, where the head is under 30 and five or more children are present, are inadequately housed, even though in absolute terms the number of such households is small. Similarly, for nonelderly single-headed households with children, 28 percent fail the standard; the presence of a large number of children only serves to increase the probability of such families being poorly housed.

Income

Seventy-five percent of households inadequately housed have "low incomes," defined here as falling below 80 percent of the median.[5] Over 4.3 million of the nearly 6 million households in inadequate housing have incomes below this level. It has been shown that a substantial number of these households are categorically ineligible for federal assistance because they are homeowners or nonelderly single persons (Isler, 1977).[6] Seventy-four percent of all households with children who live in inadequate dwellings—nearly the same proportion as that of all such households—earn less than 80 percent of the median, the measure employed here.

Not all households in inadequate dwellings are poor. The table indicates that 14 percent have "moderate incomes," defined here as falling between 80 and 120 percent of the median. In terms of number of households, the figures indicate that 16 percent of families with children

[5] This corresponds to the definition used in Section 8, the federal government's largest rental program.

[6] Some nonelderly singles are now permitted in Section 8, as long as such households do not constitute more than 10 percent of an agency's caseload.

are in this income range, compared to 13 percent of families without children. Roughly speaking, about 375,000 households with children can be labeled "moderate-income" households.

Race/Ethnicity

Minority households occupy inadequate dwellings at rates disproportionate to their numbers in the population. Although blacks were 10.5 percent of all households in 1977, 27 percent of all inadequately housed households were black. Eight percent of the Hispanic population was inadequately housed while it constituted only 4 percent of the total number of households. For both groups, more than twice the proportion of households occupy inadequate dwellings as for whites.

Tenure and Location

Like the earlier study using 1974 and 1976 data, the 1977 information confirms that a large fraction (36 percent) of all households in inadequate units are homeowners. Overall, 39 percent of families with children who were in poor housing were homeowners, compared to 35 percent of families without children. Thus, homeownership alone cannot tell us how adequately families with children are housed.

In 1977, with the single exception of husband and wife families under 30 years old with five or more children, more than half the families in all categories with children who are inadequately housed lived inside SMSAs. Thus, a sizable number of inadequate housing units exist in rural areas, and this is an especially significant problem in the South (Isler, 1977).

Table 9 shows the location of inadequate housing in the 50 largest SMSAs. Of the 2.8 million households inadequately housed within these SMSAs, more than 64 percent are located in the central cities, even though a smaller percentage (45) of all households living in these SMSAs live in the central cities. Thus, inadequate housing is disproportionately located in central cities. Furthermore, a large percentage of the largest families were located in the central cities—63 percent of the nonelderly husband and wife families with the head under age 30, and five or more children present; 42 percent of the husband and wife families with the head between 30 and 61. Lastly, more than 80 percent of the single-headed households with children who are inadequately housed live in central cities.

TABLE 9 Location of Households in Inadequate Housing, by Household Type for the 50 Largest SMSAs

Household Type	Total Households Inside SMSAs (millions)	Central City: Percent of Households Type Central City	Central City: Percent of Households in Inadequate Housing	Central City: Number of Households in Inadequate Housing (millions)	Suburbs: Percent of Households Type in Suburbs	Suburbs: Percent of Households in Inadequate Housing	Suburbs: Number of Households in Inadequate Housing (millions)
Nonelderly, with children							
Husband and wife, age under 30, less than five children	2.46	40	11	0.11	60	6	0.09
Husband and wife, age under 30, five children or more	0.02	63	17	[a]	37	29	[a]
Husband and wife, age 30–61, less than five children	9.84	33	6	0.20	67	3	0.23
Husband and wife, age 30–61, five children or more	0.39	42	11	0.02	58	11	0.03
Single head, age under 62, less than five children	3.05	55	17	0.29	45	7	0.10
Single head, age under 62, five children or more	0.13	84	30	0.03	16	5	[a]
Subtotal	15.89	39	11	0.65	612	5	0.45
Nonelderly, no children							
Husband and wife, age under 62	7.52	38	6	0.18	62	3	0.13
Single head, age under 62	8.02	56	14	0.62	44	6	0.22
Subtotal	15.54	48	11	0.80	52	4	0.35
Elderly, age over 62							
Husband and wife	4.17	44	9	0.07	56	2	0.06
Other	4.94	55	10	0.27	45	7	0.16
Subtotal	9.11	45	7	0.34	55	5	0.22
TOTAL	40.53	45	10	1.79	55	5	1.02

[a] Less than 10,000.

SOURCE: Special Tabulation, *Annual Housing Survey*, 1977.

Affordability

Much attention has been focused recently on housing affordability. Although we saw that homeownership rates continued to rise slowly in the 1970s, this probably has occurred despite increased hardship on families. The most visible manifestations of the affordability issue are average sales prices on homes, which in many areas of the country have risen astronomically. Public concern has also focused, to a lesser degree, on rent increases. Understanding the affordability issue requires treating homeowners and renters independently.

Homeownership costs are more complicated than the costs of renting and involve payments for mortgage principal and interest, property taxes, insurance, maintenance, and utilities. All these require outlays that are offset to some degree by income tax deductions of mortgage interest and property taxes. At the time of sale, the owner also achieves capital gains. During the period of high inflation in the 1970s, a major consideration for homebuyers were the "less visible" capital gains, while monthly payments that were "immediately visible" captured everyone's attention (President's Commission on Housing, 1981). The overall picture for homeowner affordability is clarified when three distinct phenomena are examined: (1) the net effective cost of homeownership, (2) the cost burden of carrying a monthly mortgage payment, and (3) the down payment.[7]

The net effective cost of homeownership is calculated by taking taxes and capital gains into account. To calculate such costs over time, a constant-quality house is used, and mortgage interest, property taxes, utilities, insurance, maintenance, and repair expenses are summed. Then tax savings and "expected" capital gains (extrapolated from actual capital gains over some previous period) are subtracted.[8] The resulting index shows that for most of the 1970s, the net effective cost of homeownership actually declined. The reasons were basically two. First, in the years following 1970, interest rates were low and expectations of appreciation accelerated. Secondly, inflation put many households in tax brackets with faster rising tax rates, making the tax advantages of homeownership even more attractive. Despite rising prices and costs of operation, the net picture was that effective costs of homeownership declined and probably reached a postwar low in 1978.

Since 1978, the index of net effective homeownership costs has begun rising sharply. Clearly, most of this increase is explained by the disap-

[7] Much of this discussion is indebted to an excellent treatment of affordability in the President's Commission on Housing (1981).

[8] For a complete description of the methodology, see Diamond (1980).

pearance of low interest rates, and current interest rates now probably also include a premium for expected rates of inflation in the future. What this means is that current carrying costs for mortgages are higher, offsetting some of the expected gains in appreciation of housing prices.

One way to calculate changes in current costs of owning is to divide the initial monthly mortgage payment by median family income for a constant-quality housing unit. This method covers financing costs but does not take into account operating and maintenance costs. Even with these omissions, however, current costs rose during the 1970s and, as a percentage of median monthly income, went from about 23 percent in 1970 to about 37 percent in 1980. Thus, although net costs decreased (until the last few years), current costs relative to income increased.

The increased rates of homeownership suggest that households are still likely to accept the burden of high carrying costs if they can qualify for the mortgage at all. One of the greatest difficulties, especially for first-time homebuyers, many of whom are young families with children, is the down payment. The President's Commission on Housing (1981) recently showed that while the real price of a constant-quality home had risen more than 30 percent between 1970 and 1979, the real incomes of young families with heads aged 25-35 had hardly changed (President's Commission on Housing, 1981).

There are several concepts applicable to the discussion of affordability among renters: (1) gross rent changes, (2) rent-income ratios, and (3) constant-quality gross rent changes. There is no doubt that gross rents have increased during the 1970s. In 1970 the median gross rent was $108 compared to $217 in 1979—a 101 percent change. However, the proper measure of rent change is the constant-quality index, which takes the consumer price index and modifies it for depreciation and utilities cost increases for units of the same quality over time. For the 1970-1979 period, the constant-quality gross rent index rose by 81 percent. During the same period, the median income for renter households increased by 59 percent (Lowry, 1981).

What this discrepancy between income and rent changes means is that rent-income ratios increased over the period. The work of the President's Commission shows that, when a longer period is observed (1950-1979), median incomes actually increased at a faster rate than the constant-quality gross rent index. But during the 1970s, the slower rate of income growth relative to rent resulted in some groups with very high rent-income ratios. In fact, almost a quarter of "very low income" households (less than 50 percent of the median family income for a family of four) pay 50 percent or more of their income in rent.

From these data, several broad conclusions can be drawn about families with children. First, even though they are not a majority of households, families with children constitute about 40 percent of all American households. In addition, it appears that the presence of children, per se, does not mean that a household is living in inadequate housing. Indeed, most households living in inadequate units do *not* have children. However, households with children represent a sizable 39 percent of inadequately housed households. Of all inadequately housed renter households, 29 percent are families with children. Of all inadequately housed homeowners, 43 percent are families with children.

Seventy-four percent of all households with children living in inadequate units earn incomes less than 80 percent of the national median. A smaller number of such households have moderate incomes. Being black or Hispanic increases the chance of living in inadequate dwellings, and it also increases the likelihood that the household will be female-headed. Race, ethnicity, single-headedness, and having large families all are related to inadequate housing.

Important for housing policy is the location of families with children living in inadequate housing. More than half of the husband and wife families with five or more children live in non-SMSA areas, but the majority of other types of families with children inadequately housed are inside SMSAs. The majority of large ill-housed families and those with single heads within SMSAs live in central cities.

The net effective cost of homeownership, which declined throughout most of the 1970s, has begun to increase since 1978. The down-payment problem facing families with children has been increasing in recent years; but this has not prevented homeownership rates for such families from keeping pace with those of other households.

Exclusionary Practices in the Housing Market

Until recently, very little was known about exclusionary practices against families with children. Most published findings pertain to housing in individual localities. For example, one study examined such practices in five California cities by surveying rental listings published in newspapers (Ashford and Eston, 1979). Another study, conducted in Dallas, went beyond vacancy listings by surveying apartments listed in the Yellow Pages. It found a sizable number of units where children were either not permitted, or accepted only with restrictions on their number and age (Greene and Blake, 1980).

The first national study of exclusionary practices for families with children was undertaken by the University of Michigan Survey Research Center (Marans and Colten, 1980). Its recent findings are the primary source of data cited in this section. The study was based on a national telephone survey with 1,007 renters and 629 managers. Included among the tenants interviewed were respondents without children in the household (in fact, they are a majority of renters in the sample, consistent with data presented earlier in this chapter). This sample permitted analysis of the attitudes of those without children toward living in apartment buildings where children are permitted.

One result of the study was to demonstrate that restrictive policies toward children go beyond the simple "no children allowed" approach. Restrictions can include limitations on the ages and the maximum number of children allowed, the sharing of bedrooms by children of the opposite sex, and designations of floors or buildings where children are not allowed. Age restrictions themselves vary, such as limits *over* a specified age as well as *under* a specified age.

The managers interviewed in this study represent a total of some 79,000 rental units. It was found that managers who indicate a simple no-children policy represented about a quarter of these units. Another half of the units are under some limitations regarding children. As expected, such policies vary depending on the size of the unit. Efficiency and one-bedroom units are more likely to be governed by no-children or other restrictions. For example, about 40 percent of one-bedroom units have no-children restrictions and 20 percent of two-bedroom units have such restrictions. About 4 percent of units with three or more bedrooms have no-children policies.

Even though strict policies of exclusion affect only a small fraction of the larger units, 60 percent of units with three or more bedrooms come under some form of restriction. Many units, for example, restrict the number or the sex of children sharing a bedroom. Such policies are more prevalent in apartment buildings and complexes than in single-family dwellings. In the former, about 77 percent of units come under some form of restriction, whereas about 53 percent of single-family homes in the rental market do so.

An important question is to what extent these patterns are associated with such market variables as vacancy rates. For example, it was suggested above that exclusionary practices are a luxury that landlords can afford in markets with low vacancy rates. The University of Michigan study, however, found that buildings with high vacancy rates are just as likely to have such policies as buildings with low vacancy rates. Other market characteristics were associated with exclusionary practices. No-children policies are more likely in urban areas than in rural areas, and they are more likely in newer units (of presumably higher quality) than in older units. Perhaps of greater interest is the fact that there was a sizable difference between predominantly black and predominantly white neighborhoods in the extent of exclusionary practices. Twenty-nine percent of units in predominantly white neighborhoods have restrictive policies, compared to only 18 percent in predominantly black neighborhoods. Finally, the trend appears to be in the direction of more rather than less exclusionary practice. By asking managers about pre-1975 practices, it was found that no-children policies covered 17 percent of the apartment complexes before that date compared to the 27 percent found in 1980. In part, this is explained by the fact that many new apartment complexes, at the time they begin occupancy, do not accept children as a matter of policy.

There are two general reasons typically cited to justify exclusionary practices. The first is that tenants *without* children prefer to live in buildings that exclude children. The second is that renting to households with children drives up maintenance costs. The University of Michigan study offers some insights into both of these rationalizations. About 25 percent of renters with no children indicate that they prefer not to live near children, a pattern that was particularly true in apartment complexes. Indeed, some 40 percent of renters in buildings with simple no-children policies claimed that they chose to live there because of those policies. Stated reasons for this preference varied. However, the most frequent response was the avoidance of noise (55 percent cited this reason), and another 17 percent indicated that they wished to avoid property destruction and/or pranks.

Any one of these figures, of course, is open to question and not sufficient to indicate much about the magnitude of the impact of exclusionary policies. However, some have interpreted the figures to "strongly suggest" that integrating families with children and households without children would not be as difficult as previously imagined (U.S. Department of Housing and Urban Development, 1980). An important consideration is how strongly held the views of managers of buildings with restrictions on children are. The survey indicated that about one-half of the no-children managers said that higher maintenance costs were a "big problem." Forty percent thought that noise was a big problem in renting to families with children.

The ultimate impact is on families with children. Almost half of renters with children reported that when they last looked for a place to live and found one they desired, they were turned down because of the presence of children. So far, we do not have systematic evidence of these impacts for a nationwide sample beyond the statements of households themselves in the Michigan study.

Conclusion

This paper has considered some of the general trends in the housing related circumstances of families with children. "Families with children" was broadly defined to include any household with children under 18 years of age. The paper discussed the relative size of such households compared to households without children and indicated the wide variety of household composition for such families.

Using these figures as a basis for discussion, the paper then considered some of the most important housing patterns for such families. Tenure and the extent to which such households live in "inadequate" units were discussed, using information calculated from the Annual Housing Survey. The measures used applied solely to the characteristics of individual housing units and not to neighborhoods. Adequate measurement of neighborhood characteristics remains an important shortcoming for housing analysis. Finally, using recent published data from a national sample of renters and managers, the extent and impact of exclusionary practices for families with children in the rental market was detailed.

The major findings are as follows:

- Families with children are a minority, although a sizable one, of all households in the population. Forty percent of households contain one or more children.
- Most such households are those with a husband and wife present. More than four-fifths of families with children are of this type.
- The fastest growing type of household with children is mother-only.
- The presence of children has not been associated directly with slower rates of increased homeownership. Families with children have experienced more than twice the rate of change in homeownership as families without children.
- Lower homeownership rates are, however, associated with race, income, and single-headedness. Families with children who are minorities, of lower income, or who are headed by women, are experiencing a disadvantage in homeownership growth.
- Vacancy rates for units with three bedrooms are several percentage points below those for all rental units, making it more difficult for large

families to locate rental housing. Furthermore, the trend has been for fewer single-family homes to be put on the rental market.

• The presence of children is not necessarily associated with living in inadequate housing. Most households in inadequate dwellings do not have children. Households with children represent about 39 percent of all inadequately housed households, about the same proportion they constitute of all households in the population.

• Race, ethnicity, single-headedness, and having large families all are related to inadequate housing. The majority of all ill-housed families with children are those with single heads that live in central cities.

• The net effective cost of homeownership has increased over the last few years, with the largest problem being that of coming up with the down payment.

• Exclusionary practices in the rental market include no-children provisions, but many rental units include limitations on the ages and the maximum number of children allowed, or other restrictions.

• About a quarter of all rental units come under a simple no-children rule. Another half of the units are under some other limitation regarding children.

References

Ashford, Dora J., and Perla Eston
1979 *The Extent and Effects of Discrimination Against Children in Rental Housing: A Study of Five Housing Cities.* Santa Monica: The Fair Housing Project, December.

Comptroller General of the United States
1979 *Rental Housing: A National Problem that Needs Immediate Attention. Report to the U.S. Congress.* Washington, D.C.: U.S. Government Printing Office, November.

Congressional Budget Office
1968 *Federal Housing Policy: Current Programs and Recurring Issues.* Washington, D.C.: U.S. Government Printing Office, June.

Diamond, D.B.
1980 Taxes, inflation, speculation, and the cost of homeownership. *Journal of the American Real Estate and Urban Economics Association* (Fall):281-298.

Greene, Jane G., and Glenda P. Blake
1980 *How Restrictive Rental Practices Affect Families With Children.* Washington, D.C.: Department of Housing and Urban Development.

Isler, Morton
1977 Housing Needs and Program Responses. FY 1978 Budget, Background Paper. Prepared for the Office of the Secretary, U.S. Department of Housing and Urban Development, Washington, D.C.

Lowry, Ira S.
1981 Rental housing in the 1970s: Searching for the crisis. Pages 23-38 in J. C.

Weicher, K. E. Villani, and E. A. Roistocher, eds., *Rental Housing: Is There a Crisis?* Washington, D.C.: The Urban Institute.

Marens, Robert W., and Mary Ellen Colten
1980 *Measuring Restrictive Rental Policies Affecting Families with Children: A National Survey*. Washington, D.C.: Office of Development and Research, U.S. Department of Housing and Urban Development.

Marshall, Sue, and James P. Zais
1980 *How Selected HUD Programs Serve the Low and Moderate Income Families with Children*. Washington, D.C.: The Urban Institute, July.

President's Commission on Housing
1981 *Interim Report*. Washington, D.C.: President's Commission on Housing, October.

Roistacher, Elizabeth, and Janet S. Young
1979 Two earner families in the housing market. *Policy Studies Journal* (8):227-240.

Ross, Heather L., and Isabel V. Sawhill
1975 *Time of Transition: The Growth of Families Headed by Women*. Washington, D.C.: The Urban Institute.

Seaman, Jeff
1979 The Changing American Household: The Use of a Household Lifecycle in the Study of Housing Characteristics. Paper presented at the Population Association of America Annual Meeting, Philadelphia, Pa., April 26-28.

Smith, Ralph E., ed.
1979 *The Subtle Revolution: Women at Work*. Washington, D.C.: The Urban Institute.

Struyk, Raymond J.
1977 *Should Government Encourage Homeownership?* Washington, D.C.: The Urban Institute.

U.S. Department of Housing and Urban Development
1980 *Housing Our Families*. Washington, D.C.: U.S. Government Printing Office.

Wireman, Peggy
1979 But that's where children have to live—Using urban social fabric for children. *HUD Challenge*, November.

DISCUSSION

In the discussion of the Zais paper, one thing became crystal clear. If the concern is to understand what is happening to families with children, one will not find out much of importance by probing farther into the issue of housing per se. There are problems relating to housing, but they are basically problems of income, wealth, and neighborhoods, not of structure.

Eugene Smolensky, the first formal discussant, made several important points. First, with respect to the capital market, any market imperfections work toward overspending on housing. "For a market already subsidized from top to bottom and side to side, the onset of inflation and the spread of homestead-tax relief has raised housing demand by more than can be explained by relative prices or earlier estimates of income elasticities. Shelter rose to 16 percent of expenditures from 14 percent between 1935 and 1973. At the same time, food and drink were falling from 42 percent to 23 percent. Expenditures on clothing fell from 11 percent to 8 percent. Of the necessities then, only the share of spending on shelter went up. At least on average, I think it is fair to say that, if children are being traded off in the utility function of households against goods, it's not housing that's giving way."

With respect to the housing market, the poorest housing goes to households headed by blacks, by women, by Hispanics. In this sense the market is relatively perfect: It matches the lowest quintile of housing quality with the lowest quintile of income. "Indeed, if we fix our definition of substandard housing according to 1963 housing consumption levels, as we fixed our definition of poverty according to 1963 food consumption levels, the number of children living in substandard housing has probably fallen faster than the proportion living in households below the poverty level. There is a poverty problem, not a housing problem. It would be a signal contribution if this conference were to conclude that housing is not now and not likely to be in the foreseeable future a threat to the nation's families and its children. Let us get the savings and loan lobby (which has received vast new subsidies in this time of budget cuts) off the backs of the poor."

It was noted in the general discussion, though, that the housing market is not perfect in another sense. There is a wide variety of evidence that strongly suggests the existence of housing discrimination. Whether one stratifies by race or by location of dwelling unit, otherwise comparable dwelling units are more expensive if they are located in black neighborhoods than in white neighborhoods. Otherwise comparable households pay more money for the same housing services if they are black households than if they are white households; otherwise comparable households have lower probabilities of purchasing homes or being homeowners if they are black households than if they are white households. These clearly have first-round income effects and, over a longer period of time, important implications for the sort of wealth portfolios of households in the economy. Since real estate values have risen faster than the general cost of living in the last 10 years, for example, this has meant that those who did not own homes at the beginning of the period did not benefit from this increase and were put at a progressively greater disadvantage in the home-buying market as the decade went on. But this is not really a housing problem—it is a wealth problem.

If there is not a housing problem, however, there is a neighborhood problem for poor families with children, as the conference participants were reminded by the second formal discussant, John Quigley. And this is a problem that has been *aggravated* by government housing policy.

Historically, housing subsidy policies have been supply-oriented; they have improved the housing conditions of the poor by new construction or by the "substantial rehabilitation" of existing dwellings. The administrative procedures surrounding new construction (and the importance of *local* planning authorities) have greatly affected the location of publicly subsidized units, and cost considerations have tended to increase the geographic concentration of dwellings providing subsidized housing to the children of poor families. Thus, in execution, these subsidies have had a strong locational component.

By increasing the isolation of the children of low-income households in particular parts of central cities, this housing subsidy policy has had special and disastrous effects on families with children. "In city after city, the 'neighborhood school' concept has meant that particular schools serve children from 'the projects.' If peer influences matter at all in education, this suggests that learning is more difficult, that levels of achievement are lower as a result of this spatial pattern of housing subsidy. Social psychologists indicate that concentrations of disadvantaged households breed social pathologies—disabilities that may well multiply more rapidly among children and young adults than among other population groups."

In addition to the schooling problem, crowding all these low-income families together has had adverse consequences for employment. The public housing projects tend to be in the center city, away from the job opportunities for the parents of these families and for their teenage offspring—creating a two-pronged employment problem. It has also had adverse consequences simply in terms of neighborhood safety, as Quigley pointed out. "We have this enormous improvement in the quality of housing, but we still have poor people packed together where the most probable problem is you get shot to death. The homicide rate is now, of course, the leading source of death for young black men. What if you did not have that kind of learning—the kind of learning where the easiest thing to learn about is not the job market but the criminal market?"

These observations suggest that housing policies that are at least neutral in their effect on the spatial concentration of poor households will improve the welfare of children. This, in turn, implies *ceteris paribus* that some new form of housing allowance or voucher program would be preferred that permitted recipients to choose freely their neighborhoods or civil divisions. Such a program would tend to disperse the children of low-income households throughout the nonpoor population and to reduce the particular disadvantages of concentrations of poverty. Clearly, housing subsidies are given in the expectation that low-income recipients will improve their housing conditions somehow. But housing is a complex bundle of attributes traded in a complicated market. The problem of designing a voucher program so that it will not rule out choice along some of these dimensions is one that needs hard and careful thought.

Some attributes of the housing bundle, such as fenestration and ventilation, are easily measurable by housing inspectors, and standards relating to them can be easily incorporated into a voucher program. Other attributes, such as the quality of the neighborhood, the local school, and public safety, are difficult to measure under the best of circumstances, and are probably impossible to incorporate into an allowance program. Both structural and locational attributes of housing are capitalized into prices, but only the structural attributes could be recognized by standards in a traditional voucher program.

As Quigley put it, "Should not recipients of housing subsidies be permitted to use these public resources to purchase better, safer neighborhoods and better schools? Even if it means that they will consume housing that is of no better physical quality and possibly worse than before the subsidy program? If the externalities associated with geographic concentrations of low-income households are large, and especially if they have significant effects on the subsequent life-chances of children, the answer to these questions should be yes. And if the answer is yes, it provides a strong argument for the reorientation of housing subsidies to low-income households, from existing programs to demand-oriented vouchers with as few strings as possible."

The other points raised in the floor discussion had to do with the attributes of particular types of housing and how they might be improved to further the well-being of families with children.

The first had to do with the increasing tendency to place "no-child" restrictions in certain areas on rental and condominium housing. This has two consequences. It tends to force families with children into having to own a home; and it makes it increasingly hard for "absent" parents to be able to find housing to which they can take their children during the periods when they are with them.

The second point concerned the disproportionate amount of housing stock in the hands of the elderly—basically people whose children have grown and who remain in the same house even though it is too large for their current needs. According to Zais, even though many cities realize this is a problem, it is politically sensitive and seldom raised explicitly as a policy concern. St. Paul, Minn., is one of the few that is tackling the problem directly, by building new small units in the areas where the elderly live, in the hope of encouraging them to move out of their big houses into the new units. In Wisconsin, the policy response has been the reverse—to help the elderly with their liquidity problem by buying their houses and amortizing them so as to enable them to remain in their houses.

These are policy responses to a problem perceived as an income support problem. Perhaps the time has come to start talking about the appropriateness of turning over the stock. As Quigley put it, "If our elderly population is going to continue to get older and more numerous, isn't there a point where the stock should be turned over to the younger households?" One problem in this connection, raised by Leobardo Estrada, is that zoning has in many areas made illegal the very subdivisions that, if allowed to operate freely, would help reallocate the housing stock in more appropriately sized units. A more effective response from the point of view of trying to match available housing to the current distribution of housing needs, as stressed by Smolensky, would be to make all these illegal subdivisions legal.

The final point discussed was the possibility of redesigning housing so that it would be more suitable (meaning convenient) for the current needs of families. Myra Strober in a previous session had mentioned the housework time that could be saved (in our current society where so many families are either one-parent or two-worker families) if there were sets of units with, say, communal eating facilities. The issue, phrased more generally, is the question of new spatial arrangements and the potential of substituting capital for labor in home production. Quigley addressed it. The statistics on new housing construction in the United States over the last decade show that the average size of dwelling has increased substantially. The number with fireplaces, even multiple fireplaces, has also increased substantially, despite the doubling in the real cost of energy. The new construction market is, thus, clearly geared to at least upper-middle-income households if not higher. The private sector seems unlikely to support the sort of capital investment that would make home production cheaper. The question then becomes: Should this kind of activity be subsidized by the public purse? The lesson from other public programs is that either building new units or reconstructing old ones is very expensive. The housework saved would have to be assigned an extremely high value to make such policies cost-effective.

7

Economic Conditions and Family Life: Contemporary and Historical Perspectives

PHYLLIS MOEN, EDWARD L. KAIN, AND GLEN H. ELDER, JR.

A long tradition of research has explored the economic vicissitudes of families. Studies of the chronically impoverished and those deprived through income loss (primarily as a consequence of unemployment) represent two primary strands of this work. From the evidence at hand, we know that drastic changes in economic status have pervasive effects, touching every aspect of family life. The experience of economic insecurity and hardships can have long-term consequences, not only for the adults experiencing them but for their offspring as well. Economic adversity and adaptations to that misfortune become a legacy for members of the next generation, structuring in turn their options and resources for dealing with adversity, as well as the very shape of their lives.

This paper moves beyond the existing case studies and cross-sectional surveys, which merely document the significance of economic factors for family well-being, by presenting a framework that can be employed to *explain* the empirical relationships detailed in this literature. A life course perspective (Elder, 1975), which underlies our analytic framework, has informed a number of studies of family history (Uhlenberg, 1974, 1979; Modell et al., 1976; Chudacoff, 1980; Hareven, 1982) and has been featured prominently in Elder's (1974, 1979) studies of families during the Great Depression.

The paper is organized around five principal sections. First, we review traditional and emerging models linking economic change with family change, culminating in an overview of the framework. From this, we go on to examine how the specific character of economic loss structures definitions and assessments of the situation, the adaptive strategies and options available to deal with such loss, and the eventual outcomes for family and individual welfare. In the third section, we explore various responses to economic loss, including the mechanisms used by families in an effort to restore equilibrium. Responses include changes in the family economy, alterations in family relations, and increases in the tensions and strains felt by individual family members. In the fourth section, we briefly discuss some direct and indirect effects of economic loss, as mediated by adaptive responses, on the well-being of children. The fifth section presents a historical perspective on economic and family change. In the concluding section, we speculate about some of the impacts of economic change upon children and families in the 1980s.

Traditional and Emerging Models

Economic conditions in family life have long been a focal point of scholarship and public concern. The main themes include: (1) the culture of poverty, which focuses on a relatively permanent poverty class and, hence, emphasizes the stability of family economic conditions rather than their fluidity (see Lewis, 1965); (2) the causes and consequences of welfare dependency (see Rainwater and Weinstein, 1960; Liebow, 1967; Rainwater, 1977; Hannan et al. 1977, 1978; MacDonald and Sawhill, 1978); (3) the varied impacts of unemployment (see Angell, 1936; Eisenberg and Lazarsfeld, 1938; Komarovsky, 1940; Cobb and Kasl, 1977; Moen, in press); (4) the effects of economic decline and family hardship (see Elder, 1974, 1979); and (5) transitions into and out of poverty (see Lane and Morgan, 1975; Duncan and Coe, 1981; Duncan et al., 1981).

In spite of this research, family studies and socioeconomic analysis have tended to "proceed along their separate narrow ways, barely acknowledging the existence of each other" (Rainwater, in Young and Wilmott, 1973:xiv). Most research that has joined these streams examines either the effects of economic change, such as job loss and economic downturns on family life, or the consequences of family change for economic well-being. Common to both approaches is a neglect of reciprocal effects.

Basic to the first perspective is the notion that change originates outside the family, in historical or macroeconomic events (e.g., recession),

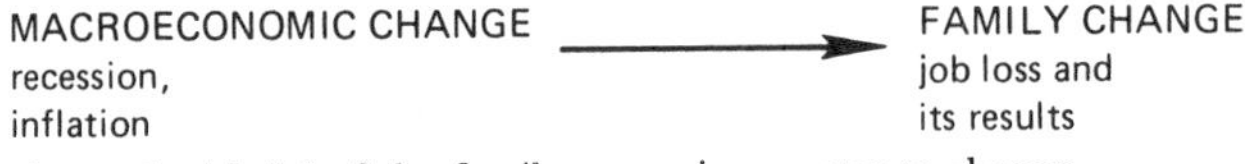

Figure 1 Model of the family as passive reactor to change.

Figure 2 Model of a family change perspective.

soon to be followed by more specific first-order effects (e.g., job loss), which significantly curtail the financial resources and status of the family. The family itself is relatively passive, viewed primarily as a hapless victim of change (Figure 1). The Depression era studies of unemployment are prime examples of this approach.

The family change perspective (Figure 2) treats the family unit itself as a potent force in the determination of its economic affairs. Changes in age structure and composition, for example, can drastically alter the family's financial welfare. Some of these changes are orderly, scheduled, and predictable, such as the birth of a planned child or the launching of young adult offspring from the home, both of which have demonstrable economic consequences (see Aldous and Hill, 1969). Other changes, such as desertion, death, or divorce, are unpredictable and often have still greater effects. In fact, longitudinal analysis of the Michigan Panel Study of Income Dynamics (Duncan and Coe, 1981; Duncan et al., 1981) have demonstrated that changes in family composition have more of an impact on the family's economic status than do the fluctuations of the economy at large or of the breadwinner's earnings.

The life course perspective combines these approaches in a process-based, dynamic model that recognizes the interplay between external economic change and internal family experience. Economic adversity prompts adaptations within the household, including alterations in family composition. These adaptive responses, in turn, serve to modify the family's resources and economic situation, which, once again, influence family decisions (Figure 3). In this manner compositional change stands as both a determinant and a result of change in economic status. Thus, divorce generally results in a lower economic position for children in an evolving one-parent household, and the economic pressures of this new situation may require doubling up with relatives in a strategy of "pooling resources."

An understanding of the financial trajectories of families is best achieved by applying the construct of the *family economy,* which views the family as a flexible unit whose economic status depends no less upon the con-

Figure 3 The interplay of household economic and compositional change.

tributions of all of its members than on the workings of the outside economy. The notion of the family economy stresses the interplay of income change and compositional change. Economic changes may necessitate the entry of multiple family members into the labor market; these changes, in turn, have a cumulative impact upon the economy at large. Thus, a dynamic model of the family economy shifts attention from static concepts, such as occupation or income status, to reciprocal effects between family units and economic conditions.

A schematic diagram of our analytic model of economic loss is presented in Figure 4. Three features of the framework deserve particular attention. First, *process and change* are stressed rather than static "snapshots" of simple correlational relationships at particular points in time. Too much research has at least implicitly assumed the permanency of poverty or hardship, treating economic status as a fixed rather than a variable state (see Mueller and Parcel, 1981). While not denying the reality of chronic deprivation in many families, we believe it is more productive analytically to deal with the *patterning* of financial resources (that is, with their alterations over the life course) than with the fact of deprivation at any one point in time. Indeed, empirical snapshots of families frequently lead to erroneous generalizations.

This perspective argues equally for attention to economic *gain* as well as loss, and the implications of both for family relationships and behavior. However, the focal point of this paper is quite deliberately one-sided, stressing loss rather than gain. The importance of *change* in the family's economic status, rather than the absolute level of financial well-being, cannot be overemphasized. Apart from the undeniable distress of the chronically poor, it appears that the deterioration of one's economic status often produces more stress than the actual state itself (Campbell, 1981). To the extent that this is true, we propose that it is because economic change seriously disrupts customary ways of living and behaving, producing *a new and painful disjuncture between family claims and the resources with which to achieve these claims.* Thomas and Znaniecki (1918-1920) advanced this perspective in their classic study, *The Polish Peasant,* and Elder (1974) used it to study families in the Great Depression.

A number of researchers have examined the relationship between socioeconomic status and a wide variety of developmental outcomes for children. Hess (1970) reviews this research and illustrates the impact of social class upon such diverse factors as parental belief systems about children, parental behavior, children's self-concept and self-esteem, personality and mental health, and differences in cognitive behavior. Hess notes that a major methodological problem in the research is that the definitions of social class employed in the research are often imprecise.

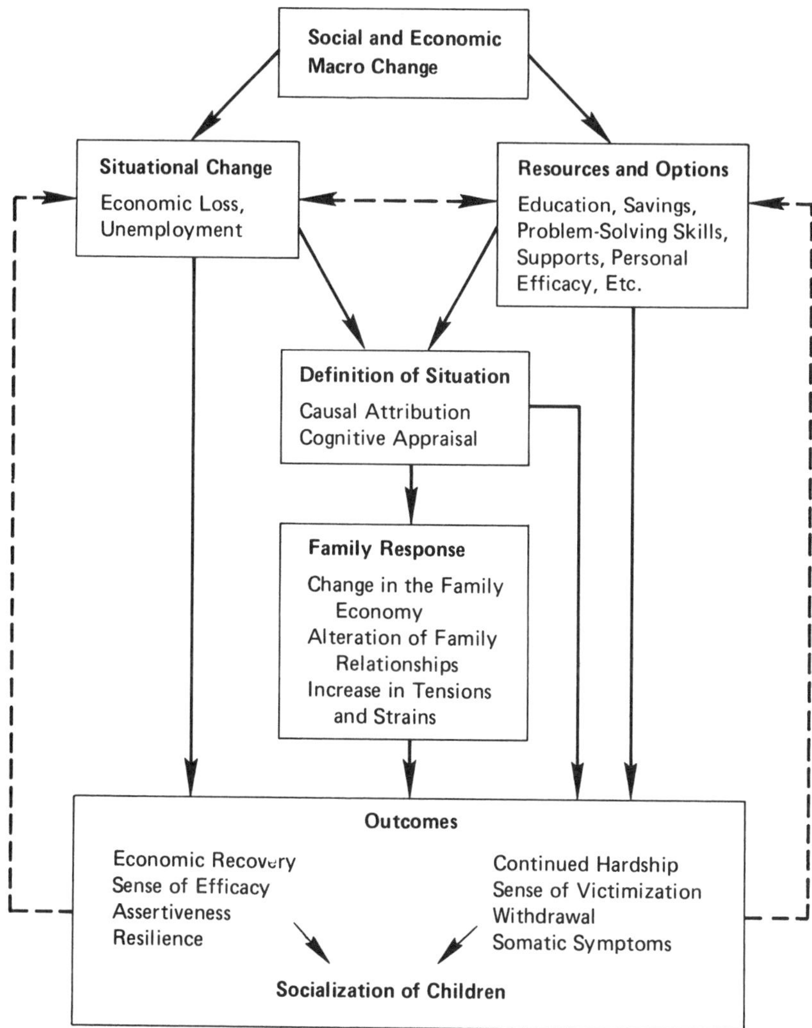

Figure 4 Analytic model relating macrosocial change to family adaptations and outcomes. Adapted from Elder and Liker (1982).

Indeed, the Hess review concentrates upon status dimensions rather than income differentials. Deutsch (1973) adds that a further weakness of the research on social class and child development is that most studies treat social class as a static concept. Our model moves beyond such a conceptualization and focuses upon change in a family's economic status. Rather than concentrating on the literature examining economic *status*, which is reviewed elsewhere, we concentrate here on research dealing explicitly with economic *change* and family functioning.

A second major feature of the model is its attention to *the options and resources available to the family prior to the occurrence of economic loss.* So far, explanations of why some families prove to be resilient in the face of economic loss while others seem unable to cope adequately with the same economic change have proved inadequate. A satisfactory answer to this question must recognize that alterations in the family economy have markedly different consequences for families differing in structure, composition, and career stage. For example, depending on the occupational status of family wage earners as well as the number of earners within a family, the repercussions of job loss can range from negligible to profound. Similarly, the *timing* of economic adversity may be a major determinant of a family's responses to it. Consider, in this regard, that young parents are less able to obtain credit and defer payments than are older couples. Similarly, new child care responsibilities make dual employment a more problematic method of coping with economic strains.

Still another consideration involves the family's past and prospective financial experiences. Recurring hard times in a family's past could lower the threat of new economic reverses, but also reduce the family's resources to survive another round of misfortune. In this case, the family has neither much to lose nor much to sustain it in time of crisis. A family's perceptions and attitudes reflect both direct and indirect experience, as in the observation or knowledge of other families and their hardships or good fortunes. Consider families that successfully avoid unemployment in a high-risk setting. Their sense of relative advantage (Barton, 1969) may be acquired at the cost of extraordinary apprehension and security consciousness, an outlook not uncommon among household heads from the Depression era of the 1930s. The essential points we wish to make are these: (1) the financial memories and expectations of a family are necessarily interrelated—projections are made in terms of the past as constructed in the present; and (2) both memories and projections structure *definitions of the situation* and, hence, determine the adaptive possibilities of the family.

The third feature of the analytic framework is its stress on the critical role played by *adaptive responses as mediating linkages between economic realities and their consequences for children.* Some of these effects are direct and straightforward: A decline in family income and corresponding reductions in consumer expenditures lead to a decline in the quality of life for all family members, including children. But still other repercussions of economic change are much less direct, a function of household adaptations to financial loss. Adaptive strategies are the mechanisms families use to regain control over desired outcomes in the face of economic change. It is important to remember that family response to financial change is itself a process, with different adaptations being played out over time as family circumstances themselves change. The range of these adaptations and their effectiveness can have significant consequences for every family member in both the short and long term. Thus, postponing the birth of a second child may effectively reduce the impact of economic loss, but it also may prove to be the decisive act in forever remaining a one-child family (Elder, 1983). Finally, it is likely that particular adaptations will have different effects on old and young, male and female, parent and child. Maternal employment, for example, has different implications for the husband (more income, greater demands for household participation, wife has more control over income), for the wife (greater independence, heavier time pressures, enhanced self-confidence), and for the children (loss of time with mother, heavier household responsibilities).

The analytic model presented here structures the remaining portion of the paper. We examine the experience and meanings of economic loss, the responses of families to deprivation, and the consequences of these family adaptations. Because of the obvious drawbacks of existing research, we have chosen not to provide a comprehensive review of the literature. Instead, we have selected a limited set of studies to illustrate the processes embodied in family responses to economic conditions. By presenting these studies as they relate, even tangentially, to our model and to our emphasis on change, we hope to elaborate both concepts and explanations contained in the empirical literature.

It is important to recognize that each stage of the model is contingent on historically grounded options and choices. The severity and significance of deprivation is shaped by the historical and cultural contexts establishing normative expectations and alternative strategies. The community and family resources available in the face of economic change vary in ethnic and racial subcultures. The risks faced by families in their economic environment, as well as the resources and options available to those confronted by economic loss, have changed markedly in this country over the last century and a half (see Modell, 1979). The definitions that families and individuals assign to their economic situations and the means they use to cope with them are similarly shaped by the historical period. Thus, observed outcomes and the interplay of economic and family changes in children's lives are best understood within specific historical settings. The meaning of economic loss in the 1980s, for example, is both similar to and different from such loss in the depressed 1930s, a point to which we will return.

Economic Loss and the Situation: Variables and Themes

The responses of families are influenced by the source and severity of economic deprivation as well as by the direct and indirect consequences of loss. Although economic deprivation is most commonly associated with job loss, cutbacks in hours worked and in wage earnings (also by-products of economic downturn) can have equally serious repercussions for families. A further manifestation is the "bumping and skidding" phenomenon (Ferman and Gardner 1979), where individuals experience downward mobility by losing jobs at one level and finding less attractive jobs with poorer pay and lower status. Economic loss is also a consequence of an inflationary economy where earnings do not keep pace with the cost of living. Moreover, even when the family's financial resources do not suffer, the *anticipation* of job and/or income loss may well be as influential as actual deprivation in fostering internal family strains. Hansen and Johnson (1979) emphasize the role of heightened ambiguity in promoting stress. We should be concerned, therefore, not only with the *fact* of economic reverses but also with the insecurity that comes from the *expectation* of loss of roles and/or resources. Both conditions may lead to the same kinds of family adaptations—the use of multiple earners, reduction of expenditures, changes in family planning, etc.

Differential risk of job loss and economic setbacks represents one of the most firmly established generalizations about economic pressures and family life. Historically this risk has been disproportionately experienced by the semiskilled and unskilled workers. Those with little seniority or job experience also rank high on vulnerability in an economic downturn. For the most part these are the workers with young children. A study of the 1975 recession (Moen, 1978) found that young families with preschool children were most likely to have an unemployed breadwinner. Fathers in two-parent families were more likely than single-parent mothers to become unemployed, since the latter tend to leave the labor market and go on welfare rather than define themselves as unemployed.

Job loss in the recession led to income loss, despite the support of unemployment insurance. The duration of unemployment among breadwinners during the 1975 recession was a major factor in determining the chances of a substantial loss of income (Moen, in press). Families with teenagers were more likely than families with younger children to have a reduced income, very probably because these are higher-income families that have more to lose before they reach the "cushion" of unemployment insurance or welfare payments. Such differences tell us something about family resources and adaptations, as does the contrast between the responses of male and female heads of households to job loss. Though male heads of households have the lowest unemployment rate of any demographic group, they also represent the highest proportion of the long-term jobless population (Flaim and Gellner, 1972). Unlike female heads, these men tend to stay in the labor force and persist in the job search following unemployment. Recent studies, including analyses by the Department of Labor, generally stress the need to examine *family* aspects of unemployment rather than simply aggregate rates (Hayghe, 1976, 1981; Moen, 1980a). By doing so we rediscover the family economy model. Families move in and out of poverty; individuals move in and out of employment and unemployment, with consequences for all family members.

Whether or not job loss results in poverty depends on both the duration of joblessness and on who in the family is unemployed. Hayghe (1979) found that, while nearly one in four husband-wife families were touched by unemployment in 1977, only one family member was jobless at any given time in most cases. When the wife or adolescent child is unemployed, the husband is usually working full time, so the financial costs of unemployment are not devastating. When the husband is laid off, on the other hand, the wife's employment and that of older children can become essential to make ends meet. The employment of wives contributes, on the average, 26 percent of the family income (U.S. Department of Labor, 1981). Less than 2 percent of two-earner families report incomes falling below the poverty level (Hayghe, 1981). Those two-income families who are in poverty tend to have earners working fewer hours than those in nonpoor families. Families with a second earner clearly are better able to adapt to economic loss than are single-earner families. Women heading families earn less, and they also have no mechanism, short of welfare and kin support, to supplement their earnings. The flexibility of the family economy is curtailed drastically when only one adult is present.

This point gains importance from three empirical observations: (1) the large income differential between two-parent households with children and one-parent households (Bianchi, 1981); (2) the substantial racial difference in children's living arrangements—12 percent of white children in 1976 resided in female-headed households, in comparison to 44 percent of black children; and (3) projections based on children born in 1975-1979 to members of the Michigan Panel Study indicating that the number reaching age 17 *without* two natural parents present is 40 percent for all white children and nearly twice that figure for all black children (Hofferth, 1981). This startling contrast provides additional incentive for thoughtful studies of the black extended family network (Shimkin et al., 1978) as an adaptive resource for single-parent households. In addition, it is important that research begin to examine the other institutional resources available in the black community, such as black churches, which can provide support in hard times.

It is important, from a perspective of change, to distinguish between those who may experience poverty or income loss at particular points in time from those who are persistently disadvantaged. Duncan et al. (1981) used the Michigan Panel data (PSID) to analyze short- and long-term poverty between the first 5 years of the survey (1969-1973) and the second 5 years (1974-1978). Economic conditions during these two periods differed considerably, with the second marked by both inflation and recessionary trends. The analysis found nearly identical proportions of families who were poor at least 1 of the 5 years in each period (17.5 percent in the first and 16.6 percent in the second 5 years). During 1969-1973 less than *2 percent* were continuously in poverty (all 5 years) and less than *4 percent* were poor every year from 1974 through 1978. The chronically poor were principally in black households and in families headed by women. More than 60 percent were black women heading their own families. Looking at the combined 10-year period, the study found a surprisingly high proportion of families in poverty at least 1 year. In fact, approximately *25 percent* of the population had incomes below the poverty level at least 1 year in the 10 years under study.

Changes in family composition—divorce, death, the launching of a child—almost invariably result in major changes in economic status. In addition to being affected by the peaks and troughs of the national economy, families also experience good times as well as hardships at *various* periods of the life course. Changes in family economic well-being are linked to the number of earners within a family and to their wage rates, as well as to the number and ages of children and other dependents. The complexity of these reciprocal relationships between family and economic change involves relations among individual life transitions, family composition, and historical conditions.

The nature of economic change, its severity and duration, serve to establish the context in which family adaptive responses are played out. It is clear that the *timing* of economic loss affects its consequences; young families are less likely than more established ones to have the resources to cope effectively with adversity. Moreover, adverse economic events tend to be concentrated in the first half of the adult life course (Pearlin et al., 1981). Yet it is also clear that most families do not remain static, but move in and out of economic hardship as their external and internal circumstances change. The implications of this movement and the family adaptations associated with it remain to be investigated in a comprehensive way. An important mediator between changing economic circumstances and family adaptations is the definition of the situation subscribed to by family members.

Definitions of the Situation

The most common types of family coping involve changes in the definitions of events (Pearlin and Schooler, 1978). Members experiencing income or job loss may engage in avoidance by selectively ignoring the seriousness of certain aspects of their situation, or they may "count their blessings," comparing their own experience with the plight of others who are even less fortunate. Another way of controlling the meaning of a problem is by devaluing the role or resource that is lost. The job or income may be claimed as not that important, or other rewards may be substituted for those no longer available. For example, nearly half of a sample of technical-professional men laid off in aerospace-defense-electronics industries in the early 1970s expressed positive attitudes toward their job loss, describing it as "not such a bad break" (Little, 1976). This positive reaction probably reflected the existence of financial reserves and perceptions of the opportunities available to middle-class professionals seeking reemployment in the early 1970s. Definitions that assign meaning to a situation are one route by which families can seek to "control" economic loss.

What individuals bring to the experience of economic hardship, in terms of personal values as well as assets and liabilities, affects both their options in the face of misfortune and their appraisal of the situation. The larger the objective severity of economic loss, the greater the likelihood of a gap between values/expectations and actual family behavior. One resource that has important family consequences is a sense of personal efficacy. Whether or not individuals feel in control of their lives inevitably shapes how they define the situation.

Campbell (1981) distinguishes between objective *welfare*, which essentially represents a sufficient income, and *well-being*, or an orientation toward and satisfaction with the quality of one's life. Welfare and well-being are not isomorphic; one does not necessarily follow the other. Analysis of large-scale surveys by the University of Michigan's Institute for Social Research documents an *uncertain* relationship between objective conditions and subjective experiences (Campbell, 1981:221):

> Feelings of well-being or ill-being are not determined exclusively either by the circumstances people find themselves in or by their own expectations,

attitudes or other personal traits. Economic position, marital status, good or bad health, employment or unemployment, and other conditions of life have clearly visible association with the way people evaluate their lives, but in no case do they account for a major part of this evaluation.

In these surveys, both low income and unemployment were found to be associated with a reduced sense of control over one's life, which, in turn, diminished reports of happiness and positive experiences. Thus, it would seem that objective conditions affect subjective feelings of well-being indirectly, through altering a sense of personal efficacy. The complexity of these relationships requires more attention to specific relations among personal efficacy, subjective orientations, objective economic conditions, and family adaptations within a model of economic change.

One method of evaluating the effects of objective versus subjective loss is to examine loss relative to social position; the meaning of a loss (say 30 percent) varies according to the family's initial position. As Elder (1974, 1982) documents in his longitudinal study of Depression era families, the meaning of income loss depended on the class-related living style and expectations of families before the 1930s. Compared to the working class, middle-class families had more in terms of coping resources, but they also had more to lose and more invested in the social status conferred by income. Appearances mattered (Elder, 1974:53). A middle-aged woman recalled that her father was "extremely stingy in providing her mother with food and clothing money, and yet spent what seemed at the time to be a huge sum of money painting the house because 'everybody could see that.'" Severe hardships were commonplace in the life histories of working-class families, and in this sense they were prepared for more of the same in the 1930s. However, they did not have the reserves to fall back upon as hard times became bad times.

Income loss also carried different meanings for men and women during the 1930s. To men, loss of income and job directly threatened their social standing, family authority, and identity in the cultural role of breadwinner. Such change did not imply personal responsibility for women. Their social importance increased as their husband's position diminished. More often than not, wives and mothers rose to the occasion, playing a vital role in the family's effort to cope with deprivation. Especially in the middle class, wives survived the hard times with greater resourcefulness and resilience (Elder, 1982), a picture that remains even in old age. By comparison, the Depression's toll in the poor health and impairment of men was large during the 1930s and persisted through the later years.

Family career stage is another important factor in defining hard times. Families with child care obligations and constraints are likely to view children as a burden; families with adolescents, on the other hand, may find their children an asset, since adolescents can manage the household while the mother is employed or earn extra income by working part time. Both objective conditions of hardship and the resources and predispositions brought to those conditions influence perceptions of the situation. All three sets of factors, in turn, structure a family's response to economic loss.

Family Response to Economic Loss

Families respond to economic pressure by restructuring roles and resources, as well as by reappraising both the present situation and prospects for the future. Families may adjust to economic loss by altering the family economy, by modifying family relationships, or by increasing the strains and tensions felt by individual family members. Some of these alterations are adaptive coping strategies, while others (such as violence or drinking) may release pressure without ameliorating the situation. Pearlin and Schooler (1978:2) define coping as "any response to external lifestrains that serves to prevent, avoid, or control emotional distress." Coping behavior, they suggest, can take three forms: eliminating or modifying problematic conditions, reducing or controlling the meaning of those conditions, or managing suffering or other emotional consequences. Changing the family economy can be viewed as an effort to eliminate or modify the problem of economic hardship. Altering family relationships can become a way of controlling the effects of economic loss or managing their emotional consequences.

Within our model, all categories of family responses are interdependent. Changes in the family economy, such as the wife's entry into the labor force, have direct implications for relationships within the family. The increased economic role of the wife changes the balance of power in marital roles, just as the entry of children into the labor force would alter their status in the family. These shifts, in turn, may result in strains and conflicts within the family unit and increased amounts of tension experienced by individual family members. The interdependence of changes in the family economy, on the one hand, and changes in family relationships and strains, on the other, underscores the contingency between deprivational consequences for parents and children and the particular adaptations chosen.

Family adaptations to economic loss reflect a series of strategies, a process rather than a single event. Different adaptations are utilized over time, as illustrated by Bakke's study of the response of families during the Great Depression (Bakke, 1940). The combination of adaptive strategies employed by families represents the process by which the family unit attempts to regain control over desired outcomes. The match between resources and claims is thrown out of balance by economic change; it is through a series of adaptations that families recover a state of balance.

All lines of adaptation followed by a family are patterned by historically structured options, as well as by the family's stage and resources at the time. Social trends and forces determine the options and choices available for family action (Elder, 1981a). For example, today's child labor laws limit the possibility of young children's employment as a response to economic adversity.

Three Adaptations in the Family Economy

Adaptations to economic loss can be divided into three broad categories: financial transactions, changes in the operations of the household (such as economizing or having the wife enter the labor force), and compositional change.

(a) *Financial Transactions*. Families faced with income loss may attempt to maintain their standard of living by using alternative sources of income. Borrowing from relatives, dipping into savings, using credit, and bank loans are strategies that can tide the family over in the short term. Social insurance, in the form of unemployment benefits, operates in a similar fashion to enable the family to endure a period of economic hardship. But not all families have the cushion of social insurance or other forms of public assistance. Moen's study (in press) of unemployed breadwinners in the 1975 recession found that unemployment compensation was received by less than half (47 percent) of the families of the unemployed and welfare benefits (AFDC) by only 5 percent. Where it was provided, unemployment compensation softened the economic blow of joblessness; more than 72 percent of those families whose breadwinner was unemployed 15 weeks or more and who had avoided an economic crisis were receiving unemployment insurance.

Working-class families are less likely than those of the middle class to have a reserve of savings or access to credit and loans (Fried, 1973). Similarly, they are less likely to be covered by unemployment insurance. The pooling of resources by families and communities is one strategy that can help families cope with economic adversity. This informal pooling of resources may be used by families who lack institutional supports (Stack, 1977), but, unless the period of economic dislocation is brief, these stop-gap financial supports must be replaced by other lines of adaptation that either reduce expenditures or increase income.

(b) *Household Operations to Make Ends Meet.* Changes in the operations of the household can range from a reduction in expenditures, to less buying of services, to a more labor intensive and multiple earner household. Budgetary reductions often involve a redefinition of "necessities" as optional and the deferral of expenditures. Particularly problematic, in this regard, are decisions to postpone medical services, including preventative medical and dental checkups for children. Generating alternative forms of income can be achieved through the use of multiple earners, the selling of assets, or receipt of welfare payments.

In addition to redefining necessities, families may improve the efficiency with which resources are managed. The magnitude of economic loss, as well as the financial resources available at the time of loss, however, have a major impact upon both the possibility of redefining what is a necessity and of improving management of resources. If a family is already at a subsistence level, belts cannot simply be tightened to weather the period of loss. Families faced with such a situation may be forced to decide which of their essential resources will be the first to be forfeited.

It is obvious that the adaptive strategies families employ are contingent on the resources they bring to the hardship situation. Single-parent families, for example, are unlikely to have an additional earner in the household. Middle-class families and homeowners are more likely than working-class families and renters to have a reserve of savings and other assets that could enable them to weather hard times. Lower-class families with few resources, on the other hand, are prime candidates for public assistance through income transfers. Career status, stage of parenthood, and class position are all associated with the particular resources and orientations that serve to structure these changes in the family economy.

(c) *Compositional Change.* Change in household composition is integrally related to change in the family economy. The absolute size of the household directly determines the number of people who can contribute to the family economy. Some compositional changes are incremental, involving marriage or remarriage, births, the addition of boarders or lodgers, and relatives as either hosts or guests in the household. Other compositional shifts are decremental (such as death, divorce, and separation, as well as the departure of family members to start their own households). Both incremental and decremental changes directly alter the pool of potential contributors to the family economy. At the same time, the birth of children or the death of elderly dependents alters the ratio of nonproductive to productive members within the household unit, thus affecting its ability to balance needs and resources.

Incremental changes in household composition are often much more open to planning and control by family members. Thus, the demands of the economic environment impinging on the family may stimulate decisions about compositional change—such as the delayed marriage of children in order to retain them in the family economy or fertility limitations to hold down the number of dependent members. Families also may have to double up in the face of economic setbacks and/or support their children for longer periods of time. Caplovitz (1979) found, for example, that 12 percent of the families he interviewed during the 1974-1975 recession had children staying at home who otherwise would have moved out. During times of economic adversity, dependent children may also be sent to the homes of kin who are more able to support them.

Overall, adaptations in the family economy may alter the *timing* or scheduling of family events and processes in ways that affect family composition (delay of marriage and childbearing) and *accentuate* existing preconditions (increasing economic strain) that lead to family separations (Elder, 1983). Theories of fertility have long included an economic component. In studies of Depression families, Elder (1974, 1983) has documented the decision to postpone or never have a second child among families that were hardpressed during the 1930s. Among adolescent children, Depression hardship tended to accelerate entry into the field of adult-life responsibilities.

The acceleration effect is suggested by Caplovitz's (1979) distinction concerning the differential effects of economic change on poor, blue-collar, and middle-class families. Inflation places poor families in an intense struggle for survival; their concern is with getting by today, not with the future. Blue-collar families may postpone some plans and curtail consumption. Middle-class families may not suffer immediately but see long-range plans to improve their lot in life being undermined.

The decisions families make in the face of economic decline can have temporary as well as enduring repercussions. Strategies beneficial to the family as a whole may have negative or, at least, far-ranging outcomes for particular family members. A more labor intensive household, for instance, has enormous implications (higher time, labor, and management demands) for the lives of women as does the decision of a wife to enter the labor force (Bennett and Elder, 1979). What seems beneficial in the short run may have negative implications for the family's future way of life. For example, financial strategies, resulting in the depletion of savings or spiraling indebtedness can, in effect, mortgage the family's financial future. The curtailment of expenditures and the entry of the wife, and possibly children, into the labor force are adaptations that impinge directly on family relationships, a domain of profound significance for the well-being of children.

All three types of adaptations (financial transactions, operations to make ends meet, and compositional change) are commonly seen as family responses coordinated by the unit itself. In this view, the family unit through the head's influence regulates the behavior of each member in a united effort. Coordination may also be achieved through prominent members of the kin system (Shimkin et al., 1978:290). A black woman describes her mother's role as leader of the extended family in Los Angeles by noting that "she takes care of the needs of our relatives." Her mother brought kin to the local church and related activities. "When a friend of the family dies, it is usually my mother who represents the family at the funeral. She is usually instrumental in getting legal advice for the family, too. My father helps her in her role as the 'leader.' Note how my father helped some of the relatives to land on jobs. They all come to my parents for advice."

Alterations in Family Relationships

The alterations in relationships among family members in response to economic loss can range from relatively minor shifts in decision-making power from husband to wife to major breaks, such as desertion, separation, and divorce. The patterns of family interaction existing prior to the deprivation event are a particularly critical determinant of subsequent family relations. This conclusion is documented by Angell's (1936) study of unemployment during the Great Depression. Integrated families, that is, families with strong bonds of common interests and affection as well as a sense of economic interdependence, were most successful in adapting to income loss. Similarly, Cavan and Ranck's (1938) study of working-class families during this same historical period found that well-organized families (e.g., those with a high degree of unity) tended to recover from unemployment more united than before, while disorganized families were likely to become even more fragmented. Still another Depression study (Komarovsky, 1940) found that unemployed husbands maintained power within the family when affection and high esteem were displayed by other family members.

Changes in family relationships can take at least two forms: Existing affiliations may be maintained but strained, or family members may alter their established roles in response to their economic pressure. There are three dyadic relationships in the traditional nuclear family (and two in the single-parent family) to consider: husband-wife, parent and child, and sibling relations. Dyadic relations are often best illuminated within the context of a triad (Bronfenbrenner, 1979), since alterations in one set of role relationships inevitably influence others. However, brevity considerations restrict our coverage to the three basic units.

(a) *The Conjugal Relationship.* Deprivational effects in marriage depend on the causes as well as the duration and severity of the hardship. Income loss may result from the job loss of husband or wife, from the departure of an employed older son or daughter, or from a lower return on investments. Each event implies different consequences for marital relations, though reliable empirical evidence is sparse. Case studies from the 1930s amply reveal the marital strains of unemployment and income loss (Cavan and Ranck, 1938; Komarovsky, 1940). However, adversity can also serve as a unifying force, drawing the couple closer together in mutual support (Gore, 1978). This may account for the unexpected conclusion of a study of marginally employed men (Brinkeroff and White, 1978) that neither low income nor unemployment adversely influenced their marital satisfaction. This interpretation is also supported by a pilot study of families (Root, 1977) who experienced a plant closing in the 1970s. A majority of the wives believed that the closing was not a completely negative event, since it brought many couples together.

Both stronger and weaker marital ties under economic pressure are consistent with an *accentuation* hypothesis that stresses the importance of initial states. Hard times are not always bad times in marriage. Weak marriages tend to disintegrate when times are difficult; strong marriages gain renewed vitality and resilience under the same circumstances. A quality marriage provides "the resources, communications and socially transmitted values that facilitate adaptation," to cite Susan Gore's (1978:2) definition of social support. Gore distinguishes between person-oriented and task-oriented dimensions of support, one providing emotional assurance and the second instrumental assistance. Both kinds of support are likely to appear when a stable, nurturant marriage is put to a test by economic pressure.

The most visible change in family structure is separation or divorce. Marital disruption is not an adaptive strategy in the sense of improving the family economy; rather, it represents the *failure* of the household to function as a viable economic unit. Studies confirm the relationship between unemployment, low income, and marital dissolution. Separation rates are twice as high among families where the husband is unemployed as in those experiencing stable employment (Ross and Sawhill, 1975). Similarly, low income also has been correlated with marital instability (Cutright, 1971). What remains unclear is the relative importance of job loss versus income loss and the process by which they lead to dissolution. Ross and Sawhill (1975) report that it is income *loss* and unemployment that are significant in predicting dissolution, not the absolute level of income. This finding is consistent with our views about the destabilizing effect of sudden disparities between the customary (and expected) living standard and the new economic situation. Research by Galligan and Bahr (1978) on wives over a 5-year period found that the level of family assets had an important effect on marital stability, while the level of income itself did not. In our model, assets represent coping resources.

An important longitudinal study (Goodwin, 1981) of men receiving unemployment compensation or welfare payments further illuminates some of the issues surrounding marital disruption. Among welfare recipients (AFDC-U), Goodwin found that men who "most strongly aspire to the goal of economic independence" are the husbands most likely to leave their wives when these aspirations are not fulfilled. Men who are most likely to stay with their wives, on the other hand, are those who report feeling most comfortable accepting welfare. For men receiving unemployment benefits, the longer the period of joblessness, the greater the likelihood of dissolution. Finally, men who had relatively high-paying jobs before their spell of unemployment were less likely than those with low wages to dissolve their marriages. Goodwin concludes that there is a direct relationship between duration of joblessness among men and marital disruption and that the effect of loss is mediated by the psychological orientations of the unemployed male when the situation requires public aid.

From the standpoint of wives, the income maintenance experiments, as well as studies of working wives, have shown that women with their own financial resources are more likely to dissolve their marriages than are wives who are totally dependent on their husband's earnings (Ross and Sawhill, 1975; Hannan et al., 1977, 1978). Despite all of this research, the actual causal process in marital dissolution remains largely a matter of speculation. As Gil Steiner (1981) points out, "Neither money, nor its absence, nor children nor their absence, nor intelligence nor its absence, is a sure indicator of family stability." Whatever the causes, it is clear that marital disruption has powerful repercussions on the family economy, with wives and children experiencing a major drop in income.

(b) *Change in Parent-Child Relations.* Some implications of economic change for parent-child relations have been noted in our discussion of change in the family economy and of relations between parents. Under conditions of economic hardship during the 1930s, older children were called upon for household tasks as families shifted toward a more labor intensive economy (Elder, 1974). Adult-like responsibilities became more a part of the lives of both boys and girls. Boys tended to seek gainful employment, while girls helped with domestic responsibilities, including child care, meal preparation, house cleaning, sewing, and ironing. The involvement of boys in work roles accelerated their liberation from parental controls.

Out of this sex-differentiated experience came a knowledge of work among boys, a valuing of dependability and self-direction, and a fund of skills for making their way in adulthood. Girls from deprived families acquired an appreciation for the special functions of family that also carried into their adult years. One might expect similar correlates of economic decline and labor intensive households to be found in contemporary society, though most of this territory remains uncharted. Even in the 1970s, the family economy is largely ignored by studies of children's work role in household and community. One of the best examples of this neglect appears in the recent survey by Goldstein and Oldham (1979).

Changes in the relationship between parents has wide-ranging implications for the parent-child relationship. Especially in discordant marriages, the combination of family income loss and mother's entry into the labor market serves to enhance the centrality of mother as a decision maker and emotional resource, and also creates the potential for greater marital discord and violence (Elder, 1974:Chapter 5). The father's role as a power and control figure diminishes accordingly. He becomes less attractive and effective as a male model in the perceptions of sons (Biller, 1971; Steinmetz, 1979). Whether expressed through contentiousness in marriage or along other paths, economic pressures qualify as a paramount factor in child abuse (Garbarino, 1976; Straus et al., 1980). Abusive parents frequently have a history of unemployment (Gil, 1970; O'Brien, 1971), but it is not clear whether the behavior of abusive parents causes or is caused by worklife instability. Parke and Collmer (1975:528) suggest that it "is not just unemployment per se, but unexpected and sudden unemployment that would be most likely to elicit violent behavior." Their review further supports our contention that it is not economic status but economic change that is the key to understanding the linkages between families and the economy. The causal ambiguity relating economic strains and child abuse is merely one facet of a larger deficiency in research on economic change: that of an underspecified or incompletely developed model. Typically the analytic framework for research is incomplete if indeed present at all.

(c) *Change in Sibling Relations*. The timing of economic setbacks or hardship in the lives of children bears most directly upon the life chances of each sibling. Economic misfortune during adolescence might permanently damage a first-born's life prospects, even though first-borns draw upon family resources before other siblings. Consistent with this observation is the relative advantage of first-borns in the middle class (Elder, 1980). The eldest son and daughter from working-class homes frequently enter the labor market as part of a family strategy of self-support. In both middle- and working-class families, the oldest sib generally carried the burden of child or sibling care. Beyond these somewhat peripheral points, however, research has little to offer on economic factors in sibling relations.

Individual Tensions and Strains

Economic change has consequences for tensions and strains on both the corporate (i.e., family) and individual level. Strains refer to the "felt difficulty in fulfilling role obligations" (Goode, 1960:483), as in the failure to meet expectations regarding the performance of economic, marital, and parental roles. The corporate effect has been noted or implied in our discussion of the family economy and marital changes: the status ambiguity and contradictions resulting from changing roles and tasks, and the marital discontent, conflict, and violence of hard times. Both marital and economic conditions have direct implications for the tensions or strains experienced by individual family members. A failing marriage may precipitate emotional depression, social withdrawal, and ineffective or punitive parenting. Denial and passive acceptance are alternative mechanisms for minimizing the emotional toll of stressful conditions (Pearlin and Schooler, 1978), as in marital conflicts and cross-pressure situations.

More direct effects of income and job loss include a reduced level of self-worth and sense of personal efficacy. Both historical and contemporary studies describe the unemployed man as lacking self-confidence, anxious, irritable, and depressed (Zawadski and Lazarsfeld, 1935; Eisenberg and Lazarsfeld, 1938; Komarovsky, 1940; Bakke, 1942; Tiffany et al., 1970; Cohn, 1978; Pearlin et al., 1981). A well-known panel study of male workers (Cobb and Kasl, 1977) who were displaced by a plant shutdown observed the adverse emotional and psycho-physiological effects of job loss and of the anticipation of such loss. However, these effects typically did not persist beyond 2 years after the shutdown and were negligible under conditions of marital support. The extent of hardship may be an important factor on the duration of effect. For example, archival work in progress (Liker and Elder, 1982) on Depression era families in the city of Berkeley, Calif., traces the family and individual effects of income loss through the male head of family to 1945. Sharp income losses substantially increased the irritability and explosiveness of men between 1930 and 1933-1935, and this change weakened the emotional quality and permanence of marriages during the 1930s and early 1940s. Even by the end of World War II, men who suffered heavy income loss during the Great Depression scored much higher on temperamental qualities and on marital discord than more fortunate men. Neither condition is promising for the welfare of children, whether older or younger.

One of the most important questions about family and health effects concerns the source of economic change and, more specifically, the *relative* effects of income and job loss. The first directs attention to the wide range of factors in economic misfortune. Family income may drop abruptly through the prolonged illness of the breadwinner or from the departure of the wife or older child from the labor force. Austustyniak and associates (1981) provide some answers in relation to men's sense of personal efficacy in their analysis of panel data on white men in the middle years (the Panel Study of Income Dynamics). They found that men's loss of earnings reduced their sense of efficacy, but that other forms of *family* income loss had no such effect. Similarly, economic gains by the men themselves enhanced their sense of personal mastery or control. These findings are consistent with theory on the psychological effects of perceived cause-effect relations. Secondly, both job *and* income loss were instrumental in producing a lower sense of personal efficacy. Unemployment has both an indirect effect on men's efficacy through earnings loss and a direct effect resulting from joblessness per se. In the long and short run, a lower sense of efficacy may have adverse consequences for family leadership, household operations, planning, and emotional health. Men who do not feel in charge of their life may communicate this outlook to family members. Individual psychology thus exerts a potent influence on the collective psychology of family units.

The connection between personal economic loss and adverse psychological effects also has been traced in women from the Depression era. By and large, the Great Depression entailed the economic losses of *men* and through them the losses come to influence family functioning and the well-being of other family members. Wives were faced with deprivations not of their own making. At least one study of the Depression generation (Elder et al., 1983) found no adverse health effect of economic loss among middle-class women during the 1930s or, years later, in their old age. However, adverse effects were observed in working-class women, especially during old age. Economic losses were more extreme and prolonged in working-class families, and lower-status women confronted this hardship without the personal and social resources of higher-status women, such as greater self-confidence and more problem-solving skills. In many respects, the health conditions of working-class women resembled those of men from the same generation. Many of these individuals suffered heavy losses in the 1930s, which created a health disadvantage that persisted to the last years of life.

We believe that the *timing* of income and job loss in the family life course is critical to an understanding of their psychological effects. Until recently, research has not done justice to the interaction of such events during the life course. Pearlin's longitudinal study (Pearlin et al., 1981) shows that younger adults are prime candidates for psychological distress through the cumulative pressures of early marriage, child care responsibilities, and occupational uncertainties. Adverse life changes tend to be concentrated during the first part of adult life. Moen (in press) found that younger men and women express a much lower sense of personal control than do middle-aged adults. And in all family stages, women were least apt to report control over their life. This general life-span trend is challenged by the studies of Andrisani and colleagues (1977, 1978), which report no age trend with respect to feelings of efficacy.

The timing issue suggests another important possibility: The immediate influence of economic change may be less significant than the manner in which it conditions future expectations in life. Rainwater (1974:36) underscores the importance of expectations in affecting the outlook and behavior of individuals, asserting that the amount of money one has at a particular moment is not nearly as critical as the "stream of resources that he has good reason to believe will be available to him in the future." Cobb and Kasl (1977), in their study of plant closings, found that one of the most distressing times experienced was the period of anticipation, where men began to contemplate the prospect of termination, an event over which they had no control. Part of the difficulty stemmed from bureaucratic procedures that made assistance conditional on actual job loss. Neither state employment agencies nor federal retraining programs would provide support until the men had received their "pink slips."

Some Implications for Children

The analytic framework used here argues for a process interpretation of the relationship between economic loss and the socialization of children. This process is governed by the expectations and options brought to the situation, by the degree and type of hardship, and by the timing of the event in the lives of both the children and their parents. To understand the impact of deprivation on the personality and behavior of children also requires an understanding of the lines of adaptation chosen and played out by their parents. Our theoretical model identifies multiple pathways between family response to economic change and the development of children within the family context. Some of these pathways are illustrated in Figure 5.

Family responses to economic distress are generally directed to immediate needs, with an eye toward specific, short-range consequences (Elder, 1974). As elements of strategies for economic survival, parental decisions are mostly geared to the short term. But what may be functional in the short run for the family unit may inadvertently have disastrous consequences for the lives of children. *It is these indirect and unanticipated outcomes that may, in fact, have the greatest significance for the life prospects of children.*

The socialization environment is altered, under conditions of deprivation, by the nature and extent of the loss. Children with an unemployed father, for example, are confronted with a parent suffering a loss of self-esteem, a far different situation from that of children experiencing deprivation as a consequence of divorce. Cultural definitions and historically structured options are also important in establishing the implications for children of economic loss. Hardship in the 1930s, when deprivation was a widely shared experience and a public issue, is interpreted differently from economic loss in a period of relative prosperity.

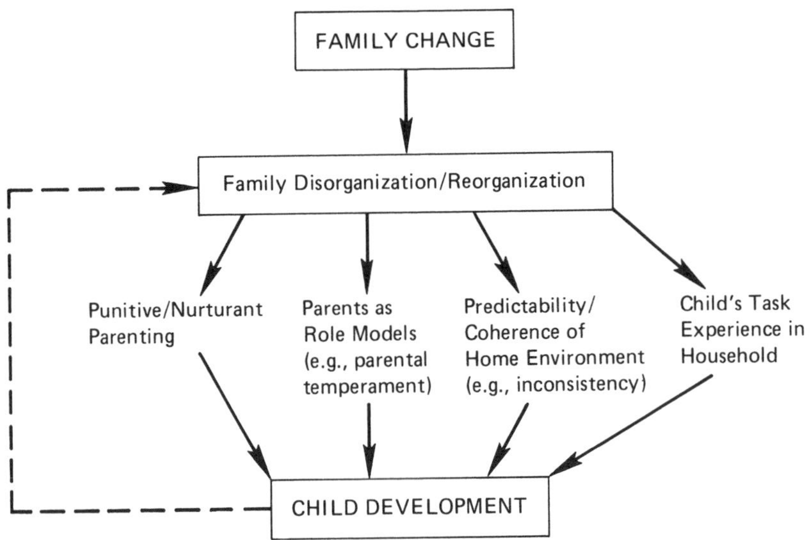

Figure 5 Model relating family change to outcomes for children. Adapted from Elder (1981c).

Similarly, when wives are traditionally homemakers, as in the 1930s, they constitute a "reserve labor force" in times of economic difficulty. Today's families usually require two earners to maintain an adequate standard of living, so that the wife's employment is increasingly less an option than a necessity. This means that families now have one less alternative in coping with increased hardship and that most children have mothers who are employed, an experience that will not change in spite of any changes in their economic situation.

Each of the paths illustrated in Figure 5 may lead to different outcomes, depending upon the timing of the loss in the life of the child. Punitive parenting may have differential effects on children at different points in their development. Younger children, for example, are more likely to be the target of abusive behavior. A similar argument applies to the second path in Figure 5. Younger children have less contact with role models outside of the home and thus would be more affected if the economic loss altered the role behavior of their parents. Research also indicates that it is younger children who would be affected by a lack of coherence in the home environment. Most of their social world is within the home. Yet, parents who are under economic pressure may be unable to provide stable guidance to their children.

Another impact of economic loss on children, now as in the 1930s, is an accelerated movement toward adulthood. Economic loss often increases the task experience of children in the household (the fourth path in Figure 5). Though youth today are less able to get jobs and thereby contribute to the family economy, the realities of economic hardship will orient them toward the adult world and convey an appreciation of life responsibilities and difficulties. Although it is unclear precisely how these changes alter the values, expectations, and aspirations of young people, it is highly likely that they are significantly influenced by the situational realities accompanying economic loss. Alterations in the interactional environment and the learning experiences of children may engender a bleak outlook for the future or anticipation of better days. The circumstances under which negative life prospects persist into the adult years are also a consequence of all the complexities surrounding economic change.

A substantial body of sociological literature has documented the relationship between educational and occupational achievements of parents and the counterpart achievements of their children (Duncan et al., 1972; Sewell and Hauser, 1975; McClendon, 1976; Hauser and Featherman, 1977). But the process by which economic difficulties serve to undermine the eventual status location of children remains obscure. Indeed, the importance of income change is ignored more often than not. Deprivation may severely restrict opportunities for education and the range of employment options from which to choose. Alternatively, the family's economic loss may underscore the importance of achievement as a means of getting ahead. The long-range consequences of economic deprivation for the lives of children cannot be estimated without taking subsequent events into account.

Children also have an impact upon family activities as indicated by the feedback loop in Figure 5. Research on child development has traditionally employed a unidirectional model of causality that examines only the impact of parents upon children. Research during the last decade has reflected a shift to a reciprocal model (Walters and Stinnett, 1971; Walters and Walters, 1980). Children who competently perform household tasks, for example, may be given even greater responsibility in the home. Thus, we can see the importance of viewing the reciprocal influences of family change upon children and children on the responses of families to economic change (see Figure 6).

The literature on punitive parenting (the first path in Figure 5) illustrates the reciprocal nature of this interaction. While economic change may increase the probability of punitive behaviors by adults, there is also evidence that certain child behaviors precipitate ineffective and punitive parenting. Gil (1970) found that one of several children is often singled out for punitive treatment. Abused infants are often whiny and have shrill, irritating cries. Abused children are often physically and verbally aggressive (Feshbach, 1970; Clark-Stewart, 1973; Martin and Beezley, 1977). This aggressive, temperamental behavior is precisely the type of child behavior that might provoke parental violence, especially under stressful economic circumstances.

Patterson et al. (1974) and Burgess and Conger (1978) provide interactional frameworks for conceptualizing negative interaction patterns that can accelerate into punitive parenting. The behaviorist social interaction theory of Patterson et al. (1974:308-309) explains how parents and their children get locked into aggressive bouts. Unpleasant or aversive behaviors by young children influence other family members to reciprocate in kind. Their explanation is that "If the coercive behavior, such as a Hit, produces a withdrawal of the unpleasant antecedent stimulus, then there is an increase in the probability that a Hit will occur in the future. However, if the coercive behavior is not followed by a removal

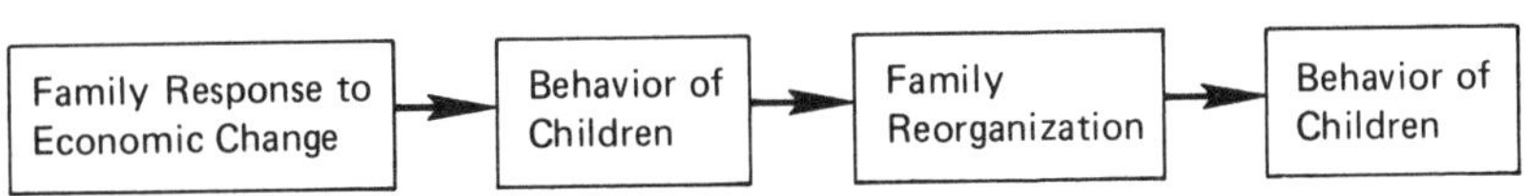

Figure 6 Model of the reciprocal influence of family change and children's behavior.

of the unpleasant stimulus, then it is likely to recur immediately and with a possible increase in amplitude. In effect, the behavior of both the victim and aggressor is under the control of negative reinforcement."

Kadushin and Martin (1981) argue that child abuse cannot be understood until it is conceptualized as an interactional event, with characteristics and behaviors of both parents and children playing a crucial part in the abuse. They review a series of studies showing the importance of characteristics and behaviors of children in child abuse. Lynch and Roberts (1977) suggest that abused children were more likely to have had atypical birth experiences. Indeed various types of physical and developmental deviation may increase the probability of abuse (Johnson and Morse, 1968; Morse et al. 1970). Abused children are less responsive to their mother, and abusive mothers seem more insensitive to signals and moods of their children (Robison and Solomon, 1979). It is clear that the interactional environment of the family must be more carefully specified and studied if we are to understand the reciprocal relations between parents and children as they respond to economic change.

Much work is required to clarify links between family responses to economic loss and the socialization of children, but it is obvious that such links do have profound consequences. For example, Pearlin has established the tie between economic loss and individual depression (Pearlin, et al., 1981), and Pearlin and others have documented the relationship between such loss and lowered feelings of self-esteem and efficacy (Cohn, 1978; Austustyniak et al., 1981). These psychological costs borne by parents may affect the socialization process both directly, through interactions between parent and child, and indirectly, as when the parent is seen as a role model with particular competencies and values to be emulated. The connections between economic hardship and deleterious child outcomes are still drawn more often by conjecture than by empirical evidence. Whether economic conditions and the family's response to those conditions result in negative effects on children's lives hinges on the timing of the loss and the options available to the family. The resilience of families and children may, in fact, be more substantial than their vulnerability.

Overview in Historical Perspective

Our analysis of economic conditions and family life returns to many of the issues and distinctions that were once prominent in the nineteenth century literature on family welfare. Work by early researchers such as Rountree brought fresh awareness concerning children in the family economy and the vacillating pattern of good and bad times across the life course of individuals and the life cycle of families.

During the first half of the twentieth century, family researchers seldom concentrated on family change or the historical content of family behavior. Sociological studies during this period stressed changes in family structure and functioning during the transition from an agricultural to an industrial economic system. The loss of functions posited by Ogburn (1933, 1937, 1955) reflected a dominant view among researchers who studied the family in isolation from economic change in its historical context (see Kain, 1980: Chapter 5, for a review of this work). This simplistic approach to linking massive economic transformation and family change was questioned by a variety of researchers in the late 1950s and early 1960s (Greenfield, 1962; Furstenberg, 1966). French and British historical demographers then began to document the nature of the family in past time, replacing the ideal images that had abounded in the literature. The early work tended to stress continuity in family patterns rather than change (Laslett, 1965; Laslett and Wall, 1972). Laslett's studies did not adequately address the issue of change over the life course of individuals within the family or variation over the family life cycle (Uhlenberg, 1974; Hareven, 1975). The importance of assuming a more dynamic approach in historical reconstruction of family patterns is illustrated in Berkner's work (1972) on Austrian peasant families.

The transition from an agricultural to an industrial economy brought about the separation of the workplace from the home. It is at this point in our history that the ideology of separate spheres for men and women developed (Welter, 1966) and the family came to be defined as a refuge from the world of work—a "haven in a heartless world" (Zaretsky, 1976; Lasch, 1977). This *physical* separation of work and family led sociologists to argue mistakenly that industrialization stripped the family of its economic functions. The family economy remained, however. Certainly it was modified with the advent of an industrial economy, as its emphasis shifted from production to consumption, but family members continued to contribute to the economic well-being of the family unit.

Each element of our analytic model varies with historical time. For example, Modell (1979) points out that the environmental risks faced by the family economy in the nineteenth century were very different from those faced today. The higher mortality rates of the nineteenth century removed more men from their families at early ages, thus taxing the emotional and material resources of their families. Modell suggests that even though voluntary family dissolution has increased over the past century as divorce rates have risen, shifts in mortality and marriage rates mean that larger proportions of recent cohorts live out their life course in family situations (see Uhlenberg, 1978). Modell further argues that the widespread growth of life insurance, improved health of workers, and changes in the nature of industrial employment have all decreased the uncertainty faced by the family economy.

Historical events such as the Great Depression and World War II brought women out of the home and into the external labor market in increasing numbers. But these strategies were not revolutionary changes. The proportion of families with two earners working outside the home has been increasing each decade since the late nineteenth century. However, the social and personal definitions of women entering the labor force have been very different for various cohorts. Unmarried women were much more likely to be in the labor force than their married counterparts in the 1890s (Kain, 1980). It was socially acceptable for never-married women (particularly if they were young) and widows to respond to economic pressures by working outside of the home. Nevertheless, this adaptive response to economic need was not viewed in the same positive light for married women.

Although substantial pressure is experienced by married women who combine career and home life today, this duality is very common in the contemporary family economy of the United States. Since 1950 the number of women with small children who are in the labor force outside the home has increased dramatically. In 1950 only 11.6 percent of married women with husbands present who had children under 6 years of age worked. By 1970 that figure was up to 30.3, and by 1978 41.6 percent of this group had entered the labor force (Bureau of Census, 1979). This trend represents a major shift in the structure of the family economy over the past three decades.

Coupled with the general increase in female labor force participation, these statistics mean that progressively smaller proportions of the population are in traditional one-earner families. In 1960, 43 percent of the households in this country consisted of married couples (with and without children) with only one worker. Twenty-three percent were married couples with two workers. Fifteen years later we find 30 percent of the households with two-worker married couples and only 25 percent with single-worker married couples. Projections (Masnick and Bane, 1980) show that by 1990 only 14 percent of U.S. households will be married couples with one worker in the labor force.

A number of other changes in the demographic structure of society also point to ways in which our model takes cognizance of the new circumstances. Declining mortality rates have drastically altered the nature of family change over the life course of individual family members.

Major reductions in the mortality of infants and women during childbirth as well as lower young adult mortality mean that fewer children lose siblings and parents during their early years and that they are more likely to know all of their grandparents than was the case in the past (see Uhlenberg, 1980). Moreover, the economic and emotional trauma of losing a spouse is much less common than it was at the turn of the century. On the other hand, the proportion of marriages ending in divorce has increased over the past century, arguing for more consideration of the economic reorganization accompanying this type of transition.

The decline in household size is still another important long-term demographic shift. In 1860 the mean household size in this country was 5.28 persons. By the turn of the century it had dropped to 4.93, and by 1978 it was down to only 2.81 (Bureau of the Census, 1976, 1979a). At the turn of the century, the modal household size was seven or more individuals. By 1978, the most common household size was two. While 45.5 percent of all households had five or more members in 1900, only 14.5 percent fell in that category by 1978. These declines reflect both a downward trend in fertility rates and fewer nonfamily members residing in the household. During rapid urbanization, the taking in of boarders and lodgers became a common adaptive strategy of the family economy, particularly at a family stage when younger members were leaving the household (Modell and Hareven, 1973). Since 1940 the decline is caused by more "empty-nest" households and, more recently, by an increasing tendency to live alone (Kobrin, 1976). This aggregate trend illustrates some of the dynamic processes accounted for by the model that result in long-term restructuring of what we define as the family in the United States. The practice of taking in boarders and lodgers is no longer a popular response to economic pressures faced by the family. On the other hand, new kinds of adaptation have grown in popularity, such as the increasing frequency of multiple earners within the household. The familial and individual implications of such shifts have not yet been thoroughly explored, but a dynamic model of the process by which families respond to economic change should be an essential element in future research.

Forecasts for the Future

Three major themes have guided the focus of this paper: an emphasis on process and change, a concern with family options and resources, and an analysis of family adaptive responses as the mediating linkages between economic hardships and their consequences for children. In concluding we return to these themes, reflecting on them in the context of the United States in the 1980s. Outlining the meaning of economic loss for families and children in the 1980s is necessarily a speculative undertaking, but one that can build on the body of knowledge accumulated about economic hardship at other historical periods.

It appears that the 1980s will be a time of continued inflation and unemployment; "stagflation" is the term given recent currency (Joint Economic Committee, 1980). Families in this decade, like families in the Depression era or the recession of 1975, are more prone to economic loss if their major breadwinners are without the job security and higher wage rates that come with seniority. This means that families with young children are still the group most vulnerable to financial hardship. Families of the unskilled and uneducated will likely continue to be hard-pressed to make ends meet. The situation of single-parent families, whose breadwinner is often without training, seniority, or job security, will remain particularly tenuous.

The historical milieu of the 1980s can be expected to exacerbate both family vulnerability to economic hardship and the consequences of that hardship. Given the dominant governmental concerns with fiscal restraint and major cutbacks in social programs, it is highly likely that more families will experience financial setbacks, either from job loss or from failure to keep pace with the spiraling cost of living, and that the average duration of economic hardship will be much longer. Recent 1980 census data bear this out: From 1979 to 1980 there was an increase of 3.2 million persons below the poverty level, one of the largest increases in any one year since poverty statistics have been kept (Bureau of the Census, 1981:1).

Unlike the period of the New Deal in the 1930s, one can expect little in the way of social services and programs to either reduce the threat of hard times or mitigate their effects. The United States is unique among the industrialized nations in failing to provide wide-ranging economic supports for families, particularly families raising children. Most American families rely exclusively on earned income in order to make ends meet. When that income is jeopardized by unemployment or inflation, the family faces financial trouble. Thus, resources and options are constrained by a political climate that limits public supports for families experiencing hard times. Family responses are also limited by the eligibility requirements of such public income transfer programs as do exist. For example, if adolescent children become employed, they may jeopardize their family's ability to receive certain welfare benefits (Perloff and Wachter, 1980). In addition, family labor reserves are far different than in the 1930s, when a wife could seek employment to enable the family to weather financial hardship. Two salaries are increasingly required to maintain an adequate standard of living, making the wife's employment essential even under relatively stable economic conditions. Wives and mothers, therefore, are less likely to be a "reserve army of the unemployed" who can enter the labor force when families face hard times.

The resiliency of the family economy can be expected to be severely tested in the 1980s. Continuous inflation and high rates of unemployment will create more strains at a time when families have fewer personal resources and can count on less institutional support. Families can be expected to respond by restructuring roles and resources as well as by reappraising both the present situation and prospects for the future. One can anticipate, for example, a decline in the goals families set for themselves. When there is a gap between aspirations and possible achievements, one can reduce the dissonance by either reaching one's goals or lowering them to a more "realistic" level. There will be little that families in the 1980s can do to ease the impact of inflation on their pocketbooks. But they can, and will, modify their plans—curtailing the dream vacation, postponing home buying or home improvements, finding low-cost recreation closer to home.

We can expect as well an increase in ambiguity and apprehension concerning the future. The erosion of the value of the dollar and the specter of employment destroy both present and future plans. Families at every economic level are increasingly unsure of what the future holds—for themselves, for their children. Those confronting economic loss will be forced to institute new styles of living as well as new role relationships to deal with the realities of their financial situation. New patterns of decision making must slowly, often painfully, be developed. In the interim, the family's time schedule for achieving important goals—owning a home, launching children into jobs and marriage, retirement—will be in disarray.

Another consequence is real as well as perceived loss of control. In the face of financial loss, families can increase debts, work more, or consume less, but there is a limit to each of these lines of adaptation. Chronic inflation as well as increased job insecurity are reducing the number of resources and options that families have. Their choices—to move or not move, to buy or build a house, to send a child to college, to have a first or second child—are more and more constrained by external factors beyond the family's control. Skills of problem solving are transmitted from generation to generation. It remains to be seen what younger generations will learn from parents who are experiencing less control.

In point of fact, the outcomes of economic loss for children of the 1980s are both obvious and problematic. What is obvious is what has happened in the past. Data from the Great Depression (Elder, 1974, 1983) inform us as to what we can expect when children's families experience deprivation. What is problematic is that the 1980s present new circumstances, the implications of which can only be speculated about.

We have established that economic downturns have their greatest impact on families with children. It is, therefore, the lives of children that are most likely to be touched by inflation and unemployment in the years ahead. Recent census statistics (Bureau of the Census, 1981) underscore this point: The highest poverty rate in 1980 was for children under age 3 (21 percent compared with 13 percent for the general population). This means that in March 1980 one child in five under 3 years of age was living in conditions of poverty.

We know that economic deprivation is translated into fewer resources devoted to the care and socialization of children. A logical adaptive response in hard times is to cut back on "frills" such as recreational opportunities, vacations, books, and toys. Educational opportunities are also likely to be curtailed as are preventative medical and dental care. Both short-term and long-range consequences of economic hardship for preschoolers were documented in Elder's Berkeley study (1981c). He found that parental behavior was an important link between economic misfortune and the experiences of children. Financial loss increased the temperamental behavior of fathers (but not of mothers), which in turn increased their punitive behavior toward children. Such punishment increased the likelihood of temper tantrums in children, which in turn increased the prospects of more punishment. Elder's analysis of the lives of children in deprived circumstances paints a picture of emotional and social difficulties, problems in school, and, later, problems at work. For many, these difficulties continued into adulthood.

As in the years of the Great Depression, adolescents in families with economic setbacks can be expected to shoulder adult concerns with their family's present and future economic plight. For many the cost of a college education may become prohibitive. But, unlike earlier periods of economic downturn, today's adolescent will find it difficult to take on adult roles in the world of work. The unemployment rate for young people, particularly black youth, is astronomical. Adolescents, then, will be saddled with adult problems but lack the wherewithal (in the form of jobs) to participate in adult solutions.

With poor educational and job opportunities, today's young people find it more difficult to make their way in society. Each generation of

Americans has assumed that it will surpass the accomplishments and status of preceding generations. Many adolescents in the 1980s will have to face the harsh reality of downward mobility, confronting the fact that in all likelihood they are not going to achieve what their parents have achieved. Adolescents and adults alike may have less confidence in the ability of society to meet their aspirations or even their needs.

Conversely, as in the Great Depression economic misfortune may have positive ramifications. Families may develop greater cohesiveness as a result of their economic plight. A more labor intensive household may upgrade the domestic responsibilities and, hence, the role of children within the family. Nurturant family ties are likely to gain value when they are threatened or fractured by economic pressures. In these respects and others, hard times are not necessarily the worst of times across all domains, yet the costly toll in children's lives is certain to rise if living conditions for less fortunate families continue to decline.

Finally, we return to the basic issue that has guided the discussion throughout this paper. "What are the impacts of economic change upon the family?" Clearly, there is no simple answer to this question. Any attempt to explain the empirical relationships reported in the literature requires knowledge of *process* and change in both the economic and family spheres. Examining the patterning of financial resources over the life course brings fresh insight to this impact on family members. The *timing* of economic adversity and the variety of options and resources available to families in meeting it must also be considered. Finally, both definitions of the situation and particular adaptations employed influence the manner in which economic conditions affect the lives of family members. It is only when we employ a dynamic model that includes such factors that we can begin to link biography and history and advance our understanding of the complex intersections among individual, family, and historical change.

References

Aldous, J. and R. Hill
1969 Breaking the poverty cycle: Strategic points for intervention. *Social Work* 14:3-12.

Andrisani, P. J.
1978 *Work Attitudes and Labor Market Experience: Evidence from the National Longitudinal Surveys*. New York: Praeger.

Andrisani, P. J., E. Appelbaum, R. Koppel, and R. C. Miljas
1977 Work Attitudes and Labor Market Experience. Report to U.S. Department of Labor, Manpower Administration, May 15.

Angell, R. C.
1936 *The Family Encounters the Depression.* New York: Scribner.
Austustyniak, S., G. J. Duncan, and J. K. Liker
1981 Income dynamics and self-conceptions: Linking theory and method in models of change. In Glen H. Elder, Jr., ed., *Life Course Dynamics: From 1968 to the 1980s.*
Bakke, E.
1940 *Citizens Without Work.* New Haven, Conn.: Yale University Press.
1942 *The Unemployed Worker.* New Haven, Conn.: Yale University Press.
Barton, A.
1969 *Communities in Disaster.* Garden City, N.Y.: Doubleday.
Bennett, S., and G. H. Elder, Jr.
1979 Women's work in the family economy: A study of depression hardship in women's lives. *Journal of Family History* 4(2):153-176.
Berkner, L.
1972 The stem family and the developmental cycle of the peasant household: An 18th century Austrian example. *American Historical Review* 77:398-418.
Bianchi, S. M.
1981 *Household Compositions and Racial Inequality.* New Brunswick, N.J.: Rutgers University Press.
Biller, H.
1971 *Father, Child, and Sex Role.* Lexington, Mass.: Lexington Books.
Brinkerhoff, D. B., and L. K. White
1978 Marital satisfaction in an economically marginal population. *Journal of Marriage and the Family* 40(2):259-268.
Bronfenbrenner, U.
1979 *The Ecology of Human Development.* Cambridge, Mass.: Harvard University Press.
Bureau of the Census
1976 *Historical Statistics of the United States, From Colonial Times to 1970.* Washington, D.C.: U.S. Government Printing Office.
1979 Current Population Reports, Series P-20, No. 340. *Households and Families by Type: March, 1978.* Washington, D.C.: U.S. Government Printing Office.
1981 Current Population Reports, Series P-60, No. 127. *Money, Income, and Poverty Studies of Families and Persons in the United States, 1980.* Washington, D.C.: U.S. Government Printing Office.
Burgess, R. L., and R. D. Conger
1978 Family interaction in abusive, neglectful, and normal families. *Child Development* 49:1163-1173.
Campbell, A.
1981 *The Sense of Well-Being in America: Recent Patterns and Trends.* New York: McGraw-Hill.
Caplovitz, D.
1979 *Making Ends Meet: How Families Cope With Inflation and Recession.* Beverly Hills: Sage.
Cavan, R., and K. Ranck
1938 *The Family and the Depression.* Chicago: University of Chicago Press.
Chudacoff, H. P.
1980 The life course of women: Age and age consciousness, 1865-1915. *Journal of Family History* 5:274-92.

Clarke-Stewart, A. K.
1973 *Interactions Between Mothers and Their Young Children: Characteristics and Consequences. Monographs of the Society for Research in Child Development* 38(6-7).

Cobb, S., and S. Kasl
1977 *Termination: The Consequences of Job Loss.* USDHEW (NIOSH) Publication No. 72-229. Washington, D.C.: U.S. Department of Health, Education, and Welfare.

Cohn, R. M.
1978 The effect of employment status change on self-attitudes. *Social Psychology Quarterly* 41:81-83.

Cutright, P.
1971 Income and family events: Marital stability. *Journal of Marriage and the Family* 33:291-306.

Deutsch, C. P.
1973 Social class and child development. Pp. 233-282 in B. M. Caldwell and H. N. Ricciuti, eds., *Review of Child Development Research,* Vol. 3. Chicago: University of Chicago Press.

Duncan, G. J., and R. D. Coe
1981 The Dynamics of Welfare. Unpublished paper, University of Michigan, Ann Arbor.

Duncan, G. J., and J. K. Liker
1981 Disentangling the Efficacy-Earnings Relationship. Unpublished paper, Cornell University, Ithaca.

Duncan, G. J., R. D. Coe, and M. S. Hill
1981 The Dynamics of Poverty. Unpublished paper, University of Michigan, Ann Arbor.

Duncan, O. D., D. L. Featherman, and B. Duncan
1972 *Socioeconomic Background and Achievement.* New York: Seminar Press.

Eisenberg, P., and P. Lazarsfeld
1938 The psychological effects of unemployment. *Psychological Bulletin* 35:358-390.

Elder, G. H., Jr.
1974 *Children of the Great Depression.* Chicago: University of Chicago Press.
1975 Age differentiation and the life course. *Annual Review of Sociology* 1:165-190.
1979 Historical changes in life patterns and personality. Pp. 117-159 in P. Baltes and O. Brim, eds., *Life-Span Development and Behavior,* Vol. 2. New York: Academic Press.
1980 *Family Structure and Socialization.* New York: Arno Press.
1981a History and the family: The discovery of complexity. *Journal of Marriage and the Family* 43(August):489-519.
1981b History and the life course. Pp. 77-115 in D. Bertaux, ed., *Biography and Society.* Beverly Hills: Sage.
1981c Family Influences and Child Behavior in Life-Span Perspective. Grant application to the National Institute of Mental Health, Washington, D.C.
1982 Historical experience in later life. Chapter 4 in T. Hareven, ed., *Aging and Life Course Transitions.* New York: Guilford Press.
1983 Families of Depression and War. Social Change Project, Cornell University, manuscript in process.

Elder, G. H., Jr., and Liker, J. K.
1982 Hard times in women's lives: Historical influences across 40 years. *American Journal of Sociology* (September).

Elder, G. H., Jr., J. K. Liker, and B. Jaworski
1983 Economic crisis and health: Historical influences from the 1930s to old age in postwar America. In J. McClusky and H. Reese, eds. *Life-Span Developmental Psychology: Historical and Generational Effects*. New York: Academic Press.

Ferman, L. A., and J. Gardner
1979 Economic deprivation, social mobility and mental health. Pp. 193-224 in L. A. Ferman and J. P. Gordus, eds., *Mental Health and the Economy*. Kalamazoo: W. E. Upjohn Institute for Employment Research.

Feshbach, S.
1970 Aggression. Pp. 159-259 in P. H. Mussen, ed., *Manual of Child Psychology*, Vol. 2. New York: John Wiley & Sons.

Flaim, P. O., and C. F. Gellner
1972 An analysis of unemployment by household relationship. *Monthly Labor Review*. 95:14-18.

Fried, M.
1973 *The World of the Urban Working Class*. Cambridge, Mass.: Harvard University Press.

Furstenberg, F.
1966 Industrialization and the American family: A look backward. *American Sociological Review* 31:327-337.

Galligen, R. J., and S. J. Bahr
1978 Economic well-being and marital stability—Implications for income-maintenance programs. *Journal of Marriage and the Family* 40(2):283-290.

Garbarino, J.
1976 Some ecological correlates of child abuse: The impact of socioeconomic stress on mothers. *Child Development* 47:178-185.

Gil, D. G.
1970 *Violence Against Children: Physical Abuse in the United States*. Cambridge, Mass.: Harvard University Press.

Goldstein, B., and J. Oldham
1979 *Children and Work: A Study of Socialization*. New Brunswick, N.J.: Transaction Books.

Goode, W. J.
1951 Economic factors and marital stability. *American Sociological Review* 16(6):802-808.
1960 A theory of role strain. *American Sociological Review* 25(4):483-496.

Goodwin, L.
1981 The Impact of Federal Income Security Programs on Work Incentives and Marital Stability. Final report to Office of Research and Development Employment and Training Administration, Grant No. 51-25-72-05, Department of Labor, Washington, D.C.

Gore, S.
1977 Support Resources for the Urban Unemployed. Paper presented at the American Sociological Association Annual Meeting, Chicago.
1978 The effect of social support on moderating the health consequences of unemployment. *Journal of Health and Social Behavior* 19:157-165.

Greenfield, S. M.
1962 Industrialization and the family in sociological theory. *American Journal of Sociology* 63:312-322.

Hannan, M. T., N. B. Tuma, and L. P. Groenveld

1977 Income and independence effects on marital dissolution. *American Journal of Sociology* 84:611-633.

1978 Income and independence effects on marital dissolution. *American Journal of Sociology* 85:653-657.

Hansen, Donald A., and Vicky A. Johnson

1979 Rethinking family stress theory: Definitional aspects. Pp. 582-603 in Burr et al., eds., *Contemporary Theories About the Family*. New York: The Free Press.

Hareven, T.

1975 Review of Laslett's *Household and Family in Past Time. History and Theory, Studies in the Philosophy of History* 14(2):242-251.

1982 *Family Time and Industrial Time: The Relationship Between the Family and Work in a New England Industrial Community*. New York: Cambridge University Press.

Hauser, R. M., and D. L. Featherman

1977 *The Process of Stratification: Trends and Analysis*. New York: Academic Press.

Hayghe, H.

1976 Research summaries: New data series on families show most jobless have working relatives. *Monthly Labor Review* 99(12).

1979 The effect of unemployment on family income in 1977. *Monthly Labor Review* 102(12):42-44.

1981 Husbands and wives as earners: An analysis of family data. *Monthly Labor Review* 104(2):46-52.

Hess, R. D.

1970 Social class and ethnic influence upon socialization. Pp. 457-557 in P. H. Mussen, ed., *Carmichael's Manual of Child Psychology*, Vol. 2, 3rd ed. New York: John Wiley & Sons.

Hofferth, S. L.

1981 Trends in the family structure and living arrangements of children: A cohort approach. In Glen H. Elder, Jr., ed., *Life Course Dynamics: From 1968 to the 1980s*. In process.

Johnson, B., and H. A. Morse

1968 Injured children and their parents. *Children* 15:147:152.

Joint Economic Committee, Congress of the United States

1980 *Stagflation: The Causes, Effects and Solutions*, Vol. 4. Special Study on Economic Change. Washington, D.C.: U.S. Government Printing Office.

Kadushin, A., and J. A. Martin

1981 *Child Abuse: An Interactional Event*. New York: Columbia University Press.

Kain, E. L.

1980 The Never-Married in the United States. Unpublished dissertation, Department of Sociology, University of North Carolina.

Kasl, S., S. Gore, and S. Cobb

1975 The experience of losing a job: Reported changes in health, symptoms, and illness behavior. *Psychosomatic Medicine* 37:106-122.

Kobrin, F.

1976 The fall in household size and the rise of the primary individual. *Demography* 13:127-138.

Komarovsky, M.

1940 *The Unemployed Man and His Family*. New York: Dryden Press.

Lane, J. P., and J. N. Morgan
1975 Patterns of change in economic status and family structure. Pp. 3-59 in G. J. Duncan and J. N. Morgan, eds., *Five Thousand American Families—Patterns of Economic Progress*, Vol. 3. Ann Arbor: Institute for Social Research.

Lasch, C.
1977 *Haven in a Heartless World: The Family Beseiged.* New York: Basic Books.

Laslett, P.
1965 *The World We Have Lost.* New York: Scribner.

Laslett, P., and R. Wall, eds.
1972 *Family and Household in Past Time.* New York: Cambridge University Press.

Lewis, O.
1965 *La Vida.* New York: Random House.

Liebow, E.
1967 *Tally's Corner.* Boston: Little Brown.

Liker, J. K., and G. H. Elder, Jr.
1982 Economic Pressures and Family Stress in the 1930s. Unpublished paper, Social Change Project, University of Ithaca.

Little, C. B.
1976 Technical-professional unemployment: Middle-class adaptability to personal crises. *The Sociological Quarterly*, 25:262-274.

Lynch, M. A. and J. Roberts
1977 Predicting child abuse: Signs of bonding failure in the maternity hospital. *Child Abuse and Neglect: The International Journal* 1:491-492.

MacDonald, M., and I. V. Sawhill
1978 Welfare policy and the family. *Public Policy* 26(1), 89-119.

McClendon, M. J.
1976 The occupational status attainment processes of males and females. *American Sociological Review* 41:52-64.

Martin, H. P., and P. Beezley
1977 Behavioral observations of abused children. *Developmental Medicine and Child Neurology* 19:373-387.

Masnick, G., and M. J. Bane
1980 *The Nation's Families 1960-1990.* Boston: Auburn.

Modell, J.
1979 Changing risks, changing adaptations: American families in the nineteenth and twentieth centuries. Pp. 119-144 in A. J. Lichtman and J. R. Challison, eds., *Kin and Communities: Families in America.* Washington, D.C.: Smithsonian Press.

Modell, J., and T. Hareven
1973 Urbanization and the malleable household: An examination of boarding and lodging in American families. *Journal of Marriage and the Family* 35(3):467-479.

Modell, J., F. F. Furstenberg, Jr., and T. Hershberg
1976 Social change and transitions to adulthood in historical perspective. *Journal of Family History* 1:7-32.

Moen, P.
1978 Family Impacts of the 1975 Recession: Unemployment Among Families With Children. Unpublished dissertation, University of Minnesota, August.
1980a Measuring unemployment: Family considerations. *Human Relations* 33(3):183-192.

1980b Developing family indicators: Financial hardship, a case in point. *Journal of Family Issues* 1 (March):5-30.

In Press Preventing financial hardship: Coping strategies of families of the unemployed. In H. McCubbin, ed., *Family Stress, Coping and Social Support.*

Morse, C., J. Sahler, and S. Friedman

1970 A three-year followup study of abused and neglected children. *American Journal of Diseases of Children* 120:439-46.

Mueller, C. W., and T. L. Parcel

1981 Measures of socioeconomic status: Alternatives and recommendations. *Child Development* 52 (March):13-30.

O'Brien, J. E.

1971 Violence in divorce prone families. *Journal of Marriage and the Family* 33:692-698.

Ogburn, W. F.

1933 *Recent Social Trends in the United States*, 2 vols. New York: McGraw-Hill.

1937 The influence of technology on American social institutions in the future. *American Journal of Sociology* 93(3):265-376.

Ogburn, W. F., with M. F. Nemkoff

1955 *Technology and the Changing Family.* Boston: Houghton Mifflin.

Parke, R. D., and C. W. Collmer

1975 Child abuse: An interdisciplinary analysis. Pp. 509-590 in E. M. Hetherington, ed., *Review of Child Development Research*, Vol. 5. Chicago: Univerisity of Chicago Press.

Patterson, G. R., J. A. Cobb, and R. S. Ray

1974 Training parents to control an aggressive child. Pp. 308-314 in S. K. Steinmetz and M. A. Straus, eds., *Violence in the Family.* New York: Harper & Row.

Pearlin, L. I., and C. Schooler

1978 The structure of coping. *Journal of Health and Social Behavior* 19:2-21.

Pearlin, L. I., M. A. Lieberman, E. G. Menaghan, and J. T. Mullan

1981 The Stress Process. Paper presented at the Annual Meetings of the American Sociological Association, Toronto, August.

Perloff, J. M., and M. L. Wachter

1980 Demographic aspects of the stagflation problem. Pp. 168-192 in Joint Economic Committee, eds., *Stagflation: The Causes, Effects and Solutions*, Vol. 4, Special Study on Economic Change. Washington, D.C.: U. S. Government Printing Office.

Rainwater, L.

1974 Work, well-being and family life. In J. O'Toole, ed., *Work and the Quality of Life.* Cambridge: MIT Press.

1977 *Welfare and Working Mothers Family Policy Note 6.* Joint Center for Urban Studies of MIT and Harvard University.

Rainwater, L., and Karol Kane Weinstein

1960 *And the Poor Get Children.* Chicago: Quadrangle Books.

Robison, E., and F. Solomon

1979 Some further findings on the treatment of the mother-child dyad in child abuse: Child abuse and neglect. *The International Journal* 3:247-51.

Root, K.

1977 Workers and Their Families in a Plant Shutdown. Paper presented at the Annual Meetings of the American Sociological Association, Chicago, September.

Ross, H. L., and I. Y. Sawhill
1975 *Time of Transition: The Growth of Families Headed by Women*. Washington, D.C.: The Urban Institute.

Sewell, W. H., and R. M. Hauser
1975 *Education, Occupation, and Earnings: Achievement in Early Career*. New York: Academic Press.

Shimkin, D. B., E. M. Shimkin and D. A. Frate, eds.
1978 *The Extended Family in Black Societies*. The Hague: Mouton.

Sorokin, P. A. and R. K. Merton
1937 Social time: A methodological and functional analysis. *American Journal of Sociology* 5:615-629.

Stack, C.
1977 *All Our Kin*. New York: Harper & Row.

Steiner, G. Y.
1981 *The Futility of Family Policy*. Washington, D.C.: Brookings Institution.

Steinmetz, S. K.
1979 Disciplinary techniques and their relationship to aggression, dependency, and conscience. Pp. 405-438 in Wesley R. Burr et al., eds., *Contemporary Theories About the Family*, Vol. I. New York: The Free Press.

Straus, M. A., R. J. Gelle, and S. K. Steinmetz
1980 *Behind Closed Doors*, New York: Doubleday.

Thomas, W. I., and F. Znaniecki
1918-1920 *The Polish Peasant in Europe and America*, Vols. 1 and 2, Chicago: University of Chicago Press.

Tiffany, D. W., J. R. Cowan, and P. M. Tiffany
1970 *The Unemployed: A Social Psychological Report*. Englewood Cliffs, N.J.: Prentice-Hall.

Uhlenberg, P.
1974 Review of Laslett's *Household and the Family in Past Time*. *Social Forces* 53:351-3.
1978 Changing configurations of the life course. Pp. 65-97 in T. Hareven, ed., *Transitions, The Family and the Life Course in Historical Perspective*. New York: Academic Press.
1979 Demographic change and problems of the aged. Pp. 153-166 in Matilda White Riley, ed., *Aging From Birth to Death*. Boulder, Colo.: Westview.
1980 Death and the family. *Journal of Family History* 5(3):313-320.

U.S. Department of Labor
1981 New income levels defining poverty. *News* 81:(March 25)156.

Walters, J., and N. Stinnett
1971 Parent-child relationships: A decade review of research. *Journal of Marriage and the Family* 33(1):70-111.

Walters, J., and L. H. Walters
1980 Parent-child relationships: A review, 1970-1979. *Journal of Marriage and the Family* 42(4):807-822.

Welter, B.
1966 The Cult of true womanhood: 1820-1860. *American Quarterly*, 18:151-174.

Young, M., and P. Wilmott
1973 *The Symmetrical Family*. New York: Pantheon.

Zaretsky, E.
1976 *Capitalism, the Family, and Personal Life*. New York: Harper & Row.

Zawadski, B., and P. Lazarsfeld
1935 The Psychological Consequences of Unemployment. *Journal of Social Psychology* 6:224-251.

DISCUSSION

The conference welcomed the paper by Moen, Kain, and Elder as an opportunity to examine some of the issues that emerged out of the various papers and discussions from a perspective that so far had only surfaced sporadically—the insight that different people react *differently* to what are objectively similar events and situations.

Edmund Gordon, the first formal discussant, focused his remarks on the model of economic loss presented in the paper as further illuminated by his own study of persons who were, at an early period in their lives, identified as at high risk of failure but who nonetheless went on to high achievement—the "defiers of negative predictions of success." The group in the study were all black or Hispanic and all born and raised in conditions of poverty.

One striking conclusion from Gordon's study that has relevance for the model in the Moen et al. paper is that objective resources or options available can only really be interpreted in light of another item in their schema—the definition of the situation. One's perception of a resource *as a resource* is important. The resource may be there, but if it is not perceived as a resource, then its utility is reduced. One's judgment that the option is a viable one is terribly important. It may be objectively viable, but, if its viability is not understood, it is not viable and is not fully utilized. "For example, in our population the extended family emerged as an important feature, but the extended family may be viewed as a resource, a responsibility, or even a liability, and my perception of it influences my utilization of it and, of course, the functions I use it for. Multiple children may be viewed either as resource producers helping the family to meet its ends or as resource consumers, a burden on the family."

Related to this is the way people perceive their position in the society. "One of our respondents was a man who grew up in Texas of a family with seven children—by all objective measures poverty-striken—but one of the comments he made was, 'We never thought of ourselves as poor. We really did not have much, but somehow we got along.' And he went through life never really thinking of himself as that poor or disadvantaged and is now a rather successful lawyer. He just thought he had to struggle a little bit more than other people."

The study also includes school-age kids, some of whom are making it and some of whom are not. "Among those who are not making it we find it a perception of self or perception of one's situation as hopeless, as excessively difficult, as not having potential for change, as a depressant on the adaptive behavior of the person."

In Gordon's view, the importance of stratification in our society should be emphasized from this perspective. The existence of a stratified society complicates adjustment to one's position in the economy and in society. It may even complicate the way we generate our theories, and it certainly complicates the way we interpret them. If research and theory development are based on too narrow and homogeneous a population, they may well distort our perception of the phenomenon we are studying. In this connection Gordon quoted a study by Carol Gilligan examining the relevance of the Kohlberg model of moral development (based on observations of a male population) for women. The burden of her argument is that the model does not fit. This has been used as evidence of inappropriate moral development in women. Gilligan argues, rather, that it may be evidence of something wrong with the theory. The Gilligan study provides a warning to the conference that arguments and conclusions should be carefully examined to be sure that they don't follow from a model or generalization developed for an overly narrow or otherwise nonapplicable population or perspective.

Adaptive strategies revealed in Gordon's study of the "defiers" include the ability of the family to manage their limited resources in such a way that they were in better shape in terms of what their resources achieved for them than others in objectively similar economic circumstances. The Gordon study bases judgments on such indicators of ability to manage as: Did anybody go hungry? Do you get dispossessed? Have you got the clothing you need? If there is illness, can you do something about it? Are the essential family functions provided for? "In my population, people poor as church mice somehow were able to do these things, while people equally as poor by objective standards were unable to do so."

The Gordon study also includes observations of the pooling phenomenon. In extended families the resources are often pooled in order to advance the chances of a single person—where everybody gets behind one child, usually a younger one. It even extends to pooling on a rotating basis. As one person moves into independence, the resources are pooled around another.

This pooling phenomenon, according to Gordon's research, is not only peculiar to extended families. It even goes into communities. "Howard Thurman, a rather distinguished black theologian who died last year, grew up in a community that put its money together to get him to school, and every summer when he came home he had to account to almost every black person in that community for what he was doing. All the time he was in school he felt, 'I cannot let them down. There are too many people back there who are counting on me.'"

There is a modern equivalent of this wider pooling, discovered by one of Gordon's students in her research. In contrast to Gordon's older black population, his student is studying a population of younger black women and finds a high degree of networking—of pooling human and material resources so that the greatest need and potential of the moment is met. This may be a new and effective coping mechanism for younger black women and their families.

Gordon also found another parallel/contrast between the older black parents in his study and younger parents in similar situations. "In an earlier period, in my older black adult male sample, the family used philanthropy; frequently the mother was rather aggressive, moving through the community to seek out philanthropic sources of support for her youngsters. In my young sample, in contrast, we are finding a lot of evidence of the use of the modern phenomenon [the irregular economy] that I prefer to call alternative economies. I call them that because I think what is legal or regular is so very relative in our society."

Gordon ended his comment by quoting research to provide further support for the point raised by both Slaughter and Ogbu in previous sessions (see discussions following Chapters 3 and 5) that the role of prior experience is crucial to one's perceptions of one's potential. Here he quoted from a study of New Jersey blacks done by Samuel Proctor. The blacks grew up in three different environments—rural New Jersey, urban New Jersey, and suburban New Jersey. What Proctor found was that the different groups went into very different careers. Those from the rural areas tended to be the unskilled workers in Newark and Jersey City. Those from the urban areas tended to be in the civil service. And those from suburban backgrounds tended to become academics or professionals. The explanation centered on what their parents had done.

"In the suburban areas the parents of most of these now-professional people had worked as domestics in white families and modeled their behavior, their socialization of their children, and their aspirations for their children on the standards of the middle- and upper-class families they were living rather intimately with. The civil service workers came out of the blue-collar and semiskilled city workers, in a political climate where upward mobility took you into the public sector for employment. The rural blacks had exposure neither to the sophistication and culture of the middle and upper class, nor to the political structures that could move one into public service. They thus remained relatively unskilled, unsophisticated. When they came to the city, of course, they moved into the first (entrance) level jobs."

James Jackson, the second formal discussant, endorsed the views of both the paper and Gordon, by emphasizing how misplaced was the assumption that "if we increase the economic well-being of families, that automatically translates into some type of personal well-being—broadly defined in terms of enjoyment of one's life." He made just one additional point of emphasis, which is a criticism not only of the Moen et al. paper but also of many of the other conference papers: The fundamental relationships among particular factors may, indeed, change as a function of looking at different subpopulations defined as different cultural groups. "This is not necessarily to say that the basic model of the effect of family characteristics is inappropriate for blacks or Hispanics, or other groups. But it is to say that the socialization processes within these different groups of families may, indeed, be different; these differences may affect the way particular factors influence people's behavior; and I think the whole issue needs to be considered more."

The discussion got somewhat of a jolt from the floor when Cherlin noted that the Elder Depression studies showed some "surprising long-run positive effects. Among the middle-class children of the Depression, for example, those whose families suffered more economically achieved a higher economic and occupational status when they got to be adults, married earlier, and had more kids. And the women in those families tended to suffer less mental depression in old age. Now, why I think that is of interest to us is because the same kinds of responses of children to deprivation in the Depression that were seen in the 1930s are now being seen in the responses of children of households to divorce, which of course has become increasingly common. To use Elder's phrasing again, there is a downward extension of adult-like experience. In other words, given the loss of a father because of divorce or the loss of the father's income because of depression, boys take on some of the typically male chores, perhaps going to work and earning some money, and girls take on some of the typically adult female roles. Elder makes the case that this downward extension of adult-like experience may be the factor that creates some of these positive effects later on.

"The historical lesson is not, of course, that we should have more depressions and more divorces in order to further children's achievements as adults, but rather that we have to differentiate clearly between the temporary economic deprivations of middle-class children and the more persistent economic deprivations of lower-class children. This is a point that we came back to in various ways again and again yesterday, and I think these historical studies have a lesson for us: The long-term, sometimes beneficial, consequences of divorce for the middle-class child may be quite different from the consequences of economic deprivation for lower-class children—one cause of which is divorce, separation, and single-parent families—and we ought to keep those distinctions in mind."

Moen added to the discussion of the so-called positive effects of the Depression by pointing out that the people who rose to the occasion were those who felt better about themselves: middle-class women who went out and got jobs, teenage boys who could get jobs and help the family economy. "But given the discussion yesterday about women's labor force participation and youth unemployment, I don't see this as a viable option for the 1980s. Most of the women are already working, and the youth cannot get jobs. So I project an increase in the sense of powerlessness in the 1980s.

"I also want to underscore what Gordon said about grounding every stage of our model in cultural options and choices. The options and choices in the United States in the 1980s will be different from those in other countries, because, as Kamerman and Kahn have pointed out, the United States is unique among industrialized countries in not providing a universal base of economic support for families in the best of times and in the worst of times."

Ogbu continued this branch of the discussion by pointing out that, though he agreed that cultural differences were an essential component to any explanation of, say, black-white differences, and that the conference has not paid sufficient attention to these cultural differences, how one treated culture was a tricky issue. "People develop cultures because of historical or structural circumstances, which then become a way of life that differentiates them. What I want to emphasize is the importance of the *structural* factors in producing cultural adaptations and reactions. An example to make my point is a study done at the World Bank showing clearly that poor children in Third World countries tend to respond to schooling differently from the way children in the ghetto respond. That is because they are coming into the system from different angles. It is important to take into account cultural differences *without* culturalizing the problem by saying it is their culture. We should link cultural differences to the overall structural factors involved."

John Modell developed the point further by saying that cross-group comparisons with respect to short-term deprivation should also take into account the material level of living people start from. "What I found lacking to a small extent in the Moen et al. paper and thoroughly lacking in most of the economists' papers is any consideration of the range of ordinary economic consumption patterns of families; they differ. Not all economic goods have the same impact on families. The particular black box of what families do ordinarily is for me the big substantive area that is missing in our discussion of how families act when circumstances are changing."

The discussion ended with Harold Watts reminding the group that focusing on the positive effects of deprivation tends to ignore what happened to those who failed to survive at all. "There is plausibility and some evidence in favor of the crucible and the forge as producing harder and tougher things and people, even in the case of disease. Polio before the vaccines is a case in point. Those who got polio tended to be better educated and from higher income families. They were also much more susceptible to polio by the time they were in the third or fourth grade. The poor were less vulnerable. That was in part because the less educated, poorer groups were more exposed earlier on to various kinds of disease-producing agents—the survivors had more immunity. But that, of course, ignores those who had been unable to survive at all to that point, and a whole lot of other things." Moen remembered Nietsche, who said it best. "As long as adversity doesn't kill you, you come out stronger."

8

The Impact of Demographic Factors on the Family Environment of Children, 1940-1995

RICHARD A. EASTERLIN

The last two decades have witnessed dramatic changes in the family environment of children and the way in which they are raised. There has been a marked increase in the percentage of children not living with both parents and of children in husband-wife (two-parent) families with mothers working outside the home and a rapid decline in the average number of siblings per child. Care of children has shifted increasingly into homes other than the children's own and into group care centers, and television has come to occupy an important share of a child's time. The aim of this paper is to assess the likelihood of continuation of these changes over the next 15 years. No attempt is made to judge the impact of these changes on child development and child welfare—indeed, it is doubtful that this is known, though clearly it is the most important question of all.

As a basis for assessing the prospective continuation of recent trends, the paper first links the changes just mentioned to their "proximate determinants"—the rate of marital dissolution, labor force participation of mothers, and the total fertility rate—and traces the record of these

This research was supported in part by NICHHD Grant HD-05427. The author is grateful for assistance to Daira E. Hill and Mahmoud S. A. Issa and Nancy Zurich and for discussions with Issa and Eileen M. Crimmins. The paper has also benefited from comments by Frank F. Furstenberg, Samuel H. Preston, Paul Taubman, and the discussants at the conference. Special thanks for assistance with official statistics are due to Gordon Green, Arthur J. Norton, Martin O'Connell, Gregory Spencer of the Bureau of the Census, and Paul O. Flaim of the Bureau of Labor Statistics.

proximate determinants and associated changes in children's circumstances over the last 40 years. The current situation is then placed in longer historical perspective by adding a comparison with conditions around the turn of the century. Following this, trends in child care over recent decades associated with these developments are described.

Next, using official projections, two pictures are constructed of how the family situation of children may change between now and 1995. One implies continued change at rates much like those of the last two decades; the other presents an outlook compared with the present in which the changes are moderate and more like those back in the 1940s and 1950s. An evaluation of the likelihood of the two alternative paths based on an interpretation of experience since 1940 is then presented. This suggests that continuation over the next 15 years of recent rates of change is unlikely, and that a return to patterns of change more like those of the 1940s and 1950s is probable. Specifically, compared with the present, the outlook through 1995 is for relatively little increase in the percentage of children not living with both parents, slower growth in the percentage of children in two-parent families with mothers working outside the home, and a moderate increase in the average number of siblings per child.

The data used are principally from official publications of the Bureau of the Census and Bureau of Labor Statistics. Recently there has been a marked advance in the demographic analysis of families (see, for example, Glick, 1957; Carter and Glick, 1970; and Glick and Norton, 1979) and a corresponding burgeoning of official statistics. Many of the features of the last two decades' experience have been noted elsewhere.[1] To the extent possible in the present analysis, the experience of both preschool age and school age children in both white and black families is considered. For whites data for all races are usually used, because they are more plentiful and are dominated by the experience of whites. At earlier dates, data for blacks are sometimes approximated by those for nonwhites.

Proximate Determinants of the Family Environment of Children: Experience Since 1940

A number of the major changes in the family environment of children and the factors immediately behind them are distilled in the figures and

[1] A number of valuable articles have appeared in the P-20 and P-23 series of the Census Bureau's Current Population Reports and in the Bureau of Labor Statistics' *Monthly Labor Review*, in addition to valuable monographs (for example, Ross and Sawhill, 1975; Cherlin, 1981).

tables that follow; the present discussion highlights some of the principal features. In this section the connections between the main proximate determinants and the family situation of children are traced. Although the analysis deals with both preschool and school age children, somewhat greater emphasis is given to the former, for whom the changes have been greater.

Marital Status

In the late 1950s, among women aged 25-34 who had been married at least once the proportion divorced or separated was about 9 percent, slightly less than 20 years earlier (Figure 1, lower left panel, solid line).[2,3] In the next 20 years, this percentage almost doubled, rising to 17 percent by 1979.

This percentage largely determines that for preschool age children not living with both parents, though the latter tends to be slightly lower, chiefly because of the below average fertility of divorced or separated women. Thus, paralleling the uptrend in marital dissolution, there was an increase in the proportion of preschool children not living with both parents, from around 7 to 14 percent (Figure 1, lower left panel, broken line).

The living arrangements of school age children are linked chiefly to the marital status of the next oldest group of women, those aged 35-44. For these women the rise in divorce or separation followed with a 10-year lag that among women 25-34, as the cohorts first experiencing the rise in marital dissolution in the 1960s entered the older age-group (Figure 1, lower right panel). At any given date, however, the percentage divorced or separated was higher among females 35-44 than those 25-34, though only slightly so, reflecting the fact that, while marital dissolution continues throughout a cohort's life cycle, most of it is concentrated in the early years of marriage when women are under 35 years old. Correspondingly, the proportion of school age children not living with both parents is only slightly higher than for preschool age children—by 1979, about 17 percent of school age children were not living with both parents.

[2] Figures 1-5 are based chiefly on reports of the decennial censuses and Current Population Surveys published by the Bureau of the Census and on Special Labor Force Reports published by the Bureau of Labor Statistics; Figures 6-8 are from Easterlin (1980).

[3] In these and subsequent marital status data, a small proportion of widows are included with those divorced and separated.

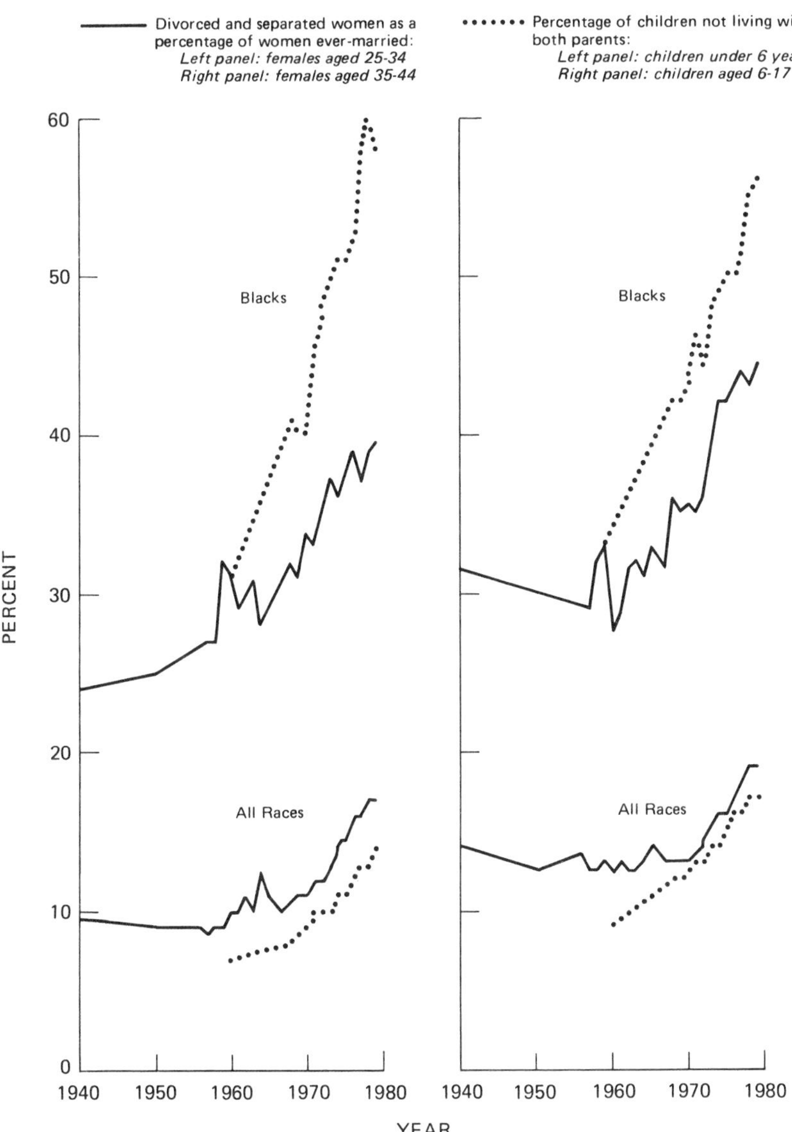

Figure 1 The impact of marital dissolution on the presence of parents in children's homes. Among both whites and blacks, the rising incidence since 1960 of divorce and separation among couples in the reproductive ages (solid lines) has caused a corresponding increase in the proportion of children not living with both parents (broken lines). Most of these children are living with their mothers (Table 1).

TABLE 1 Percent Distribution of Children According to Presence of Parents, by Race, 1960 and 1979

	White			Black[a]		
Presence of Parents	1960	1979	Change, % points (2)–(1)	1960	1979	Change, % points (5)–(4)
Total	100.0	100.0	0	100.0	100.0	0
Living with both parents	91.8	83.5	−8.3	67.7	43.4	−24.3
Not living with both parents	8.2	16.5	8.3	32.3	56.6	24.3
Living with mother only	5.5	12.5	7.0	19.6	41.9	22.3
Living with father only	0.9	1.5	0.6	1.8	2.1	0.3
Living with neither parent	1.8	2.0	0.8	10.9	11.3	1.7
Not in families		0.6			1.3	

NOTES: 1960 data are for persons under 14 years old; 1979 data, under 18 years old.

[a] 1960 data are for nonwhites.

SOURCE: Bureau of the Census, Current Population Reports, *Marital Status and Living Arrangements*, Series P–20, No. 349, and *1960 Census of Population, Persons by Family Characteristics*, PC(2)–4B, Table 1.

These trends for the population as a whole are dominated by those for whites. If one considers only blacks, there is a fair similarity to whites in regard to two features—the parallelism of the trends in marital status and children's living arrangements and the timing of the upswing in marital dissolution (Figure 1, upper panels). However, there are important differences too. At any given date the percentages both of marital dissolution and children not living with both parents are much higher for blacks than for whites. Also, in contrast to whites, the percentage of black children not living with both parents is higher than the percentage of divorced or separated wives, reflecting the higher rates of childbearing among single black women than white. In 1960, 32 percent of black children were not living with both parents; by 1979 this had risen to a staggering 57 percent, chiefly because of the rise in black rates of marital dissolution. However, among black children under 6 the rise in the proportion not living with both parents is much steeper than the trend in marital dissolution. As Andrew Cherlin pointed out in his conference comments, this reflects a trend among blacks, particularly low-income blacks, toward an increasing separation of childbearing from marriage. In addition, blacks are less likely to remarry than whites.

For both races at any given date, most children not living with both parents are living with their mother, but among blacks the proportion not living with either parent is also fairly sizable—on the order of 10 percent (Table 1; preschool and school age children show quite similar magnitudes and hence are not reported separately in the table). For both races the decline since 1960 in the percentage of children living with both parents has been taken up almost entirely by a corresponding rise in the proportion of children living with mothers only. By 1979, about one white child in eight was living only with the child's mother; among blacks the proportion living with the mother only had risen almost to equality with the percentage living with both parents—over four children in ten in each case.

Living in families headed by one's mother is likely to alter the economic circumstances of children. Divorced or separated women under age 45 are more likely to be away from home than mothers in two-parent families for two reasons. First, they are more likely to be employed or actively seeking work, and second, among women who work, those who are divorced or separated are more likely to work full time year-round. Given the fair similarity between the occupational distribution of divorced or separated women and that of wives in two-parent families, it follows that female family heads, on the average, earn more income than wives in two-parent families. However, their total family income including sources such as public assistance, alimony, and child support, but excluding noncash income, is considerably lower than for married couples—only slightly over one-third.[4] For families with children under 6 years old, the ratio is only a little more than one-fourth. It seems reasonable to infer that, so far as the economic circumstances of children are concerned, the absence of a father from the family affects them adversely by lowering family income more than it reduces demands on that income due both to the absence of the father and the smaller number of children in female-headed households. The higher-than-average poverty rate among female-headed households attests to this.[5]

It should be emphasized that the data above refer to conditions at a point in time and cannot be directly translated into the life-cycle experience of children. A child currently living with one parent is not likely to continue in this state as he grows up, because the probability of remarriage is high. According to the experience of older generations alive today, about three out of four women remarry after divorce (Cherlin, 1981). Moreover, about half of all remarriages take place within 3 years after divorce. Of course, living with a stepparent may affect a child differently from living with one's natural parent. Also, as pointed out in Chapter 2, the percentage of children who go through an episode of living with one parent is *higher* than the data for a given point in time indicate. This is because some children currently reported as living with two parents were previously living with one parent prior to that parent's remarriage. Thus the changes in Figure 1, while not directly transferable into children's life-cycle experience, clearly imply major new developments in the family circumstances of children.

Work Outside the Home

The growth in marital dissolution and consequent trend toward female-headed households has raised the proportion of mothers working outside the home, but it has not been the only factor. Even within husband-wife families, there has been a sharp rise in the labor force participation of mothers. In 1940, the proportion of mothers that worked was quite low, averaging about one in ten—somewhat less for those with preschool children and somewhat more for those with school age children. By 1980, this proportion was approaching one-half among mothers with preschool children and two-thirds among those with school age children (Figure 2, solid lines for "all races").

[4] Bureau of Labor Statistics, *Marital and Family Characteristics of the Labor Force, March 1979*, Special Labor Force Report No. 237:A-46, Table O.

[5] Bureau of the Census, Current Population Reports, Series P-60, No. 120 (1979):33.

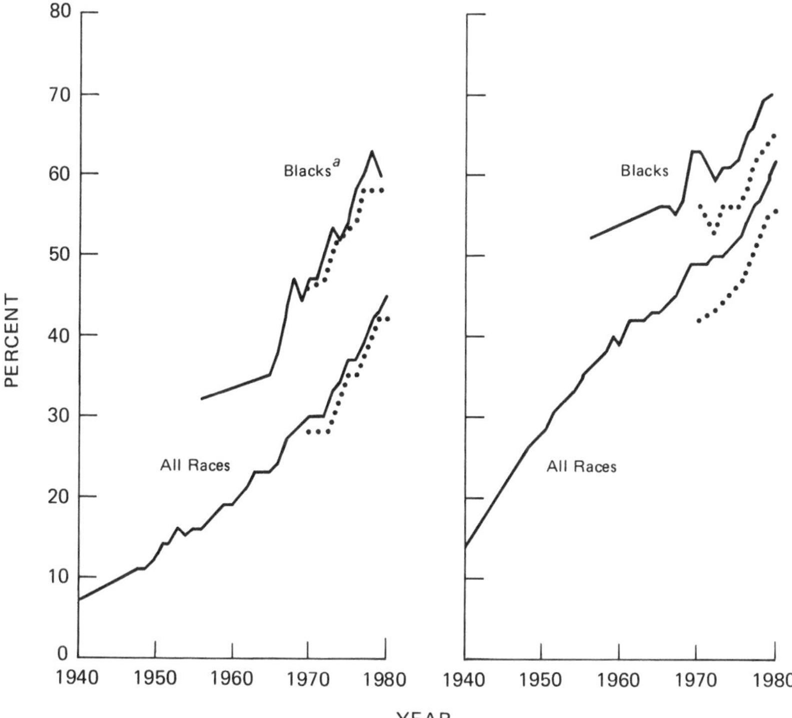

Figure 2 The impact of mothers' work outside the home on the children of married couples. Among married couples of both races, the sharp uptrend in work outside the home for mothers of both preschool and school age children (solid lines) has brought about a correspondingly dramatic change in the proportion of children with mothers in the labor force (broken lines).

[a] For 1940 and 1950, includes divorced or separated mothers in addition to those living with spouse.

For children in two-parent families, the percentage with mothers in the labor force follows the same trend as the labor-force-participation rate of mothers, but at a slightly lower level, the latter reflecting the somewhat lower fertility of working mothers relative to those not in the labor force (Figure 2, broken lines). The trends in black two-parent families are similar to those for whites, but at somewhat higher levels—

by 1979, more than 60 percent of children in black two-parent families had mothers in the labor force (Figure 2, upper panels).

A mother who is in the labor force is not necessarily away from home all day long for the whole year. The proportion of working mothers in two-parent families that hold full-time year-round jobs is considerably less than the average for all working women in husband-wife families, and this is especially true of working mothers with preschool children (Table 2). But the trend in the proportion working at such jobs over the last two decades has been steadily upward. By 1979, even among working mothers with children under 3 years old, more than one in five held a full-time year-round job. Thus, not only are a large share of mothers in two-parent families in the labor force but, among those who are, the proportion with full-time full-year jobs has grown. Among mothers with children under 3 years old, the combined effect of these trends was that almost one mother in ten was working full time year-round in 1979.

The absence of a mother from a two-parent home because of working commitments implies, of course, an addition to the family income. That this may be important to a child's welfare is suggested by the fact that low family income is correlated with bad outcomes for children, and when a husband's income is low, outside work is more frequent among mothers with children.[6] In 1978, working mothers contributed about

TABLE 2 Percentage of Those in Labor Force Who Worked at Full-Time Year-Round Jobs, Married Women, Husband Present, by Presence and Age of Children, by Race, 1960–1979

Race and Presence and Age of Children	1960	1970	1979
All persons			
All married women, husband present	32.0	40.8	43.4
No children under 18 years	41.3	51.8	52.7
Children 6–17 years only	32.2	40.6	41.9
Children 3–5 years, none under 3	25.4	29.8	34.6
Children under 3 years	10.9	15.6	22.3
Blacks			
All married women, husband present			52.3
No children under 18 years			53.4
Children 6–17 years only	not		57.3
Children 3–5 years, none under 3	available		55.1
Children under 3 years			

SOURCE: Bureau of Labor Statistics, *Special Labor Force Report: Marital and Family Characteristics of the Labor Force*, Nos. 7–237.

[6] See for example, Bureau of Labor Statistics, Special Labor Force Report No. 219: Table G.

one-fourth of the family income in lower-income households,[7] minus the expenses added by the wife's work outside the home.

Childbearing

The post-World War II period has seen a sharp turnaround in rates of childbearing—for both races a sharp "baby boom," peaking in the late 1950s, followed by an equally precipitous "baby bust." In the last few years the fertility rate has been fairly constant, close to the all-time low (Figure 3, solid lines).

This swing in fertility has had important consequences for the number of children per family and thus for the number of siblings a child has. For families with children in which the head is 30 to 34 years old, a postwar peak of almost three children under age 18 per family was reached in 1965 (Figure 3, left panel, broken line). (This peak lags that

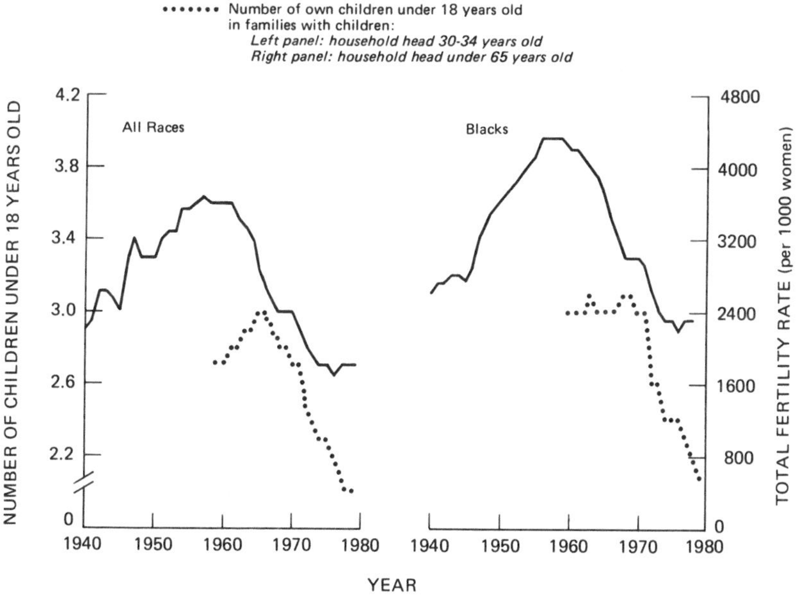

Figure 3 The impact of the declining rate of childbearing on the number of siblings children have. The "baby bust" since around 1960 (solid lines) has caused with some lag a sharp drop in the number of siblings a child has (broken lines). For example, in families that have children and are headed by a person aged 30-34, the average number of children under 18 years old has dropped from about three to two since 1965.

[7] See Bureau of Labor Statistics, Special Labor Force Report, No. 237:A-35. See also No. 189:19.

in the fertility rate, because the number of children under 18 years old at any given date is determined by fertility over the preceding 18 years; hence it takes a while before a downturn in the annual fertility rate pulls down average family size.) By 1979, the baby bust had lowered the average to about two children.

Although the average number of children per family is conceptually different from the average number of siblings per child, it happens that for the population as a whole in the period under discussion the former provides a close numerical approximation to the latter.[8] For the typical child the number of siblings was cut, on the average, by one-third—from three to two—in only 14 years. For blacks, the decline in number of siblings is even steeper, from over four to two.[9] In general, then, for both whites and blacks, not only has the presence of parents in the home declined, but so has the number of siblings. Of course, to the extent that the parents are at home, fewer siblings may mean more parental attention per child.

The decline in childbearing has been accompanied by a widening in the age gap between siblings in families of a given size. A second child about 6 months old in 1968 would typically have had an older sibling about 3.2 years old; for one born in 1979, the older sibling would have been 3.8 years old—a widening of the age gap from 2.7 to 3.3 years (Table 3). Similarly, the age difference between the oldest and youngest child has widened in large families—by 1.7 years in three-child families and 3.0 years in those with four or more children.

A Longer Historical Perspective

As far as one can judge from the imperfect data available, the current situation of young children with regard to the presence of natural par-

[8] A numerical illustration will clarify the conceptual difference. Assume that there are only two families, one with one child and one with three children. Then the average number of children per family is 2.0 [= 1/2 × (1 + 3)]; the average family size of children is 2.5 [= 1/4 × (1 + 3 + 3 + 3)]; and the average number of siblings per child is 1.5 (= 2.5 − 1.0). As Preston (1976) has shown,

$$\text{(Siblings per child)} = \text{(Average children per family)} + \text{(Variance in average children per family)} - 1.$$

For families with a head aged 30-34, the value of the variance term is approximately 1 in the period under discussion; hence, for these families in this period the last two terms in the equation cancel each other.

[9] For blacks, the variance term in the equation of the preceding footnote has a value of about 1.0 at the end of the period, but is in excess of 2.0 at the beginning.

TABLE 3 Age of Oldest Sibling of Children Aged Less Than 1 Year, by Size of Family, 1968 and 1979

Age of Oldest Child	Two Children		Three Children		Four or More	
	1968	1979	1968	1979	1968	1979
Median age (years)	3.16	3.82	5.91	7.59	8.83	11.83
Percent distribution by age						
Total	100.0	100.0	100.0	100.0	100.0	100.0
Less than 1 year	1.0	1.4	—	—	—	—
1–2 years	46.9	36.7	6.1	3.9	0.3	—
3–5 years	40.4	43.4	45.2	28.9	18.9	7.4
6–9 years	8.6	13.1	36.2	43.2	43.5	26.8
10–13 years	1.7	4.8	7.8	16.8	24.0	34.6
14–17 years	1.0	0.6	3.3	6.8	9.2	21.8
18 and over	0.2	0.1	1.6	0.5	3.9	8.7

SOURCE: Bureau of the Census, Current Population Reports, *Household and Family Characteristics*, Series P–20, Nos. 191 (October 1959) and 352 (July 1980).

ents and siblings in the home is unprecedented in this century. This is certainly true of whites and probably of blacks. Because of higher mortality at the turn of the century, widowhood was considerably more common among young wives than it is today. Among white females the decline in widowhood from 1900 to 1940 was just about offset by a corresponding rise in divorce, so that marital dissolution from these two sources combined was about the same just before World War II as at the beginning of the century (Table 4). During the next 40 years, however, as a result of the sharp upsurge in divorce in the 1960s and 1970s, the percentage widowed or divorced more than doubled among white females aged 25-34, causing an overall growth in marital dissolution including separation (compare lines 1 and 2 or 3 and 4 for whites in Table 4). At the present time, children under 6 are more likely to experience marital dissolution than were their parents or grandparents when they were young children. Exposure to marital dissolution has also increased among children 6-17, but the difference from earlier generations is less marked than for younger children (see the data for females 35-44 in Table 4).

Among black wives in the age-groups from 25 to 44, from 1900 to 1940 the percentage widowed or divorced fell, reflecting a sharp decrease in widowhood. But during the next 40 years the percentage rose sharply, as the increasing divorce rate came to predominate, until today the percentage widowed or divorced exceeds somewhat that at the beginning of the century. In contrast to whites, however, the percentage separated has also risen rapidly since 1940, and, taking this into account,

TABLE 4 Percent of Ever-Married Females Widowed and Divorced, 1900–1979, and Widowed, Divorced, and Separated, 1940–1979, by Race

	White			Black		
	1900	1940	1979	1900	1940	1979
Age 25–29						
Widowed and divorced	3.6	3.4	9.9	12.4	7.8	14.8
Widowed, divorced, and separated	n	7.0	14.4	n	21.7	38.9
Age 30–34						
Widowed and divorced	5.2	5.0	11.5	15.8	11.9	20.4
Widowed, divorced, and separated	n	8.4	15.4	n	25.9	41.2
Age 35–44						
Widowed and divorced	9.2	8.4	12.1	21.3	19.3	24.3
Widowed, divorced, and separated	n	12.0	15.8	n	31.4	44.4

SOURCES: 1900—U.S.Census Office, *Census of Population: 1900*, II:lxxxix, xc.
1940—U.S. Bureau of the Census, *Census of Population: 1950*, II, *Characteristics of the Population* (Washington, D.C.: U.S. Government Printing Office, 1953):1–179, 1–191.
1979—U.S. Bureau of the Census, Current Population Reports, *Population Characteristics*, Series P–20, No. 349 (February 1980):7.

it seems likely that as in the case of whites, exposure to marital dissolution for the present generation of black children is considerably higher than that experienced by their parents and grandparents when they were children. Only if one assumed that the percentage separated among blacks was higher in 1900 than today would this not be so, but such an assumption would imply the unlikely situation of a decline in the percentage separated from 1900 to 1940 followed by a rise to 1979.

As for work outside the home by mothers in two-parent families, the upsurge is almost wholly a product of the last 40 years, as Figure 2 makes clear. For both whites and blacks, labor force participation of *all* females aged 25-44—irrespective of marital status—was considerably lower at the beginning of the century than in 1940. Among *married* females aged 16-44 (the only age-group for which information by marital status is available), only 1 in 20 was in the labor force in 1890; for mothers, the proportion would doubtless be even lower (Long, 1958).

TABLE 5 Average Number of Siblings of Children Born to Women Aged 45–49 in Specified Year, by Race

Year	White	Black
1890	6.2	8.8
1940	4.2	5.5
1970	3.2	5.3

SOURCE: Samuel H. Preston, "Family Sizes of Children and Family Sizes of Women," *Demography* 13(1):112. Reprinted by permission.

For today's generation of children, the experience of mothers working outside the home clearly sets them apart from their predecessors in this century.

The contrast between today's children and earlier generations also stands out with regard to number of siblings. Data exactly comparable to those cited earlier are not available, but the trend in number of siblings was sharply downward for both whites and blacks before 1940 (Table 5). (The decline in siblings is overstated somewhat in the table, because it does not allow for the down trend in infant and child mortality during this period.) This decline was arrested (though not reversed) by the postwar baby boom but, as we have seen, has since resumed as a consequence of the baby bust. Thus, in all these respects, the present generation of children is being reared in family situations strikingly different from those of their parents or grandparents. Because of high marital dissolution, many more children go through a period when one of their natural parents, usually the father, is not in the home. Even in two-parent families, the growth in mothers' work outside the home implies a reduction in the presence of mothers at home. And the recent baby bust has brought the number of siblings to an all time low.

New Developments in Child Care Arrangements

What changes have occurred in the way children are cared for? For children of working mothers, valuable information on child care has been obtained in special Bureau of Census surveys conducted in 1958, 1965, and 1977 and analyzed in a forthcoming publication (O'Connell et al., 1981). The chief lesson of this analysis is quickly told: a sharp increase in care outside a child's own home—in effect, the emergence of a vast new day care "industry" (Table 6). In 1958, about 57 percent of preschoolers whose mothers held full-time jobs were cared for in their

TABLE 6 Percentage Distribution of Preschool Children of Working Mothers, by Type of Child Care Arrangement, Age of Children, and Full-Time/Part-Time Job Status of Mother, 1958–1977

	June 1958			February 1965			June 1977[a]		
	Total Under 6 Years	Under 3 Years	3 to 5 Years	Total Under 6 Years	Under 3 Years	3 to 5 Years	Total Under 5 Years	Under 3 Years	3 to 4 Years
Employed full time									
Number of children	2,039	833	1,157	2,561	1,024	1,537	2,669	1,394	1,117
Percent distribution:									
Total	100.0	100.0	100.0	100.0	100.0	100.0	100.0	100.0	100.0
Care in child's home[b]	56.6	NA	NA	47.2	46.0	48.1	28.6	29.9	26.4
By father	14.7	NA	NA	10.3	9.5	10.8	10.6	10.8	10.1
By other relative	27.7	NA	NA	18.4	18.6	18.3	11.4	12.6	10.0
By nonrelative	14.2	NA	NA	18.5	17.8	19.0	6.6	6.4	6.3
Care in another home	27.1	NA	NA	37.3	41.7	34.3	47.4	53.4	41.7
By relative	14.5	NA	NA	17.6	22.0	14.8	20.8	22.1	19.7
By nonrelative	12.7	NA	NA	19.6	19.8	19.5	26.6	31.3	22.0
Group care center[c]	4.5	NA	NA	8.2	4.8	10.5	14.6	9.1	21.2
Child cares for self	0.6	NA	NA	0.3	0.2	0.3	0.3	0.1	0.2
Mother cares for child while working[d]	11.2	NA	NA	6.7	6.4	6.9	8.2	6.8	10.1
Other arrangements		NA	NA	0.4	1.0	—	0.8	0.8	0.4

Employed part time									
Number of children	NA	NA	NA	1,233	470	763	1,458	805	611
Percent distribution:									
Total	100.0	100.0	100.0	100.0	100.0	100.0	100.0	100.0	100.0
Care in child's home[b]	NA	NA	NA	47.0	45.2	48.1	42.7	42.5	43.2
By father	NA	NA	NA	22.9	20.2	24.5	23.1	21.5	25.2
By other relative	NA	NA	NA	15.6	16.2	15.1	11.2	12.2	10.6
By nonrelative	NA	NA	NA	8.6	8.8	8.6	8.4	8.8	7.4
Care in another home	NA	NA	NA	17.0	19.7	15.5	28.8	32.2	24.7
By relative	NA	NA	NA	9.1	9.4	8.9	13.2	15.1	10.1
By nonrelative	NA	NA	NA	7.9	10.3	6.5	15.6	16.6	14.6
Group care center[c]	NA	NA	NA	2.7	0.9	3.9	9.1	5.5	14.2
Child cares for self	NA	NA	NA	0.9	0.9	1.0	0.5	—	0.2
Mother cares for child while working[d]	NA	NA	NA	32.3	33.3	31.6	18.5	19.9	16.9
Other arrangements	NA	NA	NA	—	—	—	0.4	—	0.8

NOTE: NA = Not available; — rounds to zero.

[a] Data are only for two youngest children under 5 years old. Total includes children for whom age is not known.
[b] Data exclude children whose mother cares for them while working at home.
[c] Data are for all types of group care.
[d] Data include children whose mother is working at home or away from home.

SOURCE: O'Connell et al. (1981).

own home, about a fourth of them by nonrelatives. By 1977, this figure had fallen to about one-quarter. (This understates the shift to care outside a child's home, because the 1977 figure in Table 6 is biased upwards relative to 1958 in that it omits data for 5-year-olds.) In 1958, most children not cared for at home were being cared for in another home, and use of group care centers was quite small. Similarly, with regard to the growth in care outside the home between 1958 and 1977, most of it was accounted for by care in other homes; however, the role of group care centers did rise somewhat in importance. By 1977, almost half of the children under 5 years old of full-time working mothers were cared for in other homes (somewhat over half by a nonrelative), and about one-seventh were cared for in a group center. For mothers who worked part time the trends were similar but milder—in 1977 the principal's arrangement for the children of these women was still care in the child's own home.

The role of day care facilities outside a home (whether the child's own home or not) is understated in Table 6. Trends in enrollment rates in preprimary schools for children under 6 years old parallel those for group care centers but are at a considerably higher level (Figure 4). For children 3-4 years old with mothers in the labor force, the enrollment rate in 1976 was 35 percent;[10] this compares with an average figure in 1977 only somewhat over half as large for the percentage of children in group care centers (Table 6). Taken together, however, the data in Table 6 and Figure 4 are consistent in indicating a marked shift in the locale of childrearing from a child's own home to other homes or group care facilities. Moreover, this shift occurred to some extent even among children of nonworking mothers. In 1976, the percentage of 3- to 4-year-old children of mothers not in the labor force enrolled in preprimary schools was 29 percent, only 6 points lower than that for children with mothers in the labor force.[11] Most of the children of nonworking mothers were enrolled only part of the day, however, while most of those of working mothers were enrolled for the full day.[12]

To these trends in child care should be added the influence of another major new institution in the post-World War II period, television. Estimates of the average time currently spent per week watching television by children aged 2-5 are a staggering 31 hours—about a fourth of a child's waking time (Table 7, column 1). For school age children, the figure is only moderately lower. Doubtless there is some overlap between this development and the growth in care outside the home—especially

[10] Bureau of the Census, Current Population Reports, Series P-20, No. 318: Table E.

[11] Bureau of the Census, Current Population Reports, Series P-20, No. 318: Table E.

[12] Ibid.: Table F.

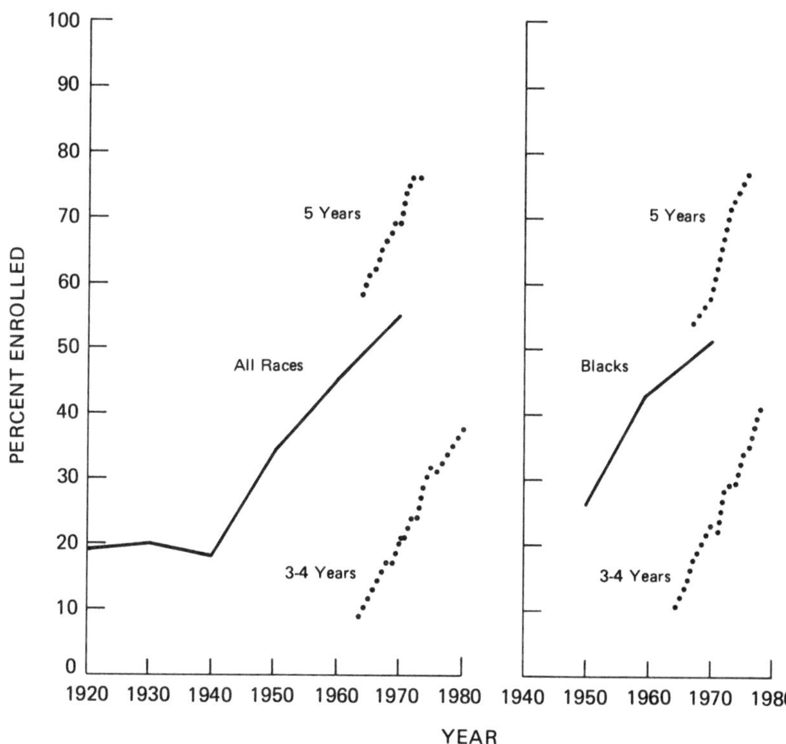

Figure 4 Preprimary school enrollment rates of children 3-4 and 5 years old, by race, 1920-1980. For both races, preprimary school enrollment rates have been rising sharply—for 5-year-olds since 1940 (solid lines), for 3- to 4-year-olds since the early sixties (broken lines). (The discontinuity in the curves for 5-year-olds is because of a shift in data source.)

in the growth of care in homes other than the child's own. But, as the distribution of viewing hours by day of week and time of day indicates, an important share of TV viewing occurs within a child's own home (Table 7). Taken together with the trends already reviewed, these data suggest a dramatic shift in the childrearing environment in less than one generation.[13]

Projections for the Family Environment of Children

What are the prospects for the family situation of children a decade and a half hence? Will the rapid changes that the last two decades have

[13] Moreover, if the reasoning of the following section is correct, then many of those retiring over the next 15 years will come from the scarcity generations born in the 1920s and 1930s and will be relatively well off.

TABLE 7 Weekly TV Viewing Activity by Preschool and School Age Children, February 1978

			Percentage Distribution of Hours by Time of Day					
				Monday–Friday		Saturday and Sunday		
	Hours per Week	Total	Prime[a] Time	4:30 p.m.– 7:30 p.m.	10:00 a.m.– 4:30 p.m.	7:00 a.m.– 1:00 p.m.	1:00 p.m.– 8:00 p.m.[b]	Other
Children aged 2–5	31.4	100	21	20	21	12	10	16
Children aged 6–11	27.3	100	31	22	12	11	11	13
Teenagers, male	27.2	100	34	17	12	7	13	17
Teenagers, female	23.4	100	36	18	16	5	11	14

[a] Monday–Saturday, 8:00–11:00 p.m.; Sunday, 7:00–11:00 p.m.
[b] 1:00 p.m.–7:00 p.m. on Sunday.

SOURCE: Data from *The 1979 Nielsen Report on Television: National Audience Demographics Report* (February 1978) were kindly provided by George Gerbner and Nancy Signorielli, Annenberg School, University of Pennsylvania.

witnessed continue unabated or even accelerate? Will they, perhaps, be reversed? No one knows the answers to these questions. The view presented here, though admittedly speculative, seeks to draw on experience since 1940 as a basis for anticipating the future.

To give quantitative shape to the discussion, the analysis starts with an attempt to assess the outlook for the situation of children implied by current official projections for the three variables that were taken in the first section as "proximate determinants." The outlook for fertility is included in the population projections of the Bureau of the Census and for marital status in the projections of families by type. Although there are no official projections of labor force status specifically for mothers, one can use the Bureau of Labor Statistics projections for labor force participation among females of childbearing age to approximate this.[14] Official projections are not predictions; rather, they offer for each magnitude several estimates of the possible future path. Actual experience has, in fact, sometimes fallen outside the range of official projections. Needless to say, the projections assume no catastrophic changes in the social, political, and economic environment. In the present analysis, the highest and lowest projections available for all three magnitudes are utilized. The analysis centers on the families of women in the 25-34 age span, and thus on children under 6 years and on the prospective experience of the population as a whole, since separate projections for whites and blacks are not available.

In 1979, the total fertility rate was a little above 1,800 births per thousand women; this compares with a value 15 years earlier of almost 3,200. The high projection of the Bureau of the Census envisages a reversal of the recent decline—namely, a rise in the total fertility rate to about 2,700 births per thousand women, still considerably below the 1964 level; the low projection anticipates a continued decline, but of fairly small magnitude, to about 1,700 births per thousand women. The smallness of the further decline projected is due to the fact that fertility is already at historically low levels.

With regard to marital status, both high and low projections anticipate a continued rise in the percentage divorced or separated among females

[14] Based on data for 1963-1979, the following regression equation was estimated: $y = 5.174 + 0.7556x$, where y is the labor force participation rate of married females, husband present, with children under 6 years old, and x is the labor force participation rate of all females aged 25-34. The period from 1963 on was chosen because a scatter diagram of the full data set revealed an almost perfect linear relation between the two variables starting in 1963. (The adjusted R^2 value is .99.) This equation was used to project the 1985, 1990, and 1995 values of y based on the "high growth" and "low growth" Bureau of Labor Statistics' projections for these dates of x (Fullerton, 1980).

aged 25-34, but the low projection anticipates only a 1-point increase over the 1979 level (to 18 percent), while the high projection foresees a rise at about the same rate as in the previous decade and a half, to about 25 percent. With regard to the percentage of mothers in the labor force with children under 6 years old, both the low and high projections of the Bureau of Labor Statistics imply a further substantial increase above the current level of 43 percent—ranging from 11 to 20 percentage points.

For discussion purposes, it is convenient to divide these projections into two sets. Projection I groups the high-fertility projection with the low projection for marital dissolution and mothers' work outside the home; projection II, the low fertility projection with the high projection for the other two variables. It should be borne in mind, however, that, in the development of these projections by the agencies responsible, no attempt was made to ensure consistency among the three variables grouped together here.

Based on this grouping, Table 8 presents the projected values for each of the three proximate determinants in 1995 and a rough estimate based on past relationships of the implied situation of children in regard to presence of parents, mother's work status, and number of siblings. Comparing the two sets, one finds that projection II implies the most radical change from current conditions. The percentage point increase in the next 15 years in young children not living with both parents would be greater than in the preceding 20 years; by 1995, over one child in five (22 percent) would be in such a situation. The proportion of young children in two-parent families whose mother works outside the home would continue growing at about the same rate as in the last decade, reaching almost two children out of three by 1995. The decline in average number of siblings would also continue, though at a somewhat slower rate because of the projected slowdown in the fertility decline. Nevertheless, by 1995, the average number of siblings in a household with head aged 30-34 would have dropped from the current value of 2.0 to 1.4.

By contrast, projection I offers a more mixed and less drastic pattern of changes from the present situation. The percentage of children not living with both parents would change very little compared with the present, rising slightly. The average number of siblings, rather than declining as in projection II, would rise to 2.25. And while the percentage of children with mothers working outside the home would rise as in projection I, the size of the increase is only about half as great. Overall, projection I does not foresee substantial changes from the present so far as the presence of children's natural parents and siblings in the home

TABLE 8 Implications of Projections of Proximate Determinants For Children's Status in 1995

	1979	1995 Projection I	1995 Projection II
Proximate determinant			
Females 25–34: Percent of ever-married women divorced or separated	17.3	18.3	24.9
Mothers in two-parent families with children under 6 years (percentage in labor force)	43.2	54.1	63.4
Total fertility rate per thousand women	1,813	2,689	1,694
Implied situation of children			
Percent of children under 6 years not living with both parents	14.2	15.2	21.8
Percent of children under 6 years with mother in labor force	41.7	52.6	61.9
Average siblings per child in families with children and head aged 30–34	2.03	2.25	1.40

SOURCE AND METHODS: For lines 1–3, sources are same as those for Figure 5. For lines 4 and 5, the sources for the 1979 values are given in Figures 1 and 2; the 1995 values were assumed to differ from those in lines 1 and 2, respectively, by the same amount as in 1979. For line 6, the source for the 1979 value is the same as for Figure 3. The 1995 value is derived from the regression equation: $y = -0.3288 + 2.1871x$, where y is the average number of own children under 18 years in families with children and a head aged 30–34 and x is the average number of persons under 18 years old in all families (including childless). A scatter diagram of y against x for 1959–1979 showed a very close linear relation except in the years 1965 and 1966, when the value of y was peaking, and the values for the latter years were consequently omitted in estimating the equation (adjuted $R^2 = 0.99$). The 1995 values of y were estimated by substituting the official projections of x corresponding to Series I and Series III fertility levels. It was assumed that the equality over the last decade of siblings per child and average family size continued to hold (see footnote 8).

is concerned, whereas projection II implies a continued considerable shrinkage.

At present it is rare for persons aged 65 and over to be living in households that are raising young children. Only about one in every 100 families with a head aged 30-34 includes a person aged 65 years or over; in families with a head 35-44, the corresponding figure is 2 in 100.[15] The aging of the population and publicity recently given to problems with the Social Security system, however, raise the question whether the welfare of young children in the next 15 years may be affected, for

[15] Bureau of the Census, *Current Population Reports,* Series P-20, No. 352, Table 3. The figures given average together childless families and those with children; separate data are not available for families with children.

better or worse, by a sizable growth in the presence of older persons in households with young children.

So far as demographic trends through 1955 are concerned, the answer suggested by the official population and labor force projections is no. In the next 15 years, the ratio of persons 65 and over to those aged 16-64 will grow from about 16 to 19 percent; if the dividing line used is age 55 rather than 65, the relative growth in the older population is negligible (Table 9, lines 1, 2, 4). The projections of these ratios are reasonably firm, because they relate only to the population 16 and over and hence do not entail projections of fertility, the most problematic component of population change. It is possible, however, that they understate somewhat the possible rise in old-age dependency, because prospective mortality among older persons is probably overestimated (Crimmins, 1981).

Probably more to the point is the ratio of older persons not in the labor force to the total labor force. The worst prospect, that given by the Bureau of Labor Statistics' "low-growth" projection, is for a mild increase in this ratio from about 29 to 31 percent between 1979 and 1995; in the case of the "high-growth" projection, the ratio actually declines (Table 9, line 3). In general, then, current population and labor force projections do not imply that the trend in old-age dependency is likely to alter seriously the family situation of young children in the next 15 years.[16]

Evaluating the Projections

While old-age dependency due to demographic factors may not imply a serious change in the environment of young children, their prospects are significantly different depending on the outlook for marital dissolution, mothers' labor force participation, and the rates of childbearing envisaged in projections I and II (Table 8). Hence the question arises: Which of these projections seems more plausible?

In thinking about this it may help to place the projections of the proximate determinants of children's family situation in historical perspective. Figure 5 presents projections I and II for each variable through 1995 against the background of experience since 1940. To aid in the discussion, vertical lines have been erected in the figure at the peak of the postwar baby boom, 1957, and the most recent observation, 1979.

[16] Moreover, if the reasoning of the following section is correct, then many of those retiring over the next 15 years will come from the scarcity generations born in the 1920s and 1930s and will be relatively well off.

TABLE 9 Ratio of Older to Working Age Population, by Race, 1975–1995 (Percent)

	1975	1979	1985	1990	1995
All races					
Population 65 and over to population 16–64	16.4	16.9	17.7	18.6	19.1
Population 55 and over to population 16–54	37.0	37.5	37.8	37.2	36.9
Persons 55 and over not in labor force to persons 16 and over in labor force:					
BLS low-growth projection	28.8	28.9	29.8	30.5	31.0
BLS high-growth projection	28.8	28.9	27.0	26.2	25.7
Nonwhites					
Population 55 and over to population 16–54	27.4	27.5	27.3	27.3	27.3

SOURCE: Fullerton (1980).

When the past four decades are divided in this way, it is clear that experience from the late 1950s to 1979 differs noticeably from that before. Before the late 1950s, the rate of marital dissolution tended to be stable or declining; thereafter it turned up sharply. With regard to mothers' work outside the home, although the trend was upward throughout the entire period from 1940 onward, the rate of increase rose after the late 1950s, and especially in the 1970s. Before 1957 fertility typically rose; thereafter, it fell. Comparing the high and low projections for each variable with experience in the periods before and after the late 1950s, one finds that, roughly speaking, projection I follows a course more like that in the earlier period, while projection II conforms more to the pattern of the second period. Thus, the issue of evaluating the alternative projections can be viewed as a matter of whether conditions in the next 15 years are likely to be closer to those of the earlier or later period.

One might answer this by dismissing the earlier period as exceptional—pointing out that fertility, after a long-term downward trend, rose dramatically in the 1940s and 1950s (Cherlin, 1981). Similarly, the previous uptrend in marital dissolution was interrupted in this period. This view leads naturally to preferring projection II, the one implying continued drastic changes in the family environment of children.

However, writing off the earlier period as atypical implies that experience *since* the late 1950s is more representative of the long-term trend. But, in fact, the recent growth in divorce rates is widely recognized

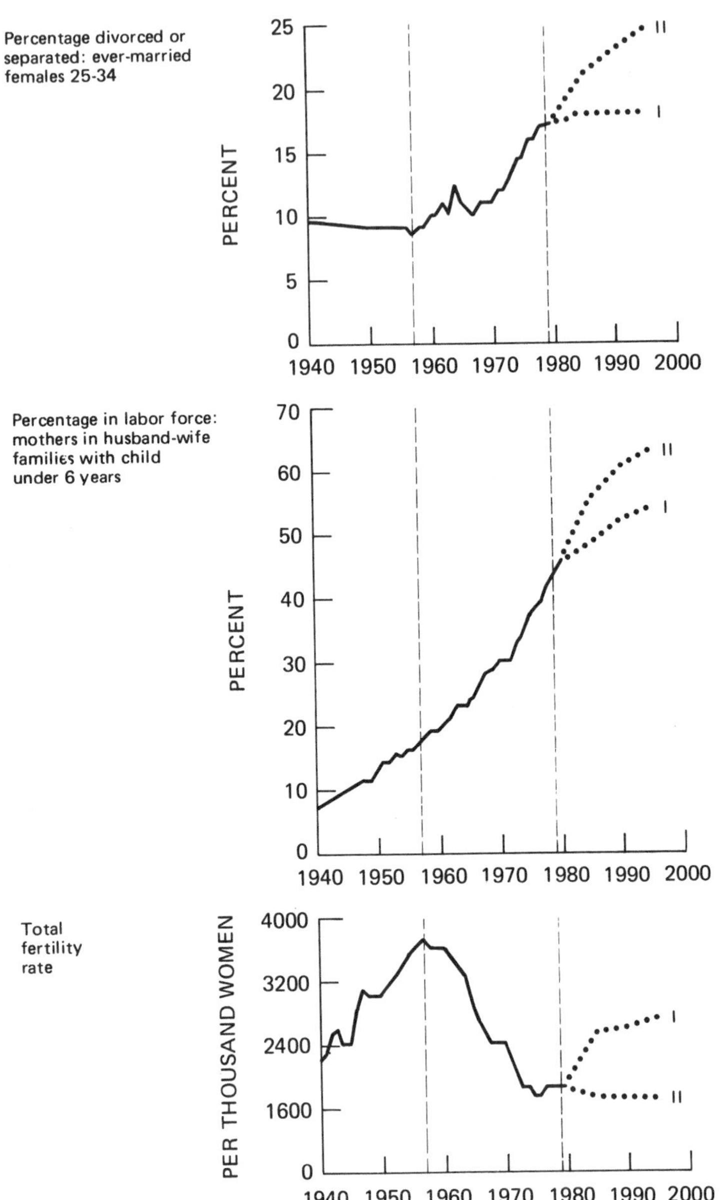

Figure 5 Recent and projected changes in marital dissolution, mothers' work outside the home, and childbearing, 1940-1995. This figure shows the high and low projections to 1995 (broken lines) for the indicated variable, compared with actual values since 1940 (solid lines).

to be at unprecedented rates, and it is far from clear that such high rates will continue (as Cherlin pointed out in this conference). Moreover, compared with experience before 1940, the growth in labor force participation of mothers with small children was exceptional both before and after the late 1950s. Although there was some difference between the two later periods, it is uncertain which of them is closer to the long-term trend. The case for dismissing the earlier period and preferring the projection that falls more into line with recent experience is far from persuasive.

Clearly, the best basis for evaluating the relevance of past experience to the future would be an interpretation of the past that can account for the contrasting patterns before and after the late 1950s. This, in fact, is the tack taken here. Instead of maintaining that one or the other of the two periods is exceptional, the present approach sees both as part of a pattern of long-term fluctuation that has emerged in the American economy since 1940—it views both periods as departures from the long-term trend, but in opposite directions.

A Cohort Size Interpretation of Recent Experience

The basis for my reasoning is, briefly, as follows (for fuller discussion, see Easterlin, 1980). The long-term trend in the three variables in Figure 5 has been shaped by a number of factors, differing in part from one variable to the other, such as changing ideology regarding sex roles and sexual relations, the continued growth in educational attainment of the population, rising demand for female labor, and so on. However, since 1940, along with such longer-term forces a new determinant has come into play, a factor that operates in cyclical fashion producing long swings around the underlying trend. This factor is the changing number of young adults relative to older—roughly the ratio of those aged 15-29 to those 30-64—termed here "relative cohort size."

Why should the relative number of young adults at a particular date influence conditions such as childbearing, mothers' work outside the home, and marital disruption? The answer to this is that all these conditions depend largely on the behavior of young adults, that such behavior is affected by (along with other things) the economic condition of young adults, and that the relative number of young adults has come to play an important part in determining their economic condition.

To see how the relative number of young adults affects their economic condition, imagine that the proportion between the jobs available for younger workers and those for older workers is constant: As the economy expands, these jobs grow at about the same rate—that is, the demand for younger and older workers grows equally. Now imagine, in contrast, that the supply of younger workers compared with older changes noticeably over a period of a decade or so. At a time when the relative supply of younger workers is high, competition among them will be intense, and employers can be choosy. Younger workers may require considerable time and effort to find satisfactory jobs, salaries may be disappointing, and advance up the career ladder may be frustratingly slow. Conversely, when younger workers are in short supply, employers find themselves competing, while younger workers pick and choose. To attract needed workers, employers will be much more likely to snap up those seeking jobs and to offer higher wages.

Experience in the last two decades illustrates this argument. Since the late 1950s, the relative number of young adults has grown rapidly, as the baby boom cohorts have reached adulthood (Figure 6). This growth in relative numbers has caused a deterioration in the relative earnings of young adults. Because older men are further up the career ladder than younger, their earnings are typically above average and younger men's are below. However, when the number of younger workers grows relative to older, the wages of the younger fall even further below the average while those of older rise further above. This is shown by the curves in Figure 7 (see also Welch, 1979).

The deterioration in the relative pay rates of young men with the growth in their relative numbers is repeated in unemployment rates. A higher unemployment rate for younger workers than for older is normal and reflects their newness in the job market, their job-seeking activity, the tentativeness of their job commitments, and so on. In the 1970s, however, the unemployment rates of younger workers compared with older were noticeably worse than in the 1950s (see Figure 8). Thus, the weight of numbers sharply aggravates the relative unemployment as well as the relative earnings disadvantage of the young (see also Wachter, 1976). The result is a noticeable deterioration in the income of young adults compared with older.

Note that it is the income of young adults *relative* to that of older that is affected by their relative numbers. An increase in the relative number of young adults, through its effects on relative rates of pay and unemployment, depresses their income relative to older adults. Conversely, a decrease raises their relative income. The relative income of young adults compared with older is especially significant for understanding the behavior of young adults. The income of younger relative to older adults can be thought of as corresponding roughly to the income of young adults relative to that of their parents; and the income of one's parents is one of the important influences shaping, however uncon-

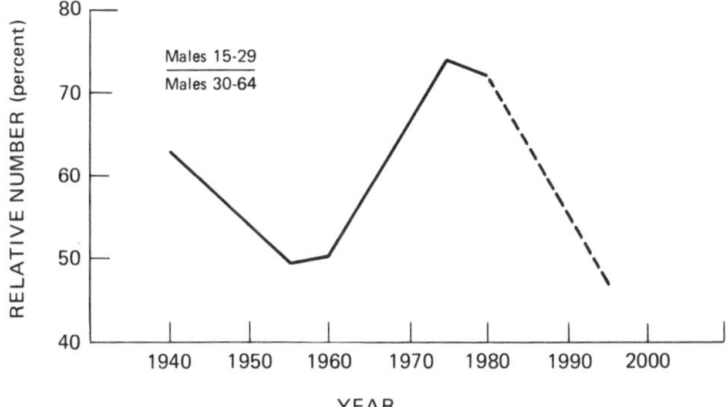

Figure 6 Recent swings in the birthrate and relative number of younger men compared with older. The proportion of younger to older men in the working age population declined from 1940 to the late 1950s and then turned sharply upward (lower panel), echoing with about a two-decade lag a corresponding swing in the birthrate (upper panel). In the next two decades, the proportion of younger to older men will decline again, as a result of the recent "baby bust."

sciously, one's life-style aspirations. This is because one's parents' income largely determines one's material environment at home, the type of neighborhood one grows up in, one's schooling, and so on. The process of "economic socialization" experienced while growing up in one's parents' home thus plays a large role in shaping one's views as to how to live as an adult. Viewed in this way, variations in the income of young adults relative to older are a rough measure of the changing success with which young adults can realize their material aspirations: The numerator is an indicator of the income-generating capacity of young

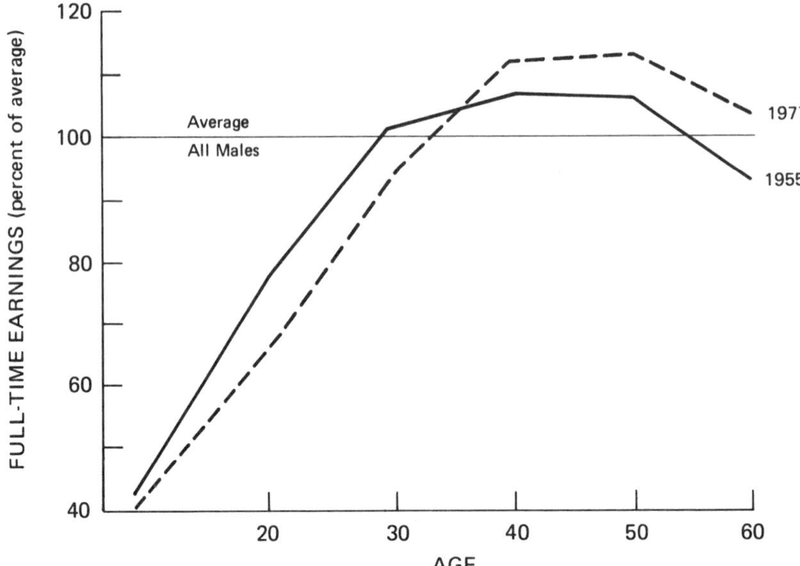

Figure 7 The earnings of younger men compared with older: the 1970s versus the 1950s. For each date, earnings at the age shown at the bottom of the chart are expressed as a percentage of the average for all ages (the horizontal broken line). At both dates, the left-hand position of the curve lies below the average, showing that younger workers earn less than older. In 1977, however, the shortfall for younger workers is greater than it was in 1955, showing that the relative position of younger workers is worse at a time when their relative numbers are greater.

adults; the denominator, of their material aspirations. When the relative income of young adults is low, they find it difficult to realize their material aspirations, are hard-pressed economically, and their psychological outlook is negative. When their relative income is high, they feel comparatively affluent and their psychological outlook is good.

If this reasoning is correct, then one might expect that indicators not only of the economic condition of young people but also of their psychological outlook would vary with changes in their relative numbers. An increase in the relative number of young adults, for example, should be associated with adverse changes in psychological outlook. This, in fact, turns out to be the case. A recent study by Joseph Veroff (1978) of the University of Michigan's Survey Research Center compared two nearly identical national surveys that inquired into feelings of well-being and distress. One of these surveys was made in 1957, when younger adults were benefiting from small cohort size, and the other in 1976, when younger adults were suffering from the disadvantages of unusually

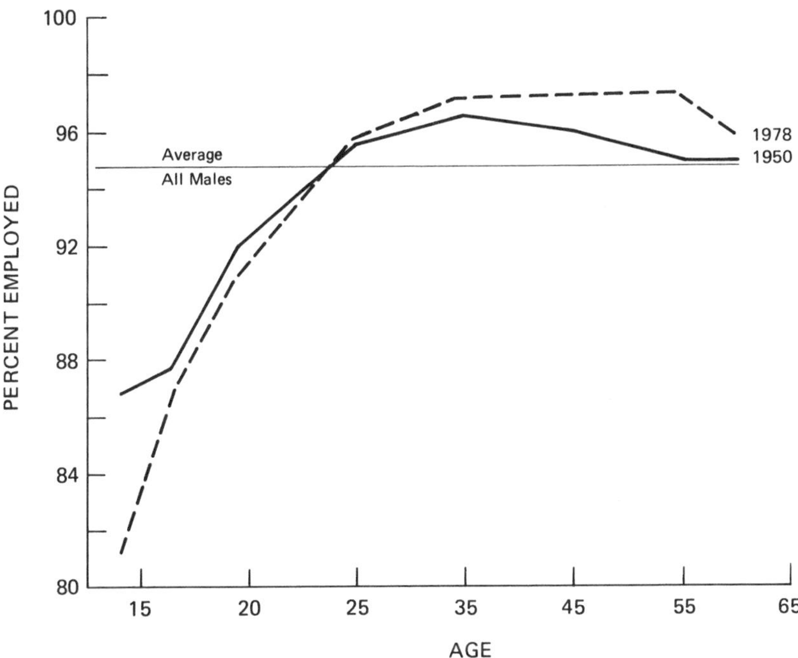

Figure 8 Employment rates of younger men compared with older: the 1970s versus the 1950s. At both dates, the left-hand portion of the curve lies below the average (the horizontal broken line), showing that younger workers have lower employment rates than older (that is, their *un*employment rates are higher). In 1978, however, the shortfall for younger workers is greater, showing that the relative position of younger men is worse when their relative numbers are greater.

large cohort size. (Veroff was not studying the effects of cohort size—it just happens that his dates work out well for the present purpose.)

His results show a marked increase in psychological stress between the two dates. The percentage of persons in their twenties reporting that they were "very happy" declined from 39 to 31 percent, and the percentage reporting that they worry "a lot" or "always" rose from 32 to 51 percent. The survey also inquired into symptoms of psychological anxiety, such as insomnia, nervousness, headaches, loss of appetite, and nausea. The percentage of young adults very high on these measures of anxiety rose over the two decades from 10 to 16 percent. A clear and consistent picture emerges of greater psychological tension among the large cohorts of the 1970s than among the small cohorts of the 1950s. Other evidence of this appears in changes since 1940 in homicide and suicide rates (O'Connell, 1975; Schapiro and Easterlin, 1979).

The foregoing reasoning should suffice to indicate the link between young adults' relative cohort size and their behavior with regard to the three key variables of childbearing, mothers' work outside the home, and marital disruption. When young adults' cohort size is large, they will feel under unusual economic pressure and their psychological outlook will be poor. As a result they will be hesitant about having children; among couples that do have children, there will be added incentive for mothers to work in order to supplement the family income; and marital strains will be greater than normal. Correspondingly, small cohort size tends to promote childbearing, to slow the growth in mothers' work outside the home, and to reduce marital disruption.

Viewed from this causal perspective, the contrasting patterns in Figure 5 in each of the proximate determinants before and after the late 1950s form a consistent picture. The former is a period in which cohort size is progressively declining; the latter, one in which it is rising (Figure 6). This swing in cohort size had the effect of modifying the long-term trend for each variable in opposite directions in each of the two subperiods. Thus, declining cohort size before the late 1950s led through the mechanisms described to a rise in childbearing and below-average growth in marital dissolution and mothers' work outside the home; after the late 1950s, increasing cohort size led to declining fertility, and above-average growth in marital dissolution and mothers' work outside the home.

It was mentioned earlier that the effect of cohort size has become important only since about 1940. This is because, before World War II, both the supply of and demand for labor were much more variable than they are today, and the effect of cohort size was dwarfed by other influences. However, with government policies stabilizing the growth of labor demand and capping immigration, variations in cohort size have come to play a much more important role in shaping the economic conditions and psychological outlook of young adults.

Implications for the Future

The foregoing reasoning has direct bearing on the issue of whether projection I or II provides a more plausible picture of how the family environment of children will change over the next 15 years. In the next two decades, the relative number of young adults will once again turn downward, a consequence of the baby bust of the last two decades (Figure 6). If experience of the past 40 years is a guide, then one may expect an amelioration in the economic situation and psychological outlook of young adults. The result should be a corresponding abatement in the growth rate of marital dissolution and mothers' work outside the home and an upturn in rates of childbearing. A shift of this type is precisely what is envisaged in projection I.

It should be emphasized that this analysis does not claim to tell the whole story of changes in marital dissolution, mothers' work outside the home, and childbearing since 1940—clearly no explanation is given of the long-term trend itself in each variable, and other factors have influenced the shorter-term movement besides relative numbers. At a minimum, however, this analysis cautions against mechanical extrapolation of the last two decades' dramatic changes into the future. For all three proximate determinants, the patterns in the two decades before 1960 contrast sharply with those thereafter. The present reasoning points to a factor that has operated systematically to produce this result and that, other things being equal, will make for a reverse toward the pre-1960 pattern in the coming two decades.

Summary

Since 1960 there has been a marked reduction in the presence of children's natural parents and siblings in their homes and a corresponding growth of a day care "industry"—care of children in the homes of others or in group care centers including private and public preprimary schools. As a result, the situation in which children are currently being raised, especially children under 6 years old, is very different from that in which their parents and grandparents were raised when they were children. The question to which this paper is principally addressed is: Will these changes continue in the next 15 years at or near their present pace?

The answer arrived at is, no. Based on an analysis that links the recent changes in the family environment of children to three proximate determinants—the rate of marital dissolution, labor force participation of mothers, and the total fertility rate—and these in turn to the effect of variations in relative cohort size (the number of younger adults relative to older), it is concluded that the economic and psychological pressures on young adults that have produced such dramatic family changes in the last two decades are likely to moderate considerably. Over the next 15 years there is likely to be only a slight increase in the percentage of children not living with both parents; the growth in the percentage of children in two-parent families with mothers working outside the home should moderate; and the average number of siblings per child, after the sharp decline in recent years, is likely to rise somewhat.

hese statements about the future refer to the population as a whole, and thus to the white population that dominates the aggregate statistics. As this paper shows, trends for blacks since 1940 have often been similar to those for whites, but there have also been important differences. The assessment here of future prospects is based on governmental projections, and because these are available only for the population as a whole, no attempt is made to judge the prospects for blacks, let alone other minority groups such as Hispanic Americans, for whom even the historical data are seriously inadequate.

References

Carter, Hugh, and Paul C. Glick
1970 *Marriage and Divorce: A Social and Economic Study*. Cambridge: Harvard University Press.

Cherlin, Andrew J.
1981 *Marriage, Divorce, Remarriage*. Cambridge: Harvard University Press.

Crimmins, Eileen M.
1981 The changing pattern of American mortality decline, 1940-77, and its implications for the future. *Population and Development Review* 7 (2):229-54.

Easterlin, Richard A.
1980 *Birth and Fortune: The Impact of Numbers on Personal Welfare*. New York: Basic Books.

Fullerton, Howard N.
1980 The 1995 labor force: A first look. *Monthly Labor Review* 103(12):11-21.

Glick, Paul C.
1957 *American Families*. New York: John Wiley & Sons.

Glick, Paul C., and Arthur J. Norton
1979 Marrying, divorcing and living together in the U. S. today. *Population Bulletin* 32(5):1-41. Washington, D.C.: Population Reference Bureau.

Kamerman, Sheila
1980 Child care and family benefits: Policies of six industrialized countries. *Monthly Labor Review* (November 1980):23-28.

Long, Clarence
1958 *The Labor Force Under Changing Income and Employment*. Princeton, N.J.: Princeton University Press.

O'Connell, Martin
1975 The Effect of Changing Age Distribution on Fertility and Suicide in Developed Countries. Unpublished Ph.D. dissertation, University of Pennsylvania.

O'Connell, Martin, Marjorie A. Lueck, and Ann C. Orr
1981 Trends in child care arrangements of working mothers. To appear in Bureau of the Census, Current Population Reports, Series P-23.

Preston, Samuel H.
1976 Family sizes of children and family sizes of women. *Demography* 13(1):112.

Ross, Heather L., and Isabel V. Sawhill
1975 *Time of Transition: The Growth of Families Headed by Women*. Washington, D.C.: The Urban Institute.

Schapiro, Morton O., and Richard A. Easterlin
1979 Homicide and fertility rates in the U.S.: A comment. *Social Biology* 26:341-343.

Veroff, Joseph
1978 General Feelings of Well Being Over a Generation. Unpublished paper presented to the American Psychological Association, September 1.

Wachter, Michael L.
1976 The changing cyclical responsiveness of wage inflation. *Brookings Papers on Economic Activity* 1:115-159.

Welch, Finis
1979 Effects of cohort size on earnings: The baby boom babies' financial bust. *Journal of Political Economy* 87(1):65-74.

DISCUSSION

Andrew Cherlin, the first formal discussant, set the framework for the discussion by noting that there were really two parts to Easterlin's predictions for the next 20 years: (a) the direction of the trends and (b) their magnitude. There is a lot of disagreement about (b), but most demographers can agree on (a). For the purposes of this conference, the main message of the Easterlin paper—a message many would agree with, including Cherlin—is that the rate of change in demographic events affecting families is going to be considerably slower in the 1980s than it was in the 1960s and 1970s.

"The rate of divorce, for example, cannot keep up its historical pace for long. The probability that a marriage will end in divorce has been increasing exponentially since the Civil War. If the long-term rate of increase were to continue, I estimate that 100 percent of all marriages begun in 2017 would end in divorce. Since even under the most pessimistic assumptions some married couples are likely to escape divorce, the increase in divorce must begin to slow in the coming years. Moreover, the increase we experienced in the 1960s and early 1970s was unusually large, even by historical standards. Thus, the increase in divorce is likely to be smaller in coming decades than in the last two decades, even if it is not as small as Easterlin expects. In fact, the trend has already started. The annual rate of divorce has increased only modestly since 1975.

"Similar arguments can be made about the recent increase in employed mothers or, conversely, about the sharp fall in the birthrate. In both cases, the pace of change in the near future is likely to be slower than in the recent past, although Easterlin and his critics can argue about the precise magnitude of future changes."

This slower pace of change is very likely to have beneficial effects on families with children in that it will enable them to catch up in their adaptations to the new reality. One reason for the emergence of the family as a source of public policy concern in recent years is that the changes in family life have occurred too rapidly for family members to find ways to adjust to them. Standard ways of coping with the everyday difficulties of family life suddenly did not apply after the wife went to work or the parents divorced. Yet there was not time to develop alternative solutions. In sociological terms, many aspects of family life became "deinstitutionalized." That is, the norms that had been taken for granted about how to conduct family lives no longer provided adequate guidelines. Once both parents worked, for example, it became difficult for wives to hold a paying job and still perform the culturally prescribed major role in childrearing and housework. Changed government and corporate policies, such as more flexible working hours, may help alleviate problems such as these, but they are unlikely to be resolved until social norms also change. (This harks back to a related point by Strober in the discussion following Chapter 1.) For instance, recent research suggests that, although fathers on flexitime like their flexibility, they don't use it to spend more time with their children—as family advocates had hoped. Instead, it appears that men will spend more time with their children only when basic norms about men's roles change. These kinds of changes—which involve reinstitutionalizing a new set of norms—take time. The respite from rapid change may provide the time for some of these changes in accepted behavior to occur.

The family lives of children in 1995 will still be quite different from their lives in 1950 or even 1970. One major factor is the increase in the number of children who will spend several years growing up in a family formed by the remarriage of their custodial parent. Everyone is aware by now that many marriages (currently about half) are expected to end in divorce, but fewer people note that most divorced people remarry. The annual rate of remarriage has fallen since the late 1960s, but evidence suggests that this decline reflects merely the tendency of divorced people to delay their remarriage by a few months, on average, compared to people divorcing a decade or so ago. This remaining high probability of remarriage means that many children will spend more of their childhood and adolescent years in a family of remarriage than in a single-parent family.

And the families formed by remarrying partners who have children from previous marriages can be quite complex. There are potentially three sets of children, several sets of grandchildren, and a large number of kin and quasi-kin. Family relationships also typically extend beyond household boundaries because of continuing ties between noncustodial parents and their children from previous marriages. In fact, each member of a household formed by remarriages may have a slightly different conception of who the members of their immediate family are. Thus, the very definition of the family becomes problematic except in relation to a particular person—the son from the wife's previous marriage, the stepfather with children from his previous marriage living elsewhere, and so forth.

Moreover, there is some suggestion in the evidence that children can have difficulty adjusting to remarriage. Having finally adjusted to the departure of the noncustodial parent, the child must now adjust to the introduction of a new stepparent.

"I do not mean to suggest that remarriages are inevitably—or even usually—a source of problems for those involved. Indeed, remarriage often provides a solution to many of the problems of life in a single-parent family, particularly the problem of low income. The stepparent and his kin expand the child's family network. But as the number of children in families of remarriages increases, we should investigate more closely the implications of this family form for children."

The last point that Cherlin emphasized, which had been mentioned previously, was the increasing divergence between blacks and whites with regard to marriage. For both races the age at marriage has been going up, and the proportion of children born out of wedlock has increased. But the trends have been much more pronounced for blacks in recent years. Until the post-World War II era, blacks used to marry earlier than whites, on average; now they marry later. Currently, less than half of all black women aged 25-44 are married with husband present, as compared to three-fourths of all white women aged 25-44. By the late 1970s, two out of three black women who gave birth to a first child were unmarried, compared to about one out of eight white women.

"What we have witnessed in the last few decades among blacks, particularly low-income blacks, is the increasing separation of childbearing from marriage. These two events, which used to be intertwined for whites and blacks, are now quite distinct for a substantial segment of the black population. It appears that among low-income blacks—the so-called underclass—the importance of marriage for family life has declined in comparison to the importance of an extended network of kin on which a mother can rely for support. The emergence of this type of family pattern on a large scale is a new phenomenon for black Americans; it was much less common just 20 years ago. In this regard, there has been a significant postwar divergence in the family patterns of blacks and whites. We know very little about the effects of this pattern on children. It will be important for us to find out more in the years ahead."

Leobardo Estrada, the second formal discussant, although subscribing to Cherlin's view that the *direction* of the trends predicted in the Easterlin paper were not in contention, did nevertheless bring up some of the arguments against Easterlin's explicit thesis of relative cohort size effects. His basic criticism centered around the fact that these relative cohort sizes have occurred at a particular historical time in conjunction with a lot of other macroeconomic changes. It is not so much that Easterlin's model gives us no insight. It is rather that other things are also likely to be important. "For example, the postwar era has been a period of economic restructuring and one in which so many things have changed at the macro level that it is difficult to separate the effects of labor supply and demand from such things as the internalization of capital, the loss of strength of the core manufacturing sector, and a convergence of wage rates among sectors."

Estrada also pointed out some specific difficulties with the theory. First, if the theory is correct one should expect to see regional job competition differences depending on the age structure. However, to the extent that they exist, they seem to go the wrong way for the Easterlin thesis—in that job competition is probably more severe where the age structure is older (in the Northeast) than where it is younger (the West). Racial differences and class differences are also relevant here.

"If one accepts the fact that the baby boom was an era in which there was a great deal of job competition and strains, psychological and sociological, then the period that is upon us or soon to be upon us as a result of the baby bust will be a period when things will become relatively better. This is very good, presumably, for some populations or subpopulations, such as the Hispanic population—which is about 8 years younger in terms of its median age and is a youthful population who will be entering their own high fertility years at the very same time that the baby bust generation will be emerging. It would follow then that the Hispanic population should be approaching the 1980s at a very good time. But there are certain factors that have to be taken into consideration that seem independent of relative cohort size. The most obvious one, for example, is language usage. The limited use of English would have an impact, I think, regardless of the relative size of cohort. Foreign birth, which is also related to language usage, would also have a clear effect, as is shown in most statistics, which also appears to be independent of relative cohort size. Finally, there are the complex issues of immigration. For a group such as Hispanics, immigration becomes a substantial part of the growth and size of the relative cohort in a flow-and-stop kind of manner. You have a situation in which immigration has to be considered and obviously, in a model like this, it may mitigate the effects of lower cohort size and fertility."

Harold Watts, the third formal discussant, focused on how meager our knowledge really is about the environment children are in and how it may be changing and enumerated three major ways in which our statistical description of that environment should be improved.

First, it is important to recognize that the child must be the unit of observation, not the family. "For example, in a population with a one-child family and a seven-child family, half the families have only one child but seven-eighths of the children have six siblings. The latter is the more relevant statistic."

Second, how various conditions affect children and how many children are affected depends a lot on *cumulative* experience. "We still suffer from a cross-section myopia that suggests that if children are in a certain condition now, they are going to be in that condition forever. Saying that, of course, one realizes immediately it is not true, but very often we don't even say that. We keep on thinking that those are permanent conditions. We may also want to distinguish in what part of a childhood career that experience occurs. There are a lot of relevant dimensions, some of which can be handled with demographic models, such as those with which Glick has worked. Surely, the kind of impact that a condition has—bad, good, or indifferent—can be expected to depend on how prevalent it is. And how deviant it is depends on how many people are affected by it and certainly for how long. Cross-section statistics are related to the cumulative picture, but we need further elaboration to know exactly how." We just don't have the facts that allow us to say, for example, how many children are in a one-parent family for, say, less than 1 year out of their childhood.

Third, a point also touched on by Cherlin, is that current statistics almost always look at families through the measuring instrument of the household at a point in time. But the household is not the family, and the two become increasingly different as family relationships become more elaborate and more complicated. "Families now, I think, ought to be regarded as multihousehold operations, much more than they were in the past. That leaves a lot of further theoretical work and the development of measuring conventions that need to be done. Tentatively, I would be inclined to try to draw the net around the family that a particular child is concerned with, having to do with the nature of commitments of time or resources that are either continually available via that person or represent some contingent claims (so that if someone gets in trouble there is this other part of the family network that can be called on.) Complex, multilayered families are becoming much more prevalent, multiplying in both number and extent. They are certainly not contained within the household as we use the word. A coresident household is an ephemeral thing. Surely a family is more permanent than that; we have got to broaden our data base to recognize this fact."

9
Implications for Policy and Research

William R. Morrill, Richard R. Nelson, and Felicity Skidmore

The picture of child poverty that has emerged from this volume is more complicated and, frankly, somewhat different from what the committee had expected. The slowdown in general growth of incomes and the rise in the overall employment rate experienced during the 1970s are reflected in the changing economic status of children and their families. We had known that overall poverty had virtually ceased to decline during the 1970s and, since we know that the elderly had continued to improve their situation during that decade, we had expected some rise in the incidence of poverty involving children. The data show this. The data also show that children of all races, in all kinds of families, in many different kinds of locales, live in poverty.

But the data show, in addition, that a very large share of poor children live in black, female-headed families in segregated urban communities. That this was part of the child poverty picture we had expected, but most members of the committee were surprised by how large a share of child poverty was of this sort. We certainly had not expected that the numbers of such children would be increasing absolutely, constituting a growing fraction of all children in poverty. The picture is more disturbing, and perplexing, than we originally had thought.

And the situation is not getting any better. The data used in most of our studies carry through to 1979 or 1980. Since then, the economic situation has become worse for many Americans, particularly for poor families with children. Between 1979 and 1981, the poverty rate for children under 18 living in families rose from 16 percent to 19.5 percent.

The last time the poverty rate for this group was higher than 19 percent was in 1965. For children in mother-only families, the poverty rate rose from 48.6 percent in 1979 to 52.3 percent in 1981. For children in black mother-only families, the poverty rate rose over the same period from 63.1 percent to 67.7 percent. In 1980, the most recent year for which the Current Population Reports are broken down by residence, there were just over 11 million poor children in the United States. Of these, 4.2 million lived inside central-city areas, and 43.6 percent of them were black. Of the 1.9 million poor children living inside the central-city areas designated as poverty areas, 59.3 percent were black. If imputations for in-kind transfers are included in the income measure, the absolute numbers become lower, but the relative proportions and the trends are provisionally estimated to be at least as severe.

The chances are high that a black child, growing up in a family with one parent at home, living in a neighborhood consisting largely of poor, black families, will be poor. When he or she reaches the middle or late teens, jobs will be hard to find. While predictions are hazardous, the chances are high that this pattern will not change over the next decade. The problem needs to be understood and not considered as merely one of a variety of possible, equally important problems related to child poverty.

What are the implications of this? What do these facts mean with respect to the policy and research agendas? The aspects are thorny, and important values are at stake. Many Americans are quite passionate about some of these values and in the last 15 years have demonstrated that their views are divergent on certain matters. We do not want to press our own values. We think it is important, however, that Americans get the facts straight and begin to rethink what they may portend for the future.

Trends of the 1970s

We would like to step back for a moment from the particulars documented in the previous chapters and consider some overall assessment of the prospective policy implications for children and families against the backdrop of the policy context of the late 1960s and early 1970s, in which these developments occurred. What emerges for the 1980s is a combination of familiar policy issues from the 1970s and earlier, plus some new or more sharply focused policy issues that should cause us to rethink the underlying assumptions and priorities of the previous period.

On the first score, the data describe some familiar conundrums that have vexed public policy in the past. Independent of other important considerations, two-parent families are likely to fare better economically than single-parent families. This is particularly true if the single parent is female, black, urban, and without strong labor market skills and experience. The disadvantaged in society, who are appropriately a special focus of policy attention, continue to present a profusion of individual circumstances and needs that defy simple or monolithic policy prescriptions or programs. This, in turn, vastly complicates the provision of equitable, efficient, and fiscally prudent public remedies. And no relief is in sight. Income maintenance and related programs mainly provide economic relief for temporary periods of hardship or for short-term problems. However, the problems for some are neither short-term nor susceptible to full remediation through individual effort combined with current U.S. income maintenance policy and available services. These problems will continue to plague the future as they have the past.

On the second score, however, the papers, both singly and even more forcefully when taken together, document the emergence of a new layer of problems, which potentially have even more disturbing consequences. Past policy prescriptions may in fact have contributed to them, leading us to urge some rethinking of the policy premises.

To oversimplify the problem (a little no doubt, but not drastically), much of the public policy of the 1960s and early 1970s was predicated on the assumption that some combination of investment in human capital and income maintenance support would permit individuals to participate in the "good life" that would emerge. Few doubted that this combination of policies, taking place in an environment of vigorous economic growth, would reduce inequities and, in consequence, close the gaps and cleavages among different groups in our society. In some ways policy programming in the late 1960s and 1970s, targeted on individual characteristics and circumstances, made sense. Had the economy been stronger, the situation for all could have been better and, conceivably, those in the worst situations might have been able to improve their lot more than proportionately. It is impossible to know.

What we do know, however, is that the reality of the 1970s was not what had been hoped. At least in the context of weakened macroeconomic performance and shifting demographic and employment patterns, the combination of human capital and income maintenance programs proved inadequate to the task. The situation for some groups of families has grown relatively much worse, and gaps between certain groups within society are widening rather than narrowing. Some may argue that poor program administration and insufficient funding were responsible for the failure. In our view, however, these are not likely to be the primary factors. The syndrome of child poverty revealed by the studies in this volume raises some disturbing questions.

Facing the 1980s

Female-Headed Families

Single-headed families now are the norm in black urban communities, and they are quite common among whites. Families of this sort account for a very significant fraction of poor children. And families of this sort are very likely to be poor. The overwhelming majority of these single-parent families with young children are female-headed. What kind of job opportunities are there for women with young children? What do these jobs pay? Where are they located? What are their hours? These variables are now important ones in determining the incidence of child poverty.

Black Poverty and Joblessness

Real median family income for the population as a whole reached a high of $24,700 a year in 1973. Real median family income for blacks reached a high of $15,820 a year in 1974 (66.4 percent of the overall median). By 1981, real median family income for the population as a whole had dropped to $22,400 a year, a decline of 9.3 percent since 1970. Real median income for blacks had dropped to $14,600 a year and—as a percentage of the overall median—had declined from a high of 66.7 percent (reached in 1978) to 65.2 percent, a lower relative position than in 1970. Why has the relative economic situation for blacks gotten worse? Is it true, as some scholars argue, that black America is now divided between those who make it and those who don't? If so, what are the factors determining a family's location on one side of the division or the other? Is poverty among blacks continued across generations? Put another way, is upward mobility, which was so strikingly evident in second-generation immigrants from so many counties, somehow blocked in second- or third-generation blacks who emigrated to the northern American cities during and after World War II?

The Urban Core

The evidence presented in this volume, and in many other studies, shows clearly that a significant fraction of black children grow up in segregated neighborhoods. As noted earlier, in these neighborhoods a very large percentage of families with young children are headed by the mother; the father lives somewhere else and may never have been part of the family. In these neighborhoods, also, a significant fraction of the jobs, goods, and services are provided by the unrecorded economy.

What is the experience these days of growing up black? How does it differ from the experience of growing up white? Does one's parents' income influence the answer to that question? One's parents' segregated or integrated community?

The Policy Dilemma

We think the experience of the 1970s that is painted in Chapters 2 through 8 provides strong grounds for reexamining the underlying policy assumptions—particularly the linkages between human development and income maintenance on one hand and macroeconomic health and development on the other. We also think the task is urgent.

First, the two demographic factors that prevented the economic experience of children and families from being even worse during the 1970s cannot be expected to have the same cushioning effect in the 1980s. Family income was increased throughout the 1970s by the enormous influx of mothers into the labor force. Such a trend cannot continue through the 1980s at anything like its rate over the last 10 years. In addition, average family size decreased (which by definition increased the per capita income of people in families). Demographic predictions agree on the slowing of this trend, if not its actual reversal.

Second, the problems over the last decade have been becoming increasingly concentrated in urban geographic centers and along racial lines. Third, employment and wage rates for women and youth in the regular labor market are conspicuously lower than those for adult men, and lower for minorities than for whites—putting single-parent families (which are almost all mother-only and more than proportionately black) at a relative disadvantage. Fourth, and obviously related at least in part to the first three, there is now a very real potential for the development of a large and continuing unrecorded economy as a permanent coping mechanism in the predominantly black, inner-city ghettos. Such an economy has separate product markets and separate labor markets and teaches different skills (some of which are antithetical to the skills needed to succeed in the regular economy).

Another decade of weak economic performance within the existing policy framework is unlikely to reverse and, indeed, may well exacerbate these growing gaps among population subgroups along racial and geographic lines. Such a development would put us far along the road to producing long-lasting dire consequences for our society, its families, and its children—and reverse America's progress toward our historic goal of equal opportunity for all in an economically, racially, and culturally integrated society.

The policy dilemma can be stated simply. It is now no longer clear that the problems of the disadvantaged can be stated predominantly in terms of individual income or human capital characteristics. This may well have been a fruitful formulation 15 years ago. And, indeed, the policy initiatives that came about as a result of this formulation have probably alleviated, at least to a degree, the remediable problems they were designed to deal with. But, in so doing, they have possibly contributed to, and certainly made more visible, a more intractable set of problems.

The United States of the early 1980s has been increasingly characterized by a geographic, racial, and economic bifurcation that was not clearly apparent in 1970. This situation leads us directly to a starker policy question: How can policies facilitate the balancing of demand and supply of labor of different skill levels in the face of significant changes in demand for skills in urban places?

The structural changes taking place in the economy in addition to the continuing cyclical swings have made it impossible to count on the overall level of economic activity—even in the long run and certainly in the shorter run—to restore enough economic activity in specific geographic areas to resolve the problems of those at the bottom. This leaves us with the problem of stimulating economic development in lagging areas and forging tighter links between policies to promote such development and policies aimed directly at this population. In particular, the view that training programs that are unrelated to the problems and opportunities of particular labor markets can still be effective is a myth we can no longer afford. This is a huge problem, and we know very little so far that is useful in the formulation of policies to solve it. There is relatively little research on how small area labor markets function, much less how to formulate labor market interventions. The data we have are weak and poorly understood. And previous policy efforts have provided weak results in the aggregate.

To the extent that such linkages between small area development and disadvantaged workers are unsuccessful, we are forced to face the problem of whether and how family mobility might be aided. We know that migration to pursue better opportunities has occurred historically, and we know that many young workers are now mobile. We have very little experience, however, with policies that provide incentives or remove disincentives to such mobility. And the problems of developing this kind of policy for the economically disadvantaged are particularly intractable. We are not talking about the very young worker. We are talking about people in their middle years, people with children, people who are poor *and* have found it hard to survive in labor markets, even in the geographical areas they are familiar with.

These are uncomfortable issues. But they are ones we think the research and policy communities should be prepared to face directly.

APPENDIX
Invited Participants, Conference on Families and the Economy

MARY JO BANE, JFK School of Government, Harvard University
BRIGITTE BERGER, Wellesley College
ORVILLE G. BRIM, JR., Foundation for Child Development
JOHN A. CALHOUN, Child Welfare League of America
ANDREW CHERLIN, Department of Sociology, Johns Hopkins University
JOHN J. CONGER, MacArthur Foundation
JOHN P. DEMOS, Department of History, Brandeis University
RICHARD A. EASTERLIN, Department of Economics, University of Pennsylvania
GLEN H. ELDER, Department of Sociology, Cornell University
DAVID T. ELLWOOD, JFK School of Government, Harvard University
LEOBARDO ESTRADA, School of Architecture and Urban Planning, University of California, Los Angeles
LOUIS A. FERMAN, Institute of Labor and Industrial Relations, University of Michigan
BARBARA D. FINBERG, Carnegie Corporation
PETER FORSYTHE, Edna McConnell Clark Foundation
EDMUND W. GORDON, Child Study Center, Yale University
ELLEN GREENBERGER, School of Social Ecology, University of California, Irvine
ROBERT J. HAGGERTY, W. T. Grant Foundation
MARTHA S. HILL, Institute of Social Research, University of Michigan

JAMES S. JACKSON, Institute for Social Research, University of Michigan

ALFRED J. KAHN, School of Social Work, Columbia University

EDWARD L. KAIN, Department of Human Development and Family Studies, Cornell University

KENNETH KENISTON, Department of Science, Technology and Society, Massachusetts Institute of Technology

FRANK LEVY, The Urban Institute

LAURENCE E. LYNN, JR., JFK School of Government, Harvard University

ELEANOR E. MACCOBY, Department of Psychology, Stanford University

JOHN MODELL, Department of History, University of Minnesota

PHYLLIS MOEN, Department of Human Development and Family Studies, Cornell University

WILLIAM A. MORRILL, Mathematica Policy Research, Inc.

RICHARD R. NELSON, Department of Economics, Yale University

JOHN U. OGBU, Department of Anthropology, University of California, Berkeley

JOHN L. PALMER, The Urban Institute

MARTHA A. PHILLIPS, Ways and Means Committee, U.S. House of Representatives

NICOLE QUESTIAUX, Minister of Solidarity, France

JOHN M. QUIGLEY, Graduate School of Public Policy, University of California, Berkeley

JULIUS RICHMOND, School of Medicine, Harvard University

ISABEL V. SAWHILL, The Urban Institute

CARL D. SIMON, Department of Economics, University of Michigan

DIANA T. SLAUGHTER, School of Education, Northwestern University

EUGENE SMOLENSKY, Institute for Research on Poverty, University of Wisconsin

MYRA H. STROBER, Department of Economics, Stanford University

HAROLD W. WATTS, Department of Economics, Columbia University

SHELDON H. WHITE, Department of Psychology and Social Relations, Harvard University

JULIE BOATRIGHT WILSON, JFK School of Government, Harvard University

WILLIAM JULIUS WILSON, Department of Sociology, University of Chicago (Center for Advanced Study in the Behavioral Sciences)

DAVID A. WISE, JFK School of Government, Harvard University

ANN D. WITTE, Department of Economics, University of North Carolina

DANIEL YANKELOVICH, Yankelovich, Shelley, and White

JAMES P. ZAIS, The Urban Institute